STRENGTHENING FORENSIC SCIENCE IN THE UNITED STATES

A PATH FORWARD

Committee on Identifying the Needs of the Forensic Science Community

Committee on Science, Technology, and Law
Policy and Global Affairs

Committee on Applied and Theoretical Statistics
Division on Engineering and Physical Sciences

NATIONAL RESEARCH COUNCIL
OF THE NATIONAL ACADEMIES

THE NATIONAL ACADEMIES PRESS
Washington, D.C.
www.nap.edu

THE NATIONAL ACADEMIES PRESS 500 Fifth Street, N.W. Washington, DC 20001

NOTICE: The project that is the subject of this report was approved by the Governing Board of the National Research Council, whose members are drawn from the councils of the National Academy of Sciences, the National Academy of Engineering, and the Institute of Medicine. The members of the committee responsible for the report were chosen for their special competences and with regard for appropriate balance.

This study was supported by Contract No. 2006-DN-BX-0001 between the National Academy of Sciences and the National Institute of Justice. Any opinions, findings, conclusions, or recommendations expressed in this publication are those of the author(s) and do not necessarily reflect the views of the organizations or agencies that provided support for the project.

Library of Congress Cataloging-in-Publication Data

Strengthening forensic science in the United States : a path forward : summary / Committee on Identifying the Needs of the Forensic Science Community, Committee on Science, Technology, and Law Policy and Global Affairs, Committee on Applied and Theoretical Statistics, Division on Engineering and Physical Sciences.
p. cm.
Includes index.
ISBN-13: 978-0-309-13135-3 (hardcover)
ISBN-10: 0-309-13135-9 (hardcover)
ISBN-13: 978-0-309-13131-5 (pbk.)
ISBN-10: 0-309-13131-6 (pbk.)
1. Forensic sciences—United States. 2. Criminal investigation—United States. 3. Evidence, Criminal—United States. I. National Research Council (U.S.). Committee on Identifying the Needs of the Forensic Science Community. II. National Research Council (U.S.). Committee on Science, Technology, and Law Policy and Global Affairs. III. National Research Council (U.S.). Committee on Applied and Theoretical Statistics.
HV8073.S7347 2009
363.250973—dc22

2009011443

Additional copies of this report are available from the National Academies Press, 500 Fifth Street, N.W., Lockbox 285, Washington, DC 20055; (800) 624-6242 or (202) 334-3313 (in the Washington metropolitan area); Internet, *http://www.nap.edu*.

Printed in the United States of America

THE NATIONAL ACADEMIES

Advisers to the Nation on Science, Engineering, and Medicine

The **National Academy of Sciences** is a private, nonprofit, self-perpetuating society of distinguished scholars engaged in scientific and engineering research, dedicated to the furtherance of science and technology and to their use for the general welfare. Upon the authority of the charter granted to it by the Congress in 1863, the Academy has a mandate that requires it to advise the federal government on scientific and technical matters. Dr. Ralph J. Cicerone is president of the National Academy of Sciences.

The **National Academy of Engineering** was established in 1964, under the charter of the National Academy of Sciences, as a parallel organization of outstanding engineers. It is autonomous in its administration and in the selection of its members, sharing with the National Academy of Sciences the responsibility for advising the federal government. The National Academy of Engineering also sponsors engineering programs aimed at meeting national needs, encourages education and research, and recognizes the superior achievements of engineers. Dr. Charles M. Vest is president of the National Academy of Engineering.

The **Institute of Medicine** was established in 1970 by the National Academy of Sciences to secure the services of eminent members of appropriate professions in the examination of policy matters pertaining to the health of the public. The Institute acts under the responsibility given to the National Academy of Sciences by its congressional charter to be an adviser to the federal government and, upon its own initiative, to identify issues of medical care, research, and education. Dr. Harvey V. Fineberg is president of the Institute of Medicine.

The **National Research Council** was organized by the National Academy of Sciences in 1916 to associate the broad community of science and technology with the Academy's purposes of furthering knowledge and advising the federal government. Functioning in accordance with general policies determined by the Academy, the Council has become the principal operating agency of both the National Academy of Sciences and the National Academy of Engineering in providing services to the government, the public, and the scientific and engineering communities. The Council is administered jointly by both Academies and the Institute of Medicine. Dr. Ralph J. Cicerone and Dr. Charles M. Vest are chair and vice chair, respectively, of the National Research Council.

www.national-academies.org

COMMITTEE ON IDENTIFYING THE NEEDS OF THE FORENSIC SCIENCE COMMUNITY

HARRY T. EDWARDS, (*Co-chair*), Judge, U.S. Court of Appeals for the District of Columbia Circuit
CONSTANTINE GATSONIS, (*Co-chair*), Director, Center for Statistical Sciences, Brown University
MARGARET A. BERGER, Suzanne J. and Norman Miles Professor of Law, Brooklyn Law School
JOE S. CECIL, Project Director, Program on Scientific and Technical Evidence, Federal Judicial Center
M. BONNER DENTON, Professor of Chemistry, University of Arizona
MARCELLA F. FIERRO, Medical Examiner of Virginia (ret.)
KAREN KAFADAR, Rudy Professor of Statistics and Physics, Indiana University
PETE M. MARONE, Director, Virginia Department of Forensic Science
GEOFFREY S. MEARNS, Dean, Cleveland-Marshall College of Law, Cleveland State University
RANDALL S. MURCH, Associate Director, Research Program Development, Virginia Polytechnic Institute and State University
CHANNING ROBERTSON, Ruth G. and William K. Bowes Professor, Dean of Faculty and Academic Affairs, and Professor, Department of Chemical Engineering, Stanford University
MARVIN E. SCHECHTER, Attorney
ROBERT SHALER, Director, Forensic Science Program, Professor, Biochemistry and Molecular Biology Department, Eberly College of Science, The Pennsylvania State University
JAY A. SIEGEL, Professor, Forensic and Investigative Sciences Program, Indiana University-Purdue University
SARGUR N. SRIHARI, SUNY Distinguished Professor, Department of Computer Science and Engineering and Director, Center of Excellence for Document Analysis and Recognition (CEDAR), University at Buffalo, State University of New York
SHELDON M. WIEDERHORN (NAE), Senior NIST Fellow, National Institute of Standards and Technology
ROSS E. ZUMWALT, Chief Medical Examiner, Office of the Medical Examiner of the State of New Mexico

Staff

ANNE-MARIE MAZZA, Study Director
SCOTT T. WEIDMAN, Director, Board on Mathematical Sciences and Their Applications
JOHN SISLIN, Program Officer, Board on Higher Education and Workforce
DAVID PADGHAM, Program Officer, Computer Science and Telecommunications Board (until 5/08)
STEVEN KENDALL, Senior Program Associate
KATIE MAGEE, Senior Program Assistant (until 9/07)
KATHI E. HANNA, Consultant Writer
SARA D. MADDOX, Editor
ROBIN ACKERMAN, Christine Mirzayan Science and Technology Policy Fellow
GEMAYEL JEAN-PAUL, Christine Mirzayan Science and Technology Policy Fellow
JOHNALYN D. LYLES, Christine Mirzayan Science and Technology Policy Fellow
SANDRA OTTENSMANN, Christine Mirzayan Science and Technology Policy Fellow
DEIRDRE PARSONS, Christine Mirzayan Science and Technology Policy Fellow
SARAH RYKER, Christine Mirzayan Science and Technology Policy Fellow
SUNBIN SONG, Christine Mirzayan Science and Technology Policy Fellow

COMMITTEE ON SCIENCE, TECHNOLOGY, AND LAW

DONALD KENNEDY (NAS/IOM), (*Co-chair*), President Emeritus and Bing Professor of Environmental Science Emeritus, Stanford University; Emeritus Editor-in-Chief, *Science*
RICHARD A. MERRILL (IOM), (*Co-chair*), Daniel Caplin Professor of Law Emeritus, University of Virginia Law School
FREDERICK R. ANDERSON, JR., Partner, McKenna, Long, & Aldridge LLP
MARGARET A. BERGER, Suzanne J. and Norman Miles Professor of Law, Brooklyn Law School
ARTHUR I. BIENENSTOCK, Special Assistant to the President for SLAC and Federal Research Policy, Stanford University
BARBARA E. BIERER, Senior Vice President for Research, Brigham and Women's Hospital
ELIZABETH H. BLACKBURN (NAS/IOM), Morris Herzstein Professor of Biology and Physiology, Department of Biochemistry and Biophysics, University of California, San Francisco
JOE S. CECIL, Project Director, Program on Scientific and Technical Evidence, Federal Judicial Center
RICHARD F. CELESTE, President, Colorado College
JOEL E. COHEN (NAS), Abby Rockefeller Mauzé Professor and Head, Laboratory of Populations, The Rockefeller University and Columbia University
KENNETH W. DAM, Max Pam Professor Emeritus of American and Foreign Law and Senior Lecturer, University of Chicago Law School
ROCHELLE COOPER DREYFUSS, Pauline Newman Professor of Law and Director, Engelberg Center on Innovation Law and Policy, New York University School of Law
ALICE P. GAST (NAE), President, Lehigh University
LAWRENCE O. GOSTIN (IOM), Associate Dean for Research and Academic Programs, Linda D. and Timothy J. O'Neill Professor of Global Health Law, Georgetown University; Professor of Public Health, The Johns Hopkins University
GARY W. HART, Wirth Chair Professor, School of Public Affairs, University of Colorado, Denver
BENJAMIN W. HEINEMAN, JR., Senior Fellow, Harvard Law School and Harvard Kennedy School of Government
DAVID BROCK HORNBY, Judge, U.S. District Court, District of Maine
DAVID KORN (IOM), Vice Provost for Research, Harvard University
RICHARD A. MESERVE (NAE), President, Carnegie Institution of Washington

DUNCAN T. MOORE (NAE), Professor, The Institute of Optics, University of Rochester
ALAN B. MORRISON, Visiting Professor, Washington College of Law, American University
HARRIET RABB, Vice President and General Counsel, Rockefeller University
PAUL D. RHEINGOLD, Senior Partner, Rheingold, Valet, Rheingold, Shkolnik & McCartney LLP
BARBARA ROTHSTEIN, Director, Federal Judicial Center
JONATHAN M. SAMET (IOM), Founding Director, Institute for Global Health and Chairman, Department of Preventive Medicine, University of Southern California
DAVID S. TATEL, Judge, U.S. Court of Appeals for the District of Columbia Circuit

Staff

ANNE-MARIE MAZZA, Director
STEVEN KENDALL, Senior Program Associate

COMMITTEE ON APPLIED AND THEORETICAL STATISTICS

KAREN KAFADAR, (*Chair*), Rudy Professor of Statistics and Physics, Indiana University
AMY BRAVERMAN, MISR Co-Investigator, Statistics and Data Analysis, Earth and Space Sciences Division, Jet Propulsion Laboratory
CONSTANTINE GATSONIS, Director, Center for Statistical Sciences, Brown University
MICHAEL GOODCHILD (NAS), Professor, Department of Geography, University of California, Santa Barbara
KATHRYN B. LASKEY, Professor, Department of Systems Engineering and Operations Research, George Mason University
MICHAEL LESK (NAE), Professor, Library and Information Sciences, Rutgers University
THOMAS A. LOUIS, Professor, Department of Biostatistics, Bloomberg School of Public Health, The Johns Hopkins University
MICHAEL A. NEWTON, Professor, Department of Biostatistics and Medical Informatics, University of Wisconsin, Madison
MICHAEL L. STEIN, Professor, Department of Statistics, The University of Chicago

Staff

SCOTT WEIDMAN, Director
NEAL GLASSMAN, Senior Program Officer
BARBARA WRIGHT, Administrative Assistant

Acknowledgments

ACKNOWLEDGMENT OF PRESENTERS

The committee gratefully acknowledges the contributions of the following individuals who made thoughtful presentations before it:

Chris Asplen, *Gordon Thomas Honeywell Government Affairs*; Peter D. Barnett, *Forensic Science Associates*; Richard E. Bisbing, *McCrone Associates, Inc.*, and *Scientific Working Group on Materials Analysis (SWGMAT)*; Joseph P. Bono, *U.S. Secret Service*; Michael R. Bromwich, *Fried, Frank, Harris, Shriver & Jacobson LLP*; Bruce Budowle, *Federal Bureau of Investigation*; James Burans, *U.S. Department of Homeland Security*; Thomas Cantwell, *U.S. Department of Defense*; Larry Chelko, *U.S. Army Criminal Investigation Laboratory*; John Collins, *DuPage County Sheriff's Office Crime Laboratory*; Charles Cooke, *Office of the Director of National Intelligence*; Robin Cotton, *Boston University School of Medicine*; Joseph A. DiZinno, *Federal Bureau of Investigation*; James Downs, *National Association of Medical Examiners* and *Consortium of Forensic Science Organizations* and *Georgia Bureau of Investigation*; Itiel Dror, *University of Southampton*; Arthur Eisenberg, *Forensic Quality Services*; Barry A. J. Fisher, *Los Angeles County Sheriff's Department*; Eric Friedberg, *Stroz Friedberg, LLC*; Robert E. Gaensslen, *University of Illinois at Chicago*; Brandon L. Garrett, *University of Virginia*; Michael D. Garris, *National Institute of Standards and Technology*; Ed German, *U.S. Army* (ret.); Paul C. Giannelli, *Case Western Reserve University School of Law*; Bruce A. Goldberger, *American Academy of Forensic Sciences*; Hank

Greely, *Stanford University*; Barbara Guttman, *National Institute of Standards and Technology*; David W. Hagy, *U.S. Department of Justice*; Randy Hanzlick, *Fulton County Medical Examiner's Center* and *Emory University School of Medicine*; Carol Henderson, *National Clearinghouse for Science, Technology and the Law* and *Stetson University*; Matthew J. Hickman, *U.S. Department of Justice*; Peter T. Higgins, *The Higgins-Hermansen Group*; Max M. Houck, *West Virginia University*; Vici Inlow, *U.S. Secret Service*; Jan L. Johnson, *Illinois State Police*; Jay Kadane, *Carnegie Mellon University*; David Kaye, *Arizona State University*; Peter D. Komarinski, *Komarinski & Associates, LLC*; Roger G. Koppl, *Farleigh Dickinson University*; Glenn Langenburg, *Minnesota Bureau of Criminal Apprehension*; Deborah Leben, *U.S. Secret Service*; John Lentini, *Scientific Fire Analysis, LLC*; Alan I. Leshner, *American Association for the Advancement of Science*; William MacCrehan, *National Institute of Standards and Technology*; Bill Marbaker, *American Society of Crime Laboratory Directors*; Kenneth F. Martin, *Massachusetts State Police*; Carole McCartney, *University of Leeds*; Stephen B. Meagher, *Federal Bureau of Investigation* and *Scientific Working Group on Friction Ridge Analysis, Study and Technology (SWGFAST)*; Jennifer Mnooken, *University of California, Los Angeles Law School*; John E. Moalli, *Exponent*; John Morgan, *U.S. Department of Justice*; Michael Murphy, *Las Vegas Office of the Coroner*; Peter Neufeld, *The Innocence Project*; John Onstwedder III, *Illinois State Police*; Garry F. Peterson, *Hennepin County Medical Examiner's Office* and *National Association of Medical Examiners*; Joseph L. Peterson, *California State University, Los Angeles*; Peter Pizzola, *New York Police Department Crime Laboratory*; Joe Polski, *Consortium of Forensic Science Organizations* and *International Association for Identification*; Larry Quarino, *Cedar Crest College*; Irma Rios, *City of Houston Crime Lab*; Michael Risinger, *Seton Hall Law School*; Michael J. Saks, *Sandra Day O'Connor College of Law, Arizona State University*; Nelson A. Santos, *Scientific Working Group for the Analysis of Seized Drugs (SWGDRUG)*; David R. Senn, *The University of Texas Health Science Center at San Antonio*; Robert Stacey, *American Society of Crime Laboratory Directors, Laboratory Accreditation Board*; David Stoney, *Stoney Forensic, Inc.*; Peter Striupaitis, *International Association for Identification* and *Scientific Working Group for Firearms and Toolmarks (SWGGUN)*; Rick Tontarski, *U.S. Army Criminal Investigation Laboratory*; Richard W. Vorder Bruegge, *Federal Bureau of Investigation*; Victor W. Weedn; and Tom Witt, *West Virginia University.*

ACKNOWLEDGMENT OF REVIEWERS

This report has been reviewed in draft form by individuals chosen for their diverse perspectives and technical expertise, in accordance with procedures approved by the National Academies' Report Review Committee. The purpose of this independent review is to provide candid and critical comments that will assist the institution in making its published report as sound as possible and to ensure that the report meets institutional standards for objectivity, evidence, and responsiveness to the study charge. The review comments and draft manuscript remain confidential to protect the integrity of the process.

We wish to thank the following individuals for their review of this report: R. Stephen Berry, University of Chicago; Christophe Champod, Universite de Lausanne, Switzerland; William Chisum, Retired, National Crime Investigation and Training; Joel Cohen, Rockefeller University; Peter DeForest, John Jay College of Criminal Justice; Stephen Fienberg, Carnegie Mellon University; Barry Fisher, Los Angeles County Sheriff's Department; Mark Flomenbaum, Boston University; Ross Gardner, Gardner Forensic Consulting; Paul Giannelli, Case Western Reserve University; Randy Hanzlick, Emory University; Keith Inman, Forensic Analytical Sciences, Inc.; Dan Kahan, Yale Law School; Roger Kahn, Harris County Medical Examiner's Office; Elizabeth Loftus, University of California, Irvine; C. Owen Lovejoy, Kent State University; Kenneth Melson, George Washington University; Michael Murphy, Office of the Coroner/Medical Examiner, Las Vegas, Nevada; Hyla Napadensky, Retired, Napadensky Energetics, Inc.; Joseph Peterson, California State University, Los Angeles; William Press, University of Texas, Austin; Jed Rakoff, U.S. District Court Southern District of New York; Carl Selavka, U.S. Army Criminal Investigation Laboratory; David Stoney, Stoney Forensic, Inc.; and Charles Wellford, University of Maryland.

Although the reviewers listed above have provided many constructive comments and suggestions, they were not asked to endorse the conclusions or recommendations, nor did they see the final draft of the report before its release. The review of this report was overseen by John Bailar, University of Chicago, and Royce Murray, University of North Carolina, Chapel Hill. Appointed by the National Academies, they were responsible for making certain that an independent examination of this report was carried out in accordance with institutional procedures and that all review comments were carefully considered. Responsibility for the final content of this report rests entirely with the authoring committee and the institution.

Contents

Preface

Recognizing that significant improvements are needed in forensic science, Congress directed the National Academy of Sciences to undertake the study that led to this report. There are scores of talented and dedicated people in the forensic science community, and the work that they perform is vitally important. They are often strapped in their work, however, for lack of adequate resources, sound policies, and national support. It is clear that change and advancements, both systemic and scientific, are needed in a number of forensic science disciplines—to ensure the reliability of the disciplines, establish enforceable standards, and promote best practices and their consistent application.

In adopting this report, the aim of our committee is to chart an agenda for progress in the forensic science community and its scientific disciplines. Because the work of forensic science practitioners is so obviously wide-reaching and important—affecting criminal investigation and prosecution, civil litigation, legal reform, the investigation of insurance claims, national disaster planning and preparedness, homeland security, and the advancement of technology—the committee worked with a sense of great commitment and spent countless hours deliberating over the recommendations that are included in the report. These recommendations, which are inexorably interconnected, reflect the committee's strong views on policy initiatives that must be adopted in any plan to improve the forensic science disciplines and to allow the forensic science community to serve society more effectively.

The task Congress assigned our committee was daunting and required serious thought and the consideration of an extremely complex and decentralized system, with various players, jurisdictions, demands, and limitations. Throughout our lengthy deliberations, the committee heard testimony from the stakeholder community, ensuring that the voices of forensic practitioners were heard and their concerns addressed. We also heard from professionals who manage forensic laboratories and medical examiner/coroner offices; teachers who are devoted to training the next generation of forensic scientists; scholars who have conducted important research in a number of forensic science fields; and members of the legal profession and law enforcement agencies who understand how forensic science evidence is collected, analyzed, and used in connection with criminal investigations and prosecutions. We are deeply grateful to all of the presenters who spoke to the committee and/or submitted papers for our consideration. These experts and their work served the committee well.

In considering the testimony and evidence that was presented to the committee, what surprised us the most was the consistency of the message that we heard:

> **The forensic science system, encompassing both research and practice, has serious problems that can only be addressed by a national commitment to overhaul the current structure that supports the forensic science community in this country. This can only be done with effective leadership at the highest levels of both federal and state governments, pursuant to national standards, and with a significant infusion of federal funds.**

The recommendations in this report represent the committee's studied opinion on how best to achieve this critical goal.

We had the good fortune to serve as co-chairs of the committee entrusted with addressing Congress' charge. The committee, formed under the auspices of the National Academies' Committee on Science, Technology, and Law and Committee on Applied and Theoretical Statistics, was composed of many talented professionals, some expert in various areas of forensic science, others in law, and still others in different fields of science and engineering. They listened, read, questioned, vigorously discussed the findings and recommendations offered in this report, and then worked hard to complete the research and writing required to produce the report. We are indebted to our colleagues for all the time and energy they gave to this effort. We are also most grateful to the staff, Anne-Marie Mazza, Scott Weidman, Steven Kendall, and the consultant writer, Kathi Hanna, for their superb work and dedication to this project; to staff members David Padgham and John Sislin, and editor, Sara Maddox, for their assistance; and to Paige Herwig, Laurie Richardson, and Judith A. Hunt for their sterling contributions in checking source materials and assisting with the final production of the report.

Harry T. Edwards and Constantine Gatsonis
Committee Co-chairs

Summary

INTRODUCTION

On November 22, 2005, the Science, State, Justice, Commerce, and Related Agencies Appropriations Act of 2006 became law.[1] Under the terms of the statute, Congress authorized "the National Academy of Sciences to conduct a study on forensic science, as described in the Senate report."[2] The Senate Report to which the Conference Report refers states:

> While a great deal of analysis exists of the requirements in the discipline of DNA, there exists little to no analysis of the remaining needs of the community outside of the area of DNA. Therefore . . . the Committee directs the Attorney General to provide [funds] to the National Academy of Sciences to create an independent Forensic Science Committee. This Committee shall include members of the forensics community representing operational crime laboratories, medical examiners, and coroners; legal experts; and other scientists as determined appropriate.[3]

The Senate Report also sets forth the charge to the Forensic Science Committee, instructing it to:

(1) assess the present and future resource needs of the forensic science community, to include State and local crime labs, medical examiners, and coroners;

---

[1] P.L. No. 109-108, 119 Stat. 2290 (2005).
[2] H.R. Rep. No. 109-272, at 121 (2005) (Conf. Rep.).
[3] S. Rep. No. 109-88, at 46 (2005).

(2) make recommendations for maximizing the use of forensic technologies and techniques to solve crimes, investigate deaths, and protect the public;
(3) identify potential scientific advances that may assist law enforcement in using forensic technologies and techniques to protect the public;
(4) make recommendations for programs that will increase the number of qualified forensic scientists and medical examiners available to work in public crime laboratories;
(5) disseminate best practices and guidelines concerning the collection and analysis of forensic evidence to help ensure quality and consistency in the use of forensic technologies and techniques to solve crimes, investigate deaths, and protect the public;
(6) examine the role of the forensic community in the homeland security mission;
(7) [examine] interoperability of Automated Fingerprint Information Systems [AFIS]; and
(8) examine additional issues pertaining to forensic science as determined by the Committee.[4]

In the fall of 2006, a committee was established by the National Academy of Sciences to implement this congressional charge. As recommended in the Senate Report, the persons selected to serve included members of the forensic science community, members of the legal community, and a diverse group of scientists. Operating under the project title "Identifying the Needs of the Forensic Science Community," the committee met on eight occasions: January 25-26, April 23-24, June 5-6, September 20-21, and December 6-7, 2007, and March 24-25, June 23-24, and November 14-15, 2008. During these meetings, the committee heard expert testimony and deliberated over the information it heard and received. Between meetings, committee members reviewed numerous published materials, studies, and reports related to the forensic science disciplines, engaged in independent research on the subject, and worked on drafts of the final report.

Experts who provided testimony included federal agency officials; academics and research scholars; private consultants; federal, state, and local law enforcement officials; scientists; medical examiners; a coroner; crime laboratory officials from the public and private sectors; independent investigators; defense attorneys; forensic science practitioners; and leadership of professional and standard setting organizations (see the Acknowledgments and Appendix B for a complete listing of presenters).

[4] Ibid.

The issues covered during the committee's hearings and deliberations included:

(a) the fundamentals of the scientific method as applied to forensic practice—hypothesis generation and testing, falsifiability and replication, and peer review of scientific publications;
(b) the assessment of forensic methods and technologies—the collection and analysis of forensic data; accuracy and error rates of forensic analyses; sources of potential bias and human error in interpretation by forensic experts; and proficiency testing of forensic experts;
(c) infrastructure and needs for basic research and technology assessment in forensic science;
(d) current training and education in forensic science;
(e) the structure and operation of forensic science laboratories;
(f) the structure and operation of the coroner and medical examiner systems;
(g) budget, future needs, and priorities of the forensic science community and the coroner and medical examiner systems;
(h) the accreditation, certification, and licensing of forensic science operations, medical death investigation systems, and scientists;
(i) Scientific Working Groups (SWGs) and their practices;
(j) forensic science practices—
pattern/experience evidence
    - fingerprints (including the interoperability of AFIS)
    - firearms examination
    - toolmarks
    - bite marks
    - impressions (tires, footwear)
    - bloodstain pattern analysis
    - handwriting
    - hair

analytical evidence
    - DNA
    - coatings (e.g., paint)
    - chemicals (including drugs)
    - materials (including fibers)
    - fluids
    - serology
    - fire and explosive analysis

digital evidence;
(k) the effectiveness of coroner systems as compared with medical examiner systems;

(l) the use of forensic evidence in criminal and civil litigation—
  - o the collection and flow of evidence from crime scenes to courtrooms
  - o the manner in which forensic practitioners testify in court
  - o cases involving the misinterpretation of forensic evidence
  - o the adversarial system in criminal and civil litigation
  - o lawyers' use and misuse of forensic evidence
  - o judges' handling of forensic evidence;

(m) forensic practice and projects at various federal agencies, including NIST, the FBI, DHS, U.S. Secret Service, NIJ, DEA, and DOD;
(n) forensic practice in state and local agencies;
(o) nontraditional forensic service providers; and
(p) the forensic science community in the United Kingdom.

The testimonial and documentary evidence considered by the committee was detailed, complex, and sometimes controversial. Given this reality, the committee could not possibly answer every question that it confronted, nor could it devise specific solutions for every problem that it identified. Rather, it reached a consensus on the most important issues now facing the forensic science community and medical examiner system and agreed on 13 specific recommendations to address these issues.

Challenges Facing the Forensic Science Community

For decades, the forensic science disciplines have produced valuable evidence that has contributed to the successful prosecution and conviction of criminals as well as to the exoneration of innocent people. Over the last two decades, advances in some forensic science disciplines, especially the use of DNA technology, have demonstrated that some areas of forensic science have great additional potential to help law enforcement identify criminals. Many crimes that may have gone unsolved are now being solved because forensic science is helping to identify the perpetrators.

Those advances, however, also have revealed that, in some cases, substantive information and testimony based on faulty forensic science analyses may have contributed to wrongful convictions of innocent people. This fact has demonstrated the potential danger of giving undue weight to evidence and testimony derived from imperfect testing and analysis. Moreover, imprecise or exaggerated expert testimony has sometimes contributed to the admission of erroneous or misleading evidence.

Further advances in the forensic science disciplines will serve three important purposes. First, further improvements will assist law enforcement officials in the course of their investigations to identify perpetrators with higher reliability. Second, further improvements in forensic science practices should reduce the occurrence of wrongful convictions, which reduces the risk that true offenders continue to commit crimes while innocent persons inappropriately serve time. Third, any improvements in the forensic science disciplines will undoubtedly enhance the Nation's ability to address the needs of homeland security.

Numerous professionals in the forensic science community and the medical examiner system have worked for years to achieve excellence in their fields, aiming to follow high ethical norms, develop sound professional standards, ensure accurate results in their practices, and improve the processes by which accuracy is determined. Although the work of these dedicated professionals has resulted in significant progress in the forensic science disciplines in recent decades, major challenges still face the forensic science community. It is therefore unsurprising that Congress instructed this committee to, among other things, "assess the present and future resource needs of the forensic science community," "make recommendations for maximizing the use of forensic technologies and techniques," "make recommendations for programs that will increase the number of qualified forensic scientists and medical examiners," and "disseminate best practices and guidelines concerning the collection and analysis of forensic evidence to help ensure quality and consistency in the use of forensic technologies and techniques." These are among the pressing issues facing the forensic science community. The best professionals in the forensic science disciplines invariably are hindered in their work because these and other problems persist.

The length of the congressional charge and the complexity of the material under review made the committee's assignment challenging. In undertaking it, the committee first had to gain an understanding of the various disciplines within the forensic science community, as well as the community's history, its strengths and weaknesses, and the roles of the people and agencies that constitute the community and make use of its services. In so doing, the committee was able to better comprehend some of the major problems facing the forensic science community and the medical examiner system. A brief review of some of these problems is illuminating.[5]

Disparities in the Forensic Science Community

There are great disparities among existing forensic science operations in federal, state, and local law enforcement jurisdictions and agencies. This is true with respect to funding, access to analytical instrumentation, the availability of skilled and well-trained personnel, certification, accreditation, and

[5] In this report, the "forensic science community," broadly speaking, is meant to include forensic pathology and medicolegal death investigation, which is sometimes referred to as "the medical examiner system" or "the medicolegal death investigation system."

oversight. As a result, it is not easy to generalize about current practices within the forensic science community. It is clear, however, that any approach to overhauling the existing system needs to address and help minimize the community's current fragmentation and inconsistent practices.

Although the vast majority of criminal law enforcement is handled by state and local jurisdictions, these entities often are sorely lacking in the resources (money, staff, training, and equipment) necessary to promote and maintain strong forensic science laboratory systems. By comparison, federal programs are often much better funded and staffed. It is also noteworthy that the resources, the extent of services, and the amount of expertise that medical examiners and forensic pathologists can provide vary widely in different jurisdictions. As a result, the depth, reliability, and overall quality of substantive information arising from the forensic examination of evidence available to the legal system vary substantially across the country.

Lack of Mandatory Standardization, Certification, and Accreditation

The fragmentation problem is compounded because operational principles and procedures for many forensic science disciplines are not standardized or embraced, either between or within jurisdictions. There is no uniformity in the certification of forensic practitioners, or in the accreditation of crime laboratories. Indeed, most jurisdictions do not require forensic practitioners to be certified, and most forensic science disciplines have no mandatory certification programs. Moreover, accreditation of crime laboratories is not required in most jurisdictions. Often there are no standard protocols governing forensic practice in a given discipline. And, even when protocols are in place (e.g., SWG standards), they often are vague and not enforced in any meaningful way. In short, the quality of forensic practice in most disciplines varies greatly because of the absence of adequate training and continuing education, rigorous mandatory certification and accreditation programs, adherence to robust performance standards, and effective oversight.[6] These shortcomings obviously pose a continuing and serious threat to the quality and credibility of forensic science practice.

The Broad Range of Forensic Science Disciplines

The term "forensic science" encompasses a broad range of forensic disciplines, each with its own set of technologies and practices. In other words, there is wide variability across forensic science disciplines with regard to

---

[6] See, e.g., P.C. Giannelli. 2007. Wrongful convictions and forensic science: The need to regulate crime labs. 86 N.C. L. Rev. 163 (2007); B. Schmitt and J. Swickard. 2008. "Detroit Police Lab Shut Down After Probe Finds Errors." *Detroit Free Press*. September 25.

techniques, methodologies, reliability, types and numbers of potential errors, research, general acceptability, and published material. Some of the forensic science disciplines are laboratory based (e.g., nuclear and mitochondrial DNA analysis, toxicology and drug analysis); others are based on expert interpretation of observed patterns (e.g., fingerprints, writing samples, toolmarks, bite marks, and specimens such as hair). The "forensic science community," in turn, consists of a host of practitioners, including scientists (some with advanced degrees) in the fields of chemistry, biochemistry, biology, and medicine; laboratory technicians; crime scene investigators; and law enforcement officers. There are very important differences, however, between forensic laboratory work and crime scene investigations. There are also sharp distinctions between forensic practitioners who have been trained in chemistry, biochemistry, biology, and medicine (and who bring these disciplines to bear in their work) and technicians who lend support to forensic science enterprises. Many of these differences are discussed in the body of this report.

The committee decided early in its work that it would not be feasible to develop a detailed evaluation of each discipline in terms of its scientific underpinning, level of development, and ability to provide evidence to address the major types of questions raised in criminal prosecutions and civil litigation. However, the committee solicited testimony on a broad range of forensic science disciplines and sought to identify issues relevant across definable classes of disciplines. As a result of listening to this testimony and reviewing related written materials, the committee found substantial evidence indicating that the level of scientific development and evaluation varies substantially among the forensic science disciplines.

Problems Relating to the Interpretation of Forensic Evidence

Often in criminal prosecutions and civil litigation, forensic evidence is offered to support conclusions about "individualization" (sometimes referred to as "matching" a specimen to a particular individual or other source) or about classification of the source of the specimen into one of several categories. With the exception of nuclear DNA analysis, however, no forensic method has been rigorously shown to have the capacity to consistently, and with a high degree of certainty, demonstrate a connection between evidence and a specific individual or source. In terms of scientific basis, the analytically based disciplines generally hold a notable edge over disciplines based on expert interpretation. But there are important variations among the disciplines relying on expert interpretation. For example, there are more established protocols and available research for fingerprint analysis than for the analysis of bite marks. There also are significant variations within each discipline. For example, not all fingerprint evidence is equally good, because the true value of the evidence is determined by the quality of the latent fingerprint image. These disparities between and within the forensic science disciplines highlight a major problem in the forensic science community: The simple reality is that the interpretation of forensic evidence is not always based on scientific studies to determine its validity. This is a serious problem. Although research has been done in some disciplines, there is a notable dearth of peer-reviewed, published studies establishing the scientific bases and validity of many forensic methods.[7]

The Need for Research to Establish Limits and Measures of Performance

In evaluating the accuracy of a forensic analysis, it is crucial to clarify the type of question the analysis is called on to address. Thus, although some techniques may be too imprecise to permit accurate identification of a specific individual, they may still provide useful and accurate information about questions of classification. For example, microscopic hair analysis may provide reliable evidence on some characteristics of the individual from which the specimen was taken, but it may not be able to reliably match the specimen with a specific individual. However, the definition of the appropriate question is only a first step in the evaluation of the performance of a forensic technique. A body of research is required to establish the limits and measures of performance and to address the impact of sources of variability and potential bias. Such research is sorely needed, but it seems to be lacking in most of the forensic disciplines that rely on subjective assessments of matching characteristics. These disciplines need to develop rigorous protocols to guide these subjective interpretations and pursue equally rigorous research and evaluation programs. The development of such research programs can benefit significantly from other areas, notably from the large body of research on the evaluation of observer performance in diagnostic medicine and from the findings of cognitive psychology on the potential for bias and error in human observers.[8]

---

[7] Several articles, for example, have noted the lack of scientific validation of fingerprint identification methods. See, e.g., J.J. Koehler. Fingerprint error rates and proficiency tests: What they are and why they matter. 59 Hastings L.J. 1077 (2008); L. Haber and R.N. Haber. 2008. Scientific validation of fingerprint evidence under *Daubert*. *Law, Probability and Risk* 7(2):87; J.L. Mnookin. 2008. The validity of latent fingerprint identification: Confessions of a fingerprinting moderate. *Law, Probability and Risk* 7(2):127.

[8] The findings of forensic science experts are vulnerable to cognitive and contextual bias. See, e.g., I.E. Dror, D. Charlton, and A.E. Péron. 2006. Contextual information renders experts vulnerable to making erroneous identifications. *Forensic Science International* 156:74, 77. ("Our study shows that it is possible to alter identification decisions on the same fingerprint, solely by presenting it in a different context."); I.E. Dror and D. Charlton. 2006. Why experts make errors. *Journal of Forensic Identification* 56(4):600; Giannelli, *supra* note 6, pp. 220-222. Unfortunately, at least to date, there is no good evidence to indicate that the forensic

The Admission of Forensic Science Evidence in Litigation

Forensic science experts and evidence are used routinely in the service of the criminal justice system. DNA testing may be used to determine whether sperm found on a rape victim came from an accused party; a latent fingerprint found on a gun may be used to determine whether a defendant handled the weapon; drug analysis may be used to determine whether pills found in a person's possession were illicit; and an autopsy may be used to determine the cause and manner of death of a murder victim. In order for qualified forensic science experts to testify competently about forensic evidence, they must first find the evidence in a usable state and properly preserve it. A latent fingerprint that is badly smudged when found cannot be usefully saved, analyzed, or explained. An inadequate drug sample may be insufficient to allow for proper analysis. And, DNA tests performed on a contaminated or otherwise compromised sample cannot be used reliably to identify or eliminate an individual as the perpetrator of a crime. These are important matters involving the proper processing of forensic evidence. The law's greatest dilemma in its heavy reliance on forensic evidence, however, concerns the question of whether—and to what extent—there is *science* in any given forensic science discipline.

Two very important questions should underlie the law's admission of and reliance upon forensic evidence in criminal trials: (1) the extent to which a particular forensic discipline is founded on a reliable scientific methodology that gives it the capacity to accurately analyze evidence and report findings and (2) the extent to which practitioners in a particular forensic discipline rely on human interpretation that could be tainted by error, the threat of bias, or the absence of sound operational procedures and robust performance standards. These questions are significant. Thus, it matters a great deal whether an expert is qualified to testify about forensic evidence and whether the evidence is sufficiently reliable to merit a fact finder's reliance on the truth that it purports to support. Unfortunately, these important questions do not always produce satisfactory answers in judicial decisions pertaining to the admissibility of forensic science evidence proffered in criminal trials.

In 1993, in *Daubert v. Merrell Dow Pharmaceuticals, Inc.*,[9] the Supreme Court ruled that, under Rule 702 of the Federal Rules of Evidence (which covers both civil trials and criminal prosecutions in the federal courts), a "trial judge must ensure that any and all scientific testimony or evidence admitted is not only relevant, but reliable."[10] The Court indicated

---

science community has made a sufficient effort to address the bias issue; thus, it is impossible for the committee to fully assess the magnitude of the problem.

[9] 509 U.S. 579 (1993).

[10] Ibid., p. 589.

that the subject of an expert's testimony should be scientific knowledge, so that "evidentiary reliability will be based upon scientific validity."[11] The Court also emphasized that, in considering the admissibility of evidence, a trial judge should focus "solely" on the expert's "principles and methodology," and "not on the conclusions that they generate."[12] In sum, *Daubert*'s requirement that an expert's testimony pertain to "scientific knowledge" established a standard of "evidentiary reliability."[13]

In explaining this evidentiary standard, the *Daubert* Court pointed to several factors that might be considered by a trial judge: (1) whether a theory or technique can be (and has been) tested; (2) whether the theory or technique has been subjected to peer review and publication; (3) the known or potential rate of error of a particular scientific technique; (4) the existence and maintenance of standards controlling the technique's operation; and (5) a scientific technique's degree of acceptance within a relevant scientific community.[14] In the end, however, the Court emphasized that the inquiry under Rule 702 is "a flexible one."[15] The Court expressed confidence in the adversarial system, noting that "[v]igorous cross-examination, presentation of contrary evidence, and careful instruction on the burden of proof are the traditional and appropriate means of attacking shaky but admissible evidence."[16] The Supreme Court has made it clear that trial judges have great discretion in deciding on the admissibility of evidence under Rule 702, and that appeals from *Daubert* rulings are subject to a very narrow abuse-of-discretion standard of review.[17] Most importantly, in *Kumho Tire Co., Ltd. v. Carmichael*, the Court stated that "whether *Daubert*'s specific factors are, or are not, reasonable measures of reliability in a particular case is a matter that the law grants the trial judge broad latitude to determine."[18]

---

[11] Ibid., pp. 590 and 591 n.9 (emphasis omitted).

[12] Ibid., p. 595. In *General Electric Co. v. Joiner*, 522 U.S. 136, 146 (1997), the Court added: "[C]onclusions and methodology are not entirely distinct from one another. Trained experts commonly extrapolate from existing data. But nothing in *Daubert* or the Federal Rules of Evidence requires a district court to admit opinion evidence that is connected to existing data only by the *ipse dixit* of the expert."

[13] *Daubert*, 509 U.S. at 589, 590 n.9, 595.

[14] Ibid., pp. 593-94.

[15] Ibid., p. 594. *In Kumho Tire Co., Ltd. v. Carmichael*, 526 U.S. 137 (1999), the Court confirmed that the *Daubert* factors do not constitute a definitive checklist or test. *Kumho Tire* importantly held that Rule 702 applies to both scientific and nonscientific expert testimony; the Court also indicated that the *Daubert* factors might be applicable in a trial judge's assessment of the reliability of nonscientific expert testimony, depending upon "the particular circumstances of the particular case at issue." Ibid., at 150.

[16] *Daubert*, 509 U.S. at 596.

[17] See *Gen. Elec. Co. v. Joiner*, 522 U.S. 136, 142-143 (1997).

[18] *Kumho Tire*, 526 U.S. at 153.

Daubert and its progeny have engendered confusion and controversy. In particular, judicial dispositions of *Daubert*-type questions in criminal cases have been criticized by some lawyers and scholars who thought that the Supreme Court's decision would be applied more rigorously.[19] If one focuses solely on reported federal appellate decisions, the picture is not appealing to those who have preferred a more rigorous application of *Daubert*. Federal appellate courts have not with any consistency or clarity imposed standards ensuring the application of scientifically valid reasoning and reliable methodology in criminal cases involving *Daubert* questions. This is not really surprising, however. The Supreme Court itself described the *Daubert* standard as "flexible." This means that, beyond questions of relevance, *Daubert* offers appellate courts no clear substantive standard by which to review decisions by trial courts. As a result, trial judges exercise great discretion in deciding whether to admit or exclude expert testimony, and their judgments are subject only to a highly deferential "abuse of discretion" standard of review. Although it is difficult to get a clear picture of how trial courts handle *Daubert* challenges, because many evidentiary rulings are issued without a published opinion and without an appeal, the vast majority of the *reported* opinions in criminal cases indicate that trial judges rarely exclude or restrict expert testimony offered by prosecutors; most *reported* opinions also indicate that appellate courts routinely deny appeals contesting trial court decisions admitting forensic evidence against criminal defendants.[20] But the reported opinions do not offer in any way a complete sample of federal trial court dispositions of *Daubert*-type questions in criminal cases.

The situation appears to be very different in civil cases. Plaintiffs and defendants, equally, are more likely to have access to expert witnesses in civil cases, while prosecutors usually have an advantage over most defendants in offering expert testimony in criminal cases. And, ironically, the appellate courts appear to be more willing to second-guess trial court judgments on the admissibility of purported scientific evidence in civil cases than in criminal cases.[21]

---

[19] See, e.g., P.J. Neufeld. 2005. The (near) irrelevance of *Daubert* to criminal justice: And some suggestions for reform. *American Journal of Public Health* 95(Supp.1):S107.

[20] Ibid., p. S109.

[21] See, e.g., *McClain v. Metabolife Int'l, Inc.*, 401 F.3d 1233 (11th Cir. 2005); *Chapman v. Maytag Corp.*, 297 F.3d 682 (7th Cir. 2002); *Goebel v. Denver & Rio Grande W. R.R. Co.*, 215 F.3d 1083 (10th Cir. 2000); *Smith v. Ford Motor Co.*, 215 F.3d 713 (7th Cir. 2000); *Walker v. Soo Line R.R. Co.*, 208 F.3d 581 (7th Cir. 2000); 1 D.L. Faigman, M.J. Saks, J. Sanders, and E.K. Cheng. 2007-2008. *Modern Scientific Evidence: The Law and Science of Expert Testimony.* Eagan, MN: Thomson/West, § 1.35, p. 105 (discussing studies suggesting that courts "employ *Daubert* more lackadaisically in criminal trials—especially in regard to prosecution evidence—than in civil cases—especially in regard to plaintiff evidence").

Prophetically, the *Daubert* decision observed that "there are important differences between the quest for truth in the courtroom and the quest for truth in the laboratory. Scientific conclusions are subject to perpetual revision. Law, on the other hand, must resolve disputes finally and quickly."[22] But because accused parties in criminal cases are convicted on the basis of testimony from forensic science experts, much depends upon whether the evidence offered is reliable. Furthermore, in addition to protecting innocent persons from being convicted of crimes that they did not commit, we are also seeking to protect society from persons who have committed criminal acts. Law enforcement officials and the members of society they serve need to be assured that forensic techniques are *reliable*. Therefore, we must limit the risk of having the reliability of certain forensic science methodologies judicially certified before the techniques have been properly studied and their accuracy verified by the forensic science community. "[T]here is no evident reason why ['rigorous, systematic'] research would be infeasible."[23] However, some courts appear to be loath to insist on such research as a condition of admitting forensic science evidence in criminal cases, perhaps because to do so would likely "demand more by way of validation than the disciplines can presently offer."[24]

The adversarial process relating to the admission and exclusion of scientific evidence is not suited to the task of finding "scientific truth." The judicial system is encumbered by, among other things, judges and lawyers who generally lack the scientific expertise necessary to comprehend and evaluate forensic evidence in an informed manner, trial judges (sitting alone) who must decide evidentiary issues without the benefit of judicial colleagues and often with little time for extensive research and reflection, and the highly deferential nature of the appellate review afforded trial courts' *Daubert* rulings. Given these realities, there is a tremendous need for the forensic science community to improve. Judicial review, by itself, will not cure the infirmities of the forensic science community.[25] The development

---

22 *Daubert*, 509 U.S. at 596-97.

23 J. Griffin and D.J. LaMagna. 2002. *Daubert* challenges to forensic evidence: Ballistics next on the firing line. *The Champion*, September-October:20, 21 (quoting P. Giannelli and E. Imwinkelried. 2000. Scientific evidence: The fallout from Supreme Court's decision in *Kumho Tire*. *Criminal Justice Magazine* 14(4):12, 40).

24 Ibid. See, e.g., *United States v. Crisp*, 324 F.3d 261, 270 (4th Cir. 2003) (noting "that while further research into fingerprint analysis would be welcome, to postpone present in-court utilization of this bedrock forensic identifier pending such research would be to make the best the enemy of the good." (internal quotation marks omitted)).

25 See J.L. Mnookin. Expert evidence, partisanship, and epistemic competence. 73 Brook. L. Rev. 1009, 1033 (2008) ("[S]o long as we have our adversarial system in much its present form, we are inevitably going to be stuck with approaches to expert evidence that are imperfect, conceptually unsatisfying, and awkward. It may well be that the real lesson is this: those who believe that we might ever fully resolve—rather than imperfectly manage—the

of scientific research, training, technology, and databases associated with DNA analysis have resulted from substantial and steady federal support for both academic research and programs employing techniques for DNA analysis. Similar support must be given to all credible forensic science disciplines if they are to achieve the degrees of reliability needed to serve the goals of justice. With more and better educational programs, accredited laboratories, certified forensic practitioners, sound operational principles and procedures, and serious research to establish the limits and measures of performance in each discipline, forensic science experts will be better able to analyze evidence and coherently report their findings in the courts. The current situation, however, is seriously wanting, both because of the limitations of the judicial system and because of the many problems faced by the forensic science community.

Political Realities

Most forensic science methods, programs, and evidence are within the regulatory province of state and local law enforcement entities or are covered by statutes and rules governing state judicial proceedings. Thus, in assessing the strengths, weaknesses, and future needs of forensic disciplines, and in making recommendations for improving the use of forensic technologies and techniques, the committee remained mindful of the fact that Congress cannot directly fix all of the deficiencies in the forensic science community. Under our federal system of government, Congress does not have free reign to amend state criminal codes, rules of evidence, and statutes governing civil actions; nor may it easily and directly regulate local law enforcement practices, state and local medical examiner units, or state policies covering the accreditation of crime laboratories and the certification of forensic practitioners.

Congress' authority to act is significant, however. Forensic science programs in federal government entities—whether within DOJ, DHS, DOD, or the Department of Commerce (DOC)—are funded by congressional appropriations. If these programs are required to operate pursuant to the highest standards, they will provide an example for the states. More importantly, Congress can promote "best practices" and strong educational, certification, accreditation, ethics, and oversight programs in the states by offering funds that are contingent on meeting appropriate standards of practice. There is every reason to believe that offers of federal funds with "strings attached" can effect significant change in the forensic science com-

deep structural tensions surrounding both partisanship and epistemic competence that permeate the use of scientific evidence within our legal system are almost certainly destined for disappointment.").

munity, because so many state and local programs currently are suffering for want of adequate resources. In the end, however, the committee recognized that state and local authorities must be willing to enforce change if it is to happen.

In light of the foregoing issues, the committee exercised caution before drawing conclusions and avoided being too prescriptive in its recommendations. It also recognized that, given the complexity of the issues and the political realities that may pose obstacles to change, some recommendations will have to be implemented creatively and over time in order to be effective.

FINDINGS AND RECOMMENDATIONS

The Fragmented System: Symptoms and Cures

The forensic science disciplines currently are an assortment of methods and practices used in both the public and private arenas. Forensic science facilities exhibit wide variability in capacity, oversight, staffing, certification, and accreditation across federal and state jurisdictions. Too often they have inadequate educational programs, and they typically lack mandatory and enforceable standards, founded on rigorous research and testing, certification requirements, and accreditation programs. Additionally, forensic science and forensic pathology research, education, and training lack strong ties to our research universities and national science assets. In addition to the problems emanating from the fragmentation of the forensic science community, the most recently published *Census of Crime Laboratories* conducted by BJS describes unacceptable case backlogs in state and local crime laboratories and estimates the level of additional resources needed to handle these backlogs and prevent their recurrence. Unfortunately, the backlogs, even in DNA case processing, have grown dramatically in recent years and are now staggering in some jurisdictions. The most recently published BJS *Special Report of Medical Examiners and Coroners' Offices* also depicts a system with disparate and often inadequate educational and training requirements, resources, and capacities—in short, a system in need of significant improvement.

Existing data suggest that forensic laboratories are underresourced and understaffed, which contributes to case backlogs and likely makes it difficult for laboratories to do as much as they could to (1) inform investigations, (2) provide strong evidence for prosecutions, and (3) avoid errors that could lead to imperfect justice. Being underresourced also means that the tools of forensic science—and the knowledge base that underpins the analysis and interpretation of evidence—are not as strong as they could be, thus hindering the ability of the forensic science disciplines to excel at informing investigations, providing strong evidence, and avoiding errors in important ways. NIJ is the only federal agency that provides direct support to crime laboratories to alleviate the backlog, and those funds are minimal. The forensic science system is underresourced also in the sense that it has only thin ties to an academic research base that could support the forensic science disciplines and fill knowledge gaps. There are many hard-working and conscientious people in the forensic science community, but this underresourcing inherently limits their ability to do their best work. Additional resources surely will be necessary to create high-quality, self-correcting systems.

However, increasing the staff within existing crime laboratories and medical examiners' offices is only part of the solution. What also is needed is an upgrading of systems and organizational structures, better training, the widespread adoption of uniform and enforceable best practices, and mandatory certification and accreditation programs. The forensic science community and the medical examiner/coroner system must be upgraded if forensic practitioners are to be expected to serve the goals of justice.

Of the various facets of underresourcing, the committee is most concerned about the knowledge base. Adding more dollars and people to the enterprise might reduce case backlogs, but it will not address fundamental limitations in the capabilities of forensic science disciplines to discern valid information from crime scene evidence. For the most part, it is impossible to discern the magnitude of those limitations, and reasonable people will differ on their significance.

Forensic science research is not well supported, and there is no unified strategy for developing a forensic science research plan across federal agencies. Relative to other areas of science, the forensic disciplines have extremely limited opportunities for research funding. Although the FBI and NIJ have supported some research in forensic science, the level of support has been well short of what is necessary for the forensic science community to establish strong links with a broad base of research universities. Moreover, funding for academic research is limited and requires law enforcement collaboration, which can inhibit the pursuit of more fundamental scientific questions essential to establishing the foundation of forensic science. The broader research community generally is not engaged in conducting research relevant to advancing the forensic science disciplines.

The forensic science enterprise also is hindered by its extreme disaggregation—marked by multiple types of practitioners with different levels of education and training and different professional cultures and standards for performance and a reliance on apprentice-type training and a guild-like structure of disciplines, which work against the goal of a single forensic science profession. Many forensic scientists are given scant opportunity for professional activities, such as attending conferences or publishing their research, which could help strengthen the professional community and offset some of the disaggregation. The fragmented nature of the enterprise raises the worrisome prospect that the quality of evidence presented in court, and its interpretation, can vary unpredictably according to jurisdiction.

Numerous professional associations are organized around the forensic science disciplines, and many of them are involved in training and education (see Chapter 8) and are developing standards and accreditation and certification programs (see Chapter 7). The efforts of these groups are laudable. However, except for the largest organizations, it is not clear how these associations interact or the extent to which they share requirements, standards, or policies. Thus, there is a need for more consistent and harmonized requirements.

In the course of its deliberations and review of the forensic science enterprise, it became obvious to the committee that, although congressional action will not remedy all of the deficiencies in forensic science methods and practices, truly meaningful advances will not come without significant concomitant leadership from the federal government. The forensic science enterprise lacks the necessary governance structure to pull itself up from its current weaknesses. Of the many professional societies that serve the enterprise, none is dominant, and none has clearly articulated the need for change or presented a vision for accomplishing it. And clearly no municipal or state forensic office has the mandate to lead the entire enterprise. The major federal resources—NIJ and the FBI Laboratory—have provided modest leadership, for which they should be commended: NIJ has contributed a helpful research program and the FBI Laboratory has spearheaded the SWGs. But again, neither entity has recognized, let alone articulated, a need for change or a vision for achieving it. Neither has the full confidence of the larger forensic science community. And because both are part of a prosecutorial department of the government, they could be subject to subtle contextual biases that should not be allowed to undercut the power of forensic science.

The forensic science enterprise needs strong governance to adopt and promote an aggressive, long-term agenda to help strengthen the forensic science disciplines. Governance must be strong enough—and independent enough—to identify the limitations of forensic science methodologies, and must be well connected with the Nation's scientific research base to effect meaningful advances in forensic science practices. The governance structure must be able to create appropriate incentives for jurisdictions to adopt and adhere to best practices and promulgate the necessary sanctions to discourage bad practices. It must have influence with educators in order to effect improvements to forensic science education. It must be able to identify standards and enforce them. A governance entity must be geared toward (and be credible within) the law enforcement community, but it must have strengths that extend beyond that area. Oversight of the forensic science community and medical examiner system will sweep broadly into areas of criminal investigation and prosecution, civil litigation, legal reform, investigation of insurance claims, national disaster planning and preparedness, homeland security, certification of federal, state, and local forensic practitioners, public health, accreditation of public and private laboratories, research to improve forensic methodologies, education programs in colleges and universities, and advancing technology.

The committee considered whether such a governing entity could be established within an existing federal agency. The National Science Foundation (NSF) was considered because of its strengths in leading research and its connections to the research and education communities. NSF is surely capable of building and sustaining a research base, but it has very thin ties to the forensic science community. It would be necessary for NSF to take many untested steps if it were to assume responsibility for the governance of applied fields of science. The committee also considered NIST. In the end analysis, however, NIST did not appear to be a viable option. It has a good program of research targeted at forensic science and law enforcement, but the program is modest. NIST also has strong ties to industry and academia, and it has an eminent history in standard setting and method development. But its ties to the forensic science community are still limited, and it would not be seen as a natural leader by the scholars, scientists, and practitioners in the field. In sum, the committee concluded that neither NSF nor NIST has the breadth of experience or institutional capacity to establish an effective governance structure for the forensic science enterprise.

There was also a strong consensus in the committee that no existing or new division or unit within DOJ would be an appropriate location for a new entity governing the forensic science community. DOJ's principal mission is to enforce the law and defend the interests of the United States according to the law. Agencies within DOJ operate pursuant to this mission. The FBI, for example, is the investigative arm of DOJ and its principal missions are to produce and use intelligence to protect the Nation from threats and to bring to justice those who violate the law. The work of these law enforcement units is critically important to the Nation, but the scope of the work done by DOJ units is much narrower than the promise of a strong forensic science community. Forensic science serves more than just law enforcement; and when it does serve law enforcement, it must be equally available to law enforcement officers, prosecutors, *and* defendants in the criminal justice system. The entity that is established to govern the forensic science community cannot be principally beholden to law enforcement. The potential for conflicts of interest between the needs of law enforcement and the broader needs of forensic science are too great. In addition, the committee determined that the research funding strategies of DOJ have not adequately served the broad needs of the forensic science community. This is understandable, but not acceptable when the issue is whether an agency is best suited to support and oversee the Nation's forensic science community. In sum, the committee concluded that advancing *science* in the forensic science enterprise is not likely to be achieved within the confines of DOJ.

Furthermore, there is little doubt that some existing federal entities are too wedded to the current "fragmented" forensic science community, which is deficient in too many respects. Most notably, these existing agencies have failed to pursue a rigorous research agenda to confirm the evidentiary reliability of methodologies used in a number of forensic science disciplines. These agencies are not good candidates to oversee the overhaul of the forensic science community in the United States.

Finally, some existing federal agencies with other missions occasionally have undertaken projects affecting the forensic science community. These entities are better left to continue the good work that defines their principal missions. More responsibility is not better for these existing entities, nor would it be better for the forensic science community or the Nation.

The committee thus concluded that the problems at issue are too serious and important to be subsumed by an existing federal agency. It also concluded that no existing federal agency has the capacity or appropriate mission to take on the roles and responsibilities needed to govern and improve the forensic science enterprise.

The committee believes that what is needed to support and oversee the forensic science community is a new, strong, and independent entity that could take on the tasks that would be assigned to it in a manner that is as objective and free of bias as possible—one with no ties to the past and with the authority and resources to implement a fresh agenda designed to address the problems found by the committee and discussed in this report. A new organization should not be encumbered by the assumptions, expectations, and deficiencies of the existing fragmented infrastructure, which has failed to address the needs and challenges of the forensic science disciplines.

This new entity must be an independent federal agency established to address the needs of the forensic science community, and it must meet the following minimum criteria:

- It must have a culture that is strongly rooted in science, with strong ties to the national research and teaching communities, including federal laboratories.
- It must have strong ties to state and local forensic entities as well as to the professional organizations within the forensic science community.

- It must not be in any way committed to the existing system, but should be informed by its experiences.
- It must not be part of a law enforcement agency.
- It must have the funding, independence, and sufficient prominence to raise the profile of the forensic science disciplines and push effectively for improvements.
- It must be led by persons who are skilled and experienced in developing and executing national strategies and plans for standard setting; managing accreditation and testing processes; and developing and implementing rulemaking, oversight, and sanctioning processes.

No federal agency currently exists that meets all of these criteria.

Recommendation 1:

To promote the development of forensic science into a mature field of multidisciplinary research and practice, founded on the systematic collection and analysis of relevant data, Congress should establish and appropriate funds for an independent federal entity, the National Institute of Forensic Science (NIFS). NIFS should have a full-time administrator and an advisory board with expertise in research and education, the forensic science disciplines, physical and life sciences, forensic pathology, engineering, information technology, measurements and standards, testing and evaluation, law, national security, and public policy. NIFS should focus on:

(a) establishing and enforcing best practices for forensic science professionals and laboratories;
(b) establishing standards for the mandatory accreditation of forensic science laboratories and the mandatory certification of forensic scientists and medical examiners/forensic pathologists—and identifying the entity/entities that will develop and implement accreditation and certification;
(c) promoting scholarly, competitive peer-reviewed research and technical development in the forensic science disciplines and forensic medicine;
(d) developing a strategy to improve forensic science research and educational programs, including forensic pathology;
(e) establishing a strategy, based on accurate data on the forensic science community, for the efficient allocation of available funds to give strong support to forensic methodologies and practices in addition to DNA analysis;

(f) funding state and local forensic science agencies, independent research projects, and educational programs as recommended in this report, with conditions that aim to advance the credibility and reliability of the forensic science disciplines;

(g) overseeing education standards and the accreditation of forensic science programs in colleges and universities;

(h) developing programs to improve understanding of the forensic science disciplines and their limitations within legal systems; and

(i) assessing the development and introduction of new technologies in forensic investigations, including a comparison of new technologies with former ones.

The benefits that will flow from a strong, independent, strategic, coherent, and well-funded federal program to support and oversee the forensic science disciplines in this country are clear: The Nation will (1) bolster its ability to more accurately identify true perpetrators and exclude those who are falsely accused; (2) improve its ability to effectively respond to, attribute, and prosecute threats to homeland security; and (3) reduce the likelihood of convictions resting on inaccurate data. Moreover, establishing the scientific foundation of the forensic science disciplines, providing better education and training, and requiring certification and accreditation will position the forensic science community to take advantage of current and future scientific advances.

The creation of a new federal entity undoubtedly will pose challenges, not the least of which will be budgetary constraints. The committee is not in a position to estimate how much it will cost to implement the recommendations in this report; this is a matter best left to the expertise of the Congressional Budget Office. What is clear, however, is that Congress must take aggressive action if the worst ills of the forensic science community are to be cured. Political and budgetary concerns should not deter bold, creative, and forward-looking action, because the country cannot afford to suffer the consequences of inaction. It will also take time and patience to implement the recommendations in this report. But this is true with any large, complex, important, and challenging enterprise.

The committee strongly believes that the greatest hope for success in this enterprise will come with the creation of the National Institute of Forensic Science (NIFS) to oversee and direct the forensic science community. The remaining recommendations in this report are crucially tied to the creation of NIFS. However, each recommendation is a separate, essential piece of the plan to improve the forensic science community in the United States. Therefore, even if the creation of NIFS is forestalled, the committee vigorously supports the adoption of the core ideas and principles embedded in each of the following recommendations.

Standardized Terminology and Reporting

The terminology used in reporting and testifying about the results of forensic science investigations must be standardized. Many terms are used by forensic scientists in scientific reports and in court testimony that describe findings, conclusions, and degrees of association between evidentiary material (e.g., hairs, fingerprints, fibers) and particular people or objects. Such terms include, but are not limited to "match," "consistent with," "identical," "similar in all respects tested," and "cannot be excluded as the source of." The use of such terms can and does have a profound effect on how the trier of fact in a criminal or civil matter perceives and evaluates scientific evidence. Although some forensic science disciplines have proposed reporting vocabulary and scales, the use of the recommended language is not standard practice among forensic science practitioners.

As a general matter, laboratory reports generated as the result of a scientific analysis should be complete and thorough. They should contain, at minimum, "methods and materials," "procedures," "results," "conclusions," and, as appropriate, sources and magnitudes of uncertainty in the procedures and conclusions (e.g., levels of confidence). Some forensic science laboratory reports meet this standard of reporting, but many do not. Some reports contain only identifying and agency information, a brief description of the evidence being submitted, a brief description of the types of analysis requested, and a short statement of the results (e.g., "the greenish, brown plant material in item #1 was identified as marijuana"), and they include no mention of methods or any discussion of measurement uncertainties.

Many clinical and testing disciplines outside the forensic science disciplines have standards, templates, and protocols for data reporting. A good example is the ISO/IEC 17025 standard (commonly called "ISO 17025"). ISO 17025 is an international standard published by the International Organization for Standardization (ISO) that specifies the general requirements for the competence to carry out tests and/or calibrations. These requirements have been used by accrediting agencies to determine what a laboratory must do to secure accreditation. In addition, some SWGs in the forensic disciplines have scoring systems for reporting findings, but these systems are neither uniformly nor consistently used. In other words, although appropriate standards exist, they are not always followed. Forensic reports, and any courtroom testimony stemming from them, must include clear characterizations of the limitations of the analyses, including measures of uncertainty in reported results and associated estimated probabilities where possible.

Recommendation 2:

The National Institute of Forensic Science (NIFS), after reviewing established standards such as ISO 17025, and in consultation with its advisory board, should establish standard terminology to be used in reporting on and testifying about the results of forensic science investigations. Similarly, it should establish model laboratory reports for different forensic science disciplines and specify the minimum information that should be included. As part of the accreditation and certification processes, laboratories and forensic scientists should be required to utilize model laboratory reports when summarizing the results of their analyses.

More and Better Research

As noted above, some forensic science disciplines are supported by little rigorous systematic research to validate the discipline's basic premises and techniques. There is no evident reason why such research cannot be conducted. Much more federal funding is needed to support research in the forensic science disciplines and forensic pathology in universities and private laboratories committed to such work.

The forensic science and medical examiner communities will be improved by opportunities to collaborate with the broader science and engineering communities. In particular, there is an urgent need for collaborative efforts to (1) develop new technical methods or provide in-depth grounding for advances developed in the forensic science disciplines; (2) provide an interface between the forensic science and medical examiner communities and basic sciences; and (3) create fertile ground for discourse among the communities. NIFS should recommend, implement, and guide strategies for supporting such initiatives.

Recommendation 3:

Research is needed to address issues of accuracy, reliability, and validity in the forensic science disciplines. The National Institute of Forensic Science (NIFS) should competitively fund peer-reviewed research in the following areas:

(a) **Studies establishing the scientific bases demonstrating the validity of forensic methods.**

(b) **The development and establishment of quantifiable measures of the reliability and accuracy of forensic analyses. Studies of the reliability and accuracy of forensic techniques should reflect actual practice on realisticcase scenarios, averaged across a representative sample of forensic scientists and laboratories. Studies also should establish the limits of reliability and accuracy that analytic methods can be expected to achieve as the conditions of forensic evidence vary. The research by which measures of reliability and accuracy are determined should be peer reviewed and published in respected scientific journals.**

(c) **The development of quantifiable measures of uncertainty in the conclusions of forensic analyses.**

(d) **Automated techniques capable of enhancing forensic technologies.**

To answer questions regarding the reliability and accuracy of a forensic analysis, the research needs to distinguish between average performance (achieved across individual practitioners and laboratories) and individual performance (achieved by the specific practitioner and laboratory). Whether a forensic procedure is sufficient under the rules of evidence governing criminal and civil litigation raises difficult legal issues that are outside the realm of scientific inquiry. (Some of the legal issues are addressed in Chapter 3.)

Best Practices and Standards

Although there have been notable efforts to achieve standardization and develop best practices in some forensic science disciplines and the medical examiner system, most disciplines still lack best practices or any coherent structure for the enforcement of operating standards, certification, and accreditation. Standards and codes of ethics exist in some fields, and there are some functioning certification and accreditation programs, but none are mandatory. In short, oversight and enforcement of operating standards, certification, accreditation, and ethics are lacking in most local and state jurisdictions.

Scientific and medical assessment conducted in forensic investigations should be independent of law enforcement efforts either to prosecute criminal suspects or even to determine whether a criminal act has indeed been committed. Administratively, this means that forensic scientists should function independently of law enforcement administrators. The best science is conducted in a scientific setting as opposed to a law enforcement setting. Because forensic scientists often are driven in their work by a need to answer a particular question related to the issues of a particular case, they sometimes face pressure to sacrifice appropriate methodology for the sake of expediency.

Recommendation 4:

> **To improve the scientific bases of forensic science examinations and to maximize independence from or autonomy within the law enforcement community, Congress should authorize and appropriate incentive funds to the National Institute of Forensic Science (NIFS) for allocation to state and local jurisdictions for the purpose of removing all public forensic laboratories and facilities from the administrative control of law enforcement agencies or prosecutors' offices.**

Recommendation 5:

> **The National Institute of Forensic Science (NIFS) should encourage research programs on human observer bias and sources of human error in forensic examinations. Such programs might include studies to determine the effects of contextual bias in forensic practice (e.g., studies to determine whether and to what extent the results of forensic analyses are influenced by knowledge regarding the background of the suspect and the investigator's theory of the case). In addition, research on sources of human error should be closely linked with research conducted to quantify and characterize the amount of error. Based on the results of these studies, and in consultation with its advisory board, NIFS should develop standard operating procedures (that will lay the foundation for model protocols) to minimize, to the greatest extent reasonably possible, potential bias and sources of human error in forensic practice. These standard operating procedures should apply to all forensic analyses that may be used in litigation.**

Recommendation 6:

> **To facilitate the work of the National Institute of Forensic Science (NIFS), Congress should authorize and appropriate funds to NIFS to work with the National Institute of Standards and Technology (NIST), in conjunction with government laboratories, universities, and private laboratories, and in consultation with Scientific Working Groups, to develop tools for advancing measurement, validation, reliability, information sharing, and proficiency testing in forensic science and to establish protocols for forensic examina-**

tions, methods, and practices. Standards should reflect best practices and serve as accreditation tools for laboratories and as guides for the education, training, and certification of professionals. Upon completion of its work, NIST and its partners should report findings and recommendations to NIFS for further dissemination and implementation.

Quality Control, Assurance, and Improvement

In a field such as medical diagnostics, a health care provider typically can track a patient's progress to see whether the original diagnosis was accurate and helpful. For example, widely accepted programs of quality control ensure timely feedback involving the diagnoses that result from mammography. Other examples of quality assurance and improvement—including the development of standardized vocabularies, ontologies, and scales for interpreting diagnostic tests and developing standards for accreditation of services—pervade diagnostic medicine. This type of systematic and routine feedback is an essential element of any field striving for continuous improvement. The forensic science disciplines likewise must become a self-correcting enterprise, developing and implementing feedback loops that allow the profession to discover past mistakes. A particular need exists for routine, mandatory proficiency testing that emulates a realistic, representative cross-section of casework, for example, DNA proficiency testing.

Recommendation 7:

Laboratory accreditation and individual certification of forensic science professionals should be mandatory, and all forensic science professionals should have access to a certification process. In determining appropriate standards for accreditation and certification, the National Institute of Forensic Science (NIFS) should take into account established and recognized international standards, such as those published by the International Organization for Standardization (ISO). No person (public or private) should be allowed to practice in a forensic science discipline or testify as a forensic science professional without certification. Certification requirements should include, at a minimum, written examinations, supervised practice, proficiency testing, continuing education, recertification procedures, adherence to a code of ethics, and effective disciplinary procedures. All laboratories and facilities (public or private) should be accredited, and all forensic science professionals should be certified, when eligible, within a time period established by NIFS.

Recommendation 8:

> **Forensic laboratories should establish routine quality assurance and quality control procedures to ensure the accuracy of forensic analyses and the work of forensic practitioners. Quality control procedures should be designed to identify mistakes, fraud, and bias; confirm the continued validity and reliability of standard operating procedures and protocols; ensure that best practices are being followed; and correct procedures and protocols that are found to need improvement.**

Codes of Ethics

A number of forensic science organizations—such as AAFS, the Midwestern Association of Forensic Scientists, ASCLD, and NAME—have adopted codes of ethics. The codes that exist are sometimes comprehensive, but they vary in content. While there is no reason to doubt that many forensic scientists understand their ethical obligations and practice in an ethical way, there are no consistent mechanisms for enforcing any of the existing codes of ethics. Many jurisdictions do not require certification in the same way that, for example, states require lawyers to be licensed. Therefore, few forensic science practitioners face the threat of official sanctions or loss of certification for serious ethical violations. And it is unclear whether and to what extent forensic science practitioners are required to adhere to ethics standards as a condition of employment.

Recommendation 9:

> **The National Institute of Forensic Science (NIFS), in consultation with its advisory board, should establish a national code of ethics for all forensic science disciplines and encourage individual societies to incorporate this national code as part of their professional code of ethics. Additionally, NIFS should explore mechanisms of enforcement for those forensic scientists who commit serious ethical violations. Such a code could be enforced through a certification process for forensic scientists.**

Insufficient Education and Training

Forensic science examiners need to understand the principles, practices, and contexts of scientific methodology, as well as the distinctive features of their specialty. Ideally, training should move beyond apprentice-like transmittal of practices to education based on scientifically valid principles. In addition to the practical experience and learning acquired during an internship, a trainee should acquire rigorous interdisciplinary education and training in the scientific areas that constitute the basis for the particular forensic discipline and instruction on how to document and report the analysis. A trainee also should have working knowledge of basic quantitative calculations, including statistics and probability, as needed for the applicable discipline.

To correct some of the existing deficiencies, it is crucially important to improve undergraduate and graduate forensic science programs. Legitimization of practices in forensic disciplines must be based on established scientific knowledge, principles, and practices, which are best learned through formal education. Apprenticeship has a secondary role, and under no circumstances can it supplant the need for the scientific basis of education in and the practice of forensic science.

In addition, lawyers and judges often have insufficient training and background in scientific methodology, and they often fail to fully comprehend the approaches employed by different forensic science disciplines and the reliability of forensic science evidence that is offered in trial. Such training is essential, because any checklist for the admissibility of scientific or technical testimony is imperfect. Conformance with items on a checklist can suggest that testimony is reliable, but it does not guarantee it. Better connections must be established and promoted between experts in the forensic science disciplines and law schools, legal scholars, and practitioners. The fruits of any advances in the forensic science disciplines should be transferred directly to legal scholars and practitioners (including civil litigators, prosecutors, and criminal defense counsel), federal, state, and local legislators, members of the judiciary, and law enforcement officials, so that appropriate adjustments can be made in criminal and civil laws and procedures, model jury instructions, law enforcement practices, litigation strategies, and judicial decisionmaking. Law schools should enhance this connection by offering courses in the forensic science disciplines, by offering credit for forensic science courses taken in other colleges, and by developing joint degree programs. And judges need to be better educated in forensic science methodologies and practices.

Recommendation 10:

> **To attract students in the physical and life sciences to pursue graduate studies in multidisciplinary fields critical to forensic science practice, Congress should authorize and appropriate funds to the National Institute of Forensic Science (NIFS) to work with appropriate organizations and educational institutions to improve and**

develop graduate education programs designed to cut across organizational, programmatic, and disciplinary boundaries. To make these programs appealing to potential students, they must include attractive scholarship and fellowship offerings. Emphasis should be placed on developing and improving research methods and methodologies applicable to forensic science practice and on funding research programs to attract research universities and students in fields relevant to forensic science. NIFS should also support law school administrators and judicial education organizations in establishing continuing legal education programs for law students, practitioners, and judges.

The Medicolegal Death Investigation System

Although steps have been taken to transform the medicolegal death investigation system, the shortage of resources and lack of consistent educational and training requirements (particularly in the coroner system)[26] prevent the system from taking full advantage of tools—such as CT scans and digital X-rays—that the medical system and other scientific disciplines have to offer. In addition, more rigorous efforts are needed in the areas of accreditation and adherence to standards. Currently, requirements for practitioners vary from nothing more than age and residency requirements to certification by the American Board of Pathology in forensic pathology.

Funds are needed to assess the medicolegal death investigation system to determine its status and needs, using as a benchmark the current requirements of NAME relating to professional credentials, standards, and accreditation. And funds are needed to modernize and improve the medicolegal death investigation system. As it now stands, medical examiners and coroners (ME/Cs) are essentially ineligible for direct federal funding and grants from DOJ, DHS, or the Department of Health and Human Services (through the National Institutes of Health). The Paul Coverdell National Forensic Science Improvement Act is the only federal grant program that names medical examiners and coroners as eligible for grants. However, ME/Cs must compete with public safety agencies for Coverdell grants; as a result, the funds available to ME/Cs are inadequate. The simple reality is that the program has not been sufficiently funded to provide significant improvements in ME/C systems.

In addition to direct funding, there are other initiatives that should be pursued to improve the medicolegal death investigation system. The Association of American Medical Colleges and other appropriate profes-

[26] Institute of Medicine. 2003. *Workshop on the Medicolegal Death Investigation System*. Washington, DC: The National Academies Press.

sional organizations should organize collaborative activities in education, training, and research to strengthen the relationship between the medical examiner community and its counterparts in the larger academic medical community. Medical examiner offices with training programs affiliated with medical schools should be eligible to compete for funds. Funding should be available to support pathologists seeking forensic fellowships. In addition, forensic pathology fellows could be allowed to apply for medical school loan forgiveness if they stay full time at a medical examiner's office for a reasonable period of time.

Additionally, NIFS should seek funding from Congress to support the joint development of programs to include medical examiners and medical examiner offices in national disaster planning, preparedness, and consequence management, involving the Centers for Disease Control and Prevention (CDC) and DHS. Uniform statewide and interstate standards of operation would be needed to assist in the management of cross-jurisdictional and interstate events. NIFS should support a federal program underwriting the development of software for use by ME/C systems for the management of multisite, multiple fatality events.

NIFS should work with groups such as the National Conference of Commissioners on Uniform State Laws, the American Law Institute, and NAME, in collaboration with other appropriate professional groups, to update the 1954 Model Post-Mortem Examinations Act and draft legislation for a modern model death investigation code. An improved code might, for example, include the elements of a competent medical death investigation system and clarify the jurisdiction of the medical examiner with respect to organ donation.

The foregoing ideas must be developed further before any concrete plans can be pursued. There are, however, a number of specific recommendations, which, if adopted, will help to modernize and improve the medicolegal death investigation system. These recommendations deserve the immediate attention of Congress and NIFS.

Recommendation 11:

To improve medicolegal death investigation:

(a) Congress should authorize and appropriate incentive funds to the National Institute of Forensic Science (NIFS) for allocation to states and jurisdictions to establish medical examiner systems, with the goal of replacing and eventually eliminating existing coroner systems. Funds are needed to build regional medical examiner offices, secure necessary equipment, improve administration, and ensure the

education, training, and staffing of medical examiner offices. Funding could also be used to help current medical examiner systems modernize their facilities to meet current Centers for Disease Control and Prevention-recommended autopsy safety requirements.

(b) Congress should appropriate resources to the National Institutes of Health (NIH) and NIFS, jointly, to support research, education, and training in forensic pathology. NIH, with NIFS participation, or NIFS in collaboration with content experts, should establish a study section to establish goals, to review and evaluate proposals in these areas, and to allocate funding for collaborative research to be conducted by medical examiner offices and medical universities. In addition, funding, in the form of medical student loan forgiveness and/or fellowship support, should be made available to pathology residents who choose forensic pathology as their specialty.

(c) NIFS, in collaboration with NIH, the National Association of Medical Examiners, the American Board of Medicolegal Death Investigators, and other appropriate professional organizations, should establish a Scientific Working Group (SWG) for forensic pathology and medicolegal death investigation. The SWG should develop and promote standards for best practices, administration, staffing, education, training, and continuing education for competent death scene investigation and postmortem examinations. Best practices should include the utilization of new technologies such as laboratory testing for the molecular basis of diseases and the implementation of specialized imaging techniques.

(d) All medical examiner offices should be accredited pursuant to NIFS-endorsed standards within a timeframe to be established by NIFS.

(e) All federal funding should be restricted to accredited offices that meet NIFS-endorsed standards or that demonstrate significant and measurable progress in achieving accreditation within prescribed deadlines.

(f) All medicolegal autopsies should be performed or supervised by a board certified forensic pathologist. This requirement should take effect within a timeframe to be established by NIFS, following consultation with governing state institutions.

AFIS and Database Interoperability

Great improvement is necessary in AFIS interoperability. Crimes may go unsolved today simply because it is not possible for investigating agencies to search across all the databases that might hold a suspect's fingerprints or that may contain a match for an unidentified latent print from a crime scene. It is also possible that some individuals have been wrongly convicted because of the limitations of fingerprint searches.

At present, serious practical problems pose obstacles to the achievement of nationwide AFIS interoperability. These problems include convincing AFIS equipment vendors to cooperate and collaborate with the law enforcement community and researchers to create and use baseline standards for sharing fingerprint data and create a common interface. Second, law enforcement agencies lack the resources needed to transition to interoperable AFIS implementations. Third, coordinated jurisdictional agreements and public policies are needed to allow law enforcement agencies to share fingerprint data more broadly.

Given the disparity in resources and information technology expertise available to local, state, and federal law enforcement agencies, the relatively slow pace of interoperability efforts to date, and the potential gains from increased AFIS interoperability, the committee believes that a broad-based emphasis on achieving nationwide fingerprint data interoperability is needed.

Recommendation 12:

Congress should authorize and appropriate funds for the National Institute of Forensic Science (NIFS) to launch a new broad-based effort to achieve nationwide fingerprint data interoperability. To that end, NIFS should convene a task force comprising relevant experts from the National Institute of Standards and Technology and the major law enforcement agencies (including representatives from the local, state, federal, and, perhaps, international levels) and industry, as appropriate, to develop:

(a) **standards for representing and communicating image and minutiae data among Automated Fingerprint Identification Systems. Common data standards would facilitate the sharing of fingerprint data among law enforcement agencies at the local, state, federal, and even international levels, which could result in more solved crimes, fewer wrongful identifications, and greater efficiency with respect to fingerprint searches; and**

(b) **baseline standards—to be used with computer algorithms—to map, record, and recognize features in fingerprint images, and a research agenda for the continued improvement, refinement, and characterization of the accuracy of these algorithms (including quantification of error rates).**

These steps toward AFIS interoperability must be accompanied by federal, state, and local funds to support jurisdictions in upgrading, operating, and ensuring the integrity and security of their systems; retraining current staff; and training new fingerprint examiners to gain the desired benefits of true interoperability. Additionally, greater scientific benefits can be realized through the availability of fingerprint data or databases for research purposes (using, of course, all the modern security and privacy protections available to scientists when working with such data). Once created, NIFS might also be tasked with the maintenance and periodic review of the new standards and procedures.

Forensic Science Disciplines and Homeland Security

Good forensic science and medical examiner practices are of clear value from a homeland security perspective, because of their roles in bringing criminals to justice and in dealing with the effects of natural and human-made mass disasters. Forensic science techniques (e.g., the evaluation of DNA fragments) enable more thorough investigations of crime scenes that have been damaged physically. Routine and trustworthy collection of digital evidence, and improved techniques and timeliness for its analysis, can be of great potential value in identifying terrorist activity. Therefore, the forensic science community has a role to play in homeland security. However, to capitalize on this potential, the forensic science and medical examiner communities must be well interfaced with homeland security efforts, so that they can contribute when needed. To be successful, this interface will require the establishment of good working relationships between federal, state, and local jurisdictions, the creation of strong security programs to protect data transmittals between jurisdictions, the development of additional training for forensic scientists and crime scene investigators, and the promulgation of contingency plans that will promote efficient team efforts on demand. Policy issues relating to the enforcement of homeland security are not within the scope of the committee's charge and, thus, are beyond the scope of the report. It can hardly be doubted, however, that improvements in the forensic science community and medical examiner system could greatly enhance the capabilities of homeland security.

Recommendation 13:

> Congress should provide funding to the National Institute of Forensic Science (NIFS) to prepare, in conjunction with the Centers for Disease Control and Prevention and the Federal Bureau of Investigation, forensic scientists and crime scene investigators for their potential roles in managing and analyzing evidence from events that affect homeland security, so that maximum evidentiary value is preserved from these unusual circumstances and the safety of these personnel is guarded. This preparation also should include planning and preparedness (to include exercises) for the interoperability of local forensic personnel with federal counterterrorism organizations.

1

Introduction

The world of crime is a complex place. Crime takes place in the workplace, schools, homes, places of business, motor vehicles, on the streets, and, increasingly, on the Internet. Crimes are committed at all hours of the day and night and in all regions of the country, in rural, suburban, and urban environments. In many cases, a weapon is used, such as a handgun, knife, or blunt object. Sometimes the perpetrator is under the influence of alcohol or illicit drugs. In other cases, no one is physically hurt, but property is damaged or stolen—for example, when burglary, theft, and motor vehicle theft occur. In recent years, information technology has provided the opportunity for identity theft and other types of cybercrime. A crime scene often is rich in information that reveals the nature of the criminal activity and the identities of those persons involved. Perpetrators and victims may leave behind blood, saliva, skin cells, hair, fingerprints, footprints, tire prints, clothing fibers, digital and photographic images, audio data, handwriting, and the residual effects and debris of arson, gunshots, and unlawful entry. Some crimes transcend borders, such as those involving homeland security, for which forensic evidence can be gathered.

Crime scene investigators, with varying levels of training and experience, search for and collect evidence at the scene, preserve and secure it in tamper-evident packaging, label it, and send it to an appropriate agency—normally a crime laboratory, where it may be analyzed by forensic examiners. If a death was sudden, unexpected, or resulted from violence, a medicolegal investigator (e.g., coroner, medical examiner, forensic pathologist, physician's assistant) will be responsible for determining whether a homicide, suicide, or accident occurred and will certify the cause and manner of death.

Crime scene evidence moves through a chain of custody in which, depending on their physical characteristics (e.g., blood, fiber, handwriting), samples are analyzed according to any of a number of analytical protocols, and results are reported to law enforcement and court officials. When evidence is analyzed, typically forensic science "attempts to uncover the actions or happenings of an event . . . by way of (1) identification (categorization), (2) individualization, (3) association, and (4) reconstruction."[1] Evidence also is analyzed for the purpose of excluding individuals or sources.

Not all forensic services are performed in traditional crime laboratories by trained forensic scientists. Some forensic tests might be conducted by a sworn law enforcement officer with no scientific training or credentials, other than experience. In smaller jurisdictions, members of the local police or sheriff's department might conduct the analyses of evidence, such as latent print examinations and footwear comparisons. In the United States, if evidence is sent to a crime laboratory, that facility might be publicly or privately operated, although private laboratories typically do not visit crime scenes to collect evidence or serve as the first recipient of physical evidence. Public crime laboratories are organized at the city, county, state, or federal level. A law enforcement agency that does not operate its own crime laboratory typically has access to a higher-level laboratory (e.g., at the state or county level) or a private laboratory for analysis of evidence.

According to a 2005 census by the Bureau of Justice Statistics (BJS),[2] 389 publicly funded forensic crime laboratories were operating in the United States in 2005: These included 210 state or regional laboratories, 84 county laboratories, 62 municipal laboratories, and 33 federal laboratories, and they received evidence from nearly 2.7 million criminal cases[3] in 2005. These laboratories are staffed by individuals with a wide range of training and expertise, from scientists with Ph.D.s to technicians who have been trained largely on the job. No data are available on the size and depth of the private forensic laboratories, except for private DNA laboratories.

In general, a traditional crime laboratory has been defined as constituting "a single laboratory or system comprised of scientists analyzing evidence

---

[1] K. Inman and N. Rudin. 2002. The origin of evidence. *Forensic Science International* 126:11-16.

[2] M.R. Durose. 2008. *Census of Publicly Funded Forensic Crime Laboratories, 2005*. U.S. Department of Justice, Office of Justice Programs, Bureau of Justice Statistics. Available at www.ojp.usdoj.gov/bjs/pub/pdf/cpffcl05.pdf.

[3] Ibid., p. 9. "A 'case' is defined as evidence submitted from a single criminal investigation. A case may include multiple 'requests' for forensic services. For example, one case may include a request for biology screening and a request for latent prints."

in one or more of the following disciplines: controlled substances, trace, biology (including DNA), toxicology, latent prints, questioned documents, firearms/toolmarks, or crime scene."[4] More recently, increasing numbers of laboratories specialize in the analysis of evidence in one area, for example, DNA or digital evidence. (See Chapter 5 for a more complete description and discussion of the forensic science disciplines.)

The capacity and quality of the current forensic science system have been the focus of increasing attention by Congress, the courts, and the media. New doubts about the accuracy of some forensic science practices have intensified with the growing number of exonerations resulting from DNA analysis (and the concomitant realization that guilty parties sometimes walk free). Greater expectations for precise forensic science evidence raised by DNA testing have forced new scrutiny on other forensic techniques. Emerging scientific advances that could benefit forensic investigation elicit concerns about resources, training, and capacity for implementing new techniques. A crisis in backlogged cases, caused by crime laboratories lacking sufficient resources and qualified personnel, raises concerns about the effectiveness and efficiency of the criminal justice system. When backlogs prolong testing time, issues involving speedy trials may arise. In addition, backlogs discourage law enforcement personnel and organizations from submitting evidence. Laboratories also may restrict submissions of evidence to reduce backlogs. All of these concerns, and more, provide the background against which this report is set.

Finally, if evidence and laboratory tests are mishandled or improperly analyzed; if the scientific evidence carries a false sense of significance; or if there is bias, incompetence, or a lack of adequate internal controls for the evidence introduced by the forensic scientists and their laboratories, the jury or court can be misled, and this could lead to wrongful conviction or exoneration. If juries lose confidence in the reliability of forensic testimony, valid evidence might be discounted, and some innocent persons might be convicted or guilty individuals acquitted.

Recent years have seen a number of concerted efforts by forensic science organizations to strengthen the foundations of many areas of testimony. However, substantial improvement is necessary in the forensic science disciplines to enhance law enforcement's ability to identify those who have or have not committed a crime and to prevent the criminal justice system from erroneously convicting or exonerating the persons who come before it.

[4] Ibid., p. 24.

WHAT IS FORENSIC SCIENCE?

Although there are numerous ways by which to categorize the forensic science disciplines, the committee found the categorization used by the National Institute of Justice to be useful:

1. general toxicology;
2. firearms/toolmarks;
3. questioned documents;
4. trace evidence;
5. controlled substances;
6. biological/serology screening (including DNA analysis);
7. fire debris/arson analysis;
8. impression evidence;
9. blood pattern analysis;
10. crime scene investigation;
11. medicolegal death investigation; and
12. digital evidence.[5]

Some of these disciplines are discussed in Chapter 5. Forensic pathology is considered a subspecialty of medicine and is considered separately in Chapter 9.

The term "forensic science" encompasses a broad range of disciplines, each with its own distinct practices. The forensic science disciplines exhibit wide variability with regard to techniques, methodologies, reliability, level of error, research, general acceptability, and published material (see Chapters 4 through 6). Some of the disciplines are laboratory based (e.g., nuclear and mitochondrial DNA analysis, toxicology, and drug analysis); others are based on expert interpretation of observed patterns (e.g., fingerprints, writing samples, toolmarks, bite marks). Some activities require the skills and analytical expertise of individuals trained as scientists (e.g., chemists or biologists); other activities are conducted by scientists as well as by individuals trained in law enforcement (e.g., crime scene investigators, blood spatter analysts, crime reconstruction specialists), medicine (e.g., forensic pathologists), or laboratory methods (e.g., technologists). Many of the processes used in the forensic science disciplines are largely empirical applications of science—that is, they are not based on a body of knowledge that recognizes the underlying limitations of the scientific principles and methodologies used for problem solving and discovery. It is therefore important to focus on ways to improve, systematize, and monitor the activities and practices

[5] National Institute of Justice. 2006. *Status and Needs of Forensic Science Service Providers: A Report to Congress*. Available at www.ojp.usdoj.gov/nij/pubs-sum/213420.htm.

in the forensic science disciplines and related areas of inquiry. Thus, in this report, the term "forensic science" is used with regard to a broad array of activities, with the recognition that some of these activities might not have a well-developed research base, are not informed by scientific knowledge, or are not developed within the culture of science.

PRESSURES ON THE FORENSIC SCIENCE SYSTEM

As mentioned above, a number of factors have combined in the past few decades to place increasing demands on an already overtaxed, inconsistent, and underresourced forensic science infrastructure. These factors have not only stressed the system's capacity, but also have raised serious questions and concerns about the validity and reliability of some forensic methods and techniques and how forensic evidence is reported to juries and courts.

The Case Backlog—Insufficient Resources

According to the 2005 BJS census report, a typical publicly funded crime laboratory ended the year with a backlog of about 401 requests for services, received another 4,328 such requests, and completed 3,980 of them. Roughly half of all requests were in the area of controlled substances. The average backlog has risen since the 2002 census,[6] with nearly 20 percent of all requests backlogged by year end. The Department of Justice (DOJ) defines a case as backlogged if it remains in the laboratory 30 days or more without the development of a report or analysis. Federal, state, and local laboratories reported a combined backlog of 435,879 requests for forensic analysis.[7] According to the census, a typical laboratory performing DNA testing in 2005 started the year with a backlog of 86 requests, received 337 new requests, completed 265 requests, and finished the year with 152 backlogged requests.

The backlog is exacerbated further by increased requests for quick laboratory results by law enforcement and prosecutors. Witnesses before the committee testified that prosecutors increasingly rely on laboratories to provide results prior to approving charges and have increased requests for additional work on the back end of a case, just before trial.[8] Backlogs are compounded by rising police agency requests for testing (e.g., for DNA evidence found on guns and from nonviolent crime scenes). Laboratories

[6] J.L. Peterson and M.J. Hickman. 2005. *Census of Publicly Funded Forensic Crime Laboratories, 2002*. U.S. Department of Justice, Office of Justice Programs, Bureau of Justice Statistics. Available at www.ojp.usdoj.gov/bjs/pub/pdf/cpffcl02.pdf.

[7] Durose, op. cit.

[8] J.L. Johnson, Laboratory Director, Illinois State Police, Forensic Science Center at Chicago. Presentation to the committee. January 25, 2007.

are thus challenged to balance requests for analyses of "older" and "cold" cases with new cases and must make choices to allocate resources by prioritizing the evidence to be analyzed. In California, voters passed Proposition 69, requiring that a DNA sample be obtained from all convicted felons. This increased the workload and resulted in 235,000 backlogged cases by the end of 2005.[9]

These backlogs can result in prolonged incarceration for innocent persons wrongly charged and awaiting trial and delayed investigation of those who are not yet charged, and they can contribute to the release of guilty suspects who go on to commit further crimes.

The Ascendancy of DNA Analysis and a New Standard

In the 1980s, the opportunity to use the techniques of DNA technologies to identify individuals for forensic and other purposes became apparent. Early concerns about the use of DNA for forensic casework included the following: (1) whether the detection methods were scientifically valid—that is, whether they correctly identified true matches and true nonmatches and (2) whether DNA analysis of forensic samples is reliable—that is, whether it yields reproducible results under defined conditions of use. A 1990 report by the congressional Office of Technology Assessment concluded that DNA tests were both reliable and valid in the forensic context but required a strict set of standards and quality control measures before they could be widely adopted.[10]

In 1990, the Federal Bureau of Investigation (FBI) established guidelines for DNA analysis and proficiency testing and four years later created the Combined DNA Index System (CODIS), which allows federal, state, and local crime laboratories to exchange and compare DNA profiles electronically, thereby linking crimes to each other and to convicted offenders.

In 1992, the National Research Council (NRC) issued *DNA Technology in Forensic Science*, which concluded that, "No laboratory should let its results with a new DNA typing method be used in court, unless it has undergone . . . proficiency testing via blind trials."[11] In addition, the report cautioned that numerous questions must be answered about using DNA evidence in a forensic context that rarely had to be considered by scientists engaged in DNA research—for example, questions involving contamination, degradation, and a number of statistical issues. While confirming that

---

[9] Durose, op. cit.

[10] U.S. Congress, Office of Technology Assessment. 1990. *Genetic Witness: Forensic Uses of DNA Tests*. OTA-BA-438. Washington, DC: U.S. Government Printing Office, NTIS order #PB90-259110.

[11] National Research Council. 1992. *DNA Technology in Forensic Science*. Washington, DC: National Academy Press, p. 55.

the science behind DNA analysis is valid, a subsequent NRC report in 1996 recommended new ways of interpreting DNA evidence to help answer a key question for jurors—the likelihood that two matching samples can come from different people.[12] This 1996 report recommended a set of statistical calculations that takes population structure into account, which enhanced the validity of the test. The report also called for independent retesting and made recommendations to improve laboratory performance and accountability through, for example, adherence to high-quality standards, accreditation, and proficiency testing.

Since then, the past two decades have seen tremendous growth in the use of DNA evidence in crime scene investigations. Currently more than 175 publicly funded forensic laboratories and approximately 30 private laboratories conduct hundreds of thousands of DNA analyses annually in the United States. In addition, most countries in Europe and Asia have forensic DNA programs. In 2003, President George W. Bush announced a 5-year, $1 billion initiative to improve the use of DNA in the criminal justice system. Called the *President's DNA Initiative*, the program pushed for increased funding, training, and assistance to ensure that DNA technology "reaches its full potential to solve crimes, protect the innocent, and identify missing persons."[13]

Thus, DNA analysis—originally developed in research laboratories in the context of life sciences research—has received heightened scrutiny and funding support. That, combined with its well-defined precision and accuracy, has set the bar higher for other forensic science methodologies, because it has provided a tool with a higher degree of reliability and relevance than any other forensic technique. However, DNA evidence comprises only about 10 percent of case work and is not always relevant to a particular case.[14] Even if DNA evidence is available, it will assist in solving a crime only if it supports an evidential hypothesis that makes guilt or innocence more likely. For example, the fact that DNA evidence of a victim's husband is found in the house in which the couple lived and where the murder took place proves nothing. The fact that the husband's DNA is found under the fingernails of the victim who put up a struggle may have a very different significance. Thus, it is essential to articulate the reasoning process and the context associated with the evidence that is being evaluated.

---

[12] National Research Council. 1996. *The Evaluation of Forensic DNA Evidence: An Update*. Washington, DC: National Academy Press.

[13] See www.dna.gov/info/e_summary.

[14] The American Society of Crime Laboratory Directors. 2004. *180 Day Study: Status and Needs of U.S. Crime Labs*. p. 7, table 2.

Questionable or Questioned Science

The increased use of DNA analysis as a more reliable approach to matching crime scene evidence with suspects and victims has resulted in the reevaluation of older cases that retained biological evidence that could be analyzed by DNA. The number of exonerations resulting from the analysis of DNA has grown across the country in recent years, uncovering a disturbing number of wrongful convictions—some for capital crimes—and exposing serious limitations in some of the forensic science approaches commonly used in the United States.

According to The Innocence Project, there have been 223 postconviction DNA exonerations in the United States since 1989 (as of November 2008).[15] Some have contested the percentage of exonerated defendants whose convictions allegedly were based on faulty science. Although the Innocence Project figures are disputed by forensic scientists who have reexamined the data, even those who are critical of the conclusions of The Innocence Project acknowledge that faulty forensic science has, on occasion, contributed to the wrongful conviction of innocent persons.[16]

The fact is that many forensic tests—such as those used to infer the source of toolmarks or bite marks—have never been exposed to stringent scientific scrutiny. Most of these techniques were developed in crime laboratories to aid in the investigation of evidence from a particular crime scene, and researching their limitations and foundations was never a top priority. There is some logic behind the application of these techniques; practitioners worked hard to improve their methods, and results from other evidence have combined with these tests to give forensic scientists a degree of confidence in their probative value. Before the first offering of the use of DNA in forensic science in 1986, no concerted effort had been made to determine the reliability of these tests, and some in the forensic science and law enforcement communities believed that scientists' ability to withstand cross-examination in court when giving testimony related to these tests was sufficient to demonstrate the tests' reliability. However, although the precise error rates of these forensic tests are still unknown, comparison of their results with DNA testing in the same cases has revealed that some of these analyses, as currently performed, produce erroneous results. The

---

[15] The Innocence Project. *Fact Sheet: Facts on Post-Conviction DNA Exonerations*. Available at www.innocenceproject.org/Content/351.php. See also B.L. Garrett. Judging innocence. 108 COLUM. L. REV. 55 (2008) (discussing the results of an empirical study of the types of faulty evidence that was admitted in more than 200 cases for which DNA testing subsequently enabled postconviction exonerations).

[16] See J. Collins and J. Jarvis. 2008. The wrongful conviction of forensic science. *Crime Lab Report*. July 16. Available at www.crimelabreport.com/library/pdf/wrongful_conviction.pdf. See also N. Rudin and K. Inman. 2008. Who speaks for forensic science? *News of the California Association of Criminalists*. Available at www.cacnews.org/news/4thq08.pdf, p. 10.

conclusions of forensic examiners may or may not be right—depending on the case—but each wrongful conviction based on improperly interpreted evidence is serious, both for the innocent person and also for society, because of the threat that may be posed by a guilty person going free. Some non-DNA forensic tests do not meet the fundamental requirements of science, in terms of reproducibility, validity, and falsifiability (see Chapters 4 through 6).

Even fingerprint analysis has been called into question. For nearly a century, fingerprint examiners have been comparing partial latent fingerprints found at crime scenes to inked fingerprints taken directly from suspects. Fingerprint identifications have been viewed as exact means of associating a suspect with a crime scene print and rarely were questioned.[17] Recently, however, the scientific foundation of the fingerprint field has been questioned, and the suggestion has been made that latent fingerprint identifications may not be as reliable as previously assumed.[18] The question is less a matter of whether each person's fingerprints are permanent and unique—uniqueness is commonly assumed—and more a matter of whether one can determine with adequate reliability that the finger that left an imperfect impression at a crime scene is the same finger that left an impression (with different imperfections) in a file of fingerprints. In October 2007, Baltimore County Circuit Judge Susan M. Souder refused to allow a fingerprint analyst to testify that a latent print was made by the defendant in a death penalty trial. In her ruling, Judge Souder found the traditional method of fingerprint analysis to be "a subjective, untested, unverifiable identification procedure that purports to be infallible."[19]

Some forensic science methods have as their goal the "individualization" of specific types of evidence (typically shoe and tire impressions, dermal ridge prints, toolmarks and firearms, and handwriting). Analysts using such methods believe that unique markings are acquired by a source item in random fashion and that such uniqueness is faithfully transmitted from the source item to the evidence item being examined (or in the case of handwriting, that individuals acquire habits that result in unique handwriting). When the evidence and putative source items are compared, a conclusion of individualization implies that the evidence originated from that source,

[17] R. Epstein. Fingerprints meet *Daubert:* The myth of fingerprint "science" is revealed. 75 *Southern California Law Review* 605 (2002).

[18] S.A. Cole. 2002. *Suspect Identities: A History of Fingerprinting and Criminal Identification.* Boston: Harvard University Press; Epstein, op. cit.

[19] *State of Maryland v. Bryan Rose.* In the Circuit Court for Baltimore County. Case No. K06-545.

to the exclusion of all other possible sources.[20,21] The determination of uniqueness requires measurements of object attributes, data collected on the population frequency of variation in these attributes, testing of attribute independence, and calculations of the probability that different objects share a common set of observable attributes.[22] Importantly, the results of research must be made public so that they can be reviewed, checked by others, criticized, and then revised, and this has not been done for some of the forensic science disciplines.[23] As recently as September 2008, the Detroit Police crime laboratory was shut down following a Michigan State Police audit that found a 10 percent error rate in ballistic evidence.[24]

The forensic science community has had little opportunity to pursue or become proficient in the research that is needed to support what it does. Few sources of funding exist for independent forensic research (see Chapter 2). Most of the studies are commissioned by DOJ and conducted by crime laboratories with little or no participation by the traditional scientific community. In addition, most disciplines in the profession are hindered by a lack of enforceable standards for interpretation of data (see Chapter 7).

Errors and Fraud

In recent years, the integrity of crime laboratories increasingly has been called into question, with some highly publicized cases highlighting the sometimes lax standards of laboratories that have generated questionable or fraudulent evidence and that have lacked quality control measures that would have detected the questionable evidence. In one notorious case, a state-mandated review of analyses conducted by West Virginia State Police laboratory employee Fred Zain revealed that the convictions of more than 100 people were in doubt because Zain had repeatedly falsified evidence in criminal prosecutions. At least 10 men had their convictions overturned as a result.[25] Subsequent reviews questioned whether Zain was ever qualified to perform scientific examinations.[26]

Other scandals, such as one involving the Houston Crime Laboratory

---

[20] M.J. Saks and J.J. Koehler. 2005. The coming paradigm shift in forensic identification science. *Science* 309:892-895.

[21] W.J. Bodziak. 1999. *Footwear Impression Evidence–Detection, Recovery, and Examination.* 2nd ed. Boca Raton, FL: CRC Press.

[22] Ibid. See also NRC, 1996, op. cit.

[23] P.C. Giannelli. Wrongful convictions and forensic science: The need to regulate crime labs. 86 N.C. L. Rev. 163 (2007).

[24] B. Schmitt and J. Swickard. 2008. Detroit Police lab shut down after probe finds errors. *Detroit Free Press* on-line. September 25.

[25] *In the Matter of an Investigation of the West Virginia State Police Crime Laboratory, Serology Division* (WVa 1993) 438 S.E.2d 501(Zaine I); and 445 S.E.2d 165 (Zain II).

[26] Ibid.

in 2003, highlight the sometimes blatant lack of proper education and training of forensic examiners. In the Houston case, several DNA experts went public with accusations that the DNA/Serology Unit of the Houston Police Department Crime Laboratory was performing grossly incompetent work and was presenting findings in a misleading manner designed to unfairly help prosecutors obtain convictions. An audit by the Texas Department of Public Safety confirmed serious inadequacies in the laboratory's procedures, including "routine failure to run essential scientific controls, failure to take adequate measures to prevent contamination of samples, failure to adequately document work performed and results obtained, and routine failure to follow correct procedures for computing statistical frequencies."[27,28]

The Innocence Project has documented instances of both intentional and unintentional laboratory errors that have lead to wrongful convictions, including:

- In the laboratory—contamination and mislabeling of evidence.
- In information provided in forensics reports—falsified results (including "drylabbing," i.e., providing conclusions from tests that were never conducted), and misinterpretation of evidence.
- In the courtroom—suppression of exculpatory evidence; providing a statistical exaggeration of the results of a test conducted on evidence; and providing false testimony about test results.[29]

Saks and Koehler have written that the testimony of forensic scientists is one of many problems in criminal cases today.[30] They cite the norms of science, which emphasize "methodological rigor, openness, and cautious interpretation of data," as norms that often are absent from the forensic science disciplines.

Although cases of fraud appear to be rare, perhaps of more concern is the lack of good data on the accuracy of the analyses conducted in forensic science disciplines and the significant potential for bias that is present in some cases. For example, the FBI was accused of bias in the case of the Madrid bombing suspect Brandon Mayfield (see Box 1-1). In that case, the Inspector General of DOJ launched an investigation. The FBI conducted its

---

[27] *Quality Assurance Audit for Forensic DNA and Convicted Offender DNA Databasing Laboratories. An Audit of the Houston Police Department Crime Laboratory-DNA/Serology Section, December 12-13, 2002.* Available at www.scientific.org/archive/Audit%20Document--Houston.pdf.

[28] See also M.R. Bromwich. 2007. *Final Report of the Independent Investigator for the Houston Police Department Crime Laboratory and Property Room.* Available at www.hpdlabinvestigation.org.

[29] The Innocence Project. Available at www.innocenceproject.org/Content/312.php.

[30] Saks and Koehler, op. cit.

Box 1-1
FBI Statement on Brandon Mayfield Case

"After the March terrorist attacks on commuter trains in Madrid, digital images of partial latent fingerprints obtained from plastic bags that contained detonator caps were submitted by Spanish authorities to the FBI for analysis. The submitted images were searched through the Integrated Automated Fingerprint Identification System (IAFIS). An IAFIS search compares an unknown print to a database of millions of known prints. The result of an IAFIS search produces a short list of potential matches. A trained fingerprint examiner then takes the short list of possible matches and performs an examination to determine whether the unknown print matches a known print in the database.

Using standard protocols and methodologies, FBI fingerprint examiners determined that the latent fingerprint was of value for identification purposes. This print was subsequently linked to Brandon Mayfield. That association was independently analyzed and the results were confirmed by an outside experienced fingerprint expert.

Soon after the submitted fingerprint was associated with Mr. Mayfield, Spanish authorities alerted the FBI to additional information that cast doubt on the findings. As a result, the FBI sent two fingerprint examiners to Madrid, who compared the image the FBI had been provided to the image the Spanish authorities had.

Upon review it was determined that the FBI identification was based on an image of substandard quality, which was particularly problematic because of the remarkable number of points of similarity between Mr. Mayfield's prints and the print details in the images submitted to the FBI."

The FBI's Latent Fingerprint Unit has reviewed its practices and adopted new guidelines for all examiners receiving latent print images when the original evidence is not included.

SOURCE: FBI. May 24, 2004, Press Release. Available at www.fbi.gov/pressrel/pressrel04/mayfield052404.htm.

own review by a panel of independent experts. The reviews concluded that the problem was not the quality of the digital images reviewed, but rather the bias and "circular reasoning" of the FBI examiners.[31]

Parts of the forensic science community have resisted the implications of the mounting criticism of the reliability of forensic analyses by investigative units such as Inspector General reports, The Innocence Project,

---

[31] U.S. Department of Justice, Office of the Inspector General. 2006. *A Review of the FBI's Handling of the Brandon Mayfield Case*. Also see R.B. Stacey. 2005. *Report on the Erroneous Fingerprint Individualization in the Madrid Train Bombing Case*. Available at www.fbi.gov/hq/lab/fsc/current/special_report/2005_special_report.htm.

and studies in the published literature. In testimony before the committee, it was clear that some members of the forensic science community will not concede that there could be less than perfect accuracy either in given laboratories or in specific disciplines, and experts testified to the committee that disagreement remains regarding even what constitutes an error. For example, if the limitations of a given technology lead to an examiner declaring a "match" that is found by subsequent technology (e.g., DNA analysis) to be a "mismatch," there is disagreement within the forensic science community about whether the original determination constitutes an error.[32] Failure to acknowledge uncertainty in findings is common: Many examiners claim in testimony that others in their field would come to the exact same conclusions about the evidence they have analyzed. Assertions of a "100 percent match" contradict the findings of proficiency tests that find substantial rates of erroneous results in some disciplines (i.e., voice identification, bite mark analysis).[33,34]

As an example, in a FBI publication on the correlation of microscopic and mitochondrial DNA hair comparisons, the authors found that even competent hair examiners can make significant errors.[35] In this study, the authors found that in 11 percent of the cases in which the hair examiners declared two hairs to be "similar," subsequent DNA testing revealed that the hairs did not match, which refers either to the competency or the relative ability of the two divergent techniques to identify differences in hair samples, as well as to the probative value of each test.

The insistence by some forensic practitioners that their disciplines employ methodologies that have perfect accuracy and produce no errors has hampered efforts to evaluate the usefulness of the forensic science disciplines. And, although DNA analysis is considered the most reliable forensic tool available today, laboratories nonetheless can make errors working with either nuclear DNA or mtDNA—errors such as mislabeling samples, losing samples, or misinterpreting the data.

Standard setting, accreditation of laboratories, and certification of individuals aim to address many of these problems, and although many laboratories have excellent training and quality control programs, even

---

[32] N. Benedict. 2004. Fingerprints and the *Daubert* standard for admission of scientific evidence: Why fingerprints fail and a proposed remedy. *Arizona Law Review* 46:519; M. Houck, Director of Forensic Science Initiative, West Virginia University. Presentation to the committee. January 25, 2007.

[33] D.L. Faigman, D. Kaye, M.J. Saks, and J. Sanders. 2002. *Modern Scientific Evidence: The Law and Science of Expert Testimony*. St. Paul, MN: Thompson/West.

[34] C.M. Bowers. 2002. The scientific status of bitemark comparisons. In: D.L. Faigman (ed.). *Science in the Law: Forensic Science Issues*. St. Paul, MN: West Publishing.

[35] M. Houck and B. Budowle. 2002. Correlation of microscopic and mitochondrial DNA hair comparisons. *Journal of Forensic Sciences* 47(5):964-967; see also Bromwich, op. cit.

accredited laboratories make mistakes. Furthermore, accreditation is a voluntary program, except in a few jurisdictions in which it is required (New York, Oklahoma, and Texas)[36] (see Chapter 7).

The "CSI Effect"

Media attention has focused recently on what is being called the "CSI Effect," named for popular television shows (such as *Crime Scene Investigation*) that are focused on police forensic evidence investigation.[37] The fictional characters in these dramas often present an unrealistic portrayal of the daily operations of crime scene investigators and crime laboratories (including their instrumentation, analytical technologies, and capabilities). Cases are solved in an hour, highly technical analyses are accomplished in minutes, and laboratory and instrumental capabilities are often exaggerated, misrepresented, or entirely fabricated. In courtroom scenes, forensic examiners state their findings or a match (between evidence and suspect) with unfailing certainty, often demonstrating the technique used to make the determination. The dramas suggest that convictions are quick and no mistakes are made.

The CSI Effect specifically refers to the real-life consequences of exposure to Hollywood's version of law and order. Jurists and crime laboratory directors anecdotally report that jurors have come to expect the presentation of forensic evidence in every case, and they expect it to be conclusive. A recent study by Schweitzer and Saks found that compared to those who do not watch CSI, CSI viewers were "more critical of the forensic evidence presented at the trial, finding it less believable. Forensic science viewers expressed more confidence in their verdicts than did nonviewers."[38] Prosecutors and defense attorneys have reported jurors second guessing them in the courtroom, citing "reasonable doubt" and refusing to convict because they believed that other evidence was available and not adequately examined.[39]

Schweitzer and Saks found that the CSI Effect is changing the manner in which forensic evidence is presented in court, with some prosecutors believing they must make their presentation as visually interesting and appealing as such presentations appear to be on television. Some are concerned that the conclusiveness and finality of the manner in which forensic evidence is

---

[36] National Institute of Justice. 2006. *Status and Needs of Forensic Science Service Providers: A Report to Congress*. Available at www.ojp.usdoj.gov/nij/pubs-sum/213420.htm.

[37] See *U.S. News & World Report*. 2005. The CSI effect: How TV is driving jury verdicts all across America. April 25.

[38] N.J. Schweitzer and M.J. Saks. 2007. The CSI Effect: Popular fiction about forensic science affects public expectations about real forensic science. *Jurimetrics* 47:357.

[39] See *U.S. News & World Report*, op. cit.

presented on television results in jurors giving more or less credence to the forensic experts and their testimony than they should, raising expectations, and possibly resulting in a miscarriage of justice.[40] The true effects of the popularization of forensic science disciplines will not be fully understood for some time, but it is apparent that it has increased pressure and attention on the forensic science community in the use and interpretation of evidence in the courtroom.

Fragmented and Inconsistent Medicolegal Death Investigation

The medicolegal death investigation system is a fragmented organization of state and local entities called upon to investigate deaths and to certify the cause and manner of unnatural and unexplained deaths. About 1 percent of the U.S. population (about 2.6 million people) dies each year. Medical examiner and coroner offices receive nearly 1 million reports of deaths, constituting between 30 to 40 percent of all U.S. deaths in 2004, and accept about one half of those (500,000, or 1 in 5 deaths) for further investigation and certification.[41] In carrying out this role, medical examiners and coroners are required to decide the scope and course of a death investigation, which may include assessing the scene of death, examining the body, determining whether to perform an autopsy, and ordering other medical tests, forensic analyses, and procedures as needed. Yet the training and skill of medical examiners and coroners and the systems that support them vary greatly. Medical examiners may be physicians, pathologists, or forensic pathologists with jurisdiction within a county, district, or state. A coroner is an elected or appointed official who might not be a physician or have had any medical training. Coroners typically serve a single county.

Since 1877, in the United States, there have been efforts to replace the coroner system with a medical examiner system.[42] In fact, more than 80 years ago, the National Academy of Sciences identified concerns regarding the lack of standardization in death investigations and called for the abolishment of the coroner's office, noting that the office "has conclusively demonstrated its incapacity to perform the functions customarily required of it."[43] In its place, the report called for well-staffed offices of a medical

---

[40] Schweitzer and Saks, op. cit.; S.A. Cole and R. Dioso-Villa. 2007. CSI and its effects: Media, juries, and the burden of proof. *New England Law Review* 41(3):435.

[41] M.J. Hickman, K.A. Hughes, K.J. Strom, and J.D. Ropero-Miller. 2007. *Medical Examiner and Coroners' Offices, 2004*. U.S. Department of Justice, Office of Justice Programs, Bureau of Justice Statistics. Available at www.ojp.usdoj.gov/bjs/pub/pdf/meco04.pdf.

[42] W.U. Spitz and R.S. Fisher. 1982. *Medicolegal Investigation of Death*, 2nd ed. Springfield, IL: Charles C. Thomas.

[43] National Research Council. 1928. *The Coroner and the Medical Examiner*. Washington, DC: National Academy Press.

examiner, led by a pathologist. In strong terms, the 1928 committee called for the professionalization of death investigation, with medical science at its center.

Despite these calls, efforts to move away from a coroner system in the United States have stalled. Currently, 11 states have coroner-only systems, 22 states have medical examiner systems, and 18 states have mixed systems—in which some counties have coroners and others have medical examiners. Some of these states have a referral system, in which the coroner refers cases to medical examiners for autopsy.[44] According to a 2003 Institute of Medicine report, in addition to the variety of systems in the United States, the location and authority of the medical examiner or coroner office also varies, with 43 percent of the U.S. population served by a medical examiner or coroner housed in a separate city, county, or state government office. Other arrangements involve an office under public safety or law enforcement. The least common placement is under a forensic laboratory or health department.[45]

Variability also is evident in terms of accreditation of death investigation systems. As of August 2008, 54 of the medical examiner offices in the United States (serving 23 percent of the population) have been accredited by the National Association of Medical Examiners, the professional organization of physician medical examiners. Most of the country is served by offices lacking accreditation.[46] Similarly, requirements for training are not mandatory. About 36 percent of the population lives where minimal or no special training is required to conduct death investigations.[47] Recently, an 18-year-old high school student was elected a deputy coroner in Indiana after completing a short training course.[48]

Additionally, funding for programs supporting death investigations vary across the country, with the cost of county systems ranging from \$0.62 to \$5.54 per capita, and statewide systems from \$0.32 to \$3.20.[49] Most funding comes from tax revenues, and with such limited funds available, the salaries of medical examiners and skilled personnel are much lower than those of other physicians and medical personnel. Consequently, recruiting and retaining skilled personnel is a constant struggle.

At a time when natural disasters or man-made disasters could create

---

[44] R. Hanzlick and D. Combs. 1998. Medical examiner and coroner systems: History and trends. *Journal of the American Medical Association* 279(11):870-874.

[45] Institute of Medicine. 2003. *Medicolegal Death Investigation System: Workshop Report*. Washington, DC: The National Academies Press.

[46] Ibid.

[47] R. Hanzlick. 1996. Coroner training needs. A numeric and geographic analysis. *Journal of the American Medical Association* 276(21):1775-1778.

[48] See www.wthr.com/Global/story.asp?S=6534514&nav=menu188_2.

[49] IOM, op. cit.

great havoc in our country, the death investigation system is one that is of increasing importance. Deaths resulting from terrorism, with the exception of any suicide perpetrators, are homicides that require robust medicolegal death investigation systems to recover and identify remains, collect forensic evidence, and determine cause of death.

Incompatible Automated Fingerprint Identification Systems

In the late 1970s and early 1980s, law enforcement agencies across the Nation began adopting Automated Fingerprint Identification Systems (AFIS) to improve their efficiency and reduce the time needed to identify (or exclude) a given individual from a fingerprint. Before the use of AFIS, the fingerprint identification process involved numerous clerks and fingerprint examiners tediously sifting through thousands of classified and cataloged paper fingerprint cards.

AFIS was an enormous improvement in the way local, state, and federal law enforcement agencies managed fingerprints and identified people. AFIS searches are much faster than manual searches and often allow examiners to search across a larger pool of candidates and produce a shorter list of possible associations of crime scene prints and unidentified persons, living or dead.

Working with a system's software, fingerprint examiners can map the details of a given fingerprint—by features that consist of "minutiae" (e.g., friction ridge endings and ridge bifurcations)—and ask the system to search its database for other records that closely resemble this pattern. Depending on the size of the database being searched and the system's workload, an examiner often can get results back within minutes.

However, even though AFIS has been a significant improvement for the law enforcement community over the last few decades, AFIS deployments and performance (operational capacities) today are still far from optimal. Many law enforcement AFIS installations are stand-alone systems or are part of relatively limited regional networks with shared databases or information-sharing agreements. Today, systems from different vendors often are incompatible and hence cannot communicate. Indeed, different versions of similar systems from the same vendor often cannot effectively share fingerprint data with one another. In addition, many law enforcement agencies also access the FBI's Integrated Automated Fingerprint Identification System database (the "largest biometric database in the world"[50]) through an entirely separate stand-alone system—a fact that often forces fingerprint examiners to enter fingerprint data for one search multiple times in multiple states (at least once for each system being searched). Additionally, searches

[50] See www.fbi.gov/hq/cjisd/iafis.htm.

between latent print to AFIS 10-print[51] files suffer by not being more fully automated: Examiners must manually encode a latent print before searching the AFIS 10-print database. Furthermore, the hit rate for latent prints searched against the AFIS database is approximately 40 percent (see Chapter 10). Much good work in recent years has improved the interoperability of AFIS installations and databases, but the pace of these efforts to date has been slow, and greater progress must be made toward achieving meaningful, nationwide AFIS interoperability.

The Growing Importance of the Forensic Science Disciplines to Homeland Security

Threats to food and transportation, concerns about nuclear and cyber security, and the need to develop rapid responses to chemical, nuclear, radiological, and biological threats underlie the need to ensure that there is a sufficient supply of adequately trained forensic specialists. At present, public crime laboratories are insufficiently prepared to handle mass disasters. In addition, demands will be increasing on the forensic science community to develop real-time plans and protocols for mass disaster responses by the network of crime laboratories and death investigation systems across the country—and internationally. The development and application of the forensic science disciplines to support intelligence, investigations, and operations aimed at the prevention, interdiction, disruption, attribution, and prosecution of terrorism has been an important component of both public health and what is now termed "homeland security" for at least two decades. With the development and deployment of enhanced capabilities came the integration of forensic science disciplines much earlier in the investigative process. As a result, the forensic science disciplines could be more fruitfully leveraged to generate investigative leads to test, direct, or redirect lines of investigation, not just in building a case for prosecution. Forensic science disciplines are essential components of the response to mass fatality events, whether natural or man made.

The Admission of Forensic Science Evidence in Litigation

As explained in Chapter 3, most forensic science disciplines are inextricably tethered to the legal system; many forensic fields (e.g., firearms analysis, latent fingerprint identification) are but handmaidens of the legal system, and they have no significant uses beyond law enforcement. There-

[51] AFIS 10-print records the fingers, thumbs, and a palm print on a large index card. These prints are carefully taken, clear, and easy to read, and they make up the bulk of the AFIS data available today.

fore, any study of forensic science necessarily must include an assessment of the legal system that it serves. As already noted, and as further amplified in Chapters 4 and 5, the forensic science system exhibits serious shortcomings in capacity and quality; yet the courts continue to rely on forensic evidence without fully understanding and addressing the limitations of different forensic science disciplines.

The conjunction between the law and forensic science is explored in detail in Chapter 3. The bottom line is simple: In a number of forensic science disciplines, forensic science professionals have yet to establish either the validity of their approach or the accuracy of their conclusions, and the courts have been utterly ineffective in addressing this problem. For a variety of reasons—including the rules governing the admissibility of forensic evidence, the applicable standards governing appellate review of trial court decisions, the limitations of the adversary process, and the common lack of scientific expertise among judges and lawyers who must try to comprehend and evaluate forensic evidence—the legal system is ill-equipped to correct the problems of the forensic science community. In short, judicial review, by itself, is not the answer. Rather, tremendous resources must be devoted to improving the forensic science community. With more and better educational programs, accredited laboratories, certification of forensic practitioners, sound operational principles and procedures, and serious research to establish the limits and measures of performance in each discipline, forensic science experts will be better able to analyze evidence and coherently report their findings in the courts. This is particularly important in criminal cases in which we seek to protect society from persons who have committed criminal acts and to protect innocent persons from being convicted of crimes that they did not commit.

ORGANIZATION OF THIS REPORT

This report begins with a series of chapters describing the current forensic science system, the use of forensic science evidence in litigation, and science and the forensic science disciplines. It then addresses systemic areas for improvement with the goal of attaining a more rigorous and robust forensic science infrastructure, including standards and best practices, education, and training. Pursuant to its charge, in three chapters the committee addresses special issues in the areas of medicolegal death investigation (Chapter 9), AFIS (Chapter 10), and the interrelationships between homeland security and the forensic science disciplines (Chapter 11).

2

The Forensic Science Community and the Need for Integrated Governance

Forensic investigations involve intelligence and information gathering, crime scene investigation, laboratory analysis, interpretation of tests and results, and reporting and communication with members of law enforcement and the judicial system. Law enforcement agencies within the United States vary in organizational structure regarding how forensic science examinations are conducted and evidence is admitted into court (see Chapter 3). Variations are attributable to the geographical size and population served by the jurisdictional authority, the types and level of crimes encountered, the funding source, and local tradition. In general, however, the forensic science community includes crime scene investigators; state and local crime laboratories; medical examiners; private forensic laboratories; law enforcement identification units; resources such as registries and databases; professional organizations; prosecutors and defense attorneys; quality system providers (i.e., accrediting and certifying organizations); and federal agencies that conduct or support research as well as provide forensic science services and training. This chapter provides an overview of the major components of the forensic science community. Data about laboratories are based largely on two surveys conducted by the Bureau of Justice Statistics (BJS) in 2002 and 2005 of publicly funded crime laboratories[1] and a more

[1] J.L. Peterson and M.J. Hickman. 2005. *Census of Publicly Funded Forensic Crime Laboratories, 2002*. U.S. Department of Justice, Office of Justice Programs, Bureau of Justice Statistics. Available at www.ojp.usdoj.gov/bjs/pub/pdf/cpffcl02.pdf; M.R. Durose. 2008. *Census of Publicly Funded Forensic Crime Laboratories, 2005*. U.S. Department of Justice, Office of Justice Programs, Bureau of Justice Statistics. Available at www.ojp.usdoj.gov/bjs/pub/pdf/cpffcl05.pdf.

recent survey of "nontraditional forensic service providers" conducted by researchers at West Virginia University.[2]

In addition to forensic laboratories, about 3,200 medical examiner and coroner offices provided death investigation services across the United States in 2004.[3] These entities—which may comprise a coroner system, a medical examiner system, or a mixed system at the county or state level—conduct death scene investigations, perform autopsies, and determine the cause and manner of death when a person has died as a result of violence, under suspicious circumstances, without a physician in attendance, or in other circumstances. These offices are described in greater detail in Chapter 9. In addition, standard setting, accrediting, and certifying organizations are described in greater detail in Chapter 7, and education and training programs are described in Chapter 8.

The committee's first recommendation, appearing at the end of this chapter, calls for a more central, strategic, and integrated approach to forensic science at the national level.

CRIME SCENE INVESTIGATION

Evidence recovery and interpretation at the crime scene is the essential first step in forensic investigations. Several organizational approaches to crime scene investigation and subsequent forensic laboratory activity exist, sometimes involving a large number of personnel with varied educational backgrounds. Conversely, in some jurisdictions, a single forensic examiner might also be the same investigator who goes to the crime scene, collects evidence, processes the evidence, conducts the analyses, interprets the evidence, and testifies in court. In other jurisdictions, the investigators submit the evidence to a laboratory where scientists conduct the analyses and prepare the reports. Crime scene evidence collectors can include uniformed officers, detectives, crime scene investigators, criminalists, forensic scientists, coroners, medical examiners, hospital personnel, photographers, and arson investigators.[4] Thus, the nature and process of crime scene investiga-

---

[2] T.S. Witt, Director, Bureau of Business and Economic Research, West Virginia University. "Survey of Non-Traditional Forensic Service Providers." Presentation to the committee. December 6, 2007.

[3] R. Hanzlick, Fulton County Medical Examiner's Center and Emory University School of Medicine. 2007. "An Overview of Medical Examiner/Coroner Systems in the United States—Development, Current Status, Issues, and Needs." Presentation to the committee. June 5, 2007. The Bureau of Justice (2004) omits Louisiana and classifies Texas as a medical examiner state, and accordingly reports the total as 1,998. According to Hanzlick, many of Texas's 254 counties maintain justice of the peace/coroners offices. The total number includes Justices of the Peace in Texas.

[4] B. Fisher, Director, Scientific Services Bureau, Los Angeles County Sheriff's Department. Presentation to the committee. April 24, 2007.

tion varies dramatically across jurisdictions, with the potential for inconsistent policies and procedures and bias. Some analysts say that the lack of standards and oversight can result in deliberate deception of suspects, witnesses, and the courts; fraud; and "honest mistakes" made because of haste, inexperience, or lack of a scientific background.[5]

In 1978, the U.S. Supreme Court held for the first time in *Monell v. Department of Social Services of the City of New York*[6] that a municipality can be held directly liable for violating a person's constitutional rights under 42 U.S.C. section 1983. Partly in response to this liability, most large cities and metropolitan areas created their own professionally trained crime scene units. However, in smaller suburban and rural communities, evidence from a crime scene may be collected and preserved by a patrol officer or investigator. Even in large metropolitan areas, most crime scene investigation units are composed of sworn officers.

Recognizing that some agencies did not have the resources to adequately train all personnel in crime scene processing, in 2000 the National Institute of Justice (NIJ) and its Technical Working Group on Crime Scene Investigation (TWGCSI) developed *Crime Scene Investigation: A Guide for Law Enforcement*, which stated that "successful implementation of this guide can be realized only if staff possess basic (and in some cases advanced) training in the fundamentals of investigating a crime scene."[7] However, there remains great variability in crime scene investigation practices, along with persistent concerns that the lack of standards and proper training at the crime scene can contribute to the difficulties of drawing accurate conclusions once evidence is subjected to forensic laboratory methods. (See Chapter 5 for a discussion of methodologies and Chapter 7 for further discussion of standards and ethics.)

FORENSIC SCIENCE LABORATORIES AND SERVICE PROVIDERS

The configuration of forensic laboratories varies by jurisdiction. Some are located within a state police department as part of a statewide system of laboratories and training programs. For example, in Illinois, state law mandates that the laboratory system provide forensic services to law enforcement agencies in all 102 counties (population 12.7 million). Although the forensic laboratory system is part of the Illinois State Police, 98 percent

[5] See J.I. Thornton. 2006. Crime reconstruction—ethos and ethics. In: W.J. Chisum and B.E. Turvey (eds.). *Crime Reconstruction.* Boston: Elsevier Science, pp. 37-50.

[6] 436 U.S. 658 (1978).

[7] Available at www.ncjrs.gov/pdffiles1/nij/178280.pdf, p. 2.

of the casework completed is for the 1,200 local and county police agencies across the state.[8]

Not all forensic services are performed in traditional crime laboratories—they may be conducted by a sworn law enforcement officer with no scientific training (e.g., some latent print examiners). Thus, forensic service providers may be located in law enforcement agencies, may be crime scene investigators, or may be a for-profit entity. There are no good data on the entire universe of forensic science entities, although there have been efforts to gather data on publicly funded crime laboratories and nonlaboratory-based providers. The committee could find no data regarding for-profit forensic science service providers, except for DNA laboratories, of which there are approximately 30 in the United States.

Publicly Funded Laboratories

BJS has conducted two censuses of publicly funded forensic crime laboratories. The first census, administered in 2002, established baseline information on the operations and workload of the Nation's public crime laboratories.[9] The 2005 census documented changes in workload and backlog that have occurred since the 2002 census. According to the 2005 census, 389 publicly funded forensic crime laboratories were operating in the United States in 2005—210 state or regional laboratories, 84 county laboratories, 62 municipal laboratories, and 33 federal laboratories. The estimated budget for all 389 crime laboratories exceeded $1 billion, nearly half of which funded state laboratories. The BJS report cites a total of nearly 2.7 million new cases[10] in 2005, including a much larger number of separate requests for forensic services. Some laboratories are full-service facilities; others might conduct only the more common analyses of evidence (see Chapter 5).

Funding Sources

According to the 2005 BJS census, in addition to federal, state, or local support, 28 percent of publicly funded laboratories charged fees for service, and 65 percent reported receiving some funding from grants. However, funding for laboratories has not increased with increasing demands. Some

[8] J. Johnson, Illinois State Police Forensic Science Center at Chicago. Presentation to the committee. January 25, 2007.

[9] Peterson and Hickman, op. cit.

[10] Durose, op. cit. "A 'case' is defined as all physical evidence submitted from a single criminal investigation submitted for crime laboratory analysis," p. 9.

laboratory directors appearing before the committee cited budget cuts as high as 22 percent over the past five years.[11]

Personnel and Equipment

The 2005 BJS census estimated that publicly funded crime laboratories employed more than 11,900 full-time equivalent (FTE) personnel in 2005. Most crime laboratories are relatively small: the median staff size in 2005 was 16. Distinctly different professional tracks exist within forensic laboratories, ranging from laboratory technicians and general examiners to scientists. According to the census data, analysts or examiners—persons who typically prepare evidence, conduct tests, interpret results, sign laboratory reports, and testify in court—comprised 58 percent of all crime laboratory FTEs in 2005. Technical support personnel, who typically assist analysts or examiners in preparing evidence and conducting tests, accounted for 10 percent of all FTEs. Thirteen percent of FTEs were managerial personnel, 8 percent were in clerical positions, and 6 percent were crime scene technicians. Similar ranges in the distribution of personnel are evident among laboratories by type of jurisdiction served. (The uncertainties in these reported percentages depend on the number of laboratories that responded to the FTE survey questions.) A 2006 NIJ report cited equipment shortages (which may include insufficient equipment maintenance) as a limiting factor in processing cases.[12] It cited equipment needs at the 50 largest laboratories in the disciplines of controlled substances, trace evidence, firearms, questioned documents, latent prints, toxicology, and arson. Evidence submission may or may not be automated, depending on the laboratory. Lack of automation increases the time the laboratory spends on logging in evidence.

A 2005 survey of public crime laboratories conducted by researchers at the State University of New York at Albany found that the number of FTEs in a laboratory ranged from 2 to 280, with an average of 34, the majority of whom have bachelor's degrees.[13] Because of the distinctly different professional tracks within larger laboratories, for example, technicians perform tests with defined protocols, and credentialed scientists conduct specialized testing and interpretation. Unlike many other professions, the forensic science disciplines have no organized control over entry into the profession, such as by degree, boards or exams, or licensure (see Chapter

---

[11] Johnson, op. cit.

[12] NIJ. 2006. *Status and Needs of Forensic Science Service Providers: A Report to Congress.* Available at www.ojp.usdoj.gov/nij/pubs-sum/213420.htm.

[13] W.S. Becker, W.M. Dale, A. Lambert, and D. Magnus. 2005. Letter to the editor—Forensic lab directors' perceptions of staffing issues. *Journal of Forensic Sciences* 50(5):1255-1257.

7). Control mechanisms traditionally have been held through employment and job function.[14]

Of the laboratories surveyed by the State University of New York at Albany, only 21 percent reported having a sufficient number of FTEs to complete their workload. The authors concluded that "as total number of cases increases, scientists do not have proper equipment, enough time, adequate resources, enough information from the DA [district attorney], enough time to prepare for courtroom testimony, and the needed resources to provide courtroom testimony."[15] In addition, "as casework capacity increases, pressure to complete cases too quickly increases significantly, and pressure to extend opinions beyond the scientific method and pressure to get a particular result also increases significantly."[16]

The National Association of Medical Examiners (NAME) also reports acute personnel shortages in the death investigation system, with a critical need for significantly more board-certified forensic pathologists than are currently available. (See Chapter 9 for a discussion of the medicolegal death investigation system.)

Laboratory Functions

According to the 2002 BJS data, almost all public crime laboratories examine controlled substances (90 percent). Sixty-three percent examine firearms and toolmarks, 65 percent screen biological samples (usually in preparation for DNA analysis on selected exhibits), and 61 percent examine latent prints.[17] Fifty-nine percent of laboratories examine one or more forms of trace evidence (e.g., hairs, fibers, glass, or paint). Fewer laboratories examine questioned documents (26 percent) or conduct computer crime investigations (11 percent). As would be expected, larger laboratories are able to perform a broader range of examinations.

In terms of crime scene investigation, 62 percent of laboratories report having sent examiners directly to crime scenes, although most forensic examiners did not visit crime scenes. Twenty-five percent of the laboratories reported that laboratory personnel also served as crime scene investigators. However, more than half of laboratories (62 percent) reported that agencies or persons not affiliated with the laboratory handled most major investigations—usually a police unit with specialized evidence technicians

---

[14] D.S. Stoney. Chief Scientist, Stoney Forensic, Inc. Presentation to the committee. January 26, 2007.

[15] Becker, et al., op. cit., p. 1255.

[16] Ibid., p. 1256.

[17] Peterson and Hickman, op. cit.

or crime scene search officers who go onsite to take photographs and locate, preserve, label, and gather physical evidence.

CASE BACKLOGS

According to the 2005 BJS data, the Nation's 389 crime laboratories received an estimated 2.7 million new cases during 2005. Almost half were submitted to state laboratories. Laboratories serving local jurisdictions received about 1.3 million cases in 2005, including 727,000 cases received by county laboratories and 566,000 by municipal laboratories.

> An estimated 359,000 cases were backlogged (not completed within 30 days) at the end of 2005, compared to 287,000 at yearend 2002. This represents a 24 percent increase in backlogged cases between 2002 and 2005. State laboratories accounted for more than half of the backlog in both years. Among the 288 laboratories that reported this information, the median number of cases received in 2005 was about 4,100. Overall, laboratories ended the year with a median backlog of about 400 cases. Six percent of laboratories that received cases in 2005 reported having no backlog at yearend.[18]

In 2005, federal laboratories received the fewest cases.

Fifty-one percent of the laboratories reported outsourcing one or more types of forensic services to private laboratories in 2005, primarily DNA casework, toxicology, Combined DNA Index System (CODIS) samples, and controlled substances.

In a communication with the committee, Los Angeles County Sheriff's Department Crime Laboratory Director Barry Fisher warned that to manage backlogs, laboratories triage cases:

> Murders, rapes, aggravated assaults and the like have priority, as do cases going to court, cases where a suspect is being held on an arrest warrant, highly publicized cases, etc. Property crimes, such as burglaries, are often far down the list. This makes the likelihood of examining evidence from property crime cases unlikely. Oddly, the police and prosecutors are rarely consulted about how priorities are determined. The use of triage is the lab's best effort to manage its own scarce resources. Another factor at play in case management is that the "squeaky wheel gets the grease." This means that a persistent investigator who calls the lab often enough will get his case done more quickly than the investigator who just sends the case down to the lab expecting that it will be done.[19]

---

[18] Ibid., pp. 3, 4. The committee notes that the 30-day turnaround metric is an arbitrary metric useful for comparative purposes only.

[19] Letter to the committee from B.A.J. Fisher. June 12, 2007.

Fisher also cautioned that backlog data are not entirely reliable, saying that one of the reasons for the lack of data is that laboratories count backlogs, case submissions, tests, output, and outcomes differently. Additionally, many laboratories lack automated information management systems to "capture the very data that might support their case for more assistance."[20] Finally, it is difficult to track cases for which forensic work has moved all the way through the criminal justice system: Police, prosecutors, and forensic laboratories use different tracking systems.

NIJ'S COVERDELL FORENSIC SCIENCE IMPROVEMENT GRANT PROGRAM

Through the Paul Coverdell National Forensic Science Improvement Act (P.L. 106-561), the Justice Department operates the Paul Coverdell Forensic Science Improvement Grants Program (the Coverdell program), which awards grants to states and units of local government to help improve the quality and timeliness of forensic science and medical examiner services.[21] The program provides funding for expenses related to facilities, personnel, equipment, computerization, supplies, accreditation, certification, and education and training. In 2004, the Justice for All Act (P.L. 108-405) expanded the Coverdell program, with the aim of reducing the backlog.

A state or unit of local government that receives a Coverdell grant must use the grant for one or more of three purposes:

(1) To carry out all or a substantial part of a program intended to improve the quality and timeliness of forensic science or medical examiner services in the state, including those services provided by laboratories operated by the state and those operated by units of local government within the state.
(2) To eliminate a backlog in the analysis of forensic science evidence, including, among other things, a backlog with respect to firearms examination, latent prints, toxicology, controlled substances, forensic pathology, questioned documents, and trace evidence.
(3) To train, assist, and employ forensic laboratory personnel as needed to eliminate such a backlog.[22]

---

20 Ibid.

21 P.L. 106-561 (December 21, 2000). An Act to improve the quality, timeliness, and credibility of forensic science services for criminal justice purposes and for other purposes. Cited as the Paul Coverdell National Forensic Sciences Improvement Act.

22 See www.ojp.usdoj.gov/nij/topics/forensics/nfsia/welcome.htm.

The expectation for those receiving grants is "demonstrated improvement over current operations in the quality and/or timeliness of forensic science or medical examiner services provided in the state, including services provided by laboratories operated by the state and services provided by laboratories operated by units of local government within the State."[23] The output measures for Coverdell awards are:

(1) Change in the number of days between submission of a sample to a forensic science laboratory and delivery of test results to a requesting office or agency.
(2) The number of backlogged forensic cases analyzed with Coverdell funds, if applicable to the grant.
(3) The number of forensic science or medical examiner personnel who completed appropriate training or educational opportunities with Coverdell funds, if applicable to the grant.[24]

States may be eligible for both "base" (formula) and competitive funds from NIJ for forensic science programs. Units of local government within states may be eligible for competitive funds and may apply directly to NIJ. The Coverdell law (42 U.S.C. § 3797k(4)) requires that, to request a grant, an applicant for Coverdell funds must submit:

- A certification and description regarding a plan for forensic science laboratories.
- A certification regarding use of generally accepted laboratory practices.
- A certification and description regarding costs of new facilities.
- A certification regarding external investigations into allegations of serious negligence or misconduct.

Program funding was $10 million in Fiscal Year (FY) 2004, $15 million in FY 2005, and $18.5 million in FY 2006. Funds may be used for personnel, computerization, laboratory equipment, supplies, accreditation, education, training, certification, or facilities.

FORENSIC SERVICES BEYOND THE TRADITIONAL LABORATORY

Many forensic examiners do not work in a traditional crime laboratory. Often they work within law enforcement offices in units called "identifica-

---

[23] Ibid.
[24] Ibid.

tion units" or "fingerprint units." For example, a 2004 study conducted by the American Society of Crime Laboratory Directors (ASCLD) for NIJ reported that two-thirds of fingerprint identifications take place outside of traditional crime laboratories.[25] Insufficient data are available on the size and expertise of this population of forensic examiners who are not employed in publicly funded forensic science laboratories. Therefore, in 2006, a survey instrument modeled after the BJS census was developed by researchers at West Virginia University in collaboration with the International Association for Identification (IAI).[26] Its survey was sent to 5,353 IAI U.S. members in April 2007,[27] targeting forensic scientists working outside the crime laboratories surveyed by BJS.

Of the units responding to the IAI survey, most were publicly funded (e.g., city, borough, village, town, county, state, or federal), with half working at the local level. Units at the city, borough, village, or town level had a median annual budget of $168,850, compared to $387, 413 at the county level. Half are small units, with one to five full- and part-time employees. The units primarily conduct crime scene investigations, latent print and 10-print examinations, photography, and bloodstain pattern analyses. A smaller number are involved in other forensic functions, such as the analysis of digital evidence, footwear, tire track impressions, firearms, forensic art, questioned documents, polygraph tests, and dental evidence.

For the responding units, the mean number of cases received per year was 2,780. The mean backlog was 9.4 percent of the annual caseload, with the backlog for latent prints being higher, at 12.3 percent of the caseload. More than half of the units report outsourcing work, primarily firearms, latent print, and footwear analyses. Although 69 percent of respondents replied that they had some system for verifying results, only 15 percent are accredited.

FEDERAL FORENSIC SCIENCE ACTIVITIES

Several federal agencies either provide support for forensic infrastructure, certification, and training, or conduct or fund forensic science in support of their missions. Brief descriptions follow.

---

[25] American Society of Crime Laboratory Directors. 2004. *180-Day Study Report: Status and Needs United States Crime Laboratories*. Available at www.ncjrs.gov/pdffiles1/nij/grants/213422.pdf.

[26] Witt, op. cit.

[27] Ibid. Of the 815 surveys returned, 308 represented responses from active forensic service provider organizations (i.e., only 1 response per organization was included) outside of publicly funded crime laboratories.

Federal Forensic Science Laboratories

The largest publicly funded forensic laboratory in the country is the Federal Bureau of Investigation (FBI) Laboratory in Quantico, Virginia. Other federal agencies have smaller crime laboratories, for example, the U.S. Secret Service, the U.S. Army, the Drug Enforcement Administration, the Bureau of Alcohol, Tobacco, Firearms, and Explosives (known as ATF), the U.S. Postal Service, the Internal Revenue Service, and the U.S. Fish and Wildlife Service. In addition, the Department of Commerce's National Institute of Standards and Technology (NIST) conducts research in support of standard setting for gunshot residue analysis, trace explosives detectors, DNA analysis, and more. Some of these efforts are described below.

The FBI Laboratory

The types of cases investigated by the FBI include terrorism, espionage, public corruption, civil rights, criminal organizations and enterprises, white collar crime, and violent crime. Investigative case work services include those involving:

- chemistry
- cryptanalysis and racketeering records
- DNA analysis
- explosives
- evidence response
- firearms-toolmarks
- hazardous materials
- investigative and prosecutive graphics
- latent prints
- photographic operations and imaging services
- questioned documents
- structural design
- trace evidence
- specialty units

According to the 2005 BJS report, the FBI Laboratory had approximately 600 employees in 2005, and it partners with state and local crime laboratories throughout the country. Its FY 2007 budget was $63 million. The FBI Laboratory provides a full range of forensic services and handles a large volume of fingerprint work, receiving approximately 50,000 fingerprint submissions every day. In July 1999, the FBI updated its fingerprint databases with the Integrated Automated Fingerprint Identification System (IAFIS). Previously, all prints arrived on paper fingerprint cards that had to be processed by hand. With the introduction of IAFIS, prints and pictures can be submitted electronically.

According to the 2005 BJS census, the FBI laboratory began 2003 with an estimated backlog of 3,062 requests for forensic services. About two-thirds of the backlog was attributable to latent print requests. During 2003, the FBI laboratory received 6,994 new requests and completed 7,403 requests. The estimated year end backlog was 2,653 requests, a 13 percent reduction over the previous year. Latent print requests comprised half of the year end 2003 backlog. No data were provided in the 2005 census.

By the end of the first quarter of 2004, the FBI Laboratory reported a total backlog of 2,585 requests. This included 1,216 latent print requests, or 47 percent of the total. The FBI Laboratory reported a need for additional equipment and 249 additional FTEs in order to have achieved a 30-day turnaround on all 2003 requests. The cost of the additional equipment was estimated to be $40 million. Based on starting salaries for analyst/examiners, the estimated cost of the additional FTEs exceeds $17.5 million.

The FBI Laboratory also has working partnerships with the forensic science community's Scientific Working Groups (SWGs) that are tasked with generating guidelines and standards for specific forensic disciplines (see Chapter 7). The FBI also provides training for the forensic science community and conducts and funds research (see later discussion).

In addition, the FBI collects and maintains data and materials for multiple databases and registries (see Box 2-1). The largest is CODIS, which is composed of three components: the forensic database, the missing persons database, and the convicted felon database. The FBI CODIS Unit is responsible for developing, providing, and supporting the CODIS Program to federal, state, and local crime laboratories in the United States and selected international law enforcement crime laboratories to foster the exchange and comparison of forensic DNA evidence from violent crime investigations. The CODIS Unit also provides administrative management and support to the FBI for various advisory boards, Department of Justice (DOJ) grant programs, and legislation regarding DNA.

U.S. Secret Service (Department of Homeland Security [DHS])

The U.S. Secret Service laboratory examines evidence, develops investigative leads, and provides expert courtroom testimony. As part of the 1994 Crime Bill (P.L. 103-322), Congress mandated that the U.S. Secret Service provide forensic/technical assistance in matters involving missing and exploited children. On April 30, 2003, President George W. Bush signed the PROTECT Act of 2003 (P.L. 108-21), known as the "Amber Alert Bill," which gave full authorization to the U.S. Secret Service in this area. The

Box 2-1
FBI Databases and Reference Libraries

The CODIS Program consists of the development, enhancement, and support of software that enables forensic DNA laboratories to store, maintain, and search DNA profiles from crime scenes, offenders, and missing persons. Support of the CODIS software includes training for DNA analysts and help-desk services, as well as a yearly national meeting for all CODIS administrators. The unit also provides CODIS software to international law enforcement laboratories to assist them in establishing a DNA database program. Forty law enforcement laboratories in 25 countries now have the CODIS software. CODIS consists of a three-tiered hierarchy of databases: the NDIS [National DNA Index System], the State DNA Index System, and the Local DNA Index System. The highest level in the CODIS hierarchy is NDIS, which contains the DNA profiles contributed by participating federal, state, and local forensic DNA laboratories. There are more than 170 NDIS participating sites across the United States, including the FBI Laboratory, the U.S. Army Criminal Investigation Laboratory, and a laboratory in Puerto Rico.

The NDIS contains 6.2 million offender profiles and 233,454 forensic profiles as of August 2008. Its operation requires determining the eligibility of samples for the National Index in accordance with applicable federal law, developing procedures for laboratories participating in the Index, and monitoring the participating laboratories' compliance with federal law. The CODIS Unit also provides administrative management and support for the NDIS Procedures Board and other DNA working groups. As of August 2008, CODIS has produced more than 74,500 hits, assisting in more than 74,700 investigations.[a]

The National Automotive Paint File contains entries dating as far back as the 1930s. The Paints and Polymers Subunit also serves as the U.S. repository for the Paint Data Query database, which is a Canadian database. State and local law enforcement agencies investigating hit-and-run homicides rely on both the National Automotive Paint File and the Paint Data Query database.

The FBI Explosives Reference File contains several thousand standards that help examiners identify the components and manufacturers of explosive and incendiary devices. The Explosives Reference Tools database (EXPeRT) combines the text of FBI Laboratory reports with evidentiary photographs from bombing cases and permits the rapid retrieval of information on any aspect of the forensic examination. The database also contains manufacturer data and open-source literature on the construction and use of explosives and explosive devices. An examiner can search EXPeRT, find similar devices, and identify similarities in the components used in the construction of an improvised explosive device.8

The Reference Firearms Collection contains more than 5,500 handguns and shoulder firearms; and the Standard Ammunition File, a collection of more than 15,000 military and commercial ammunition specimens from both domestic and international manufacturers.

---

[a]See www.fbi.gov/hq/lab/codis/clickmap.htm.
SOURCE: FBI Web site at www.fbi.gov/hq/lab/html/ipgu1.htm.

forensic services utilized by the Secret Service include identification, forensic automation, polygraph, questioned documents, and visual information.

Bureau of Alcohol, Tobacco, Firearms and Explosives (ATF)

The ATF Laboratories reside within DOJ. Currently, the ATF Laboratories have more than 100 employees working in 4 laboratories in 3 cities. In FY 2005, ATF Laboratories performed more than 2,600 forensic examinations with an authorized staff of 106 positions and a budget of approximately $16 million.

In FY 2006, the ATF Laboratories:

- analyzed 64 samples related to alcohol and tobacco diversion;
- processed 3,086 forensic cases;
- spent 171 days providing expert testimony in the courts;
- spent 242 days at crime scenes; and
- spent 371 days providing training to federal, state, and local investigators and examiners.

A new $135 million National Laboratory Center in suburban Maryland was opened in 2003. The National Laboratory Center contains a unique fire testing facility, designed to support fire investigations. Each ATF Laboratory also has a mobile laboratory designed to support the examination of evidence at the scene of a fire or explosion. In FY 2006, ATF established a DNA analysis capability at the National Laboratory Center.[28] The Laboratories are ASCLD/Laboratory Accreditation Board (LAB) accredited in the disciplines of trace evidence, biology (serology only), questioned documents, firearms/toolmarks, and latent prints.

In a 2006 semiannual report from the DOJ Office of the Inspector General (OIG), the OIG's Audit Division evaluated whether the ATF Laboratories managed workloads effectively to provide timely services to ATF field divisions. The audit report stated the following:

> Our audit found that processing times have not significantly improved in the past 4 years. Two-thirds of completed forensic examinations continued to take more than 30 days to complete and about one-third of examinations took more than 90 days.
>
> Improvements in the timeliness of laboratory examinations have been limited because ATF has not accomplished actions it committed to in 2001, such as increasing the number of examiner positions in the forensic laboratories, implementing a new priority system, implementing a new

[28] See www.atf.treas.gov/labs/index.htm.

> information management system, and significantly reducing the size of its backlog of examination requests. Laboratory staffing generally was adequate to manage the incoming workload, but backlogged requests continued to interfere with the timely analysis of incoming examination requests. The audit found that the backlog could increase as a result of unusually resource-intensive cases. We concluded that if these conditions are not addressed serious consequences may result, such as delays in making arrests and bringing offenders to trial.[29]

Department of Defense (DOD)

DOD's forensic requirements are growing beyond the traditional realm of criminal investigations, casualty investigations, and medical examiner functions toward more intelligence and counterintelligence functions. DOD's activities are primarily mission oriented, but they also serve specific functional roles in criminal investigations. A DOD Forensic Sciences Committee provides advice on forensic science activities across the department.

Like other crime laboratories, DOD has capabilities in most of the forensic science disciplines. Its major forensic entities include the Criminal Investigation Laboratory, the Armed Forces Institute of Pathology, the Cyber Crime Center ($20 million annually), and the Central Identification Laboratory ($1 million annually), all of which are ASCLD/LAB accredited.[30] The Army also maintains the Armed Forces Repository of Specimen Samples for the Identification of Remains, with more than 5 million DNA samples primarily from military service members. It also maintains a searchable database of DNA profiles from detainees and known or suspected terrorists. The Criminal Investigation Laboratory provides worldwide forensic laboratory services, training, and research and development (R&D) to all DOD investigative agencies.

DOD currently is developing a "Defense Forensic Enterprise System" to more centrally manage, integrate, and coordinate across the Services for both criminal investigation and warfighter operations, as well as to serve homeland security functions.[31] Part of the system is the Joint Expeditionary Forensic Facilities, which are modular by design for deployment purposes

[29] Office of the Inspector General. *Semiannual Report to Congress*, October 1, 2005-March 31, 2006. April 8, 2006. Available at www.usdoj.gov/oig/semiannual/0605/message.htm. Also see U.S. Department of Justice Office of the Inspector General Audit Division, Audit Report 06-15. March 2006. *Follow-Up Audit of the Bureau of Alcohol, Tobacco, Firearms and Explosives Forensic Science Laboratories Workload Management.*

[30] L.C. Chelko, Director, U.S. Army Criminal Investigation Laboratory. Presentation to the committee. September 21, 2007.

[31] R. Tontarski, Chief, Forensic Analysis Division, CID Command, U.S. Army Criminal Investigation Laboratory. Presentation to the committee. September 21, 2007.

but which are also designed for expansion to full-spectrum analyses. The Defense Forensic Network connects all DOD forensic operations virtually and synchronizes worldwide DOD forensic operations. A Forensic Training and Research Academy is responsible for all DOD forensic examiner training and serves as DOD's certification authority. In addition to conducting its own research, DOD partners with academia, industry, and other federal agencies. It is collaborating with the National Forensic Science Technology Center to leverage its work in deployable forensic instrumentation and technologies and with NIJ on technology transfer strategies.

National Bioforensic Analysis Center (NBFAC), DHS

NBFAC is a component of the National Biodefense Analysis and Countermeasures Center (NBACC), which is operated by a contractor on behalf of DHS, with a proposed budget of $28.3 million for FY 2009. NBFAC and NBACC are not federal agencies. Their prime customer for their services is the FBI. They do not perform complete forensic analyses on evidence from biocrimes and bioterrorism; they do perform or direct the performance (by one or more of their affiliated laboratories) of analyses targeting biological materials and biotoxins. NBFAC provides the laboratories and training for FBI Laboratory examiners in several disciplines to safely and effectively conduct their standard examinations on contaminated traditional evidence. It is also charged with establishing and maintaining reference collections of biological agents.[32]

National Counterproliferation Center

The National Counterproliferation Center, a policy and program oversight organization within the Office of the Director of National Intelligence, is seeking to bring a unified, strategic perspective to microbial forensics (bioforensics) research and development and its application to intelligence purposes. Microbial forensics is a "developing interdisciplinary field of microbiology devoted to the development, assessment, and validation of methods to fully characterize microbial samples for the ultimate purpose of high confidence comparative analysis."[33]

---

[32] J. Burans, Bioforensics Program Manager, National Bioforensics Analysis Center. Presentation to the committee. September 21, 2007.

[33] C.L. Cooke, Jr., Office of the Deputy Director for Strategy and Evaluation, National Counterproliferation Center. Presentation to the committee. September 21, 2007.

RESEARCH FUNDING

Nearly all forensic science research funds are channeled through DOJ. NIJ and the FBI are the two primary federal sources of funding for forensic science research.

National Institute of Justice (NIJ)

NIJ provides the bulk of funds for research. The BJS 2002 census found that of the 12 percent of laboratories that had resources dedicated to research, the primary source of funding for this research was NIJ.

NIJ has two operating offices: (1) the Office of Research and Evaluation develops, conducts, directs, and supervises research and evaluation activities across a wide variety of issues and (2) the Office of Science and Technology manages technology research and development, the development of technical standards, testing, forensic science capacity building, and technology assistance to state and local law enforcement and corrections agencies.[34] NIJ's forensic science programs relevant to research include the President's DNA Initiative; General Forensics R&D; the Forensic Resource Network; and Electronic Crime. These programs vary in their direct support of research. Research decisions are managed through a peer-review process.[35] Total expenditures for forensic research were $78 million in FY 2002, but they decreased to $33 million by FY 2009. According to John Morgan, Deputy Director, NIJ, the agency is able to fund 5 to 7 percent of the applications submitted.[36] Commentators have noted that NIJ funds often are not awarded to working members of the forensic science community.[37]

In 2003, the President announced a five-year, $1 billion initiative to improve the use of DNA in the criminal justice system. The President's DNA Initiative pushed for increased funding, training, and assistance to ensure that DNA technology "reaches its full potential to solve crimes, protect the innocent, and identify missing persons."[38] Congress has appropriated more than $300 million to date for the initiative, although only a small fraction is directed toward research. Since 2003, DOJ has made grants in excess of $26 million for new research on forensic tools and techniques,[39] with grants tending to go to population geneticists, medical geneticists, molecular biolo-

---

[34] See www.ojp.gov/nij/about_rsrchpri.htm#1.

[35] J. Morgan, Deputy Director National Institute of Justice, Office of Justice Programs, U.S. Department of Justice. Presentation to the committee. January 25, 2007.

[36] Ibid.

[37] K. Pyrek. 2007. *Forensic Science Under Siege: The Challenges of Forensic Laboratories and the Medico-Legal Investigation System.* Burlington, MA: Academic Press (Elsevier), p. 448.

[38] See www.dna.gov/info/e_summary.

[39] Morgan, op. cit.

gists, technology experts, and crime laboratory personnel. The bulk of the funding has gone to state and local law enforcement agencies to support the examination of nearly 104,000 DNA cases from 2004 to 2007 and 2,500,000 convicted offender and arrestee samples, which will be added to the national DNA database. More than 5,000 "hits," or matches to unknown profiles or other cases, have resulted from these efforts. In 2008, NIJ expects to fund the testing of an additional 9,000 backlogged cases and more that 834,000 backlogged convicted offender and arrestee samples.[40]

Under the General Forensics R&D Program, 53 awards have been made through 2007 for the development of "tools and technologies that will allow faster, more reliable, more robust, less costly, or less labor-intensive identification, collection, preservation, and/or analysis of forensic evidence; tools that provide a quantitative measure or statistical evaluation of forensic comparisons; and identification or characterization of new analytes of forensic importance."[41] In FY 2007, solicitations were issued for proposals in Research and Development on Crime Scene Tools, Techniques, and Technologies; Research and Development on Impression Evidence; Research and Development in the Forensic Analysis of Fire and Arson Evidence; and Forensic Toxicology Research and Development.

The size of the NIJ research program warrants comparison with other research programs. In FY 2007, NIJ awarded 21 grants for forensic research and development (not including awards for DNA research) (see Box 2-2). As will be seen in Chapter 5, the number of open research questions about the more common forensic science methods greatly exceeds 21, and none of these open questions appear to be squarely addressed by the projects listed in Box 2-2. The 2007 NIJ awards totaled nearly $6.6 million, with an average award size of $314,000. As a comparison, in the same year, the National Institutes of Health awarded 37,275 research project grants, averaging $359,000, for a total of $15 billion.[42] Also in FY 2007, the National Science Foundation made over 11,500 research project awards for a total of $6.0 billion.[43]

NIJ's Forensic Resource Network is a system of four forensic centers whose mission is to assist state and local forensic service providers in achieving their service delivery goals through research and development, testing and evaluation, training, technology transfer, and technology assistance.

The NIJ Electronic Crime Portfolio addresses "the practical needs of the criminal justice community in its efforts to respond to electronic crime,

[40]Statement of J.S. Morgan, Deputy Director National Institute of Justice, Office of Justice Programs, U.S. Department of Justice, before the U.S. Senate Committee on the Judiciary concerning "Oversight of the Justice For All Act: Has the Justice Department Effectively Administered the Bloodsworth and Coverdell DNA Grant Programs?" January 23, 2008.

[41]Morgan, 2007, op. cit.

[42]See http://report.nih.gov/index.aspx?section=NIHFunding.

[43]See www.nsf.gov/news/news_summ.jsp?cntn_id=105803.

aiding/assisting law enforcement in the discovery, analysis, presentation and preservation of digital evidence of probative value."[44]

In September 2007, NIJ announced the addition of four Technology Centers of Excellence to serve as resources within their respective technology focus areas by providing technology assistance to law enforcement personnel as well as by working with technology developers and users to test and evaluate equipment in operational environments. In addition, NIJ set aside $5 million for grants to support the development of forensic science standards at NIST.[45]

Federal Bureau of Investigation (FBI)

The FBI Laboratory also receives roughly $33 million per year for its own research. To set priorities, the laboratory consults with its own staff and with working-level scientists in the SWGs they support.

The FBI's Counterterrorism and Forensic Science Research Unit "provides technical leadership/advancement of counterterrorism and forensic sciences for the FBI as well as for state and local law enforcement agencies through the development and validation of new technologies/techniques by both internal and outsourced research efforts and through advanced scientific training in specialized forensic procedures."[46] It fulfills its research mission through two core programs.

The Research and Development Program creates and coordinates the development of new forensic techniques, instrumentation, and protocols for FBI Laboratory units to use in terrorism and violent crime cases. The program focuses its efforts in the areas of DNA analysis, trace organic chemical analysis, toxicology, explosives, fingerprints, drug and materials analysis (e.g., paints, tapes, inks, glass, and metals), database development, anthropology, microbial forensics, and field instrumentation. The committee was told that the program publishes some of its results in scientific journals. The Research Partnership Program transfers new forensic technologies and procedures to case-working examiners at state and local crime laboratories through collaborative studies and implements SWG-defined protocols and national forensic databases. Workshops include those involving the use of an automotive carpet fiber database, messenger RNA (mRNA) profiling of human semen, the visualization and identification of pepper spray on evidentiary materials, 1-step purification of DNA from different matrices, and the permanence of friction ridge skin detail.

---

[44] Ibid.

[45] J. Morgan, Deputy Director for Science and Technology, NIJ. Presentation to the committee. January 25, 2007.

[46] See www.fbi.gov/hq/lab/html/cterror1.htm.

Box 2-2
FY 2007 NIJ Awards for Forensic Science Research and Development

Biometric Technologies

Automatic Fingerprint Matching Using Extended Feature Set, Michigan State University, $260,038
Selective Feature-Based Quality Measure Plug-In for Iris Recognition System, Indiana University, $84,858
Site-Adaptive Face Recognition at a Distance, General Electric Co., $496,341

Forensic DNA Research and Development

A Low-Cost Microfluidic Microarray Instrument for Typing Y-Chromosome Single Nucleotide Polymorphisms (SNPs), Akonni Biosystems, Inc., $448,466
A Rapid, Efficient and Effective Assay to Determine Species Origin in Biological Materials, Bode Technology Group, Inc., $170,212
DNA Profiling of the Semen Donor in Extended Interval Post-Coital Samples, University of Central Florida, $271,504
Microfabricated Capillary Array Electrophoresis Genetic Analysis for Forensic Short Tandem Repeat DNA Profiling, Regents of the University of California, $592,183
National Institute of Justice Forensic DNA Research and Development, Network Biosystems, Inc., $497,346
National Institute of Justice Forensic DNA Research and Development in Vermont for Fiscal Year 2007,Vermont Department of Public Safety, $112,481
Population Genetics of Single Nucleotide Polymorphisms (SNPs) for Forensic Purposes, Yale University, $680,516
Sperm Capture Using Aptamer-Based Technology, Denver, City and County of, $370,813

PROFESSIONAL ASSOCIATIONS

Numerous professional organizations are focused on the forensic science disciplines (see Box 2-3). The Consortium of Forensic Science Organizations, founded in 2000, includes the largest of these organizations—the American Academy of Forensic Sciences (AAFS), ASCLD, ASCLD/LAB, IAI, NAME, and Forensic Quality Services (FQS).

AAFS, with 6,000 members worldwide, was founded in 1948. It created and supports the Forensic Specialties Accreditation Board, which accredits

Tools for Improving the Quality of Aged, Degraded, Damaged or Otherwise Compromised DNA Evidence, Louisiana State University, $580,337
Y Chromosome Whole Genome Analysis Strategies: Improved Detection of Male DNA, University of Central Florida, $324,705

Research and Development on Crime Scene Tools, Techniques and Technologies

Detecting Buried Firearms Using Multiple Geophysical Technologies, University of Central Florida, $89,584
Developing Fluorogenic Reagents for Detecting and Enhancing Bloody Fingerprints, Portland State University, $168,904
Electronic Fingerprint Development Device "Fuma-Room," Mountain State University, $61,152
Investigations on the Use of Sample Matrix to Collect and Stabilize Crime Scene Biological Evidence for Optimized Analysis and Room Temperature Storage, California State University, Los Angeles, University Auxiliary Services, $353,449
Rapid Visualization of Biological Fluids at Crime Scenes Using Optical Spectroscopy, University of South Carolina Research Foundation, $382,394

Research and Development on Impression Evidence

Analysis of Footwear Impression Evidence, Research Foundation of the State University of New York, $350,172
The Use of Infrared Imaging, a Robust Matching Engine and Associated Algorithms to Enhance Identification of Both 2-D and 3-D Impressions: Phase 1, SED Technology, LLC, $295,247

SOURCE: www.ojp.usdoj.gov/nij/awards/2007.htm#solvingcoldcaseswithdna.

certification organizations.[47] Membership includes physicians, attorneys, dentists, toxicologists, physical anthropologists, document examiners, psychiatrists, physicists, engineers, criminalists, educators, and others. AAFS sponsors an annual scientific meeting, publishes the *Journal of Forensic Sciences*, and promotes research, education, and training. It also operates the Forensic Science Education Programs Accreditation Commission (see Chapter 8 for further discussion).[48]

[47] See www.thefasb.org.
[48] B.A. Goldberger, AAFS President-Elect. Presentation to the committee. January 25, 2007.

Box 2-3
Forensic Associations and Societies

American Academy of Forensic Sciences
American Board of Criminalistics
American Board of Forensic Anthropology
American Board of Forensic Odontology
American Board of Forensic Toxicology
American Society for Quality
American Society for Testing and Materials
American Society of Crime Laboratory Directors
American Society of Questioned Document Examiners
AOAC International
Association of Firearm & Tool Marks Examiners
Association of Forensic Quality Assurance Managers
California Association of Criminalistics
Canadian Society of Forensic Sciences
Council of Federal Forensic Crime Laboratory Directors
Forensic Science Society
International Association for Identification
International Association of Arson Investigators
International Association of Bloodstain Pattern Analysts
International Association of Coroners and Medical Examiners
International Association of Forensic Nurses
International Association of Forensic Toxicologists
Mid-Atlantic Association of Forensic Scientists
Midwestern Association of Forensic Scientists
National Association of Medical Examiners
National Center of Forensic Science
National Forensic Science Technology Center
New Jersey Association of Forensic Scientists
Northeastern Association of Forensic Scientists
Northwest Association of Forensic Scientists
Society of Forensic Toxicologists
Southern Association of Forensic Science
Southwestern Association of Forensic Scientists
Wisconsin Association for Identification

IAI was founded in 1915 and has 6,700 members worldwide. Its members tend to be involved at the "front end" of the process—crime scene investigation, evidence collection, and evidence preservation.[49] It operates certification programs in seven disciplines and publishes the *Journal of*

[49] J. Polski, IAI Chief Operations Officer. Presentation to the committee. January 25, 2007.

Forensic Identification. The focus of its activities is pattern evidence—for example, fingerprint, footwear, tire track, questioned documents, forensic photography, and forensic art.

ASCLD/LAB and FQS accredit crime laboratories and are discussed in greater detail in Chapter 7. Chapter 9 describes the activities of NAME.

CONCLUSIONS AND RECOMMENDATION

The fragmented nature of the forensic science community makes it difficult to gather data on the entire universe of forensic service entities and activities, although efforts have been made to collect data on publicly funded crime laboratories and nonlaboratory-based providers. For example, the committee could find no data available on for-profit forensic service providers, other than on DNA laboratories. Thus, attempts to construct effective policies are hampered by the lack of coherent and consistent information on the forensic science infrastructure in the United States. However, the large amount of information provided to the committee by people engaged in the forensic science enterprise and by experts who have studied how well that enterprise functions all points to a system that lacks coordination and that is underresourced in many ways.

By using the term "underresourced," the committee means to imply all of its dimensions. Existing data suggest that forensic laboratories are underresourced and understaffed, which contributes to a backlog in cases and likely makes it difficult for laboratories to do as much as they could to inform investigations, provide strong evidence for prosecutions, and avoid errors that could lead to imperfect justice. But underresourced also means that the tools of forensic science are not as strong as they could be. The knowledge base that underpins analysis and the interpretation of evidence—which enable the forensic science disciplines to excel at informing investigations, providing strong evidence for prosecutions, and avoiding errors that could lead to imperfect judgment—is incomplete in important ways. NIJ is the only federal agency that provides direct support to crime laboratories to alleviate the backlog, and those funds are minimal. The enterprise also is underresourced in the sense that it has only thin ties to an academic research base that could undergird the forensic science disciplines and fill knowledge gaps. This underresourcing limits the ability of the many hard-working and conscientious people in the forensic science community to do their best work.

Among the various facets of underresourcing, the committee is most concerned about the knowledge base, which is further examined in Chapter 5. Adding more dollars and people to the enterprise might reduce case backlogs, but it will not address fundamental limitations in the capability of the forensic science disciplines to discern valid information from crime scene evidence. For the most part, it is impossible to discern the magnitude of those limitations, and reasonable people will differ on their significance.

Forensic science research is not well supported, and there is no unified strategy for developing a forensic science research plan across federal agencies. Relative to other areas of science, the forensic science disciplines have extremely limited opportunities for research funding. Although the FBI and NIJ have supported some research in the forensic science disciplines, the level of support has been well short of what is necessary for the forensic science community to establish strong links with a broad base of research universities and the national research community. Moreover, funding for academic research is limited and requires law enforcement collaboration, which can inhibit the pursuit of more fundamental scientific questions essential to establishing the foundation of forensic science. Finally, the broader research community generally is not engaged in conducting research relevant to advancing the forensic science disciplines.

The forensic science community also is hindered by its extreme disaggregation—marked by multiple types of practitioners with different levels of education and training and different professional cultures and standards for performance. Many forensic scientists are given scant opportunity for professional activities such as attending conferences or publishing their research, which could help strengthen that professional community. Furthermore, the fragmented nature of the forensic science community raises the worrisome prospect that the quality of evidence presented in court, and its interpretation, can vary unpredictably according to jurisdiction.

Numerous professional associations are organized around the forensic science disciplines, and many of them are involved in training and education (see Chapter 8) and developing standards and accreditation and certification programs (see Chapter 7). The efforts of these groups are laudable. However, except for the largest organizations, it is not clear how these associations interact or the extent to which they share requirements, standards, or policies. Thus, there is a need for more consistent and harmonized requirements.

In the course of its deliberations and review of the forensic science community, it became obvious to the committee that truly meaningful advances will not come without significant leadership from the federal government. The forensic science community lacks the necessary governance structure to pull itself up from its current weaknesses. Insufficiencies in the current system cannot be addressed simply by increasing the staff within existing crime laboratories and medical examiners offices. Of the many professional societies that serve the forensic science community, none is dominant, and none has clearly articulated the need for change or presented a vision for accomplishing it. And clearly no municipal or state forensic office has the mandate to lead the entire community. The major federal resources—NIJ and the FBI Laboratory—have provided modest leadership, for which they should be commended. NIJ has contributed a helpful research program and the FBI Laboratory has spearheaded the SWGs. But again, neither entity has recognized, let alone articulated, a need for change or a vision for affecting it. Neither has the full confidence of the larger forensic science community. And because both are part of a prosecutorial department of the government, they could be subject to subtle contextual biases that should not be allowed to undercut the power of forensic science.

The forensic science community needs strong governance to adopt and promote an aggressive, long-term agenda to help strengthen forensic science. Governance must be strong enough—and independent enough—to identify the limitations of forensic science methodologies and must be well connected with the Nation's scientific research base in order to affect meaningful advances in forensic science practices. The governance structure must be able to create appropriate incentives for jurisdictions to adopt and adhere to best practices and promulgate the necessary sanctions to discourage bad practices. It must have influence with educators in order to effect improvements to forensic science education. It must be able to identify standards and enforce them. The governance entity must be geared toward (and be credible within) the law enforcement community, but it must have strengths that extend beyond that area. Oversight of the forensic science community and medical examiner system will sweep broadly into areas of criminal investigation and prosecution, civil litigation, legal reform, investigation of insurance claims, national disaster planning and preparedness, homeland security, certification of federal, state, and local forensic practitioners, public health, accreditation of public and private laboratories, research to improve forensic methodologies, education programs in colleges and universities, and advancing technology.

The committee considered whether such a governing entity could be established within an existing federal agency. The National Science Foundation (NSF) was considered because of its strengths in leading research and its connections to the research and education communities. NSF is surely capable of building and sustaining a research base, but it has very thin ties to the forensic science community. It would be necessary for NSF to take many untested steps if it were to assume responsibility for the governance of applied fields of science. The committee also considered NIST. In the end analysis, however, NIST did not appear to be a viable option. It has a good program of research targeted at forensic science and law enforcement, but the program is modest. NIST also has strong ties to industry and academia, and it has an eminent history in standard setting and method development. But its ties to the forensic science community are still limited, and it would not be seen as a natural leader by the scholars, scientists, and practitioners in the field. In sum, the committee concluded that neither NSF nor NIST has the breadth of experience or institutional capacity to establish an effective governance structure for the forensic science enterprise.

There was also a strong consensus in the committee that no existing or new division or unit within DOJ would be an appropriate location for a new entity governing the forensic science community. DOJ's principal mission is to enforce the law and defend the interests of the United States according to the law. Agencies within DOJ operate pursuant to this mission. The FBI, for example, is the investigative arm of DOJ and its principal missions are to produce and use intelligence to protect the Nation from threats and to bring to justice those who violate the law. The work of these law enforcement units is critically important to the Nation, but the scope of the work done by DOJ units is much narrower than the promise of a strong forensic science community. Forensic science serves more than just law enforcement; and when it does serve law enforcement, it must be equally available to law enforcement officers, prosecutors, and defendants in the criminal justice system. The entity that is established to govern the forensic science community cannot be principally beholden to law enforcement. The potential for conflicts of interest between the needs of law enforcement and the broader needs of forensic science are too great. In addition, the committee determined that the research funding strategies of DOJ have not adequately served the broad needs of the forensic science community. This is understandable, but not acceptable when the issue is whether an agency is best suited to support and oversee the Nation's forensic science community. In sum, the committee concluded that advancing science in the forensic science enterprise is not likely to be achieved within the confines of DOJ. Moreover, DHS is too focused on national security to embed a new entity within it.

The committee thus concluded that no existing agency has the capacity or appropriate mission to take on the roles and responsibilities needed to govern and improve the forensic science community. The tasks assigned to it require that it be unfettered and objective and as free from bias as possible. What is needed is a new, strong, and independent entity with no ties to the past and with the authority and resources to implement a fresh agenda designed to address the many problems found by the committee and discussed in the remainder of this report.

The proposed entity must meet the following minimum criteria:

- It must have a culture that is strongly rooted in science, with strong ties to the national research and teaching communities, including federal laboratories.
- It must have strong ties to state and local forensic entities, as well as to the professional organizations within the forensic science community.

- It must not be in any way committed to the existing system, but should be informed by its experiences.
- It must not be part of a law enforcement agency.
- It must have the funding, independence, and sufficient prominence to raise the profile of the forensic science disciplines and push effectively for improvements.
- It must be led by persons who are skilled and experienced in developing and executing national strategies and plans for standard setting; managing accreditation and testing processes; and developing and implementing rulemaking, oversight, and sanctioning processes.

No federal agency currently exists that meets all of these criteria.

Recommendation 1:

To promote the development of forensic science into a mature field of multidisciplinary research and practice, founded on the systematic collection and analysis of relevant data, Congress should establish and appropriate funds for an independent federal entity, the National Institute of Forensic Science (NIFS). NIFS should have a full-time administrator and an advisory board with expertise in research and education, the forensic science disciplines, physical and life sciences, forensic pathology, engineering, information technology, measurements and standards, testing and evaluation, law, national security, and public policy. NIFS should focus on:

(a) establishing and enforcing best practices for forensic science professionals and laboratories;
(b) establishing standards for the mandatory accreditation of forensic science laboratories and the mandatory certification of forensic scientists and medical examiners/forensic pathologists—and identifying the entity/entities that will develop and implement accreditation and certification;
(c) promoting scholarly, competitive peer-reviewed research and technical development in the forensic science disciplines and forensic medicine;
(d) developing a strategy to improve forensic science research and educational programs, including forensic pathology;
(e) establishing a strategy, based on accurate data on the forensic science community, for the efficient allocation of

available funds to give strong support to forensic methodologies and practices in addition to DNA analysis;

(f) funding state and local forensic science agencies, independent research projects, and educational programs as recommended in this report, with conditions that aim to advance the credibility and reliability of the forensic science disciplines;

(g) overseeing education standards and the accreditation of forensic science programs in colleges and universities;

(h) developing programs to improve understanding of the forensic science disciplines and their limitations within legal systems; and

(i) assessing the development and introduction of new technologies in forensic investigations, including a comparison of new technologies with former ones.

The benefits that will flow from a strong, independent, strategic, coherent, and well-funded federal program to support and oversee the forensic science disciplines in this country are clear: The Nation will (1) bolster its ability to more accurately identify true perpetrators and exclude those who are falsely accused; (2) improve its ability to effectively respond to, attribute, and prosecute threats to homeland security; and (3) reduce the likelihood of convictions resting on inaccurate data. Moreover, establishing the scientific foundation of the forensic science disciplines, providing better education and training, and requiring certification and accreditation will position the forensic science community to take advantage of current and future scientific advances.

The creation of a new federal entity undoubtedly will pose challenges, not the least of which will be budgetary constraints. The committee is not in a position to estimate how much it will cost to implement the recommendations in this report; this is a matter best left to the expertise of the Congressional Budget Office. What is clear, however, is that Congress must take aggressive action if the worst ills of the forensic science community are to be cured. Political and budgetary concerns should not deter bold, creative, and forward-looking action, because the country cannot afford to suffer the consequences of inaction. It will also take time and patience to implement the recommendations in this report. But this is true with any large, complex, important, and challenging enterprise.

The committee strongly believes that the greatest hope for success in this enterprise will come with the creation of NIFS to oversee and direct the forensic science community. The remaining recommendations in this report are crucially tied to the creation of NIFS. However, each recommendation is a separate, essential piece of the plan to improve the forensic science community in the United States. Therefore, even if the creation of NIFS is forestalled, the committee vigorously supports the adoption of the core ideas and principles embedded in the additional recommendations that appear in this report.

3

The Admission of Forensic Science Evidence in Litigation

This chapter describes the legal system's reliance on forensic science evidence in criminal prosecutions and examines the existing adversarial process for admitting this type of evidence. The report describes and analyzes the current situation and makes recommendations for the future. No judgment is made about past convictions and no view is expressed as to whether courts should reassess cases that already have been tried. The report finds that the existing legal regime—including the rules governing the admissibility of forensic evidence, the applicable standards governing appellate review of trial court decisions, the limitations of the adversary process, and judges and lawyers who often lack the scientific expertise necessary to comprehend and evaluate forensic evidence—is inadequate to the task of curing the documented ills of the forensic science disciplines. This matters a great deal, because "forensic science is but the handmaiden of the legal system."[1] As explained in Chapters 4 and 5, there are serious issues regarding the capacity and quality of the current forensic science system; yet, the courts continue to rely on forensic evidence without fully understanding and addressing the limitations of different forensic science disciplines. This profound conjunction of law and science, especially in the context of law enforcement, underscores the need for improvement in the

[1] 4 D.L. Faigman, M.J. Saks, J. Sanders, and E.K. Cheng. 2007-2008. *Modern Scientific Evidence: The Law and Science of Expert Testimony*. Eagan, MN: Thomson/West, § 29.4, p.6. See also P.C. Giannelli and E.J. Imwinkelried. 2007. *Scientific Evidence*, 4th ed. Albany, NY: Lexis Publishing Co., on the latest forensic techniques and scientific concepts used in collecting and evaluating evidence.

forensic science community. The report concludes that every effort must be made to limit the risk of having the reliability of certain forensic science methodologies judicially certified before the techniques have been properly studied and their accuracy verified.

LAW AND SCIENCE

Science and law always have had an uneasy alliance:

> Since as far back as the fourteenth century, scientific evidence has posed profound challenges for the law. At bottom, many of these challenges arise from fundamental differences between the legal and scientific processes. . . . The legal system embraces the adversary process to achieve "truth," for the ultimate purpose of attaining an authoritative, final, just, and socially acceptable resolution of disputes. Thus law is a normative pursuit that seeks to define how public and private relations *should* function. . . . In contrast to law's vision of truth, however, science embraces empirical analysis to discover truth as found in verifiable facts. Science is thus a descriptive pursuit, which does not define how the universe should be but rather describes how it actually *is*.
>
> These differences between law and science have engendered both systemic and pragmatic dilemmas for the law and the actors within it. . . . Moreover, in almost every instance, scientific evidence tests the abilities of judges, lawyers, and jurors, all of whom may lack the scientific expertise to comprehend the evidence and evaluate it in an informed manner.[2]

Nowhere are these dilemmas more evident than in decisions pertaining to the admissibility of forensic science evidence proffered in criminal trials.

Forensic science experts and evidence are routinely used in the service of the criminal justice system. DNA testing may be used to determine whether sperm found on a rape victim came from an accused party; a latent fingerprint found on a gun may be used to determine whether a defendant handled the weapon; drug analysis may be used to determine whether pills found in a person's possession were illicit; and an autopsy may be used to determine the cause of death of a murder victim. In order for qualified forensic science experts to testify competently about forensic evidence, they must first find the evidence in a usable state and properly preserve it. A latent fingerprint that is badly smudged when found cannot be usefully saved, analyzed, or explained. An inadequate drug sample may be insufficient to allow for proper analysis. And, DNA tests performed on a contaminated

[2] Developments in the law—confronting the new challenges of scientific evidence. 108 Harv. L. Rev. 1481, 1484 (1995) (hereinafter "Developments in the law") (footnotes omitted); see also M.A. Berger and L.M. Solan. The uneasy relationship between science and law: An essay and introduction. 73 Brook. L. Rev. 847 (2008).

or otherwise compromised sample cannot reliably identify or eliminate an individual as the perpetrator of a crime. These are important matters having to do with the proper "processing" of forensic evidence. The law's greatest dilemma in its heavy reliance on forensic evidence, however, concerns the question of whether—and to what extent—there is *science* in any given "forensic science" discipline.[3]

The degree of science in a forensic science method may have an important bearing on the reliability of forensic evidence in criminal cases. There are two very important questions that *should* underlie the law's admission of and reliance upon forensic evidence in criminal trials: (1) the extent to which a particular forensic discipline is founded on a reliable scientific methodology that gives it the capacity to accurately analyze evidence and report findings and (2) the extent to which practitioners in a particular forensic discipline rely on human interpretation that could be tainted by error, the threat of bias, or the absence of sound operational procedures and robust performance standards. These questions are significant:[4] The goal of law enforcement actions is to identify those who have committed crimes and to prevent the criminal justice system from erroneously convicting the innocent. So it matters a great deal whether an expert is qualified to testify about forensic evidence and whether the evidence is sufficiently reliable to merit a fact finder's reliance on the truth that it purports to support.

As discussed in Chapters 4 and 5, no forensic method other than nuclear DNA analysis has been rigorously shown to have the capacity to consistently and with a high degree of certainty support conclusions about "individualization" (more commonly known as "matching" of an unknown item of evidence to a specific known source). In terms of scientific basis, the analytically based disciplines generally hold a notable edge over disciplines based on expert interpretation. But there also are important variations among the disciplines relying on expert interpretation. For example, there are more established protocols and available research for the analysis of fingerprints than for bite marks. In addition, there also are significant variations within each discipline. Thus, not all fingerprint evidence is equally good, because the true value of the evidence is determined by the quality of the latent fingerprint image. In short, the interpretation of forensic evidence is not infallible. Quite the contrary. This reality is not always fully appre-

[3] Principles of science are discussed in Chapter 4.

[4] Descriptions and assessments of different forensic science disciplines are set forth in Chapters 5 and 6.

ciated or accepted by many forensic science practitioners, judges, jurors, policymakers, or lawyers and their clients.[5]

THE *FRYE* STANDARD AND RULE 702 OF THE FEDERAL RULES OF EVIDENCE

During the twentieth century, as science advanced, the legal system "attempted to develop coherent tests for the admissibility of scientific evidence."[6] The first notable development occurred in 1923 with the issuance of the landmark decision in *Frye v. United States*.[7] The *Frye* case involved a murder trial in which the defendant sought to demonstrate his innocence through the admission of a lie detector test that measured systolic blood pressure. The court rejected the evidence, stating:

> Just when a scientific principle or discovery crosses the line between the experimental and demonstrable stages is difficult to define. Somewhere in this twilight zone the evidential force of the principle must be recognized, and while courts will go a long way in admitting expert testimony deduced from a well-recognized scientific principle or discovery, the thing from which the deduction is made must be sufficiently established to have gained general acceptance in the particular field in which it belongs.[8]

The *Frye* decision held that the lie detector test was unreliable because it had not gained "general acceptance" in the relevant scientific community. The meaning of the *Frye* test is elusive. Indeed, "[t]he merits of the *Frye* test have been much debated, and scholarship on its proper scope and application is legion."[9] For many years, the *Frye* test was cited in both civil and criminal cases, but it was applied most frequently in criminal cases.[10] "In the 70 years since its formulation in the *Frye* case, the 'general acceptance'

---

[5] See 4 Faigman et al., op. cit., *supra* note 1, §29.3, p. 6 ("Few forensic scientists harbor serious misgivings about the expectation of good science on the part of their clients, be they the police, the prosecution, or the defense bar. . . . The clients want good science and the truth if it will help their case."); S. Scarborough. 2005. They keep putting fingerprints in print. *The CACNews*. California Association of Criminalists, 2nd Quarter. Available at www.cacnews.org/news/2ndq05.pdf, p. 19 ("As scientists we are confident that any 'critic' that tries to prove the fallibility of fingerprints will actually find the opposite. Just as we testify to everyday.").

[6] Developments in the law, *supra* note 2, p. 1486.

[7] *Frye v. United States*, 54 App. D.C. 46, 293 F. 1013 (1923).

[8] Ibid., p. 1014.

[9] *Daubert v. Merrell Dow Pharm., Inc.*, 509 U.S. 579, 586 & n.4 (1993) (citing authorities).

[10] P.C. Giannelli. 1993. "Junk science": The criminal cases. *Journal of Criminal Law and Criminology* 84:105, 111, and n.35.

test [was] the dominant standard for determining the admissibility of novel scientific evidence at trial."[11]

In 1975, more than a half-century after *Frye* was decided, the Federal Rules of Evidence were promulgated to guide criminal and civil litigation in federal courts. The first version of Federal Rule of Evidence 702 provided that:

> If scientific, technical, or other specialized knowledge will assist the trier of fact to understand the evidence or to determine a fact in issue, a witness qualified as an expert by knowledge, skill, experience, training, or education, may testify thereto in the form of an opinion or otherwise.[12]

In place of *Frye*'s requirement of general scientific acceptance, mere "assistance" to the trier of fact appeared to be "the touchstone of admissibility under Rule 702."[13]

After the promulgation of Rule 702, litigants, judges, and legal scholars remained at odds over whether the rule embraced the *Frye* standard or established a new standard.[14] There was also much controversy surrounding the application of Rule 702 in civil cases. Most notably, Peter Huber popularized the now well-known phrase "junk science" to criticize the judiciary's acceptance of unreliable expert testimony in support of tort claims.[15] Huber's study was sharply criticized,[16] but it nonetheless spurred a debate over the use of expert testimony in the courts. However, "[d]espite the highly visible efforts to reform the rules governing experts in the civil arena, the 'junk science' debate . . . all but ignored criminal prosecutions."[17] The "neglect of the problems of expert testimony in criminal prosecutions" was seen by some as "deplorable."[18]

---

[11] *Daubert*, 509 U.S. at 585.

[12] FED. R. EVID. 702, P.L. No. 93-595, § 1, 88 Stat. 1926 (effective January 2, 1975).

[13] Giannelli, op. cit., *supra* note 10, p. 107.

[14] T. Lyons. 1997. *Frye, Daubert* and where do we go from here? *Rhode Island Bar Journal* 45(5):21 (stating that "the vast majority of federal circuit and other courts adopted *Frye* as the standard of admissibility in their jurisdictions").

[15] P.W. Huber. 1991. *Galileo's Revenge: Junk Science in the Courtroom.* New York: Basic Books.

[16] See, e.g., K.J. Chesebro. *Galileo's* retort: Peter Huber's junk scholarship. 42 AM. U. L. REV. 1637 (1993); Book Note: Rebel without a cause. 105 HARV. L. REV. 935 (1992).

[17] Giannelli, op. cit., *supra* note 10, p. 110.

[18] Ibid., pp. 110-111. Over time, a number of courts and commentators found the "general acceptance" test seriously wanting. See 1 Faigman et al., op. cit., *supra* note 1, § 1:6, pp. 13-17; P.C. Giannelli. The admissibility of novel scientific evidence: *Frye v. United States*, a half-century later. 80 COLUM. L. REV. 1197, 1207-1208 (1980) ("[T]he problems *Frye* has engendered—the difficulties in applying the test and the anomolous results it creates—so far outweigh [its] advantages that the argument for adopting a different test has become overwhelming."); M. McCormick. Scientific evidence: Defining a new approach to admissibility. 67 IOWA L. REV. 879, 915 (1982) (*Frye*'s "main drawbacks are its inflexibility, confusion of

THE *DAUBERT* DECISION AND THE SUPREME COURT'S CONSTRUCTION OF RULE 702

In 1993, in *Daubert v. Merrell Dow Pharmaceuticals, Inc.*, the Supreme Court finally clarified that Rule 702, not *Frye*, controlled the admission of expert testimony in the federal courts.[19] *Daubert* was a civil case brought by two minor children and their parents, alleging that the children's serious birth defects had been caused by their mothers' prenatal ingestion of Bendectin, a prescription drug marketed by the defendant pharmaceutical company. In support of a motion for summary judgment, the drug company submitted an affidavit from a qualified expert, who stated that he had reviewed all the literature on Bendectin and human birth defects and had found no study showing Bendectin to be a human teratogen (i.e., an agent that can cause malformations of an embryo or fetus). The plaintiffs countered with experts of their own, each of whom concluded that Bendectin could cause birth defects. Their conclusions were based on animal studies that found a link between Bendectin and malformations; pharmacological studies of the chemical structure of Bendectin that purported to show similarities between the structure of the drug and that of other substances known to cause birth defects; and the "reanalysis" of previously published epidemiological (human statistical) studies. The district court held that the expert testimony proffered by the plaintiffs was inadmissible, because their scientific evidence was not sufficiently established to have general acceptance in the field to which it belonged.[20] The court of appeals, citing *Frye*, affirmed the judgment of the district court, declaring that expert opinion based on a methodology that diverges significantly from the procedures accepted by recognized authorities in the field cannot be shown to be generally accepted as a reliable technique.[21] The Supreme Court reversed, holding that the trial court had applied the wrong standard in assessing the expert testimony proffered by the plaintiffs. The case was then remanded for further proceedings.

In construing and applying Rule 702, the *Daubert* Court ruled that a "trial judge must ensure that any and all scientific testimony or evidence admitted is not only relevant, but reliable."[22] The Court rejected the *Frye* test, noting that the drafting history of Rule 702 made no mention of *Frye*,

---

issues, and superfluity."); J.W. Strong. Questions affecting the admissibility of scientific evidence. U. ILL. L.F. 1, 14 (1970) ("The *Frye* standard, however, tends to obscure these proper considerations by asserting an undefinable general acceptance as the principal if not sole determinative factor.").

[19] 509 U.S. 579 (1993).

[20] *Daubert v. Merrell Dow Pharm, Inc.*, 727 F. Supp. 570, 575 (S.D. Cal. 1989).

[21] *Daubert v. Merrell Dow Pharm., Inc.*, 951 F.2d 1128, 1129-30 (9th Cir. 1991).

[22] *Daubert,* 509 U.S. at 589.

"and a rigid 'general acceptance' requirement would be at odds with the 'liberal thrust' of the Federal Rules and their 'general approach of relaxing the traditional barriers to 'opinion' testimony.'"[23] The Court indicated that the subject of expert testimony should be "scientific knowledge," so "evidentiary reliability will be based upon scientific validity."[24] The Court also emphasized that, in considering the admissibility of evidence, trial judges should focus "solely" on experts' "principles and methodology," and "not on the conclusions that they generate."[25] In sum, *Daubert*'s requirement that expert testimony pertain to "scientific knowledge" established a standard of "evidentiary reliability."

In explaining this evidentiary standard, the *Daubert* Court pointed to several factors that might be considered by a trial judge: (1) whether a theory or technique can be (and has been) tested; (2) whether the theory or technique has been subjected to peer review and publication; (3) the known or potential rate of error of a particular scientific technique; (4) the existence and maintenance of standards controlling the technique's operation; and (5) a scientific technique's degree of acceptance within a relevant scientific community.[26] In the end, however, the Court emphasized that the inquiry under Rule 702 is "a flexible one."[27] The Court also rejected the suggestion that its liberal construction of Rule 702 would "result in a 'free-for-all' in which befuddled juries are confounded by absurd and irrational pseudoscientific assertions."[28] Rather, the Court expressed confidence in the adversary system, noting that "[v]igorous cross-examination, presentation of contrary evidence, and careful instruction on the burden of proof are the traditional and appropriate means of attacking shaky but admissible evidence."[29]

---

[23] Ibid., p. 588 (internal citations omitted).

[24] Ibid, p. 590 and n.9 (emphasis omitted).

[25] Ibid., p. 595. In *General Electric Co. v. Joiner*, 522 U.S. 136, 146 (1997), the Court added: "[C]onclusions and methodology are not entirely distinct from one another. Trained experts commonly extrapolate from existing data. But nothing in *Daubert* or the Federal Rules of Evidence requires a district court to admit opinion evidence that is connected to existing data only by the *ipse dixit* of the expert."

[26] Ibid., pp. 592-94.

[27] Ibid., p. 594. In *Kumho Tire Co., Ltd. v. Carmichael*, 526 U.S. 137 (1999), the Court confirmed that the *Daubert* factors do not constitute a definitive checklist or test. *Kumho Tire* importantly held that Rule 702 applies to both scientific and nonscientific expert testimony; the Court also indicated that the *Daubert* factors might be applicable in a trial judge's assessment of the reliability of nonscientific expert testimony, depending upon "the particular circumstances of the particular case at issue." 526 U.S. at 150.

[28] *Daubert*, 509 U.S. at 595.

[29] Ibid., p. 596.

Daubert-type questions may be raised by the parties pretrial,[30] or during the course of trial,[31] or *sua sponte* by the trial judge.[32] Sometimes a trial judge will conduct a formal "*Daubert* hearing" before ruling on a party's objection to expert testimony; sometimes, however, the judge will simply entertain a party's objection, hear arguments, and then rule.[33] Judges sometimes rule on the briefs alone, without the benefit of formal arguments. There are any number of questions that might arise concerning the testimony of a forensic science expert or about the forensic evidence itself. These questions might include, *inter alia*, issues relating to one of the five *Daubert* factors or other factors appropriate to the forensic evidence, the relevance of the evidence, the qualifications of the expert, the adequacy of the evidentiary sample about which the expert will be testifying, and the procedures followed in the handling and processing of the evidence. After considering the matter at issue, a trial judge may exclude the evidence in whole or in part, prevent or limit the testimony of the expert witness, or deny the challenge. The Supreme Court has made it clear that trial judges have great discretion in deciding on the admissibility of evidence under Rule 702, and that appeals from *Daubert* rulings are subject to a very narrow abuse-of-discretion standard of review.[34] Most importantly, in *Kumho Tire Co., Ltd. v. Carmichael*, the Court made it clear that "whether *Daubert*'s specific factors are, or are not, reasonable measures of reliability in a particular case is a matter that the law grants the trial judge broad latitude to determine."[35]

THE 2000 AMENDMENT OF RULE 702

In 2000, Rule 702 was amended "in response to *Daubert*."[36] The revised rule provides:

---

[30] See, e.g., *Alfred v. Caterpillar, Inc.*, 262 F.3d 1083, 1087 (10th Cir. 2001). ("[B]ecause *Daubert* generally contemplates a 'gatekeeping' function, not a 'gotcha' junction, [the case law] permits a district court to reject as untimely *Daubert* motions raised late in the trial process.")

[31] See, e.g., *United States v. Alatorre*, 222 F.3d 1098, 1100 (9th Cir. 2000) (holding trial courts are not compelled to conduct pretrial hearings in order to discharge the gatekeeping function under *Daubert* as to expert testimony).

[32] See, e.g., *Hoult v. Hoult*, 57 F.3d 1, 4 (1st Cir. 1995) ("We think *Daubert* does instruct district courts to conduct a preliminary assessment of the reliability of expert testimony, even in the absence of an objection.").

[33] 1 Faigman et al., op. cit., *supra* note 1, § 1.8, p. 23 (stating "[i]n general, most courts considering the matter hold that a separate hearing to determine the validity of the basis for scientific evidence is not required" and discussing cases).

[34] See *Gen. Elec. Co. v. Joiner*, 522 U.S. 136, 142-43 (1997).

[35] *Kumho Tire Co., Ltd. v. Carmichael*, 526 U.S. 137, 153 (1999).

[36] Fed. R. Evid. 702 advisory committee's note (2000 Amendments).

> If scientific, technical, or other specialized knowledge will assist the trier of fact to understand the evidence or to determine a fact in issue, a witness qualified as an expert by knowledge, skill, experience, training, or education, may testify thereto in the form of an opinion or otherwise, if (1) the testimony is based upon sufficient facts or data, (2) the testimony is the product of reliable principles and methods, and (3) the witness has applied the principles and methods reliably to the facts of the case.[37]

The commentary accompanying the revised rule[38] recites the "*Daubert* factors" and then goes on to explain that:

> Courts both before and after *Daubert* have found other factors relevant in determining whether expert testimony is sufficiently reliable to be considered by the trier of fact. These factors include:
>
> (1) Whether experts are proposing to testify about matters growing naturally and directly out of research they have conducted independent of the litigation, or whether they have developed their opinions expressly for purposes of testifying.
> (2) Whether the expert has unjustifiably extrapolated from an accepted premise to an unfounded conclusion.[39]
> (3) Whether the expert has adequately accounted for obvious alternative explanations.
> (4) Whether the expert is being as careful as he would be in his regular professional work outside his paid litigation consulting.
> (5) Whether the field of expertise claimed by the expert is known to reach reliable results for the type of opinion the expert would give.[40]

All of these factors remain relevant to the determination of the reliability of expert testimony under the rule as amended.

The commentary accompanying the revised rule also notes that:

---

[37] Fed. R. Evid. 702.

[38] Fed. R. Evid. 702 advisory committee's note (2000 Amendments) (citations and quotation marks omitted).

[39] The commentary cites *General Electric*, 522 U.S. at 146 (noting that in some cases a trial court "may conclude that there is simply too great an analytical gap between the data and the opinion proffered").

[40] The commentary cites *Kumho Tire*, 526 U.S. at 150 (*Daubert*'s general acceptance factor does not "help show that an expert's testimony is reliable where the discipline itself lacks reliability, as for example, do theories grounded in any so-called generally accepted principles of astrology or necromancy."); *Moore v. Ashland Chem., Inc.*, 151 F.3d 269 (5th Cir. 1998) (en banc) (clinical doctor was properly precluded from testifying to the toxicological cause of the plaintiff's respiratory problem, where the opinion was not sufficiently grounded in scientific methodology); *Sterling v. Velsicol Chem. Corp.*, 855 F.2d 1188 (6th Cir. 1988) (rejecting testimony based on "clinical ecology" as unfounded and unreliable).

[T]he amendment [to Rule 702] does not distinguish between scientific and other forms of expert testimony. The trial court's gatekeeping function applies to testimony by any expert. While the relevant factors for determining reliability will vary from expertise to expertise, the amendment rejects the premise that an expert's testimony should be treated more permissively simply because it is outside the realm of science. An opinion from an expert who is not a scientist should receive the same degree of scrutiny for reliability as an opinion from an expert who purports to be a scientist. Some types of expert testimony will be more objectively verifiable, and subject to the expectations of falsifiability, peer review, and publication, than others. Some types of expert testimony will not rely on anything like a scientific method, and so will have to be evaluated by reference to other standard principles attendant to the particular area of expertise. The trial judge in all cases of proffered expert testimony must find that it is properly grounded, well-reasoned, and not speculative before it can be admitted. The expert's testimony must be grounded in an accepted body of learning or experience in the expert's field, and the expert must explain how the conclusion is so grounded.

The amendment requires that the testimony must be the product of reliable principles and methods that are reliably applied to the facts of the case. While the terms "principles" and "methods" may convey a certain impression when applied to scientific knowledge, they remain relevant when applied to testimony based on technical or other specialized knowledge. For example, when a law enforcement agent testifies regarding the use of code words in a drug transaction, the principle used by the agent is that participants in such transactions regularly use code words to conceal the nature of their activities. The method used by the agent is the application of extensive experience to analyze the meaning of the conversations. So long as the principles and methods are reliable and applied reliably to the facts of the case, this type of testimony should be admitted.

Nothing in this amendment is intended to suggest that experience alone—or experience in conjunction with other knowledge, skill, training or education—may not provide a sufficient foundation for expert testimony. To the contrary, the text of Rule 702 expressly contemplates that an expert may be qualified on the basis of experience. In certain fields, experience is the predominant, if not sole, basis for a great deal of reliable expert testimony. *See, e.g., United States v. Jones*, 107 F.3d 1147 (6th Cir. 1997) (no abuse of discretion in admitting the testimony of a handwriting examiner who had years of practical experience and extensive training, and who explained his methodology in detail). . . . *See also Kumho Tire Co. v. Carmichael*, 119 S. Ct.1167, 1178 (1999) (stating that "no one denies that an expert might draw a conclusion from a set of observations based on extensive and specialized experience.").[41]

[41] Fed. R. Evid. 702 advisory committee's note (2000 Amendments).

Given this view of Rule 702—which makes clear that "technical or other specialized knowledge" may be credited as expert testimony "so long as the principles and methods are reliable and applied reliably to the facts of the case"—it is not surprising that the courts might be hard pressed, under existing standards of admissibility, to hold some forensic science practitioners to the more demanding standards of the traditional sciences.[42]

AN OVERVIEW OF JUDICIAL DISPOSITIONS OF *DAUBERT*-TYPE QUESTIONS

Assessing the admission of forensic evidence in litigation is no small undertaking, given the huge number of cases in which such evidence is proffered. Moreover, although *Daubert* remains the standard by which admissibility in federal cases is measured under Federal Rule of Evidence 702, states remain free to apply other evidentiary standards. Some states still apply some version of the *Frye* standard, while others have adopted *Daubert* or some version of the *Daubert* test.[43] Considering the patchwork of state standards and the fact that "[s]tate courts receive 200 times more criminal prosecutions than federal courts," because "[f]orensic science is used most commonly in crimes of violence, and most crimes of violence are tried in state court,"[44] a comprehensive overview would be difficult to create.

The focus of this section and succeeding sections of this chapter will be on judicial dispositions of *Daubert*-type questions in criminal cases in the federal courts. The reason for this is that, although not every state has adopted the *Daubert* standard, there is little doubt that *Daubert* has effectively set a norm that applies in every federal court and in a great many state jurisdictions. It cannot be ignored, and the reported federal cases give the best evidence of how *Daubert* is applied by the judiciary.

Judicial dispositions of *Daubert*-type questions in criminal cases have been criticized by some lawyers and scholars who thought that the Supreme Court's decision would be applied more rigorously to protect the rights of accused parties:

> [*Daubert*] obligated trial court judges to assume the role of "gatekeepers" and to exclude proffered scientific evidence unless it rested on scientifically valid reasoning and methodology. Many thought *Daubert* would be the

---

[42] See generally Giannelli and Imwinkelried, op. cit., for thoughtful discussions of the admissibility of some forms of forensic science testimony as technical or other specialized knowledge under Rule 702.

[43] See generally D.E. Bernstein and J.D. Jackson. The *Daubert* trilogy in the states. 44 JURIMETRICS J. 351 (2004).

[44] P.J. Neufeld. 2005. The (near) irrelevance of *Daubert* to criminal justice: And some suggestions for reform. *American Journal of Public Health* 95(Supp. 1):S107, S110.

> meaningful standard that was lacking in criminal cases and that it would serve to protect innocent defendants.
>
> . . .
>
> [However, a]n analysis of post-*Daubert* decisions demonstrates that whereas civil defendants prevail in their *Daubert* challenges, most of the time criminal defendants almost always lose their challenges to government proffers. But when the prosecutor challenges a criminal defendant's expert evidence, the evidence is almost always kept out of the trial. . . . In the first 7 years after *Daubert*, there were 67 reported federal appellate decisions reviewing defense challenges to prosecution experts. The government prevailed in all but 6, and even among the 6, only 1 resulted in the reversal of a conviction. In contrast, in the 54 cases in which the defense appealed a trial court ruling to exclude the defendant's expert, the defendant lost in 44 cases. In 7 of the remaining 10, the case was remanded for a *Daubert* hearing.[45]

This critique of reported federal appellate decisions cannot be the end of the analysis, however. First, there are two sides to any discussion concerning the admissibility and reliability of forensic evidence: (1) enhancing the ability of law enforcement to identify persons who commit crimes and (2) protecting innocent persons from being convicted of crimes that they did not commit. It is easier to assess the latter than the former, because there are no good studies indicating how many convictions are lost because of faulty forensic science evidence. Second, if one focuses solely on federal appellate decisions, the picture is not appealing to those who have preferred a more rigorous application of *Daubert*. Federal appellate courts have not with any consistency or clarity imposed standards ensuring the application of scientifically valid reasoning and reliable methodology in criminal cases involving *Daubert* questions.[46] This is not really surprising. The Supreme Court itself described the *Daubert* standard as "flexible." This means that, beyond questions of relevance, *Daubert* offers appellate courts no clear substantive standard pursuant to which to review decisions by trial courts.[47] As a result, trial judges exercise great discretion in deciding whether to

---

45 Ibid., p. S109. See also P.C. Giannelli. Wrongful convictions and forensic science: The need to regulate crime labs. 86 N.C. L. Rev. 163 (2007).

46 See, e.g., *United States v. Brown*, 415 F.3d 1257 (11th Cir. 2005); *United States v. Havvard*, 260 F.3d 597 (7th Cir. 2001). The *Havvard* decision has been described as "[a]n excellent, albeit deeply troubling, example of a court straining scientific credulity for the sake of a venerable forensic science." See 1 Faigman et al., op. cit., *supra* note 1, § 1:30, pp. 85-86.

47 As noted above, "whether *Daubert*'s specific factors are, or are not, reasonable measures of reliability in a particular case is a matter that the law grants the trial judge broad latitude to determine." *Kumho Tire*, 526 U.S. at 153.

admit or exclude expert testimony, and their judgments are subject only to a highly deferential "abuse of discretion" standard of review.[48]

To get a clearer picture of judicial dispositions of *Daubert*-type questions, we need to know how these matters are handled by trial courts. Unfortunately, the picture is unclear. There are countless *Daubert*-type, evidentiary challenges in criminal cases, some resulting in formal *Daubert* hearings, and many others not. There is no way to know with any degree of certainty how many of these challenges are entirely or partially sustained, because many trial court judgments on evidentiary matters are issued without published opinions[49] and with no appeal. If a defendant's challenge is sustained and is followed by an acquittal, no appeal ensues and the matter is over. If a defendant's challenge is sustained and is followed by a conviction, the defendant obviously will not appeal the favorable evidentiary ruling. If a defendant's challenge is rejected and is followed by an acquittal, no appeal ensues and the matter is over. *Reported* opinions in criminal cases indicate that trial judges sometimes exclude or restrict expert testimony offered by prosecutors;[50] *reported* opinions also indicate that appellate courts routinely deny appeals contesting trial court decisions admitting forensic evidence against criminal defendants.[51] But the reported opinions do not offer in any way a complete sample of federal trial court dispositions of *Daubert*-type questions in criminal cases.[52]

---

[48] *Gen. Elec. Co. v. Joiner*, 522 U.S. 136, 142-43 (1997); see also H.T. Edwards and L.A. Elliott. 2007. *Federal Standards of Review.* St. Paul, MN: Thomson/West, pp. 72-74 (explaining that when a trial judge acts pursuant to broad discretion, appellate court scrutiny is necessarily very limited).

[49] See, e.g., *Hoult*, 57 F.3d at 5 (district courts are not required "to make explicit on-the-record rulings regarding the admissibility of expert testimony"); *United States v. Locascio*, 6 F.3d 924, 938-939 (2d Cir. 1993) ("We decline . . . to shackle the district court with a mandatory and explicit trustworthiness analysis. . . . In fact, we assume that the district court consistently and continually performed a trustworthiness analysis *sub silentio* of all evidence introduced at trial. We will not, however, circumscribe this discretion by burdening the court with the necessity of making an explicit determination for all expert testimony.").

[50] See, e.g., *United States v. Green*, 405 F. Supp. 2d 104 (D. Mass. 2005) (toolmark analysis); *United States v. Mikos*, No. 02-137, 2003 WL 22922197 (N.D. Ill. Dec. 9, 2003) (expert testimony relating to comparative bullet lead analysis); *United States v. Horn*, 185 F. Supp. 2d 530 (D. Md. 2002) (evidence of defendant's performance on field sobriety tests); *United States v. Rutherford*, 104 F. Supp. 2d 1190 (D. Neb. 2000) (handwriting analysis).

[51] See, e.g., *United States v. Ford*, 481 F.3d 215 (3d Cir. 2007); *United States v. Moreland*, 437 F.3d 424 (4th Cir. 2006); *United States v. Brown*, 415 F.3d 1257 (11th Cir. 2005); *United States v. Davis*, 397 F.3d 173 (3d Cir. 2005); *United States v. Conn*, 297 F.3d 548 (7th Cir. 2002); *United States v. Havvard*, 260 F.3d 597 (7th Cir. 2001); *United States v. Malveaux*, 208 F.3d 223 (9th Cir. 2000); *United States v. Harris*, 192 F.3d 580 (6th Cir. 1999).

[52] In 2000, Michael Risinger published a study in which he found that, "as to proffers of asserted expert testimony, civil defendants win their *Daubert* reliability challenges to plaintiffs' proffers most of the time, and that criminal defendants virtually always lose their reliability challenges to government proffers. And, when civil defendants' proffers are challenged by

The situation is very different in civil cases. The party who loses before the trial court in a nonfrivolous civil case always has the right and incentive to appeal to contest the admission or exclusion of expert testimony. In addition, plaintiffs and defendants, equally, are more likely to have access to expert witnesses in civil cases, whereas prosecutors usually have an advantage over most defendants in offering expert testimony in criminal cases. And, ironically, the appellate courts appear to be more willing to second-guess trial court judgments on the admissibility of purported scientific evidence in civil cases than in criminal cases.[53]

---

plaintiffs, those defendants usually win, but when criminal defendants' proffers are challenged by the prosecution, the criminal defendants usually lose." D. M. Risinger Navigating expert reliability: Are criminal standards of certainty being left on the dock? 64 ALB. L. REV. 99, 99 (2000). However, the sample of federal district court decisions included "only sixty-five . . . criminal cases, and only fifty-four dealt with dependability issues in a guilt-or-innocence context . . . . These fifty-four cases represented *twelve opinions on defense challenges to prosecution proffers*, and forty-two opinions on government challenges to defense proffers. Of the twelve defense challenges, the government's challenged evidence was fully admitted eleven times, and admitted with restrictions once." Ibid., p. 109 (emphasis added) (footnotes omitted). The study did not include any sample of trial court dispositions of *Daubert*-type claims in which no opinion was issued, which might explain why the study included only 12 dispositions of defense challenges to prosecution proffers. The author speculated that "one can be relatively confident that virtually any decision totally excluding government proffered expertise on dependability grounds would have been the subject of some sort of opinion, at least the first time the decision was made in regard to a particular kind of proffer." Ibid. But there is no reason to believe that this assumption is correct. Trial judges routinely issue evidentiary rulings without reported opinions, and many such rulings might implicate *Daubert*-type questions. Merely because a defense attorney fails to state "I object on *Daubert* grounds" says very little about whether the objection raises an issue that is cognizable under *Daubert*.

[53] See, e.g., *McClain v. Metabolife Int'l, Inc.*, 401 F.3d 1233 (11th Cir. 2005); *Chapman v. Maytag Corp.*, 297 F.3d 682 (7th Cir. 2002); *Goebel v. Denver & Rio Grande W. R.R. Co.*, 215 F.3d 1083 (10th Cir. 2000); *Smith v. Ford Motor Co.*, 215 F.3d 713 (7th Cir. 2000); *Walker v. Soo Line R.R. Co.*, 208 F.3d 581 (7th Cir. 2000); see also 1 Faigman et al., op. cit., *supra* note 1, § 1:35, p. 105 (discussing studies suggesting that courts "employ *Daubert* more lackadaisically in criminal trials—especially in regard to prosecution evidence—than in civil cases—especially in regard to plaintiff evidence"); Risinger, op. cit., *supra* note 52, p. 100 ("The system shipwreck I fear is that in ten years we will find that civil cases are subject to strict standards of expertise quality control, while criminal cases are not. The result would be that the pocketbooks of civil defendants would be protected from plaintiffs' claims by exclusion of undependable expert testimony, but that criminal defendants would not be protected from conviction based on similarly undependable expert testimony. Such a result would seem particularly unacceptable given the law's claim that inaccurate criminal convictions are substantially worse than inaccurate civil judgments, reflected in the different applicable standards of proof.").

SOME EXAMPLES OF JUDICIAL DISPOSITIONS OF QUESTIONS RELATING TO FORENSIC SCIENCE EVIDENCE

Judicial Dispositions of Questions Relating to DNA Evidence

> DNA typing has been subjected to the most rigorous scrutiny by the courts, presumably because its discriminating power is so great and so much is at stake when a suspect is associated to a crime scene only through DNA typing. Or perhaps because (at least some) modern courts or lawyers are more literate about science than they were in the past.[54]

Unlike many forensic techniques that were developed empirically within the forensic community, with little foundation in scientific theory or analysis, DNA analysis is a fortuitous byproduct of cutting-edge science. From the beginning, eminent scientists contributed their expertise to ensuring that DNA evidence offered in a courtroom would be valid and reliable,[55] and by 1996 the National Academy of Sciences had convened two committees that issued influential recommendations on the use of DNA technology in forensic science.[56] As a result, principles of statistics and population genetics that pertain to DNA evidence were clarified, the methods for conducting DNA analyses and declaring a match became less subjective, and quality assurance and quality control protocols were designed to improve laboratory performance.

Although some courts initially refused to admit the results of DNA testing because of perceived flaws,[57] DNA evidence is now universally admit-

---

[54] 4 Faigman et al., op. cit., *supra* note 1, § 29:35, p. 41.

[55] See, e.g., *United States v. Yee*, 134 F.R.D. 161 (N.D. Ohio 1991) (hearings held over 6 weeks featuring a total of 12 expert witnesses on the admissibility of DNA evidence); *People v. Castro*, 545 N.Y.S.2d 985 (N.Y. Sup. Ct. 1989) (hearings held over 12 weeks featuring a total of 10 expert witnesses on the admissibility of DNA evidence).

[56] National Research Council, Committee on DNA Forensic Science. 1996. *The Evaluation of Forensic DNA Evidence*. Washington, DC: National Academy Press; National Research Council, Committee on DNA Technology in Forensic Science. 1992. *DNA Technology in Forensic Science*. Washington, DC: National Academy Press.

[57] See *Castro*, 545 N.Y.S.2d at 999 (finding after a pretrial hearing that the "DNA identification evidence of inclusion" was inadmissible because "[t]he testing laboratory failed in several major respects to use the generally accepted scientific techniques and experiments for obtaining reliable results, within a reasonable degree of scientific certainty"). Decided a few years before the *Daubert* decision was handed down, *Castro* applied a modified *Frye* standard to determine the admissibility of DNA evidence. Later federal cases, both pre- and post-*Daubert*, held that alleged errors in handling and interpreting specific DNA samples would not render the evidence inadmissible as a matter of law, but should instead be raised at trial as factors for the jury to weigh in determining the credibility of the DNA evidence. See, e.g., *United States v. Jakobetz*, 955 F.2d 786, 800 (2d Cir. 1992); *United States v. Trala*, 162 F. Supp. 2d 336, 349 (D. Del. 2001), *aff'd*, 386 F.3d 536 (3rd Cir. 2004), *vacated on other grounds*, 546

ted by courts in the United States. When 2 profiles are found to "match" in a search of the Federal Bureau of Investigation's (FBI's) Combined DNA Index System (CODIS) database using 13 short tandem repeat (STR) loci, the likelihood that the profiles came from different people is extremely small. In other words, assuming the samples were properly collected and analyzed, an observer may state with a high degree of confidence that the two profiles likely came from the same person.

Among existing forensic methods, only nuclear DNA analysis has been rigorously shown to have the capacity to consistently, and with a high degree of certainty, demonstrate a connection between an evidentiary sample and a specific individual or source. Indeed, DNA testing has been used to exonerate persons who were convicted as a result of the misapplication of other forensic science evidence.[58] However, this does not mean that DNA evidence is always unassailable in the courtroom. There may be problems in a particular case with how the DNA was collected,[59] examined in the laboratory,[60] or interpreted, such as when there are mixed samples, limited amounts of DNA, or biases due to the statistical interpretation of data from partial profiles.[61]

Courts were able to subject DNA evidence to rigorous evaluation

---

U.S. 1086 (2006); *United States v. Shea*, 957 F. Supp. 331, 340-41 (D.N.H. 1997), *aff'd*, 159 F.3d 37 (1st Cir. 1998).

[58] According to The Innocence Project, there have been 220 postconviction DNA exonerations in the United States since 1989. See The Innocence Project, Fact Sheet: Facts on Post-Conviction DNA Exonerations. Available at www.innocenceproject.org/Content/351.php; see also B.L. Garrett. Judging innocence. 108 COLUM. L. REV. 55 (2008) (discussing the results of an empirical study of the types of faulty evidence that was admitted in more than 200 cases for which DNA testing subsequently enabled postconviction exonerations); but see J. Collins and J. Jarvis. 2008. *The Wrongful Conviction of Forensic Science*. CRIME LAB REPORT. Available at www.crimelabreport.com/library/pdf/wrongful_conviction.pdf (contesting the percentage of exonerated defendants whose convictions allegedly were based on faulty forensic science).

[59] See, e.g., W.C. Thompson. DNA evidence in the O.J. Simpson trial. 67 U. COLO. L. REV. 827 (1996) (detailing the defense counsel's theory that proper procedures were not followed in the collection or handling of the DNA samples at various points in the murder investigation).

[60] See, e.g., L. Hart. 2003. "DNA Lab's Woes Cast Doubt on 68 Prison Terms." *Los Angeles Times*. March 31, at 19; A. Liptak. 2003. "Houston DNA Review Clears Convicted Rapist, and Ripples in Texas Could Be Vast." *New York Times*. March 11, at A14; R. Tanner. 2003. "Crime Labs Stained by a Shadow of a Doubt." *Los Angeles Times*. July 13, at 18.

[61] See, e.g., *Coy v. Renico*, 414 F. Supp. 2d 744, 761-63 (E.D. Mich. 2006) (rejecting habeas petitioner's claim that he was denied a fair trial because the statistical techniques used to evaluate mixed DNA samples were insufficiently reliable); see also B.S. Weir. 2007. The rarity of DNA profiles. *Annals of Applied Statistics* 1(2):358-370 (suggesting that wholesale searches of large DNA databases for solving cold cases might yield false positives with some regularity).

standards from the beginning,[62] because scientific groundwork for DNA analysis had been laid outside the context of law enforcement. The National Institutes of Health (NIH) and other respected institutions funded and conducted extensive basic research, followed by applied research. Serious studies on DNA analysis preceded the establishment and implementation of "individualization" criteria and parameters for assessing the probative value of claims of individualization. This history stands in sharp contrast to the history of research involving most other forensic science disciplines, which have not benefitted from extensive basic research, clinical applications, federal oversight, vast financial support from the private sector for applied research, and national standards for quality assurance and quality control. The goal is not to hold other disciplines to DNA's high standards in all respects; after all, it is unlikely that most other current forensic methods will ever produce evidence as discriminating as DNA. However, using *Daubert* as a guide, the least that the courts should insist upon from any forensic discipline is certainty that practitioners in the field adhere to enforceable standards, ensuring that any and all scientific testimony or evidence admitted is not only relevant, but reliable.

Judicial Dispositions of Questions Relating to Drug Identification

Over the years, there have been countless instances in which trial judges have assessed the admissibility of expert testimony relating to drug analyses, either *sua sponte* or pursuant to objections raised by defense counsel. Because trial court decisions in these matters often are resolved without published written opinions and with no challenges on appeal, there is no sure way to know how often trial judges deny the admissibility of the evidence. Trial judges may sometimes sustain challenges to the admissibility of expert testimony, especially in instances where the defense can show defects in the foundational laboratory reports.[63] But there are very few such reported cases.

In addition to alleged defects in laboratory reports and sampling procedures, trial courts routinely consider whether experts possess the necessary qualifications to testify and, more generally, whether expert testimony is sufficiently reliable to be admitted under *Daubert* and Federal Rule of Evidence 702. However, in published opinions addressing expert testimony based on drug identification, federal appellate courts rarely reverse trial

[62] See *supra* text accompanying note 54; see also *Gov't of V.I. v. Byers*, 941 F. Supp. 513 (D.V.I. 1996); *United States v. Jakobetz*, 747 F. Supp. 250 (D. Vt. 1990), *aff'd*, 955 F.2d 786 (2d Cir. 1992).

[63] See, e.g., *United States v. Diaz*, 2006 WL 3512032 (N.D. Cal. 2006).

court decisions rejecting *Daubert* challenges.[64] Why? First, as noted above, in cases where the evidence is excluded at trial, no appeal will be taken. Second, the scientific methodology supporting many drug tests is sound. This means that, regardless of the standard of review, most decisions by trial courts will withstand scrutiny. Finally, courts of appeals owe great deference to trial court judgments on questions relating to the admission of evidence.[65]

The importance of the limited standard of review was clearly explained in *United States v. Brown*:[66]

> Immersed in the case as it unfolds, a district court is more familiar with the procedural and factual details and is in a better position to decide *Daubert* issues. The rules relating to *Daubert* issues are not precisely calibrated and must be applied in case-specific evidentiary circumstances that often defy generalization. And we don't want to denigrate the importance of the trial and encourage appeals of rulings relating to the testimony of expert witnesses. All of this explains why the task of evaluating the reliability of expert testimony is uniquely entrusted to the district court under *Daubert*, and why we give the district court considerable leeway in the execution of its duty. That is true whether the district court admits or excludes expert testimony. *Joiner*, 522 U.S. at 141-42 ("A court of appeals applying 'abuse-of-discretion' review to [*Daubert*] rulings may not categorically distinguish between rulings allowing expert testimony and rulings disallowing it."). And it is true where the *Daubert* issue is outcome determinative.[67]

Judicial Dispositions of Questions Relating to Fingerprint Analyses

Over the years, the courts have admitted fingerprint evidence, even though this evidence has "made its way into the courtroom without empirical validation of the underlying theory and/or its particular application."[68] The courts sometimes appear to assume that fingerprint evidence is irrefutable. For example, in *United States v. Crisp*, the court noted that "[w]hile the principles underlying fingerprint identification have not attained the

---

[64] See, e.g., *United States v. Moreland*, 437 F.3d 424, 430-31 (4th Cir. 2006), *cert. denied*, 547 U.S. 1142 (2006); *United States v. Scalia*, 993 F.2d 984, 988-90 (1st Cir. 1993).

[65] See, e.g., *United States v. Gaskin*, 364 F.3d 438, 460 n.8 (2d Cir. 2004) (holding that "when a party questions whether sound scientific methodology provides a basis for an expert opinion, it may move to preclude the admission of the opinion" under *Daubert*; however, when a defendant makes no such motion and instead stipulates to the admissibility of the expert opinion, "he cannot complain on appeal that the opinion lacks foundation").

[66] 415 F.3d 1266 (11th Cir. 2005).

[67] Ibid., pp. 1265-66 (alteration in original) (internal quotation marks, other internal citations omitted).

[68] M.A. Berger. Procedural paradigms for applying the *Daubert* test. 78 MINN. L. REV. 1345, 1354 (1994).

status of scientific law, they nonetheless bear the imprimatur of a strong general acceptance, not only in the expert community, but in the courts as well."[69] The court went on to say:

> [E]ven if we had a more concrete cause for concern as to the reliability of fingerprint identification, the Supreme Court emphasized in *Daubert* that "[v]igorous cross-examination, presentation of contrary evidence, and careful instruction on the burden of proof are the traditional and appropriate means of attacking shaky but admissible evidence." *Daubert*, 509 U.S. at 596. Ultimately, we conclude that while further research into fingerprint analysis would be welcome, "to postpone present in-court utilization of this bedrock forensic identifier pending such research would be to make the best the enemy of the good."[70]

Opinions of this sort have drawn sharp criticism:

> [M]any fingerprint decisions of recent years . . . display a remarkable lack of understanding of certain basic principles of the scientific method. Court after court, for example, [has] repeated the statement that fingerprinting met the *Daubert* testing criterion by virtue of having been tested by the adversarial process over the last one-hundred years. This silly statement is a product of courts' perception of the incomprehensibility of actually limiting or excluding fingerprint evidence. Such a prospect stilled their critical faculties. It also transformed their admissibility standard into a *Daubert*-permissive one, at least for that subcategory of expertise.[71]

This is a telling critique, especially when one compares the judicial decisions that have pursued rigorous scrutiny of DNA typing with the decisions that have applied less stringent standards of review in cases involving fingerprint evidence.

In holding that fingerprint evidence satisfied *Daubert*'s reliability and relevancy standards for admissibility, the Fourth Circuit's decision in *Crisp* noted approvingly that "the Seventh Circuit [in *United States v. Havvard*, 260 F.3d 597 (7th Cir. 2001)] determined that *Daubert*'s 'known error rate' factor was satisfied because the expert in *Havvard* had testified that the error rate for fingerprint comparison was 'essentially zero.'"[72] This statement appears to overstate the expert's testimony in *Havvard*, and gives fuel to the misconception that the forensic discipline

---

69 324 F.3d 261, 268 (4th Cir. 2003).

70 Ibid., pp. 269-70 (second alteration in original) (other internal citation omitted).

71 1 Faigman et al., op. cit., *supra* note 1, § 1:1, p. 4; see also J.J. Koehler. Fingerprint error rates and proficiency tests: What they are and why they matter. 59 HASTINGS L.J. 1077 (2008).

72 324 F.3d at 269 (quoting *Havvard*, 260 F.3d at 599).

of fingerprinting is infallible. The *Havvard* opinion actually described the expert's testimony as follows:

> [The expert] testified that the error rate for fingerprint comparison is essentially zero. Though conceding that a small margin of error exists because of differences in individual examiners, he opined that this risk is minimized because print identifications are typically confirmed through peer review. [The expert] did acknowledge that fingerprint examiners have not adopted a single standard for determining when a fragmentary latent fingerprint is sufficient to permit a comparison, but he suggested that the unique nature of fingerprints is counterintuitive to the establishment of such a standard and that through experience each examiner develops a comfort level for deciding how much of a fragmentary print is necessary to permit a comparison.[73]

This description of the expert's equivocal testimony calls into question any claim that fingerprint evidence is infallible.

The decision in *Crisp* also pointed out that "[f]ingerprint identification has been admissible as reliable evidence in criminal trials in this country since at least 1911."[74] The court, however, pointed to no studies supporting the reliability of fingerprint evidence. When forensic DNA first appeared, it was sometimes called "DNA fingerprinting" to suggest that it was as reliable as fingerprinting, which was then viewed as the premier identification science and one that consistently produced irrefutable results. During the effort to validate DNA evidence for courtroom use, however, it became apparent that assumptions about fingerprint evidence had been reached without the scientific scrutiny being accorded DNA. When the Supreme Court decided *Daubert* in 1993, with its emphasis on validation, legal commentators turned their attention to fingerprinting and began questioning whether experts could match and attribute fingerprints with a zero error rate as the FBI expert claimed in *Havvard*, and whether experts should be allowed to testify and make these claims in the absence of confirmatory studies. As noted above, most of these challenges have thus far failed, but the questions persist.

The 2004 Brandon Mayfield case refueled the debate over fingerprint evidence. The chronology of events in the Mayfield case is as follows:

---

[73] *Havvard*, 260 F.3d at 599. The *Havvard* decision is sharply criticized by 1 Faigman et al., op. cit., *supra* note 1, § 1:30, pp. 86-89.

[74] *Crisp*, 324 F.3d at 266. The decision cites a number of other legal references, including, *inter alia*: *People v. Jennings*, 96 N.E. 1077 (1911); J.L. Mnookin. Fingerprint evidence in an age of DNA profiling. 67 BROOK. L. REV. 13 (2001) (discussing history of fingerprint identification evidence).

> March 11, 2004: Terrorists detonate bombs on a number of trains in Madrid, Spain, killing approximately 191 people, and injuring thousands more, including a number of United States citizens.
>
> May 6, 2004: Brandon Bieri Mayfield, a 37-year-old civil and immigration lawyer, practicing in Portland, Oregon, is arrested as a material witness with respect to a federal grand jury's investigation into that bombing. An affidavit signed by FBI Special Agent Richard K. Werder, submitted in support of the government's application for the material witness arrest warrant, [avers] that Mayfield's fingerprint has been found on a bag in Spain containing detonation devices similar to those used in the bombings, and that he has to be detained so that he cannot flee before the grand jury has a chance to obtain his testimony.
>
> May 24, 2004: The government announces that the FBI has erred in its identification of Mayfield and moves to dismiss the material witness proceeding.[75]

In March 2006, the Office of the Inspector General of the U.S. Department of Justice issued a comprehensive analysis of how the misidentification occurred.[76] And in November 2006, the federal government agreed to pay Mayfield $2 million for his wrongful jailing in connection with the 2004 terrorist bombings in Madrid.[77] The Mayfield case and the resulting report from the Inspector General surely signal caution against simple, and unverified, assumptions about the reliability of fingerprint evidence.

In *Maryland v. Rose*, a Maryland State trial court judge found that the Analysis, Comparison, Evaluation, and Verification (ACE-V) process (see Chapter 5) of latent print identification does not rest on a reliable factual foundation.[78] The opinion went into considerable detail about the lack of error rates, lack of research, and potential for bias. The judge ruled that the State could not offer testimony that any latent fingerprint matched the prints of the defendant. The judge also noted that, because the case involved

[75] S.T. Wax and C.J. Schatz. 2004. A multitude of errors: The Brandon Mayfield case. *The Champion*. September-October, p. 6. The facts of the case and Mayfield's legal claims against the government are fully reported in *Mayfield v. United States*, 504 F. Supp. 2d 1023 (D. Or. 2007).

[76] Office of the Inspector General, Oversight and Review Division, U.S. Department of Justice. 2006. *A Review of the FBI's Handling of the Brandon Mayfield Case*. Available at www.usdoj.gov/oig/special/s0601/exec.pdf.

[77] E. Lichtblau. 2006. "U.S. Will Pay $2 Million To Lawyer Wrongly Jailed." *New York Times*. November 30, at A18.

[78] *Maryland v. Rose*, Case No. K06-0545, mem. op. at 31 (Balt. County Cir. Ct. Oct. 19, 2007) (holding that the ACE-V methodology of latent fingerprint identification was "a subjective, untested, unverifiable identification procedure that purports to be infallible" and therefore ruling that fingerprint evidence was inadmissible). The ACE-V process is described in Chapter 5.

the possibility of the death penalty, the reliability of the evidence offered against the defendant was critically important.[79]

The same concerns cited by the judge in *Maryland v. Rose* can be raised with respect to other forensic techniques that lack scientific validation and careful reliability testing.

Judicial Dispositions of Questions Relating to Other Forensic Disciplines

Review of reported judicial opinions reveals that, at least in criminal cases, forensic science evidence is not routinely scrutinized pursuant to the standard of reliability enunciated in *Daubert*. The Supreme Court in *Daubert* indicated that the subject of an expert's testimony should be "scientific knowledge"—which implies that such knowledge is based on scientific methods—to ensure that "evidentiary reliability will be based upon scientific validity." The standard is admittedly "flexible," but that does not render it meaningless. Any reasonable reading of *Daubert* strongly suggests that, when faced with forensic evidence, "trial judge[s] must ensure that any and all scientific testimony or evidence admitted is not only relevant, but reliable." As the reported cases suggest, however, *Daubert* has done little to improve the use of forensic science evidence in criminal cases.

> For years in the forensic science community, the dominant argument against regulating experts was that every time a forensic scientist steps into a courtroom, his work is vigorously peer reviewed and scrutinized by opposing counsel. A forensic scientist might occasionally make an error in the crime laboratory, but the crucible of courtroom cross-examination

---

[79] Professor Jennifer Mnookin has also highlighted an important concern over "the rhetorical dimensions of the testimony . . . provide[d] in court" by members of the fingerprint community:

> At present, fingerprint examiners typically testify in the language of absolute certainty. Both the conceptual foundations and the professional norms of latent fingerprinting prohibit experts from testifying to identification unless they believe themselves certain that they have made a correct match. Experts therefore make only what they term "positive" or "absolute" identifications—essentially making the claim that they have matched the latent print to the one and only person in the entire world whose fingertip could have produced it. In fact, if a fingerprint examiner testifies on her own initiative that a match is merely "likely" or "possible" or "credible," rather than certain, she could possibly be subject to disciplinary sanction! Given the general lack of validity testing for fingerprinting; the relative dearth of difficult proficiency tests; the lack of a statistically valid model of fingerprinting; and the lack of validated standards for declaring a match, such claims of absolute, certain confidence in identification are unjustified, the product of hubris more than established knowledge. Therefore, in order to pass scrutiny under *Daubert*, fingerprint identification experts should exhibit a greater degree of epistemological humility. Claims of "absolute" and "positive" identification should be replaced by more modest claims about the meaning and significance of a "match."

J.L. Mnookin. 2008. The validity of latent fingerprint identification: Confessions of a fingerprinting moderate. *Law, Probability and Risk* 7(2):127; see also Koehler, *supra* note 71.

> would expose it at trial. This "crucible," however, turned out to be utterly ineffective.
>
> . . .
>
> Unlike the extremely well-litigated civil challenges, the criminal defendant's challenge is usually perfunctory. Even when the most vulnerable forensic sciences—hair microscopy, bite marks, and handwriting—are attacked, the courts routinely affirm admissibility citing earlier decisions rather than facts established at a hearing. Defense lawyers generally fail to build a challenge with appropriate witnesses and new data. Thus, even if inclined to mount a *Daubert* challenge, they lack the requisite knowledge and skills, as well as the funds, to succeed.[80]

The reported decisions dealing with judicial dispositions of *Daubert*-type questions appear to confirm this assessment. As noted above, the courts often "affirm admissibility citing earlier decisions rather than facts established at a hearing." Much forensic evidence—including, for example, bite marks[81] and firearm and toolmark identifications[82]—is introduced in

---

[80] Neufeld, *supra* note 44, at S109, S110.

[81] There is nothing to indicate that courts review bite mark evidence pursuant to *Daubert*'s standard of reliability. See, e.g., *Milone v. Camp*, 22 F.3d 693, 702 (7th Cir. 1994) (denying habeas petition after finding, in part, that the inclusion of bite mark testimony against the defendant had not denied him a fair trial, and stating that "while the science of forensic odontology might have been in its infancy at the time of trial . . . certainly there is some probative value to comparing an accused's dentition to bite marks found on the victim."). Two recent cases might, at first glance, seem to indicate that courts were beginning to seriously evaluate the general credibility of bite mark testimony, but this is not in fact the case. In *Burke v. Town of Walpole*, 405 F.3d 66 (1st Cir. 2005), the court denied summary judgment to police officers in a 42 U.S.C. § 1983 action where exculpatory DNA evidence that directly contradicted inculpatory bite mark evidence was "intentionally or recklessly withheld from the officer who was actually preparing the warrant application," ibid., p. 84, resulting in petitioner being wrongfully imprisoned for 41 days. However, the *Burke* court rejected the petitioner's claim that the inclusion of bite mark evidence in the arrest warrant had demonstrated "reckless disregard for the truth," because the method was generally unreliable. Ibid., pp. 82-83. In *Ege v. Yukins*, 380 F. Supp. 2d 852 (E.D. Mich. 2005), *aff'd in part and rev'd in part*, 485 F.3d 364 (6th Cir. 2007), the court granted the habeas petition of a defendant whose conviction was based in significant part on bite mark testimony from a later-discredited expert witness. But the disposition in *Ege* rested primarily on the flaws of one "particular witness and his particular testimony," not on a judicial evaluation of "*the* [bite mark] *field's* more general shortcomings." 4 Faigman et al., op. cit., *supra* note 1, § 36:6, p. 662.

[82] There is little to indicate that courts review firearms evidence pursuant to *Daubert*'s standard of reliability. See e.g., *United States v. Hicks*, 389 F.3d 514 (5th Cir. 2004) (upholding defendant's conviction after finding, in part, that it was not an abuse of discretion for the court to admit testimony on shell casing comparisons by the Government's firearms expert); *United States v. Foster*, 300 F. Supp. 2d 375 (D. Md. 2004) (denying defendant's motion to exclude expert firearms testimony). Several federal trial judges, however, have subjected expert firearm testimony to rigorous analysis under *Daubert*. In *United States v. Monteiro*, 407 F. Supp. 2d 351 (D. Mass. 2006), Judge Saris concluded that toolmark identification testimony was

criminal trials without any meaningful scientific validation, determination of error rates, or reliability testing to explain the limits of the discipline. One recent judicial decision highlights the problem. In *United States v. Green*, Judge Gertner acknowledged that toolmark identification testimony *ought not be considered admissible* under *Daubert*.[83] But the judge pointed out that "the problem for the defense is *that every single court* post-*Daubert* has admitted this testimony, sometimes without any searching review, much less a hearing."[84] Judge Gertner allowed the prosecution's expert to describe the similarities between the shell casings at issue, but prohibited him from testifying that there was a definitive match. Obviously feeling bound by circuit precedent, the judge stated:

> I reluctantly [admit the evidence] because of my confidence that any other decision will be rejected by appellate courts, in light of precedents across the country, regardless of the findings I have made. While I recognize that the *Daubert-Kumho* standard does not require the illusory perfection of a television show (CSI, this wasn't), when liberty hangs in the balance—and, in the case of the defendants facing the death penalty, life itself—the standards should be higher than were met in this case, and than have been imposed across the country. The more courts admit this type of toolmark evidence without requiring documentation, proficiency testing, or evidence of reliability, the more sloppy practices will endure; we should require more.[85]

"[T]he undeniable reality is that the community of forensic science

---

generally admissible under *Daubert*, but excluded the specific testimony at issue, because the experts failed to properly document their basis for identification, and because an independent examiner had not verified the experts' conclusions. Likewise, in *United States v. Diaz*, No. 05-CR-167, 2007 WL 485967, at *14 (N.D. Cal. Feb. 12, 2007), Judge Alsup allowed firearm identification testimony under *Daubert*, but prevented experts from testifying to their conclusions "to the exclusion of all other firearms in the world" and only allowed testimony "to a reasonable degree of certainty." *Cf. United States v. Glynn*, 578 F. Supp. 2d 569 (S.D.N.Y. 2008), where Judge Rakoff precluded testimony that a bullet and shell casings came from a firearm linked to the defendant "to a reasonable degree of ballistics certainty," because "whatever else ballistics identification analysis could be called, it could not fairly be called 'science.'" However, the judge ruled that although inadmissible under *Daubert*, testimony that the evidence was "more likely than not" from the firearm was admissible under Federal Rule of Evidence 401. See also *Green*, 405 F. Supp. 2d 104, discussed in the text.

[83] 405 F. Supp. 2d at 107-08.

[84] Ibid., p. 108.

[85] Ibid., p. 109 (footnotes omitted). "The case law on the admissibility of toolmark identification and firearms identification expert evidence is typified by decisions admitting such testimony with little, and usually no, reference to legal authority beyond broad 'discretion' and an adroit sidestepping of any judicial duty to assure that experts' claims are valid. Appellate courts defer to trial courts, and trial courts defer to juries. Later appellate courts simply defer to earlier appellate courts." 4 Faigman et al., op. cit., *supra* note 1, § 34:5, p. 589.

professionals has not done nearly as much as it reasonably could have done to establish either the validity of its approach or the accuracy of its practitioners' conclusions,"[86] and the courts have been "utterly ineffective" in addressing this problem.[87]

CONCLUSION

Prophetically, the *Daubert* decision observed that "there are important differences between the quest for truth in the courtroom and the quest for truth in the laboratory. Scientific conclusions are subject to perpetual revision. Law, on the other hand, must resolve disputes finally and quickly."[88] But because accused parties in criminal cases are convicted on the basis of testimony from forensic science experts, much depends upon whether the evidence offered is reliable. Furthermore, in addition to protecting innocent persons from being convicted of crimes that they did not commit, we are also seeking to protect society from persons who have committed criminal acts. Law enforcement officials and the members of society they serve need to be assured that forensic techniques are *reliable*. Therefore, we must limit the risk of having the reliability of certain forensic science methodologies condoned by the courts before the techniques have been properly studied and their accuracy verified. "[T]here is no evident reason why ['rigorous, systematic'] research would be infeasible."[89] However, some courts appear to be loath to insist on such research as a condition of admitting forensic science evidence in criminal cases, perhaps because to do so would likely "demand more by way of validation than the disciplines can presently offer."[90]

Some legal scholars think that, "[o]ver time, if *Daubert* does not come

---

[86] Mnookin, op. cit., *supra* note 79.

[87] Neufeld, op. cit., *supra* note 44, p. S109. In *Green*, 405 F. Supp. 2d at 109 n.6, Judge Gertner also noted that:

> [R]ecent reexaminations of relatively established forensic testimony have produced striking results. Saks and Koehler, for example, report that forensic testing errors were responsible for wrongful convictions in 63% of the 86 DNA Exoneration cases reported by the Innocence Project at Cardozo Law School. Michael Saks and Jonathan Koehler, The Coming Paradigm Shift in Forensic Identification Science, 309 Science 892 (2005). This only reinforces the importance of careful analysis of expert testimony in this case.

See also S.R. Gross, *Convicting the Innocent* (U. Mich. Law Sch. Pub. Law & Legal Theory Working Paper Series, Working Paper No. 103, 2008). Available at http://papers.ssrn.com/sol3/papers.cfm?abstract_id=1100011 (forthcoming in *Annual Review of Law & Social Science* 2008).

[88] *Daubert v. Merrell Dow Pharm., Inc.*, 509 U.S. 579, 596-97 (1993).

[89] J. Griffin and D.J. LaMagna. 2002. *Daubert* challenges to forensic evidence: Ballistics next on the firing line. *The Champion*. September-October:21.

[90] Ibid. See, e.g., *Crisp*, 324 F.3d at 270.

to be diluted or distorted, . . . courts will increasingly appreciate its power and flexibility to evaluate proffered expert testimony."[91] However, at least with respect to criminal cases, this may reflect an unrealistic assessment of the problem. "The principal difficulty, it appears, is that many [forensic science] techniques have been relied on for so long that courts might be reluctant to rethink their role in the trial process. . . . In many forensic areas, effectively no research exists to support the practice."[92]

As the discussion in this chapter indicates, the adversarial process relating to the admission and exclusion of scientific evidence is not suited to the task of finding "scientific truth." The judicial system is encumbered by, among other things, judges and lawyers who generally lack the scientific expertise necessary to comprehend and evaluate forensic evidence in an informed manner, trial judges (sitting alone) who must decide evidentiary issues without the benefit of judicial colleagues and often with little time for extensive research and reflection, and the highly deferential nature of the appellate review afforded trial courts' *Daubert* rulings. Furthermore, the judicial system embodies a case-by-case adjudicatory approach that is not well suited to address the systematic problems in many of the various forensic science disciplines. Given these realities, there is a tremendous need for the forensic science community to improve. Judicial review, by itself, will not cure the infirmities of the forensic science community.[93] The development of scientific research, training, technology, and databases associated with DNA analysis have resulted from substantial and steady federal support for both academic research and programs employing techniques for DNA analysis. Similar support must be given to all credible forensic science disciplines if they are to achieve the degrees of reliability needed to serve the goals of justice. With more and better educational programs, accredited laboratories, certified forensic practitioners, sound operational principles and procedures, and serious research to establish the limits and measures of performance in each discipline, forensic science experts will be better able to analyze evidence and coherently report their findings in the courts. The present situation, however, is seriously wanting, both because of the limitations of the judicial system and because of the many problems faced by the forensic science community.

---

[91] 1 Faigman et al., op. cit., *supra* note 1, § 1:1, p. 5 n. 9.

[92] Ibid. § 1:30, p. 85 (footnotes omitted).

[93] See J.L. Mnookin. Expert evidence, partisanship, and epistemic competence. 73 BROOK. L. REV. 1009, 1033 (2008) ("[S]o long as we have our adversarial system in much its present form, we are inevitably going to be stuck with approaches to expert evidence that are imperfect, conceptually unsatisfying, and awkward. It may well be that the real lesson is this: those who believe that we might ever fully resolve—rather than imperfectly manage—the deep structural tensions surrounding both partisanship and epistemic competence that permeate the use of scientific evidence within our legal system are almost certainly destined for disappointment.").

4

The Principles of Science and Interpreting Scientific Data

> Scientific method refers to the body of techniques for investigating phenomena, acquiring new knowledge, or correcting and integrating previous knowledge. It is based on gathering observable, empirical and measurable evidence subject to specific principles of reasoning.
>
> Isaac Newton (1687, 1713, 1726)
> "Rules for the study of natural philosophy,"
> *Philosophiae Naturalis Principia Mathematica*

Forensic science actually is a broad array of disciplines, as will be seen in the next chapter. Each has its own methods and practices, as well as its strengths and weaknesses. In particular, each varies in its level of scientific development and in the degree to which it follows the principles of scientific investigation. Adherence to scientific principles is important for concrete reasons: they enable the reliable inference of knowledge from uncertain information—exactly the challenge faced by forensic scientists. Thus, the reliability of forensic science methods is greatly enhanced when those principles are followed. As Chapter 3 observes, the law's admission of and reliance on forensic evidence in criminal trials depends critically on (1) the extent to which a forensic science discipline is founded on a reliable scientific methodology, leading to accurate analyses of evidence and proper reports of findings and (2) the extent to which practitioners in those forensic science disciplines that rely on human interpretation adopt procedures and performance standards that guard against bias and error. This chapter discusses the ways in which science more generally addresses those goals.

FUNDAMENTAL PRINCIPLES OF THE SCIENTIFIC METHOD

The scientific method presumes that events occur in consistent patterns that can be understood through careful comparison and systematic study. Knowledge is produced through a series of steps during which data are accumulated methodically, strengths and weaknesses of information are assessed, and knowledge about causal relationships is inferred. In the process, scientists also develop an understanding of the limits of that knowledge (such as the precision of the observations), the inferred nature of relationships, and key assumptions behind the inferences. Hypotheses are developed, are measured against the data, and are either supported or refuted.

Scientists continually observe, test, and modify the body of knowledge. Rather than claiming absolute truth, science approaches truth either through breakthrough discoveries or incrementally, by testing theories repeatedly. Evidence is obtained through observations and measurements conducted in the natural setting or in the laboratory. In the laboratory, scientists can control and vary the conditions in order to isolate exclusive effects and thus better understand the factors that influence certain outcomes. Typically, experiments or observations must be conducted over a broad range of conditions before the roles of specific factors, patterns, or variables can be understood. Methods to reduce errors are part of the study design, so that, for example, the size of the study is chosen to provide sufficient statistical power to draw conclusions with a high level of confidence or to understand factors that might confound results. Throughout scientific investigations, the investigator must be as free from bias as possible, and practices are put in place to detect biases (such as those from measurements, human interpretation) and to minimize their effects on conclusions.

Ultimately, the goal is to construct explanations ("theories") of phenomena that are consistent with broad scientific principles, such as the laws of thermodynamics or of natural selection. These theories, and investigations of them through experiments and observed data, are shared through conferences, publications, and collegial interactions, which push the scientist to explain his or her work clearly and which raise questions that might not have been considered. The process of sharing data and results requires careful recordkeeping, reviewed by others. In addition, the need for credibility among peers drives investigators to avoid conflicts of interest. Acceptance of the work comes as results and theories continue to hold, even under the scrutiny of peers, in an environment that encourages healthy skepticism. That scrutiny might extend to independent reproduction of the results or experiments designed to test the theory under different conditions. As credibility accrues to data and theories, they become accepted as established fact and become the "scaffolding" upon which other investigations are constructed.

This description of how science creates new theories illustrates key elements of good scientific practice: precision when defining terms, processes, context, results, and limitations; openness to new ideas, including criticism and refutation; and protections against bias and overstatement (going beyond the facts). Although these elements have been discussed here in the context of creating new methods and knowledge, the same principles hold when applying known processes or knowledge. In day-to-day forensic science work, the process of formulating and testing hypotheses is replaced with the careful preparation and analysis of samples and the interpretation of results. But that applied work, if done well, still exhibits the same hallmarks of basic science: the use of validated methods and care in following their protocols; the development of careful and adequate documentation; the avoidance of biases; and interpretation conducted within the constraints of what the science will allow.

Validation of New Methods

One particular task of science is the validation of new methods to determine their reliability under different conditions and their limitations. Such studies begin with a clear hypothesis (e.g., "new method X can reliably associate biological evidence with its source"). An unbiased experiment is designed to provide useful data about the hypothesis. Those data—measurements collected through methodical prescribed observations under well-specified and controlled conditions—are then analyzed to support or refute the hypothesis. The thresholds for supporting or refuting the hypothesis are clearly articulated before the experiment is run. The most important outcomes from such a validation study are (1) information about whether or not the method can discriminate the hypothesis from an alternative, and (2) assessments of the sources of errors and their consequences on the decisions returned by the method. These two outcomes combine to provide precision and clarity about what is meant by "reliably associate."

For a method that has not been subjected to previous extensive study, a researcher might design a broad experiment to assist in gaining knowledge about its performance under a range of conditions. Those data are then analyzed for any underlying patterns that may be useful in planning or interpreting tests that use the new method. In other situations, a process already has been formulated from existing experimental data, knowledge, and theory (e.g., "biological markers A, B, and C can be used in DNA forensic investigations to pair evidence with suspect").

To confirm the validity of a method or process for a particular purpose (e.g., for a forensic investigation), validation studies must be performed.

The International Organization for Standardization (ISO) and the International Electrotechnical Commission (IEC) developed a joint document,

"General requirements for the competence of testing and calibration laboratories" (commonly referred to as "ISO 17025"), which includes a well-established list of techniques that can be used, alone or in combination, to validate a method:

- calibration using reference standards or reference materials;
- comparison of results achieved with other methods;
- interlaboratory comparisons;
- systematic assessment of the factors influencing the result; and
- assessment of the uncertainty of the results based on scientific understanding of the theoretical principles of the method and practical experience.[1]

A critical step in such validation studies is their publication in peer-reviewed journals, so that experts in the field can review, question, and check the repeatability of the results. These publications must include clear statements of the hypotheses under study, as well as sufficient details about the experiments, the resulting data, and the data analysis so that the studies can be replicated. Replication will expose not only additional sources of variability but also further aspects of the process, leading to greater understanding and scientific knowledge that can be used to improve the method. Methods that are specified in more detail (such as DNA analysis, where particular genetic loci are to be compared) will have greater credibility and also are more amenable to systematic improvement than those that rely more heavily on the judgments of the investigator.

The validation of results over time increases confidence. Moreover, the scientific culture encourages continued questioning and improvement. Thus, the relevant scientific community continues to check that established results still hold under new conditions and that they continue to hold in the face of new knowledge. The involvement of graduate student researchers in scientific research contributes greatly to this diligence, because part of their education is to read carefully and to question so-called established methods. This culture leads to continued reexamination of past research and hence increased knowledge.

In the case of DNA analysis, studies have evaluated the precision, reliability, and uncertainties of the methods. This knowledge has been used to define standard procedures that, when followed, lead to reliable evidence. For example, below is a brief sample of the specifications required by the Federal Bureau of Investigation's (FBI's) Quality Assurance Standards for

[1] Quoted from Section 5.4.5 2 (Note 2) of ISO/IEC 17025, "General requirements for the competence of testing and calibration laboratories" (2nd ed., May 15, 2005).

Forensic DNA Testing Laboratories[2] in order to ensure reliable DNA forensic analysis:

- Testing laboratories must have a standard operating protocol for each analytical technique used, specifying reagents, sample preparation, extraction, equipment, and controls that are standard for DNA analysis and data interpretation.
- The laboratory shall monitor the analytical procedures using appropriate controls and standards, including quantitation standards that estimate the amount of human nuclear DNA recovered by extraction, positive and negative amplification controls, and reagent blanks.
- The laboratory shall check its DNA procedures annually or whenever substantial changes are made to the protocol(s) against an appropriate and available NIST standard reference material or standard traceable to a NIST standard.
- The laboratory shall have and follow written general guidelines for the interpretation of data.
- The laboratory shall verify that all control results are within established tolerance limits.
- Where appropriate, visual matches shall be supported by a numerical match criterion.
- For a given population(s) and/or hypothesis of relatedness, the statistical interpretation shall be made following the recommendations 4.1, 4.2, or 4.3 as deemed applicable of the National Research Council report entitled *The Evaluation of Forensic DNA Evidence* (1996) and/or a court-directed method. These calculations shall be derived from a documented population database appropriate for the calculation.[3]

This level of specificity is consistent with the spirit of the guidelines presented in ISO 17025. The second edition (May 15, 2005) of those guidelines includes the following minimum set of information for properly specifying the process of any new analytical method:

(a) appropriate identification;
(b) scope;
(c) description of the type of item to be tested or calibrated;

---

[2] DNA Advisory Board. 2000. *Forensic Science Communications* 2(3). Available at www.bioforensics.com/conference04/TWGDAM/Quality_Assurance_Standards_2.pdf.

[3] Paraphrased from Section 9 of the FBI's Quality Assurance Standards for Forensic DNA Testing Laboratories.

(d) parameters or quantities and ranges to be determined;
(e) apparatus and equipment, including technical performance requirements;
(f) reference standards and reference materials required;
(g) environmental conditions required and any stabilization period needed;
(h) description of the procedure, including
   - affixing of identification marks, handling, transporting, storing and preparation of items;
   - checks to be made before the work is started;
   - checks that the equipment is working properly and, where required, calibration and adjustment of the equipment before each use;
   - the method of recording the observations and results;
   - any safety measures to be observed;
(i) criteria and/or requirements for approval/rejection;
(j) data to be recorded and method of analysis and presentation;
(k) the uncertainty or the procedure for estimating uncertainty.[4]

Uncertainty and Error

Scientific data and processes are subject to a variety of sources of error. For example, laboratory results and data from questionnaires are subject to measurement error, and interpretations of evidence by human observers are subject to potential biases. A key task for the scientific investigator designing and conducting a scientific study, as well as for the analyst applying a scientific method to conduct a particular analysis, is to identify as many sources of error as possible, to control or to eliminate as many as possible, and to estimate the magnitude of remaining errors so that the conclusions drawn from the study are valid. Numerical data reported in a scientific paper include not just a single value (point estimate) but also a range of plausible values (e.g., a confidence interval, or interval of uncertainty).

Measurement Error

As with all other scientific investigations, laboratory analyses conducted by forensic scientists are subject to measurement error. Such error reflects the intrinsic strengths and limitations of the particular scientific technique. For example, methods for measuring the level of blood alcohol in an individual or methods for measuring the heroin content of a sample

[4] Quoted from Section 5.4.4 of ISO/IEC 17025, "General requirements for the competence of testing and calibration laboratories" (2nd ed., May 15, 2005).

can do so only within a confidence interval of possible values. In addition to the inherent limitations of the measurement technique, a range of other factors may also be present and can affect the accuracy of laboratory analyses. Such factors may include deficiencies in the reference materials used in the analysis, equipment errors, environmental conditions that lie outside the range within which the method was validated, sample mix-ups and contamination, transcriptional errors, and more.

Consider, for example, a case in which an instrument (e.g., a breathalyzer such as Intoxilyzer) is used to measure the blood-alcohol level of an individual three times, and the three measurements are 0.08 percent, 0.09 percent, and 0.10 percent. The variability in the three measurements may arise from the internal components of the instrument, the different times and ways in which the measurements were taken, or a variety of other factors. These measured results need to be reported, along with a confidence interval that has a high probability of containing the true blood-alcohol level (e.g., the mean plus or minus two standard deviations). For this illustration, the average is 0.09 percent and the standard deviation is 0.01 percent; therefore, a two-standard-deviation confidence interval (0.07 percent, 0.11 percent) has a high probability of containing the person's true blood-alcohol level. (Statistical models dictate the methods for generating such intervals in other circumstances so that they have a high probability of containing the true result.) The situation for assessing heroin content from a sample of white powder is similar, although the quantification and limits are not as broadly standardized. The combination of gas chromatography and mass spectrometry (GC/MS) is used extensively in identifying controlled substances. Those analyses tend to be more qualitative (e.g., identifying peaks on a spectrum that appear at frequencies consistent with the controlled substance and which stand out above the background "noise"), although quantification is possible.

Error Rates

Analyses in the forensic science disciplines are conducted to provide information for a variety of purposes in the criminal justice process. However, most of these analyses aim to address two broad types of questions: (1) can a particular piece of evidence be associated with a particular class of sources? and (2) Can a particular piece of evidence be associated with one particular source? The first type of question leads to "classification" conclusions. An example of such a question would be whether a particular hair specimen shares physical characteristics common to a particular ethnic group. An affirmative answer to a classification question indicates only that the item belongs to a particular *class* of similar items. Another example might be whether a paint mark left at a crime scene is consistent (according to some collection of relevant measurements) with a particular paint sample in a database, from which one can infer the class of vehicle (e.g., model(s) and production year(s)) that could have left the mark. The second type of question leads to "individualization" conclusions—for example, does a particular DNA sample belong to individual X?

Although the questions addressed by forensic analyses are not always binary (yes/no) or as crisply stated as in the previous paragraph, the paradigm of yes/no conclusions is useful for describing and quantifying the accuracy with which forensic science disciplines can provide answers.[5] In such situations, results from analyses for which the truth is known can be classified in a two-way table as follows:

	Analysis Results	
Truth	yes	no
yes	a (true positives)	b (false negatives)
no	c (false positives)	d (true negatives)

The conceptual framework and terminology for evaluating the accuracy of forensic analyses is illustrated using a *hypothetical* example from microscopic analysis of head hair. In this situation, multiple features, both qualitative and quantitative, on each sample of hair are assessed. Qualitative features include color (e.g., blonde, brown, red), coloring (natural or treated), form (straight, wavy, curved, kinked), texture (smooth, medium, coarse). Quantitative features include length and diameter. Undoubtedly, these features will vary from hair to hair, even from the same individual, but features that vary *less* for the *same* individual (i.e., within-individual variability) and *more* for *different* individuals (i.e., between-individual variability) are needed for purposes of class identification and discrimination. These features may also be combined in some fashion to result in some overall score, or set of scores, for each sample, and these scores are then compared with those from the target sample. In the final analysis, however, a binary conclusion is often required. For example, "Did this hair come from the head of a Caucasian person?"

As in the case of all analyses leading to classification conclusions (e.g., diagnostic tests in medicine), the microscopic hair analysis process must be subjected to performance and validation studies in which appropriate error rates can be defined and estimated. Consider a hypothetical study in

[5] More complete discussion of the questions addressed by forensic science may be found in references such as K. Inman and N. Rudin. 2002. The origin of evidence. *Forensic Science International* 126:11-16; and R. Cook, I.W. Evett, G. Jackson, P.J. Jones, and J.A. Lambert. 1998. A hierarchy of propositions: Deciding which level to address in casework. *Science and Justice* 38:231-239.

which 100 samples (each with multiple hairs) are taken from the heads of 100 individuals from class C, and another 100 samples are taken from the heads of individuals not in class C. The analyst is asked to determine, for each of the 200 samples, whether it does or does not come from a person in class C, and the true answer is known. The validation study returns the following results:

Hypothetical Hair Analysis Validation Study

	Analysis of Hair Samples Indicates:		
	Class C	Not Class C	Row Total
Sample is from Class C Persons	95 True Positive (correct determination)	5 False Negative	100
Sample is not from Class C Persons	2 False Positive	98 True Negative (correct determination)	100
Column Total	97	103	Overall total 200

The accuracy of a test (here, microscopic hair analysis) can be assessed in different ways. Borrowing terminology from the evaluation of medical diagnostic tests, four characterizations and their associated measures are given below. Each one is useful in its own way: the first two emphasize the ability to *detect* an association; the last two emphasize the ability to *predict* an association:[6]

- Among samples from persons in Class C, the fraction that is correctly identified by the test is called the "sensitivity" or the "true positive rate" (TPR) of the test. In this table, the sensitivity would be estimated as $[95/(95+5)] \times 100=95$ percent.
- Among samples from persons not in Class C, the fraction that is correctly identified by the test is called the "specificity" or the "true

[6] See, e.g., X-H. Zhou, N. Obuchowski, and D. McClish. 2002. *Statistical Methods in Diagnostic Medicine*. Hoboken, NJ. Wiley & Sons, for a general account of methods for diagnostic tests. A series of NAS/NRC reports have applied such methods to the examination of forensic disciplines. See, e.g., NRC. Committee to Review the Scientific Evidence on the Polygraph. 2003. *The Polygraph and Lie Detection*. Washington, DC: The National Academies Press; NRC. 2004. *Forensic Analysis: Weighing Bullet Lead Evidence*. Washington, DC: The National Academies Press; NAS. 2005. *The Sackler Colloquium on Forensic Science: The Nexus of Science and the Law*, November 16-18, 2005.

negative rate" (TNR) of the test. In this table, the specificity would be estimated as [98/(2+98)] × 100=98 percent.

- Among samples classified by the test as coming from persons in Class C, the fraction that actually turns out to be from Class C is called the "positive predictive value (PPV)" of the test. In this table, the PPV would be estimated as [95/(95+ 2)] × 100=98 percent.
- Among samples classified by the test as coming from persons not in Class C, the fraction that actually turns out to not be persons from Class C is called the "negative predictive value (NPV)" of the test. In this table, the NPV would be estimated as [98/(5+98)] × 100=95 percent.

The above four measures emphasize the ability of the analysis to make correct determinations.[7] "Error rates" are defined as proportions of cases in which the analysis led to a false conclusion. For example, the complement of sensitivity (100 percent minus the sensitivity) is the percent of false negative cases in which the sample was from class C but the analysis reached the opposite conclusion. In the above table, this would be estimated as 5 percent. Similarly, the complement of specificity (100 percent minus the specificity) is the percent of false positive cases in which the sample was not from class C but the analysis concluded that it was. In the above table this would be estimated as 2 percent. A global error rate could be defined as the percent of incorrectly identified cases among all those analyzed. In the above table this would be estimated as [(5+2)/200] × 100=3.5 percent.

Importantly, whether the test answer is correct or not depends on which question is being addressed by the test. In this hair comparison example, the purpose is to determine whether the hair came from the head of an individual from class C. Thus, the analysis should be evaluated on the accuracy of the classification. In this example, if the analysis indicated "Class C" but the hair actually came from a "non-Class C" individual, then the analysis returned an incorrect classification. This accuracy evaluation does not apply to other tasks that are beyond the goal of the particular analysis, such as pinpointing the individual from whom the specimen was obtained. In the paint example about paint marks left by a vehicle, if the question is whether a vehicle under investigation was a model A made by manufacturer B in 2000, then a correct answer is limited to only the model, manufacturer, and year.

---

[7] Each estimate (of sensitivity, specificity, PPV, NPV) is associated with an interval that has a high probability of containing the true sensitivity, specificity, PPV, NPV. The larger the study, the more precise the estimate (i.e., the narrower the interval of uncertainty about the estimate).

Although only illustrations, these examples serve to demonstrate the importance of:

- the careful and precise characterization of the scientific procedure, so that others can replicate and validate it;
- the identification of as many sources of error as possible that can affect both the accuracy and precision of a measurement;
- the quantification of measurements (e.g., in the example of GC/MS analysis of possible heroin, reporting peak area, as well as appropriate calibration data, including the response area for a known amount of analyte standard, rather than merely "peak is present/absent");
- the reporting of a measurement with an interval that has a high probability of containing the true value;
- the precise definition of the question addressed by the method (e.g., classification versus individualization), and the recognition of its limitations; and
- the conducting of validation studies of the performance of a forensic procedure to assess the percentages of false positives and false negatives.

Clearly, better understanding of the measuring equipment and the measurement process leads to more improvements to every process and ultimately to fewer false positive and false negative results. Most importantly, as stated above, whether the test answer is correct or not depends on the question the test is being used to address. In the case of microscopic hair analysis, the validation study may confirm its value in identifying *class characteristics* of an individual, but not in identifying the specific person.

It is also important to note that errors and corresponding error rates can have more complex sources than can be accommodated within the simple framework presented above. For example, in the case of DNA analysis, a declaration that two samples match can be erroneous in at least two ways: The two samples might actually come from different individuals whose DNA appears to be the same within the discriminatory capability of the tests, or two different DNA profiles could be mistakenly determined to be matching. The probability of the former error is typically very low, while the probability of a false positive (different profiles wrongly determined to be matching) may be considerably higher. Both sources of error need to be explored and quantified in order to arrive at reliable error rate estimates for DNA analysis.[8]

---

[8] C. Aitken and F. Taroni. 2004. *Statistics and the Evaluation of Evidence for Forensic Scientists*. Chichester, UK: John Wiley & Sons.

The existence of several types of potential error rates makes it absolutely critical for all involved in the analysis to be explicit and precise in the particular rate or rates referenced in a specific setting. The estimation of such error rates requires rigorously developed and conducted scientific studies. Additional factors may play a role in analyses involving human interpretation, such as the experience, training, and inherent ability of the interpreter, the protocol for conducting the interpretation, and biases from a variety of sources, as discussed in the next section. The assessment of the accuracy of the conclusions from forensic analyses and the estimation of relevant error rates are key components of the mission of forensic science.

Sources of Bias

Human judgment is subject to many different types of bias, because we unconsciously pick up cues from our environment and factor them in an unstated way into our mental analyses. Those mental analyses might also be affected by unwarranted assumptions and a degree of overconfidence that we do not even recognize in ourselves. Such cognitive biases are not the result of character flaws; instead, they are common features of decisionmaking, and they cannot be willed away.[9] A familiar example is how the common desire to please others (or avoid conflict) can skew one's judgment if co-workers or supervisors suggest that they are hoping for, or have reached, a particular outcome. Science takes great pains to avoid biases by using strict protocols to minimize their effects. The 1996 National Academies DNA report, for example, notes, "[l]aboratory procedures should be designed with safeguards to detect bias and to identify cases of true ambiguity. Potential ambiguities should be documented."[10]

A somewhat obvious cognitive bias that may arise in forensic science is a willingness to ignore base rate information in assessing the probative value of information. For example, suppose carpet fibers from a crime scene are found to match carpet fibers found in a suspect's home. The probative value of this information depends on the rate at which such fibers are found in homes in addition to that of the suspect. If the carpet fibers are extremely common, the presence of matching fibers in the suspect's home will be of little probative value.[11]

A common cognitive bias is the tendency for conclusions to be affected by how a question is framed or how data are presented. In a police line-up,

---

[9] See, e.g., M.J. Saks, D.M. Risinger, R. Rosenthal, and W.C. Thompson. 2003. Context effects in forensic science: A review and application of the science of science to crime laboratory practice in the United States. *Science and Justice* 43(2):77-90.

[10] NRC. 1996. *The Evaluation of Forensic DNA Evidence*. Washington, DC: National Academy Press.

[11] C. Guthrie, J.J. Rachlinski, and A.J. Wistrich. 2001. Inside the judicial mind. *Cornell Law Review* 86:777-830.

for instance, an eyewitness who is presented with a pool of faces in one batch might assume that the suspect is among them, which may not be correct. If the mug shots are presented together at one time and the witness is asked to identify the suspect, the witness may choose the photograph that is most similar to the perpetrator, even if the perpetrator's picture is not among those presented. Similarly, if the photographs are presented sequentially and the witness knows that only a limited number will be presented, the eyewitness might tend to "identify" one of the last photographs under the assumption that the suspect must be in that batch. (This is also driven by the common bias toward reaching closure.) A series of studies has shown that judges can be subject to errors in judgment resulting from similar cognitive biases.[12] Forensic scientists also can be affected by this cognitive bias if, for example, they are asked to compare two particular hairs, shoeprints, fingerprints—one from the crime scene and one from a suspect—rather than comparing the crime scene exemplar with a pool of counterparts.

Another potential bias is illustrated by the erroneous fingerprint identification of Brandon Mayfield as someone involved with the Madrid train bombing in 2004. The FBI investigation determined that once the fingerprint examiner had declared a match, both he and other examiners who were aware of this finding were influenced by the urgency of the investigation to affirm repeatedly this erroneous decision.[13]

Recent research provided additional evidence of this sort of bias through an experiment in which experienced fingerprint examiners were asked to analyze fingerprints that, unknown to them, they had analyzed previously in their careers. For half the examinations, contextual biasing was introduced. For example, the instructions accompanying the latent prints included information such as the "suspect confessed to the crime" or the "suspect was in police custody at the time of the crime." In 6 of the 24 examinations that included contextual manipulation, the examiners reached conclusions that were consistent with the biasing information and different from the results they had reached when examining the same prints in their daily work.[14]

Other cognitive biases may be traced to common imperfections in our reasoning ability. One commonly recognized bias is the tendency to avoid cognitive dissonance, such as persuading oneself through rational argument that a purchase was a good value once the transaction is complete. A scientist encounters this unconscious bias if he/she becomes too wedded to a preliminary conclusion, so that it becomes difficult to accept new infor-

---

[12] Ibid.

[13] R.B. Stacey. 2004. A report on the erroneous fingerprint individualization in the Madrid train bombing case. *Journal of Forensic Identification* 54:707.

[14] I.E. Dror and D. Charlton. 2006. Why experts make errors. *Journal of Forensic Identification* 56(4):600-616.

mation fairly and unduly difficult to conclude that the initial hypotheses were wrong. This is often manifested by what is known as "anchoring," the well-known tendency to rely too heavily on one piece of information when making decisions. Often, the piece of information that is weighted disproportionately is one of the very first ones encountered. One tends to seek closure and to view the initial part of an investigation as a "sunk cost" that would be wasted if overturned.

Another common cognitive bias is the tendency to see patterns that do not actually exist. This bias is related to our tendency to underestimate the amount of complexity that can really exist in nature. Both tendencies can lead one to formulate overly simple models of reality and thus to read too much significance into coincidences and surprises. More generally, human intuition is not a good substitute for careful reasoning when probabilities are concerned. As an example, consider a problem commonly posed in beginning statistics classes: How many people must be in a room before there is a 50 percent probability that at least two will share a common birthday? Intuition might suggest a large number, perhaps over 100, but the actual answer is 23. This is not difficult to prove through careful logic, but intuition is likely to be misleading.

All of these sources of bias are well known in science, and a large amount of effort has been devoted to understanding and mitigating them. The goal is to make scientific investigations as objective as possible so the results do not depend on the investigator. Certain fields of science (most notably, biopharmaceutical clinical trials of treatment protocols and drugs) have developed practices such as double-blind tests and independent (blind) verification to minimize the impact of biases. Additionally, science seeks to publish its discoveries, findings, and conclusions so that they are subjected to independent peer review; this enables others to study biases that may exist in the investigative method or attempt to replicate unexpected results. Avoiding, or compensating for, a bias is an important task. Even fields with well-established protocols to minimize the effects of bias can still bear improvement. For example, a recent working paper[15] has raised questions about the way cognitive dissonance has been studied since 1956. Although these results must be considered preliminary because the paper has yet to be published, they do demonstrate that continual vigilance is needed. Research has been sparse on the important topic of cognitive bias in forensic science—both regarding their effects and methods for minimizing them.[16]

---

[15] M.K. Chen. 2008. *Rationalization and Cognitive Dissonance: Do Choices Affect or Reflect Preferences?* Available at www.som.yale.edu/Faculty/keith.chen/papers/CogDisPaper.pdf.

[16] See, e.g., I.E. Dror, D. Charlton, and A.E. Peron. 2006. Contextual information renders experts vulnerable to making erroneous identifications. *Forensic Science International* 156:74-78; I.E. Dror, A. Peron, S. Hind, and D. Charlton. 2005. When emotions get the better of us:

The Self-Correcting Nature of Science

The methods and culture of scientific research enable it to be a self-correcting enterprise. Because researchers are, by definition, creating new understanding, they must be as cautious as possible before asserting a new "truth." Also, because researchers are working at a frontier, few others may have the knowledge to catch and correct any errors they make. Thus, science has had to develop means of revisiting provisional results and revealing errors before they are widely used. The processes of peer review, publication, collegial interactions (e.g., sharing at conferences), and the involvement of graduate students (who are expected to question as they learn) all support this need. Science is characterized also by a culture that encourages and rewards critical questioning of past results and of colleagues. Most technologies benefit from a solid research foundation in academia and ample opportunity for peer-to-peer stimulation and critical assessment, review and critique through conferences, seminars, publishing, and more. These elements provide a rich set of paths through which new ideas and skepticism can travel and opportunities for scientists to step away from their day-to-day work and take a longer-term view. The scientific culture encourages cautious, precise statements and discourages statements that go beyond established facts; it is acceptable for colleagues to challenge one another, even if the challenger is more junior. The forensic science disciplines will profit enormously by full adoption of this scientific culture.

CONCLUSION

The way in which science is conducted is distinct from, and complementary to, other modes by which humans investigate and create. The methods of science have a long history of successfully building useful and trustworthy knowledge and filling gaps while also correcting past errors. The premium that science places on precision, objectivity, critical thinking, careful observation and practice, repeatability, uncertainty management, and peer review enables the reliable collection, measurement, and interpretation of clues in order to produce knowledge.

The effects of contextual top-down processing on matching fingerprints. *Journal of Applied Cognitive Psychology* 19:799-809; and B. Schiffer and C. Champod. 2007. The potential (negative) influence of observational biases at the analysis stage of fingerprint individualization. *Forensic Science International* 167:116-120.

5

Descriptions of Some Forensic Science Disciplines

This chapter describes the methods of some of the major forensic science disciplines. It focuses on those that are used most commonly for investigations and trials as well as on those that have been cause for concern in court or elsewhere because their reliability has not been sufficiently established in a systematic (scientific) manner in accordance with the principles discussed in Chapter 4. The chapter focuses primarily on the forensic science disciplines' capability for providing evidence that can be presented in court. As such, there is considerable discussion about the reliability and precision of results—attributes that factor into probative value and admissibility decisions. It should be recalled, however, that forensic science also provides great value to law enforcement investigations, and even those forensic science disciplines whose scientific foundation is currently limited might have the capacity (or the potential) to provide probative information to advance a criminal investigation.[1] This chapter also provides the committee's summary assessment of each of these disciplines.[2]

---

[1] For example, forensic odontology might not be sufficiently grounded in science to be admissible under *Daubert*, but this discipline might be able to reliably exclude a suspect, thereby enabling law enforcement to focus its efforts on other suspects. And forensic science methods that do not meet the standards of admissible evidence might still offer leads to advance an investigation.

[2] The chapter does not discuss eyewitness identification or line-ups, because these techniques do not normally rely on forensic scientists for analysis or implementation. They clearly are of major importance for investigations and trials, and their effective use and interpretation relies on scientific knowledge and continuing research. For similar reasons, this chapter does not delve into the polygraph. The validity of polygraph testing for security screening was addressed

Because forensic science aims to glean information from a wide variety of clues and evidence associated with a crime, it deals with a broad range of tools and with evidence of highly variable quality. In general, the forensic science disciplines are pragmatic, with practitioners adopting, adapting, or developing whatever tools and technological aids they can to distill useful information from crime scene evidence. Many forensic science methods have been developed in response to such evidence—combining experience-based knowledge with whatever relevant science base exists in order to create a procedure that returns useful information. Although some of the techniques used by the forensic science disciplines—such as DNA analysis, serology, forensic pathology, toxicology, chemical analysis, and digital and multimedia forensics—are built on solid bases of theory and research, many other techniques have been developed heuristically. That is, they are based on observation, experience, and reasoning without an underlying scientific theory, experiments designed to test the uncertainties and reliability of the method, or sufficient data that are collected and analyzed scientifically.

In the course of its deliberations, the committee received testimony from experts in many forensic science disciplines concerning current practices, validity, reliability and errors, standards, and research.[3] From this testimony and from many written submissions, as well as from the personal experiences of the committee members, the committee developed the consensus views presented in this chapter.

BIOLOGICAL EVIDENCE

Biological evidence is provided by specimens of a biological origin that are available in a forensic investigation. Such specimens may be found at the scene of a crime or on a person, clothing, or weapon. Some—for example, pet hairs, insects, seeds, or other botanical remnants—come from the crime scene or from an environment through which a victim or suspect has recently traversed. Other biological evidence comes from specimens obtained directly from the victim or suspect, such as blood, semen, saliva, vaginal secretions, sweat, epithelial cells, vomitus, feces, urine, hair, tissue, bones, and microbiological and viral agents. The most common types of biological evidence collected for examination are blood, semen, and saliva. Human biological evidence that contains nuclear DNA can be particularly valuable because the possibility exists to associate that evidence with one individual with a degree of reliability that is acceptable for criminal justice.

in National Research Council, Committee to Review the Scientific Evidence on the Polygraph. 2003. *The Polygraph and Lie Detection*. Washington, DC: The National Academies Press. It does not cover forensic pathology, because that field is addressed in Chapter 9.

[3] A complete list of those who provided testimony to the committee is included in Appendix B.

Sample Data and Collection

At the crime scene, biological evidence is located, documented, collected, and preserved for subsequent analysis in the crime laboratory. Locating and recognizing biological evidence can be more difficult than a layperson would presume. For example, blood is not always red, some red substances are not blood, and most biological evidence, such as saliva or semen, is not readily visible. Crime scene investigators locate biological evidence through tests that screen for the presence of a particular biological fluid (e.g., blood, semen, saliva), and investigators have a choice of techniques.[4] For blood they might use an alternate light source (ALS) at 415nm, the wavelength under which bloodstains absorb light and are thus more visible to the naked eye. Most commonly, though, the screening test for blood is a catalytic chemical test that turns color or luminesces in the presence of blood. Scene investigators may also use Luminol, fluorescein, or crystal violet to identify areas at the scene where attempts were made to clean a bloody crime scene.

These tests for blood may also locate other evidence that should be collected and taken to the laboratory for analysis. Recently, immunological tests that can identify human hemoglobin or glycophorin A have become available. These are blood-specific proteins that can be demonstrated to be of human origin. At some point in the future, these immunological tests may replace standard chemical tests, and, although more expensive, they are more specific because they identify blood conclusively instead of just presumptively. Investigators also have several techniques for locating semen at the crime scene. Commonly they rely on an ALS, under which semen, other biological fluids, and some other evidence will luminesce. More recently, immunological tests can be used to identify seminal plasma proteins, for example, prostate specific antigen (p30 or PSA) or semenogelin.[5]

Finding saliva at the scene is mostly happenstance. Although it luminesces with the ALS at specific wavelengths, the glow is not as strong, and a weaker ALS light source may not highlight it well and possibly not at all. Thus, it can be easily missed. Screening tests for saliva are chemical tests that identify amylase, an enzyme occurring in high concentrations in saliva. But the screening is not definitive, because other types of tissue also

---

[4] Interpreting the results of any screening test requires expertise and experience. Many crime scene investigators have the requisite experience, but they may lack a scientific background, and it is not always straightforward to correctly interpret the results of screening tests. Crime scene investigations that require science-based screening tools are most reliable if someone is involved who understands the physics and chemistry of those tools.

[5] I. Sato, M. Sagi, A. Ishiwari, H. Nishijima, E. Ito, and T. Mukai. 2002. Use of the "SMITEST" PSA card to identify the presence of prostate-specific antigen in semen and male urine. *Forensic Science International* 127(1-2):71-74.

contain amylase, including the particular type (AMY 1) that is associated with saliva.

Analyses

Although the forensic use of nuclear DNA is barely 20 years old, DNA typing is now universally recognized as the standard against which many other forensic individualization techniques are judged. DNA enjoys this preeminent position because of its reliability and the fact that, absent fraud or an error in labeling or handling, the probabilities of a false positive are quantifiable and often miniscule. However, even a very small (but nonzero) probability of false positive can affect the odds that a suspect is the source of a sample with a matching DNA profile.[6] The scientific bases and reliability of other types of biological analysis are also well established, but absent nuclear DNA, they can only narrow the field of suspects, not suggest any particular individual.

Testing biological evidence in the laboratory involves the use of a logical sequence of analyses designed to identify what a substance is and then from whom it came. The sequence begins with a forensic biologist locating the substance on the evidence. This is followed by a presumptive test that would give more information about the substance, typically using the same tests employed by scene investigators: the ALS, enzymatic, chemical, or immunological tests. Once the material (e.g., blood, semen, or saliva) is known, an immunological test or a human DNA test is run to determine whether the sample comes from a human or an animal.

The final step in the analytical sequence procedure is to identify the source of the biological material. If a sufficient sample is present and is probative, the forensic biologist prepares the material for DNA testing. The analyst who conducts the DNA test may or may not be the same person who examines the original physical evidence, depending on laboratory policies.

A decision might be required regarding the type of DNA testing to employ. Two primary types of DNA tests are conducted in U.S. forensic laboratories: nuclear testing and mitochondrial DNA (mtDNA) testing, with several variations of the former. For most biological evidence having evidentiary significance, forensic DNA laboratories employ nuclear testing routinely,[7] and testing for the 13 core Short Tandem Repeat (STR)

---

[6] W.C. Thompson, F. Taroni, and C.G.G. Aitken. 2003. How the probability of a false positive affects the value of DNA evidence. *Journal of Forensic Sciences* 48(1):47-54.

[7] T.R. Moretti, A.L. Baumstark, D.A. Defenbaugh, K.M. Keys, J.B. Smerick, and B. Budowle B. 2001. Validation of short tandem repeats (STRs) for forensic usage: Performance testing of fluorescent multiplex STR systems and analysis of authentic and simulated forensic samples. *Journal of Forensic Sciences* 46(3):647-660.

polymorphisms is the first line of attack.[8] The results are entered into the Federal Bureau of Investigation's (FBI's) Combined DNA Indexing System (CODIS) and are searched against DNA profiles already in one of three databases: a convicted felon database, a forensic database containing DNA profiles from crime scenes, and a database of DNA from unidentified persons.

Sometimes the evidence dictates testing just for Y STRs, which assesses only the Y (male) chromosome. In sexual assaults for which only small amounts of male nuclear DNA are available (e.g., a large excess of vaginal DNA), it is possible to obtain a Y STR profile of the male who left the semen. Unlike the 13 core loci used in CODIS searches, where a match of all 13 is a strong indicator that both samples come from the same individual, Y STR testing is not as definitive with respect to identifying a single person. A third nuclear test involves the analysis of single nucleotide polymorphisms (SNPs). Although no public forensic DNA laboratory in the United States is routinely analyzing forensic evidence for SNPs, the utility of this genomic information for cases in which the DNA is too damaged to allow standard testing has garnered attention since its use in the World Trade Center identification effort.[9]

If insufficient nuclear DNA is present for STR testing, or if the existing nuclear DNA is degraded, two options potentially are available. One technique amplifies the amount of DNA available, although this technique is not widely available in U.S. forensic laboratories. A second alternative is to sequence mitochondrial DNA (mtDNA). Since 1996, it has been possible to compare single-source crime scene samples and samples from the victim or defendant on the basis of mtDNA. Four FBI-supported mtDNA laboratories and a few private mtDNA laboratories conduct DNA casework. This technique has been particularly helpful with regard to hairs—which do not contain enough nuclear DNA to enable analysis with current methods unless the root is present—and bones and teeth. Because it measures only a single locus of the genome, mtDNA analysis is much less discriminating than nuclear DNA analysis; all people with a common female ancestor (within the past few generations) share a common profile. But mtDNA testing has forensic value in its ability to include or exclude an individual as its source.

Laboratories entering the results of forensic DNA testing into CODIS must meet specific quality guidelines, which include the requirement that

[8] Some laboratories are now using 16 loci, 13 of which are the original core loci.

[9] B. Leclair, R. Shaler, G.R. Carmody, K. Eliason, B.C.Hendrickson, T. Judkins, M.J. Norton, C. Sears, and T. Scholl. 2007. Bioinformatics and human identification in mass fatality incidents: The World Trade Center disaster. *Journal of Forensic Sciences* 52(4):806-819. Epub May 25, 2007.

the laboratory be accredited and that specific procedures be in place and followed. In accredited laboratories, forensic DNA personnel must take proficiency tests and must meet specific educational and training requirements. (See Chapter 8 for further discussion.) Laboratory analyses are conducted by scientists with degrees ranging from a bachelor's degree in science to a doctoral degree. Each forensic DNA laboratory has a technical leader, who normally must meet additional experience and educational requirements.

Although DNA laboratories are expected to conduct their examinations under stringent quality controlled environments, errors do occasionally occur. They usually involve situations in which interpretational ambiguities occur or in which samples were inappropriately processed and/or contaminated in the laboratory. Errors also can occur when there are limited amounts of DNA, which limits the amount of test information and increases the chance of misinterpretation. Casework reviews of mtDNA analysis suggest a wide range in the quality of testing results that include contamination, inexperience in interpreting mixtures, and differences in how a test is conducted.[10]

Reporting of Results

FBI quality guidelines require that reports from forensic DNA analysis must contain, at a minimum, a description of the evidence examined, a listing of the loci analyzed, a description of the methodology, results and/or conclusions, and an interpretative statement (either quantitative or qualitative) concerning the inference to be drawn from the analysis.[11]

---

[10] Personal communication, Terry Melton, Mitotyping Laboratory. December 2007. See also L. Prieto; A. Alonso; C. Alves; M. Crespillo; M. Montesino; A. Picornell; A. Brehm; J.L. Ramirez; M.R. Whittle; M.J. Anjos; I. Boschi; J. Buj; M. Cerezo; S. Cardoso; R. Cicarelli; D. Comas; D. Corach; C. Doutremepuich; R.M. Espinheira; I. Fernandez-Fernandez; S. Filippini; Julia Garcia-Hirschfeld; A. Gonzalez; B. Heinrichs; A. Hernandez; F.P.N. Leite; R.P. Lizarazo; A.M. Lopez-Parra; M. Lopez-Soto; J.A. Lorente; B. Mechoso; I. Navarro; S. Pagano; J.J. Pestano; J. Puente; E. Raimondi; A. Rodriguez-Quesada; M.F. Terra-Pinheiro; L. Vidal-Rioja; C. Vullo; A. Salas. 2008. GEP-ISFG collaborative exercise on mtDNA: Reflections about interpretation, artefacts and DNA mixtures. *Forensic Science International: Genetics* 2(2):126-133; and A. Salas, L. Prieto, M. Montesino, C. Albarrán, E. Arroyo, M. Paredes-Herrera, A. Di Lonardo, C. Doutremepuich, I. Fernández-Fernández, A. de la Vega. 2005. Mitochondrial DNA error prophylaxis: Assessing the causes of errors in the GEP'02-03 proficiency testing trial. *Forensic Science International* 148(2-3):191-198.

[11] DNA Advisory Board. 2000. Quality assurance standards for forensic DNA testing laboratories. *Forensic Science Communications* 2(3). Available at www.bioforensics.com/conference04/TWGDAM/Quality_Assurance_Standards_2.pdf.

Summary Assessment

Unlike many forensic techniques that were developed empirically within the forensic science community, with limited foundation in scientific theory or analysis, DNA analysis is a fortuitous by-product of cutting-edge science. Eminent scientists contributed their expertise to ensuring that DNA evidence offered in a courtroom would be valid and reliable (e.g., in the 1989 New York case, *People v. Castro*), and by 1996 the National Academy of Sciences had convened two committees that issued influential recommendations on handling DNA forensic science.[12] As a result, principles of statistics and population genetics that pertain to DNA evidence were clarified, the methods for conducting DNA analyses and declaring a match became less subjective, and quality assurance and quality control protocols were designed to improve laboratory performance.

DNA analysis is scientifically sound for several reasons: (1) there are biological explanations for individual-specific findings; (2) the 13 STR loci used to compare DNA samples were selected so that the chance of two different people matching on all of them would be extremely small; (3) the probabilities of false positives have been explored and quantified in some settings (even if only approximately); (4) the laboratory procedures are well specified and subject to validation and proficiency testing; and (5) there are clear and repeatable standards for analysis, interpretation, and reporting. DNA analysis also has been subjected to more scrutiny than any other forensic science discipline, with rigorous experimentation and validation performed prior to its use in forensic investigations. As a result of these characteristics, the probative power of DNA is high. Of course, DNA evidence is not available in every criminal investigation, and it is still subject to errors in handling that can invalidate the analysis. In such cases, other forensic techniques must be applied. The probative power of these other methods can be high, alone or in combination with other evidence. This power likely can be improved by strengthening the methods' scientific foundations and practice, as has occurred with forensic DNA analysis.

ANALYSIS OF CONTROLLED SUBSTANCES

The term "illicit drugs" is widely used to describe abused substances. Other terms that are used include "abused drugs," "illegal drugs," "street drugs," and, in the United States, "controlled substances." The latter term refers specifically to drugs that are controlled by federal and state laws.[13]

---

[12] National Research Council. 1992. *DNA Technology in Forensic Science*. Washington, DC: National Academy Press; National Research Council. 1996. *The Evaluation of Forensic DNA Evidence: An Update*. Washington, DC: National Academy Press.

[13] See, e.g., 21 U.S.C.A. § 802(6).

The analysis of controlled substances is a mature forensic science discipline and one of the areas with a strong scientific underpinning. The analytical methods used have been adopted from classical analytical chemistry, and there is broad agreement nationwide about best practices.[14] In 1997, the U.S. Drug Enforcement Administration and the Office of National Drug Control Policy co-sponsored the formation of the Technical Working Group for the Analysis of Seized Drugs, now known as the Scientific Working Group for the Analysis of Seized Drugs (SWGDRUG). This organization brings together more than 20 forensic practitioners from all over the world to develop standards for the analysis and reporting of illicit drug cases. Their standards are being widely adopted by drug analysis laboratories in the United States and worldwide.

Sample Data and Collection

Controlled substances typically are seized by police officers, narcotics agents, and detectives through undercover buys, raids on drug houses and clandestine drug laboratories, and seizures on the streets. In some cases, forensic chemists are sent to clandestine laboratory operations to help render the laboratory safe and help with evidence collection. The seized drugs may be in the form of powders or adulterated powders, chunks of smokeable or injectable material, legitimate and clandestine tablets and capsules, or plant materials or plant extracts.

Analyses

Controlled substances are analyzed by well-accepted standard schemes or protocols. Few drug chemists have the requisite botanical background to identify any common illicit plants other than marijuana; thus, in cases that require botanical identification, the assistance of outside experts is enlisted.

Sampling can be a major issue in the analysis of controlled substances. Although sometimes only trace amounts of a drug are present (e.g., in a syringe used to inject heroin), at other times there are hundreds or thousands of packages of drugs or very large bags or bales. SWGDRUG and others have proposed statistical and nonstatistical methods for sampling,[15] and a wide variety of methods are used.

Most controlled substances are subjected first to a field test for pre-

---

[14] See F. Smith and J.A. Siegel (eds.). 2004. *Handbook of Forensic Drug Analysis*. Burlington, MA: Academic Press.

[15] Scientific Working Group for the Analysis of Seized Drugs (SWGDRUG) Recommendations. Available at www.swgdrug.org/approved.htm.

sumptive identification. This is followed by gas chromatography-mass spectrometry (GC-MS), in which chromatography separates the drug from any diluents or excipients, and then mass spectrometry is used to identify the drug. This is the near universal test for identifying unknown substances. Marijuana is an exception, because it is identified normally through a sequence of tests—a presumptive color test, followed by low-powered microscopic identification, and finally by thin-layer chromatography.

Reporting of Results

Most drug chemists produce terse reports for attorneys and courts. The reports contain administrative data and a short description of the evidence. The weight or number of exhibits is stated and then the results of the analysis. A typical report for a marijuana case might read as follows:

Received:	Item 1—a sealed plastic bag containing 25.6 g of green-brown plant material.
Results:	The green-brown plant material in item 1 was identified as marijuana.

Some laboratories might mention the tests that were conducted, but in most cases the spectra, chromatograms, and other evidence of the analysis and the chemist's notes are not submitted. Likewise, possible sources of error and statistical data are not commonly included. From a scientific perspective, this style of reporting is often inadequate, because it may not provide enough detail to enable a peer or other courtroom participant to understand and, if needed, question the sampling scheme, process(es) of analysis, or interpretation.

Summary Assessment

The chemical foundations for the analysis of controlled substances are sound, and there exists an adequate understanding of the uncertainties and potential errors. SWGDRUG has established a fairly complete set of recommended practices.[16] It also provides pointers to a number of guidelines for statistical sampling, both for illegal drugs per se (created by the European Network of Forensic Science Institutes) and for materials more generally (created by the American Society for Testing and Materials).

The SWGDRUG recommendations include a menu of analytical chemistry techniques that are considered acceptable in certain circumstances. Because this menu was constructed to be applicable worldwide, it includes

[16] See www.swgdrug.org/approved.htm.

options that allow laboratories to substitute a concatenation of simple methods if they do not have access to the preferred analytical equipment (e.g., GC-MS). It is questionable, however, whether all of the possible combinations recommended by SWGDRUG would be acceptable in a scientific sense, if one's goal were to identify and classify a completely unknown substance. The committee has been told that experienced forensic chemists and good forensic laboratories understand which tests (or combinations of tests) provide adequate reliability, but the SWGDRUG recommendations do not ensure that these tests will be used. This ambiguity would be a less significant issue if the reports presented in court contained sufficient detail about the methods of analysis.

FRICTION RIDGE ANALYSIS

Fingerprints, palm prints, and sole prints have been used to identify people for more than a century in the United States. Collectively, the analysis of these prints is known as "friction ridge analysis," which consists of experience-based comparisons of the impressions left by the ridge structures of volar (hands and feet) surfaces. Friction ridge analysis is an example of what the forensic science community uses as a method for assessing "individualization"—the conclusion that a piece of evidence (here, a pattern left by friction ridges) comes from a single unambiguous source. Friction ridge analysis shares similarities with other experience-based methods of pattern recognition, such as those for footwear and tire impressions, toolmarks, and handwriting analysis, all of which are discussed separately below.

Friction ridge analysis is performed in various settings, including accredited crime laboratories and nonaccredited facilities. Nonaccredited facilities may be crime laboratories, police "identification units," or private practice (consultants). In some instances, the latent print examiner is employed solely to perform latent print casework. Some examiners may also perform other types of forensic casework (e.g., footwear and tire impressions, firearms analysis). In some agencies, fingerprint examiners also are required to respond to crime scenes and can be sworn officers who also perform police officer/detective duties.

The training of personnel to perform latent print identifications varies from agency to agency. Agencies may have a formalized training program, may use an informal mentoring process, or may send new examiners to a one- to two-week course. The International Association for Identification (IAI) offers a training publication, "Friction Ridge Skin Identification Training Manual,"[17] and the Scientific Working Group on Friction Ridge

[17] International Association for Identification. *Friction Ridge Skin Identification Training Manual.* Available at www.theiai.org.

Analysis, Study and Technology (SWGFAST) offers a guideline, "Training to Competency for Latent Print Examiners."[18] Although these are excellent resources, they are not required, and there is no auditing of the content of training programs developed by nonaccredited agencies. The IAI also offers a certification test that measures both the knowledge and skill of latent print examiners; however, not all agencies require latent print examiners to achieve and maintain certification.

Method of Data Collection and Analysis

The technique used to examine prints made by friction ridge skin is described by the acronym ACE-V: "Analysis, Comparison, Evaluation, and Verification."[19] It has been described in forensic literature as a means of comparative analysis of evidence since 1959.[20] The process begins with the **analysis** of the unknown friction ridge print (now often a digital image of a latent print). Many factors affect the quality and quantity of detail in the latent print and also introduce variability in the resulting impression. The examiner must consider the following:

(1) Condition of the skin—natural ridge structure (robustness of the ridge structure), consequences of aging, superficial damage to the skin, permanent scars, skin diseases, and masking attempts.
(2) Type of residue—natural residue (sweat residue, oily residue, combinations of sweat and oil); other types of residue (blood, paint, etc.); amount of residue (heavy, medium, or light); and where the residue accumulates (top of the ridge, both edges of the ridge, one edge of the ridge, or in the furrows).
(3) Mechanics of touch—underlying structures of the hands and feet (bone creates areas of high pressure on the surface of the skin); flexibility of the ridges, furrows, and creases; the distance adjacent ridges can be pushed together or pulled apart during lateral movement; the distance the length of a ridge might be compressed or stretched; the rotation of ridge systems during torsion; and the effect of ridge flow on these factors.
(4) Nature of the surface touched—texture (rough or smooth), flexibility (rigid or pliable), shape (flat or curved), condition (clean or dirty), and background colors and patterns.

---

[18] SWGFAST. 2002. *Training to Competency for Latent Print Examiners*. Available at www.SWGFAST.org.

[19] Ashbaugh, op. cit.; Triplette and Cooney, op. cit.; J. Vanderkolk. 2004. ACE-V: A model. *Journal of Forensic Identification* 54(1):45-52; SWGFAST. 2002. *Friction Ridge Examination Methodology for Latent Print Examiners*. Available at www.SWGFAST.org.

[20] R.A. Huber. 1959-1960. Expert witness. *Criminal Law Quarterly* 2:276-296.

(5) Development technique—chemical signature of the technique and consistency of the chemical signature across the impression.
(6) Capture technique—photograph (digital or film) or lifting material (e.g., tape or gelatin lifter).
(7) Size of the latent print or the percentage of the surface that is available for comparison.

The examiner also must perform an analysis of the known prints (taken from a suspect or retrieved from a database of fingerprints), because many of the same factors that affect the quality of the latent print can also affect the known prints.

If the latent print does not have sufficient detail for either identification or exclusion, it does not undergo the remainder of the process (comparison and evaluation). These insufficient prints are often called "of no value" or "not suitable" for comparison. Poor-quality known prints also will end the examination. If the examiner deems that there is sufficient detail in the latent print (and the known prints), the comparison of the latent print to the known prints begins.

Visual **comparison** consists of discerning, visually "measuring," and comparing—within the comparable areas of the latent print and the known prints—the details that correspond. The amount of friction ridge detail available for this step depends on the clarity of the two impressions. The details observed might include the overall shape of the latent print, anatomical aspects, ridge flows, ridge counts, shape of the core, delta location and shape, lengths of the ridges, minutia location and type, thickness of the ridges and furrows, shapes of the ridges, pore position, crease patterns and shapes, scar shapes, and temporary feature shapes (e.g., a wart).

At the completion of the comparison, the examiner performs an **evaluation** of the agreement of the friction ridge formations in the two prints and evaluates the sufficiency of the detail present to establish an identification (source determination).[21] Source determination is made when the examiner concludes, based on his or her experience, that sufficient quantity and quality of friction ridge detail is in agreement between the latent print and the known print. Source exclusion is made when the process indicates sufficient disagreement between the latent print and known print. If neither an identification nor an exclusion can be reached, the result of the comparison is inconclusive. **Verification** occurs when another qualified examiner repeats the observations and comes to the same conclusion, although the second examiner may be aware of the conclusion of the first. A more complete de-

[21] Ashbaugh, op. cit.; SWGFAST. 2002. *Friction Ridge Examination Methodology for Latent Print Examiners.*

scription of the steps of ACE-V and an analysis of its limitations is provided in a paper by Haber and Haber.[22]

Although some Automated Fingerprint Identification Systems (AFIS) permit fully automated identification of fingerprint records related to criminal history (e.g., for screening job applicants), the assessment of latent prints from crime scenes is based largely on human interpretation. Note that the ACE-V method does not specify particular measurements or a standard test protocol, and examiners must make subjective assessments throughout. In the United States, the threshold for making a source identification is deliberately kept subjective, so that the examiner can take into account both the quantity and quality of comparable details. As a result, the outcome of a friction ridge analysis is not necessarily repeatable from examiner to examiner. In fact, recent research by Dror[23] has shown that experienced examiners do not necessarily agree with even their own past conclusions when the examination is presented in a different context some time later.

This subjectivity is intrinsic to friction ridge analysis, as can be seen when comparing it with DNA analysis. For the latter, 13 specific segments of DNA (generally) are compared for each of two DNA samples. Each of these segments consists of ordered sequences of the base pairs, called A, G, C, and T. Studies have been conducted to determine the range of variation in the sequence of base pairs at each of the 13 loci and also to determine how much variation exists in different populations. From these data, scientists can calculate the probability that two DNA samples from different people will have the same permutations at each of the 13 loci.

By contrast, before examining two fingerprints, one cannot say a priori which features should be compared. Features are selected during the comparison phase of ACE-V, when a fingerprint examiner identifies which features are common to the two impressions and are clear enough to be evaluated. Because a feature that was helpful during a previous comparison might not exist on these prints or might not have been captured in the latent impression, the process does not allow one to stipulate specific measurements in advance, as is done for a DNA analysis. Moreover, a small stretching of distance between two fingerprint features, or a twisting of angles, can result from either a difference between the fingers that left the prints or from distortions from the impression process. For these reasons, population statistics for fingerprints have not been developed, and friction ridge analysis relies on subjective judgments by the examiner. Little research

---

[22] L. Haber and R.N. Haber. 2008. Scientific validation of fingerprint evidence under *Daubert*. *Law, Probability, and Risk* 7(2):87-109.

[23] I.E. Dror and D. Charlton. 2006. Why experts make errors. *Journal of Forensic Identification* 56(4):600-616.

has been directed toward developing population statistics, although more would be feasible.[24]

Methods of Interpretation

The determination of an exclusion can be straightforward if the examiner finds detail in the latent print that does not match the corresponding part of the known print, although distortions or poor image quality can complicate this determination. But the criteria for identification are much harder to define, because they depend on an examiner's ability to discern patterns (possibly complex) among myriad features and on the examiner's experience judging the discriminatory value in those patterns. The clarity of the prints being compared is a major underlying factor. For 10-print fingerprint cards, which tend to have good clarity, even automated pattern-recognition software (which is not as capable as human examiners) is successful enough in retrieving matching sets from databases to enjoy widespread use. When dealing with a single latent print, however, the interpretation task becomes more challenging and relies more on the judgment of the examiner. The committee heard presentations from friction ridge experts who assured it that friction ridge identification works well when a careful examiner works with good-quality latent prints. Clearly, the reliability of the ACE-V process could be improved if specific measurement criteria were defined. Those criteria become increasingly important when working with latent prints that are smudged and incomplete, or when comparing impressions from two individuals whose prints are unusually similar.

The fingerprint community continues to assert that the ability to see latent print detail is an acquired skill attained only through repeated exposure to friction ridge impressions. In their view, a lengthy apprenticeship (typically two years, at the FBI Laboratory) with an experienced latent print examiner enables a new examiner to develop a sense of the rarity of features and groups of features; the rarity of particular kinds of ridge flows; the frequency of features in different areas of the hands and feet; the degree to which differences can be accounted for by mechanical distortion of the skin; a sense of how to extract detail from background noise; and a sense of how much friction ridge detail could be common to two prints from different

---

[24] See, e.g., E. Gutiérrez, V. Galera, J.M. Martínez, and C. Alonso. 2007. Biological variability of the minutiae in the fingerprints of a sample of the Spanish population. *Forensic Science International* 172(2-3):98-105. For information about the basic availability of data, see C. Champod, C.J. Lennard, P.A. Margot, and M. Stoilovic. 2004. *Fingerprints and other ridge skin impressions*. Boca Raton, FL: CRC Press; D.A. Stoney. 2001. "Measurement of Fingerprint Individuality." In: H.C. Lee and R.E. Gaensslen (eds.). *Advances in Fingerprint Technology*. 2nd ed. Boca Raton, FL: CRC Press; pp. 327-387.

sources.[25] From this base of experience, the fingerprint community asserts that the latent print examiner learns to judge whether there is sufficient detail (which varies with image quality) to make a source determination during the evaluation phase of ACE-V.

The latent print community in the United States has eschewed numerical scores and corresponding thresholds, because those developed to date[26] have been based only on minutia, not on the unique features of the friction ridge skin (e.g., lengths of ridges, shapes of ridges, crease lengths and shapes, scar lengths and shapes). Additionally, thresholds based on counting the number of features that correspond, lauded by some as being more "objective," are still based on primarily subjective criteria—an examiner must have the visual expertise to discern the features (most important in low-clarity prints) and must determine that they are indeed in agreement. A simple point count is insufficient for characterizing the detail present in a latent print; more nuanced criteria are needed, and, in fact, likely can be determined.

Reporting of Results

SWGFAST has promulgated three acceptable conclusions resulting from latent print comparison: individualization (or identification), exclusion, or inconclusive.[27] Although adherence to this standard is common, some latent print examiners report either "identification" or "negative" results. "Negative" (or sometimes "not identified") is an ambiguous conclusion, and it could mean excluded, inconclusive, or unable to locate after exhaustive search. It is problematic that the meaning of "negative" may be specific to a particular agency, examiner, or case.

Latent print examiners report an individualization when they are confident that two different sources could not have produced impressions with the same degree of agreement among details. This is a subjective assessment. There has been discussion regarding the use of statistics to assign match probabilities based on population distributions of certain friction ridge features. Current published statistical models, however, have not matured past counts of corresponding minutia and have not taken clarity into consideration. (This area is ripe for additional research.) As a result, the friction ridge community actively discourages its members from testifying in terms of the probability of a match; when a latent print examiner testifies that two

---

[25] T. Busey and J. Vanderkolk. 2005. Behavioral and electrophysiological evidence for configural processing in fingerprint experts. *Vision Research* 45:431-448.

[26] See, e.g., I.W. Evett and R.A. Williams. 1996. A review of the sixteen points fingerprint standard in England and Wales. *Journal of Forensic Identification* 46(1):49-73.

[27] SWGFAST. 2002. *Friction Ridge Examination Methodology for Latent Print Examiners.* Available at www.swgfast.org/Training_to_Competency_for_Latent_Print_Examiners_2.1.pdf.

impressions "match," they are communicating the notion that the prints could not possibly have come from two different individuals.

As noted in Chapter 3, Jennifer Mnookin of the University of California, Los Angeles School of Law summarized the reporting of fingerprint analyses as follows:

> At present, fingerprint examiners typically testify in the language of absolute certainty. Both the conceptual foundations and the professional norms of latent fingerprinting prohibit experts from testifying to identification unless they believe themselves certain that they have made a correct match. Experts therefore make only what they term 'positive' or 'absolute' identifications—essentially making the claim that they have matched the latent print to the one and only person in the entire world whose fingertip could have produced it . . . Given the general lack of validity testing for fingerprinting; the relative dearth of difficult proficiency tests; the lack of a statistically valid model of fingerprinting; and the lack of validated standards for declaring a match, such claims of absolute, certain confidence in identification are unjustified . . . Therefore, in order to pass scrutiny under Daubert, fingerprint identification experts should exhibit a greater degree of epistemological humility. Claims of 'absolute' and 'positive' identification should be replaced by more modest claims about the meaning and significance of a 'match.'[28]

Summary Assessment

Historically, friction ridge analysis has served as a valuable tool, both to identify the guilty and to exclude the innocent. Because of the amount of detail available in friction ridges, it seems plausible that a careful comparison of two impressions can accurately discern whether or not they had a common source. Although there is limited information about the accuracy and reliability of friction ridge analyses, claims that these analyses have zero error rates are not scientifically plausible.

ACE-V provides a broadly stated framework for conducting friction ridge analyses. However, this framework is not specific enough to qualify as a validated method for this type of analysis. ACE-V does not guard against bias; is too broad to ensure repeatability and transparency; and does not guarantee that two analysts following it will obtain the same results. For these reasons, merely following the steps of ACE-V does not imply that one is proceeding in a scientific manner or producing reliable results. A recent

---

[28] J.L. Mnookin. 2008. The validity of latent fingerprint identification: Confessions of a fingerprinting moderate. *Law, Probability and Risk* 7:127. See also the discussion in C. Champod. 2008. Fingerprint examination: Towards more transparency. *Law Probability and Risk* 7:111-118.

paper by Haber and Haber[29] presents a thorough analysis of the ACE-V method and its scientific validity. Their conclusion is unambiguous: "We have reviewed available scientific evidence of the validity of the ACE-V method and found none."[30] Further, they state:

> [W]e report a range of existing evidence that suggests that examiners differ at each stage of the method in the conclusions they reach. To the extent that they differ, some conclusions are invalid. We have analysed the ACE-V method itself, as it is described in the literature. We found that these descriptions differ, no single protocol has been officially accepted by the profession and the standards upon which the method's conclusions rest have not been specified quantitatively. As a consequence, at this time the validity of the ACE-V method cannot be tested.[31]

Recent legal challenges, *New Hampshire vs. Richard Langill*[32] and *Maryland vs. Bryan Rose*,[33] have also highlighted two important issues for the latent print community: documentation and error rate. Better documentation is needed of each step in the ACE-V process or its equivalent. At the very least, sufficient documentation is needed to reconstruct the analysis, if necessary. By documenting the relevant information gathered during the analysis, evaluation, and comparison of latent prints and the basis for the conclusion (identification, exclusion, or inconclusive), the examiner will create a transparent record of the method and thereby provide the courts with additional information on which to assess the reliability of the method for a specific case. Currently, there is no requirement for examiners to document which features within a latent print support their reasoning and conclusions.

Error rate is a much more difficult challenge. Errors can occur with any judgment-based method, especially when the factors that lead to the ultimate judgment are not documented. Some in the latent print community argue that the method itself, if followed correctly (i.e., by well-trained examiners properly using the method), has a zero error rate. Clearly, this assertion is unrealistic, and, moreover, it does not lead to a process of method improvement. The method, and the performance of those who use it, are inextricably linked, and both involve multiple sources of error (e.g., errors in executing the process steps, as well as errors in human judgment).

Some scientific evidence supports the presumption that friction ridge patterns are unique to each person and persist unchanged throughout a

[29] Mnookin, op. cit.

[30] Ibid., p. 19.

[31] Ibid.

[32] 157 N.H. 77, 945 A.2d 1 (N.H., April 04, 2008).

[33] No. K06-0545 (MD Cir. Ct. Oct. 19, 2007).

lifetime.[34] Uniqueness and persistence are necessary conditions for friction ridge identification to be feasible, but those conditions do not imply that anyone can reliably discern whether or not two friction ridge impressions were made by the same person. Uniqueness does not guarantee that prints from two different people are always sufficiently different that they cannot be confused, or that two impressions made by the same finger will also be sufficiently similar to be discerned as coming from the same source. The impression left by a given finger will differ every time, because of inevitable variations in pressure, which change the degree of contact between each part of the ridge structure and the impression medium. None of these variabilities—of features across a population of fingers or of repeated impressions left by the same finger—has been characterized, quantified, or compared.[35]

To properly underpin the process of friction ridge identification, additional research is also needed into ridge flow and crease pattern distributions on the hands and feet. This information could be used to limit the possible donor population of a particular print in a statistical approach and could provide examiners with a more robust understanding of the prevalence of different ridge flows and crease patterns. Additionally, more research is needed regarding the discriminating value of the various ridge formations and clusters of ridge formations.[36] This would provide examiners with a solid basis for the intuitive knowledge they have gained through experience and provide an excellent training tool. It also would lead to a good framework for future statistical models and provide the courts with additional information to consider when evaluating the reliability of the science. Recently, research has begun to build some of this basis.[37]

---

[34] F. Galton. 1892. *Fingerprints*. New York: MacMillan; H. Cummins and C. Midlo. 1943. *Finger Prints, Palms and Soles: An Introduction of Dermatoglyphics*. Philadelphia: The Blakiston Company; A. Hale. 1952. Morphogenesis of volar skin in the human fetus. *The American Journal of Anatomy* 91:147-173; S. Holt and L.S. Penrose. 1968. *The Genetics of Dermal Ridges*. Springfield, IL: Charles C Thomas Publishing; W. Montagna and P. Parakkal. 1974. *The Structure and Function of Skin*. New York: Academic Press; J. Raser and E. O'Shea. 2005. Noise in gene expression: Origins, consequences, and control. *Science* 39:2010-2013.

[35] Some in the friction ridge community point to an unpublished 1999 study by the Lockheed-Martin Corporation, the "50K vs. 50K Fingerprint Comparison Test," as evidence of the scientific validity of fingerprint "matchup." But that study has several major design and analysis flaws, as pointed out in D.H. Kaye. 2003. Questioning a courtroom proof of the uniqueness of fingerprints. *International Statistical Review* 71(3):524. Moreover, even if it were valid, the study provides only a highly optimistic estimate of the reliability of friction ridge analyses, biased toward highly favorable conditions.

[36] Haber and Haber also provide a sensible research agenda for enhancing the validity of fingerprint comparisons.

[37] E.g., C. Neumann, C. Champod, R. Puch-Solis, N. Egli, A. Anthonioz, and A. Bromage-Griffiths. 2007. Computation of likelihood ratios in fingerprint identification for configurations of any number of minutiae. *Journal of Forensic Sciences* 52(1):54-64; N.M. Egli,

There is also considerable room for research on the various factors that affect the quality of latent prints (e.g., condition of the skin, residue, mechanics of touch). Formal research could provide examiners with additional tools to support or refute distortion explanations. Currently, distortion and quality issues are typically based on "common sense" explanations or on information that is passed down through oral tradition from examiner to examiner. A criticism of the latent print community is that the examiners can too easily explain a "difference" as an "acceptable distortion" in order to make an identification.[38]

OTHER PATTERN/IMPRESSION EVIDENCE: SHOEPRINTS AND TIRE TRACKS

Other pattern evidence, also referred to as impression evidence, occurs when an object such as a shoe or a tire leaves an impression at the crime scene or on another object or a person. Impressions can be either two dimensional, such as shoeprints in dust, or three dimensional, such as tire track impressions in mud. Shoeprints and tire tracks are common types of impression evidence examined by forensic examiners, but the list of potential types of impression evidence is long. Examples include bite marks, markings on bullets and cartridge cases, ear prints, lip prints, toolmarks, some bloodstain patterns, and glove prints.[39] Although there are general approaches concerning the analytical sequence of various types of impression evidence, each has its own set of characteristics. For example, some types of impression evidence, such as those arising from footwear and tires, require knowledge of manufacturing and wear, while other types, such as ear prints and bloodstain patterns, do not. Because footwear and tire track impressions comprise the bulk of the examinations conducted, the remarks in this section are specifically focused on these analyses. Bite marks, markings on bullets and cartridge cases, and bloodstain patterns are covered in later sections in this chapter.

C. Champod, and P. Margot. 2007. Evidence evaluation in fingerprint comparison and automated fingerprint identification systems—Modelling within finger variability. *Forensic Science International* 167(2-3):189-195.

[38] U.S. Department of Justice, Office of the Inspector General. 2006. *A Review of the FBI's Handling of the Brandon Mayfield Case.* Office of the Inspector General Oversight and Review Division, January.

[39] M. Liukkonen, H. Majamaa, and J. Virtanen. 1996. The role and duties of the shoeprint/toolmark examiner in forensic laboratories. *Forensic Science International* 82:99-108.

Sample Data and Collection

Impression evidence at the scene is generally of two types: latent (invisible to the naked eye) or patent (visible). The quality of impression evidence left at the scene cannot be controlled, but failures in the initial scene work used to collect, preserve, and possibly enhance the evidence will degrade the quality of the evidence eventually used for comparative analysis. After documentation at the scene, the evidence is preserved and possibly enhanced using techniques such as those based on chemistry (e.g., metal detection), physical characteristics (e.g., super glue fuming, powder dusting, casting), or transfer onto a contrasting surface (e.g., electrostatic transfer or gel lifting). The quality of the enhanced impression that is used for comparison will depend largely on the experience, training, and scientific knowledge of the scene investigator as well as the agency's resources.

Although some analysis of impression evidence might begin at the scene, the comparison of scene evidence to known exemplars occurs in the laboratory. The educational background of forensic scientists who examine shoeprints and tire track impressions runs the gamut from a high school diploma to scientists with Ph.D.s. Identifications are largely subjective and are based on the examiner's experience and on the number of individual, identifying characteristics in common with a known standard.

Analyses

The goal of impression evidence analysis is to identify a specific source of the impression, and the analytical process that this follows generally is an accepted sequence: identifying the class (group) characteristics of the evidence, followed by locating and comparing individual, identifying (also termed accidental or random) characteristics.[40]

Class characteristics of footwear and tires result from repetitive, controlled processes that are typically mechanical, such as those used to manufacture items in quantity. Although defined similarly by various authors, Bodziak describes footwear class characteristics as "an intentional or unavoidable characteristic that repeats during the manufacturing process and is shared by one or more other shoes."[41] For tires, Nause defines class characteristics as, "[p]hysical characteristics acquired during the manufacturing process (made from the same mold) that tires have in common."[42] He continues, "Class characteristics can often be combined to limit a tire impression to a very select group within the overall group bearing similar class

---

[40] Ibid.

[41] W.J. Bodziak. 1999. *Footwear Impression Evidence–Detection, Recovery, and Examination.* Boca Raton, FL: CRC Press, 2nd ed., p. 329.

[42] Nause, op. cit.

characteristics. (In the field of forensic tire evidence, class characteristics often refer to such things as design, pattern, size, shape, mold variations, etc.)."[43] Regardless of the type of impression evidence, class characteristics are not sufficient to conclude that any one particular shoe or tire made the impression. That latter step—which is not always possible—requires comparison of the individual identifying characteristics on the impression evidence with those on a shoe or tire that is suspected of leaving the impression. These individual characteristics occur during the normal use of an item, sometimes called wear and tear,[44] and are created by "random, uncontrolled processes."[45] For footwear, Bodziak writes that "individual identifying characteristics are characteristics that result when something is randomly added to or taken away from a shoe outsole that either causes or contributes to making that shoe outsole unique."[46] Such characteristics might include cuts, scratches, gouges, holes, or random inclusions that result from manufacturing, such as bubbles, and those that result from adherent substances, such as rocks, chewing gum, papers, or twigs.

Following analysis of the impression, an identification is determined or ruled out according to the number of individual characteristics the evidence has in common with the suspected source. But there is no defined threshold that must be surpassed, nor are there any studies that associate the number of matching characteristics with the probability that the impressions were made by a common source. It is generally accepted that the specific number of characteristics needed to assign a definite positive identification depends on the quality and quantity of these accidental characteristics and the criteria established by individual laboratories.[47] According to Cassidy, many factors and accidental characteristics are required before a positive identification can be established; however, the most important are the examiner's experience, the clarity of the impression, and the uniqueness of the characteristic.[48] Proficiency testing for examiners of impression evidence is available through Collaborative Testing Service, Inc., but the proficiency tests for footwear impressions include samples that are either a match or not a match[49]—that is, none of the samples included in the tests have the sort of ambiguities that would lead an experienced examiner to an "inconclusive"

---

[43] Ibid.

[44] M.J. Cassidy. 1980. *Footwear Identification*. Quebec, Canada: Government Printing Office Centre.

[45] K. Inman and N. Rudin. 2001. *Principles and Practice of Criminalistics*. Boca Raton, FL: CRC Press, p. 129.

[46] Ibid., p. 335.

[47] Liukkonen, Majamaa, and Virtanen, op. cit.

[48] Cassidy, op. cit.

[49] H. Majamaa and Y. Anja. 1996. Survey of the conclusions drawn of similar footwear cases in various crime laboratories. *Forensic Science International* 82:109-120.

conclusion. IAI has a certification program for footwear and tire track examiners.[50] The group's recommended course of study has 13 segments, and each segment includes a suggested reading list and practical and/or written exercises. The student must pass an examination. This course of study does not require an understanding of the scientific basis of the examinations, and it does not recommend the use of a scientific method. Also, there is no provision or recommendation for proficiency testing or continuing education. SWGTREAD, a group of footwear and tire track examiners formed by the FBI, recommends that a trainee candidate have (1) a bachelor's degree (preferably in a physical or natural science) from an accredited college or university; or (2) an associate degree or 60 college semester hours, plus two years of job-related forensic experience; or (3) a high school diploma or equivalent, plus four years of job-related forensic experience.[51]

Scientific Interpretation and Reporting of Results

For footwear evidence, Fawcett[52] and Bodziak[53] have attempted to assign probabilistic or statistical significance to impression comparisons. Generally, shoeprint and tire track examiners prefer nonstatistical language to report or to testify to the result of their findings. Terms such as "positive identification" and "nonidentification" can be used to indicate an identification or nonidentification, respectively, and "nonconclusive" would indicate situations in which the analysis falls short of either of the other two.[54]

In a European survey, examiners were given identical mock cases. Accidental, identifying characteristics were purposely put onto the sole of new shoes, and examiners were asked to make a statement concerning the strength of matches. The results of the survey concluded that there were considerable differences in the conclusions reached by different laboratories examining identical cases."[55] SWGTREAD recommends terminology such as:

- "identification" (definite conclusion of identity)
- "probably made" (very high degree of association)

---

[50] Recommended Course of Study for Footwear & Tire Track Examiners. 1995. Mendota Heights, MN: International Association for Identification.

[51] SWGTread. 2006. *Guide for Minimum Qualifications and Training for a Forensic Footwear and/or Tire Tread Examiner.* Available at www.theiai.org/guidelines/swgtread/qualifications_final.pdf.

[52] A.S. Fawcett. 1970. The role of the footmark examiner. *Journal of the Forensic Science Society* 10:227-244.

[53] Bodziak, op. cit., pp. 342-346.

[54] Ibid.

[55] H. Majamaa and Y. Anja., op. cit.

- "could have made" (significant association of multiple class characteristics)
- "inconclusive" (limited association of some characteristics)
- "probably did not make" (very high degree of nonassociation)
- "elimination" (definite exclusion)
- "unsuitable" (lacks sufficient detail for a meaningful comparison).

Additionally, SWGTREAD discourages the use of once common terminology, such as "consistent with" (acceptable when used to describe a similarity of characteristics), "match/no match," "responsible for/not responsible for," and "caused with/not caused with."[56] Neither the IAI nor SWGTREAD address the statistical evaluation of impression evidence.

Summary Assessment

The scientific basis for the evaluation of impression evidence is that mass-produced items (e.g., shoes, tires) pick up features of wear that, over time, individualize them. However, because these features continue to change as they are worn, elapsed time after a crime can undercut the forensic scientist's certainty. At the least, class characteristics can be identified, and with sufficiently distinctive patterns of wear, one might hope for specific individualization. However, there is no consensus regarding the number of individual characteristics needed to make a positive identification, and the committee is not aware of any data about the variability of class or individual characteristics or about the validity or reliability of the method. Without such population studies, it is impossible to assess the number of characteristics that must match in order to have any particular degree of confidence about the source of the impression.

Experts in impression evidence will argue that they accumulate a sense of those probabilities through experience, which may be true. However, it is difficult to avoid biases in experience-based judgments, especially in the absence of a feedback mechanism to correct an erroneous judgment. These problems are exacerbated with the less common types of impression evidence. For example, a European survey found that 42 laboratories conducted 28,093 shoeprint examinations and 41 laboratories conducted 591 tire track examinations, but only 14 laboratories conducted a total of 21 lip print examinations and 17 laboratories conducted a total of 100 ear print examinations.[57] Although one might argue that those who perform the

[56] SWGTREAD. 2006. *Standard Terminology for Expressing Conclusions of Forensic Footwear and Tire Impression Examinations*. Available at www.theiai.org/guidelines/swgtread/terminology_final.pdf.

[57] Liukkonen, Majamaa, and Virtanen, op. cit.

work in laboratories that conduct hundreds or thousands of evaluations of impression evidence develop useful experience and judgment, it is difficult to assert that the field has enough collective judgment about the variabilities in lip prints and ear prints based on tens of examinations. The community simply does not have enough data about the natural variability of those less frequent impressions, absent the presence of a clear deformity or scar, to infer whether the observed degree of similarity is significant.

Most of the research in the field is conducted in forensic laboratories, with the results published in trade journals, such as the *Journal of Forensic Identification*. With regard to reporting, SWGTREAD is moving toward the use of standard language to convey the conclusions reached.[58] But neither IAI nor SWGTREAD addresses the issue of what critical research should be done or by whom, critical questions that should be addressed include the persistence of individual characteristics, the rarity of certain characteristic types, and the appropriate statistical standards to apply to the significance of individual characteristics. Also, little if any research has been done to address rare impression evidence. Much more research on these matters is needed.

TOOLMARK AND FIREARMS IDENTIFICATION

Toolmarks are generated when a hard object (tool) comes into contact with a relatively softer object. Such toolmarks may occur in the commission of a crime when an instrument such as a screwdriver, crowbar, or wire cutter is used or when the internal parts of a firearm make contact with the brass and lead that comprise ammunition. The marks left by an implement such as a screwdriver or a firearm's firing pin depend largely on the manufacturing processes—and manufacturing tools—used to create or shape it, although other surface features (e.g., chips, gouges) might be introduced through post-manufacturing wear. Manufacturing tools experience wear and abrasion as they cut, scrape, and otherwise shape metal, giving rise to the theory that any two manufactured products—even those produced consecutively with the same manufacturing tools—will bear microscopically different marks. Firearms and toolmark examiners believe that toolmarks may be traced to the physical heterogeneities of an individual tool—that is, that "individual characteristics" of toolmarks may be uniquely associated with a specific tool or firearm and are reproduced by the use of that tool and only that tool.

The manufacture and use of firearms produces an extensive set of

---

[58] SWGTREAD. 2006. *Standard Terminology for Expressing Conclusions of Forensic Footwear and Tire Impression Examinations*. Available at www.theiai.org/guidelines/swgtread/terminology_final.pdf.

specialized toolmarks. Gun barrels typically are rifled to improve accuracy, meaning that spiral grooves are cut into the barrel's interior. The process of cutting these grooves into the barrel leaves marks and scrapes on the relatively softer metal of the barrel.[59] In turn, these markings are transferred to the softer metal of a bullet as it exits the barrel. Over time, with repeated use (and metal-to-metal scraping), the marks on a barrel (and the corresponding "stria" imparted to bullets) may change as individual imperfections are formed or as cleanliness of the barrel changes. The brass exterior of cartridge cases receive analogous toolmarks during the process of gun firing: the firing pin dents the soft primer surface at the base of the cartridge to commence firing, the primer area is forced backward by the buildup of gas pressure (so that the texture of the gun's breech face is impressed on the cartridge), and extractors and ejectors leave marks as they expel used cartridges and cycle in new ammunition.

Firearms examination is one of the more common functions of crime laboratories. Even small laboratories with limited services often perform firearms analysis. In addition to the analysis of marks on bullets and cartridges, firearms examination also includes the determination of the firing distance, the operability of a weapon, and sometimes the analysis of primer residue to determine whether someone recently handled a weapon. These broader aspects are not covered here.

Sample and Data Collection

When a tool is used in a crime, the object that contains the tool marks is recovered when possible. If a toolmark cannot be recovered, it can be photographed and cast. Test marks made by recovered tools can be made in a laboratory and compared with crime scene toolmarks.

In the early 1990s, the FBI and the Bureau of Alcohol, Tobacco, Firearms, and Explosives (ATF) developed separate databases of images of bullet and cartridge case markings, which could be queried to suggest possible matches. In 1996, the National Institute of Standards and Technology (NIST) developed data exchange standards that permitted the integration of the FBI's DRUGFIRE database (cartridge case images) and the ATF's CEASEFIRE database (then limited to bullet images). The current National Integrated Ballistic Information Network (NIBIN) includes images from both cartridge cases and bullets that are associated with crime scenes and is maintained by the ATF.

Periodically—and particularly in the wake of the Washington, DC,

---

[59] Although the metal and initial rifling are very similar, the cutting of the individual barrels, the finishing machining, and the cleaning and polishing begin the process of differentiation of the two sequentially manufactured barrels.

sniper attacks in 2002—the question has been raised of expanding the scope of databases like NIBIN to include images from test firings of newly manufactured firearms. In concept, this would permit downstream investigators who recover a cartridge case or bullet at a crime scene to identify the likely source firearm. Though two states (Maryland and New York) instituted such reference ballistic image databases for newly manufactured firearms, proposals to create such a database at the national level did not make substantial progress in Congress. A recent report of the National Academies, *Ballistic Imaging*, examined this option in great detail and concluded that "[a] national reference ballistic image database of all new and imported guns is not advisable at this time."[60]

Analyses

In both firearm and toolmark identification, it is useful to distinguish several types of characteristics that are considered by examiners. "Class characteristics" are distinctive features that are shared by many items of the same type. For example, the width of the head of a screwdriver or the pattern of serrations in the blade of a knife may be class characteristics that are common to all screwdrivers or knives of a particular manufacturer and/or model. Similarly, the number of grooves cut into the barrel of a firearm and the direction of "twist" in those grooves are class characteristics that can filter and restrict the range of firearms that match evidence found at a crime scene. "Individual characteristics" are the fine microscopic markings and textures that are said to be unique to an individual tool or firearm. Between these two extremes are "subclass characteristics" that may be common to a small group of firearms and that are produced by the manufacturing process, such as when a worn or dull tool is used to cut barrel rifling.

Bullets and cartridge cases are first examined to determine which class characteristics are present. If these differ from a comparison bullet or cartridge, further examination may be unnecessary. The microscopic markings on bullets and cartridge cases and on toolmarks are then examined under a comparison microscope (made from two compound microscopes joined by a comparison bridge that allows viewing of two objects at the same time). The unknown and known bullet or cartridge case or toolmark surfaces are compared visually by a firearms examiner, who can evaluate whether a match exists.

---

[60] National Research Council. 2008. *Ballistic Imaging*. Washington, DC: The National Academies Press, p. 5.

Scientific Interpretation

The task of the firearms and toolmark examiner is to identify the individual characteristics of microscopic toolmarks apart from class and subclass characteristics and then to assess the extent of agreement in individual characteristics in the two sets of toolmarks to permit the identification of an individual tool or firearm.

Guidance from the Association of Firearm and Tool Mark Examiners (AFTE)[61] indicates that an examiner may offer an opinion that a specific tool or firearm was the source of a specific set of toolmarks or a particular bullet striation pattern when "sufficient agreement" exists in the pattern of two sets of marks. The standards then define agreement as significant "when it exceeds the best agreement demonstrated between tool marks known to have been produced by different tools and is consistent with the agreement demonstrated by tool marks known to have been produced by the same tool."[62]

Knowing the extent of agreement in marks made by different tools, and the extent of variation in marks made by the same tool, is a challenging task. AFTE standards acknowledge that these decisions involve subjective qualitative judgments by examiners and that the accuracy of examiners' assessments is highly dependent on their skill and training. In earlier years, toolmark examiners relied on their past casework to provide a foundation for distinguishing between individual, class, and subclass characteristics. More recently, extensive training programs using known samples have expanded the knowledge base of examiners.

The emergence of ballistic imaging technology and databases such as NIBIN assist examiners in finding possible candidate matches between pieces of evidence, including crime scene exhibits held in other geographic locations. However, it is important to note that the final determination of a match is always done through direct physical comparison of the evidence by a firearms examiner, not the computer analysis of images. The growth of these databases also permits examiners to become more familiar with similarities in striation patterns made by different firearms. Newer imaging techniques assess toolmarks using three-dimensional surface measurement data, taking into account the depth of the marks. But even with more training and experience using newer techniques, the decision of the toolmark examiner remains a subjective decision based on unarticulated

---

[61] Theory of identification, range of striae comparison reports and modified glossary definitions—An AFTE Criteria for Identification Committee report. 1992. *Journal of the Association of Firearm and Tool Mark Examiners* 24:336-340.

[62] Ibid., p. 336.

standards and no statistical foundation for estimation of error rates.[63] The National Academies report, *Ballistic Imaging*, while not claiming to be a definitive study on firearms identification, observed that, "The validity of the fundamental assumptions of uniqueness and reproducibility of firearms-related toolmarks has not yet been fully demonstrated." That study recognized the logic involved in trying to compare firearms-related toolmarks by noting that, "Although they are subject to numerous sources of variability, firearms-related toolmarks are not completely random and volatile; one can find similar marks on bullets and cartridge cases from the same gun," but it cautioned that, "A significant amount of research would be needed to scientifically determine the degree to which firearms-related toolmarks are unique or even to quantitatively characterize the probability of uniqueness."[64]

Summary Assessment

Toolmark and firearms analysis suffers from the same limitations discussed above for impression evidence. Because not enough is known about the variabilities among individual tools and guns, we are not able to specify how many points of similarity are necessary for a given level of confidence in the result. Sufficient studies have not been done to understand the reliability and repeatability of the methods. The committee agrees that class characteristics are helpful in narrowing the pool of tools that may have left a distinctive mark. Individual patterns from manufacture or from wear might, in some cases, be distinctive enough to suggest one particular source, but additional studies should be performed to make the process of individualization more precise and repeatable.

---

[63] Recent research has attempted to develop a statistical foundation for assessing the likelihood that more than one tool could have made specific marks by assessing consecutive matching striae, but this approach is used in a minority of cases. See A.A. Biasotti. 1959. A statistical study of the individual characteristics of fired bullets. *Journal of Forensic Sciences* 4:34; A.A. Biasotti and J. Murdock. 1984. "Criteria for identification" or "state of the art" of firearms and tool marks identification. *Journal of the Association of Firearms and Tool Mark Examiners* 16(4):16; J. Miller and M.M. McLean. 1998. Criteria for identification of tool marks. *Journal of the Association of Firearms and Tool Mark Examiners* 30(1):15; J.J. Masson. 1997. Confidence level variations in firearms identification through computerized technology. *Journal of the Association of Firearms and Tool Mark Examiners* 29(1):42. For a critique of this area and a comparison of scientific issues involving toolmark evidence and DNA evidence, see A. Schwartz. 2004-2005. A systemic challenge to the reliability and admissibility of firearms and tool marks identification. *Columbia Science and Technology Law Review* 6:2. For a rebuttal to this critique, see R.G. Nichols. 2007. Defending the scientific foundations of the firearms and tool mark identification discipline: Responding to recent challenges. *Journal of Forensic Sciences* 52(3):586-594.

[64] All quotes from National Research Council. 2008. *Ballistic Imaging*. Washington, DC: The National Academies Press, p. 3.

A fundamental problem with toolmark and firearms analysis is the lack of a precisely defined process. As noted above, AFTE has adopted a theory of identification, but it does not provide a specific protocol. It says that an examiner may offer an opinion that a specific tool or firearm was the source of a specific set of toolmarks or a bullet striation pattern when "sufficient agreement" exists in the pattern of two sets of marks. It defines agreement as significant "when it exceeds the best agreement demonstrated between tool marks known to have been produced by different tools and is consistent with the agreement demonstrated by tool marks known to have been produced by the same tool." The meaning of "exceeds the best agreement" and "consistent with" are not specified, and the examiner is expected to draw on his or her own experience. This AFTE document, which is the best guidance available for the field of toolmark identification, does not even consider, let alone address, questions regarding variability, reliability, repeatability, or the number of correlations needed to achieve a given degree of confidence.

Although some studies have been performed on the degree of similarity that can be found between marks made by different tools and the variability in marks made by an individual tool, the scientific knowledge base for toolmark and firearms analysis is fairly limited. For example, a report from Hamby, Brundage, and Thorpe[65] includes capsule summaries of 68 toolmark and firearms studies. But the capsule summaries suggest a heavy reliance on the subjective findings of examiners rather than on the rigorous quantification and analysis of sources of variability. Overall, the process for toolmark and firearms comparisons lacks the specificity of the protocols for, say, 13 STR DNA analysis. This is not to say that toolmark analysis needs to be as objective as DNA analysis in order to provide value. And, as was the case for friction ridge analysis and in contrast to the case for DNA analysis, the specific features to be examined and compared between toolmarks cannot be stipulated a priori. But the protocols for DNA analysis do represent a precisely specified, and scientifically justified, series of steps that lead to results with well-characterized confidence limits, and that is the goal for all the methods of forensic science.

ANALYSIS OF HAIR EVIDENCE

The basis for hair analyses as forensic evidence stems from the fact that human and animal hairs routinely are shed and thus are capable of being

[65] J.E. Hamby, D.J. Brundage, and J.W. Thorpe. 2009. The identification of bullets fired from 10 consecutively rifled 9mm Ruger pistol barrels—A research project involving 468 participants from 19 countries. Available online at http://www.fti-ibis.com/DOWNLOADS/Publications/10%20Barrel%20Article-%20a.pdf.

transferred from an individual to the crime scene, and from the crime scene to an individual. Forensic hair examiners generally recognize that various physical characteristics of hairs can be identified and are sufficiently different among individuals that they can be useful in including, or excluding, certain persons from the pool of possible sources of the hair. The results of analyses from hair comparisons typically are accepted as class associations; that is, a conclusion of a "match" means only that the hair could have come from any person whose hair exhibited—within some levels of measurement uncertainties—the same microscopic characteristics, but it cannot uniquely identify one person. However, this information might be sufficiently useful to "narrow the pool" by excluding certain persons as sources of the hair.

Although animal hairs might provide useful evidence in certain cases (e.g., animal poaching), animal hair analysis often can lead to an identification of only the type of animal, not the specific breed[66]; consequently, most (90 to 95 percent) of hair analyses refer to analyses of human hair. Human hairs from different parts of the body have different characteristics; Houck cautions strongly against drawing conclusions about hairs from one part of the body based on analyses of hairs from a different body part.[67]

Houck and Bisbing recommend as minimal training for hair examiners a bachelor's degree in a natural or applied science (e.g., chemistry, biology, forensic science), on-the-job training programs, and an annual proficiency test.[68]

Sample Data and Collection

Sample hairs received for analysis initially are examined macroscopically for certain broad features such as color, shaft form (e.g., straight, wavy, curved, kinked), length, and overall shaft thickness (e.g., fine, medium, coarse).

In the second stage of analysis, hairs are mounted on microscopic slides using a mounting medium that has the same refractive index (about 1.54) as the hair, to better view the microscopic features (see next section). One hair or multiple hairs from the same source may be mounted on a glass microscope slide with an appropriate cover slip, as long as each mounted hair is clearly visible. It is most important that questioned and known hairs are mounted in the same type of mounting medium.

During this examination, the hair analyst attempts to identify the part of the body from which the hair might have come, based on certain de-

---

[66] P.D. Barnett and R.R. Ogle. 1982. Probabilities and human hair comparison. *Journal of Forensic Sciences* 27(2):272-278.

[67] M.M. Houck and R.E. Bisbing. 2005. Forensic human hair examination and comparison in the 21st century. *Forensic Science Review* 17(1):7.

[68] Ibid., p. 12.

finable characteristics that distinguish hairs from various body locations. Occasionally, suspects can be eliminated on the basis of these simple microscopic characteristics.

A "control" or "comparison" group of hairs must be collected from a known hair source. A known head hair sample should consist of hairs from the five different areas of the scalp (top, front, back including nape, and both sides). Known hair samples should be obtained by a combination of pulling and combing from the sampled region. Ideally, a total of 50 hairs should be obtained from the scalp. A known pubic hair sample or a sample from any other somatic region should ideally consist of 25 hairs obtained by pulling and combing from different regions. A comparison can still be performed with less than the recommended number of hairs, but this may increase the likelihood of a false exclusion.[69]

Features from human hair analyses can be divided broadly into "major characteristics" and "secondary characteristics." The former category includes features such as color, treatment (e.g., dyed, bleached, curled, permed), pigment aggregation (e.g., streaked, clumped, patchy), and shaft form (e.g., wavy, straight, curly). Other major characteristics may include pigment distribution (e.g., uniform, peripheral, clustered), medulla appearance, if present (e.g., continuous, interrupted, or fragmented—and opaque or translucent), hair diameter, medullary index, and presence or absence of cortical fusi (e.g., root or shaft). Secondary characteristics include cuticular margin (e.g., smooth, serrated, looped, or cracked), pigment density (e.g., absent, sparse, heavy), pigment size (e.g., absent, fine, coarse), tip shape (e.g., tapered, cut, rounded, frayed, split), and shaft diameter (e.g., narrow or wide).[70]

Studies of Accuracy in Identification

In 1974, investigators Gaudette and Keeping described a system of hair analysis and used it in a study of pairwise comparisons among 861 hairs from 100 different persons.[71] They acknowledged that "the hair samples were not chosen from the population at random, but were selected so that the probability of two hairs being similar would be greater, if anything, than in the population at large."[72] From their assignment of probabilities, the authors estimated that the chance of asserting a difference between two

[69] Scientific Working Group on Materials Analysis (SWGMAT). 2005. Forensic human hair examination guidelines. *Forensic Science Communications* 7(2). Available at www.fbi.gov/hq/lab/fsc/backissu/april2005/standards/2005_04_standards02.htm.

[70] Ibid.

[71] B.D. Gaudette and E.S. Keeping. 1974. An attempt at determining probabilities in human scalp hair comparison. *Journal of Forensic Sciences* 19(3):599-606.

[72] Ibid., p. 65.

hairs from the same person is small, about 1 in 4,500.[73] This assignment of probabilities has since been shown to be unreliable.[74] Moreover, the study does not confirm the chance of asserting a match between two dissimilar hairs, and the authors acknowledge that, "due to the fact that so many of the characteristics coded are subjective—for example, color, texture—it was not possible to get complete reproducibility between two or more examiners coding the same hair."[75]

Barnett and Ogle raised four concerns with the Gaudette and Keeping study: (1) it relied on idealized (not from real life) test scenarios; (2) there was no objective basis for selecting the features; (3) the statistical analysis of data from the study was questionable; and (4) there was a possible examiner bias.[76] Gaudette attempted to address these concerns through a further study. However, this additional study involved only three hair examiners, in addition to the author. The author concluded that:

> . . . whereas hair is not generally a basis for positive personal identification, the presence of abnormalities or unusual features or the presence of a large number of different unknown hairs all similar to the standard can lead to a more positive conclusion. The problem, at present, lies in finding suitable additional characteristics [of hair, for effecting individualization]. Although there is basic agreement as to the value of the macroscopic and microscopic characteristics used, other characteristics are either unreliable or controversial. Physical characteristics such as refractive index, density, scale counts, tensile strength, and electrical properties have been proposed by some workers but have been attacked by others, and the general consensus is that they are of little use in hair comparison.[77]

In 1990, Wickenheiser and Hepworth attempted a study to address examiner bias in a small study with only two examiners. They reported that "no incorrect associations were made by either examiner."[78] But a study with only two examiners cannot offer accurate and precise estimates of bias in the population of examiners.

An attempt at an objective system for identifying "matches" among hair samples is presented in Verma et al., based on a neural network.[79]

---

[73] A later study on human pubic hairs (Caucasian only) estimated this probability as "about 1 in 800." B.D. Gaudette. 1976. Probabilities and human pubic hair comparisons. *Journal of Forensic Sciences* 21(3):514-517.

[74] P.D. Barnett and R.R. Ogle. 1982. Probabilities and human hair comparison. *Journal of Forensic Sciences* 27(2):272-278.

[75] Gaudette and Keeping, op. cit.

[76] Barnett and Ogle, op. cit.

[77] B.D. Gaudette. 1978. Some further thoughts on probabilities and human hair comparisons. *Journal of Forensic Sciences* 23(4):758-763, pp. 761-762.

[78] Wickenheiser and Hepworth, op. cit., p. 1327.

[79] M.S. Verma, L. Pratt, C. Ganesh, and C. Medina. 2002. Hair-MAP: A prototype automated system for forensic hair comparison and analysis. *Forensic Science International* 129:168-186.

According to the authors of this article, "The system accurately judged whether two populations of hairs came from the same person or from different persons 83 percent of the time."[80] The article states that 83 percent was obtained by testing the neural network on all possible pairs among 9 samples of hairs from 9 people (i.e., 81 combinations, of which 9 are "true matches" and 72 are "true mismatches"). Their *Table 3*[81] can be summarized as follows:

	System said "same"	System said "different"	
Same person	5	4	Total= 9
Different persons	9	64	Total=73

Because the total of these 4 numbers is 82, not 81, one presumes a typographical error in the table; as stated, the number of correct calls is (5 + 64)/81=0.85, or 85 percent. (If one of the counts, 5 or 64, is off by 1, the percentage would be 84 percent.) However, the table also shows that the neural network claimed 9 of the 73 different pairs as "same," for a false positive rate of 9/73=12 percent, and 4 sets of hairs from the same person as "different," for a false negative rate of 4/9=44 percent. With such high error rates, one would want to study improvements to such systems before putting them into routine practice.

Houck et al. indicate that proficiency testing is conducted regularly for hair experts in crime laboratories.[82] Collaborative Testing Services[83] offers hair and fiber proficiency tests annually. Unfortunately, mass production of test samples such as hair is problematic. Because known samples exhibit a range of characteristics within each of the major and secondary characteristics, it is not possible to provide comparable samples to multiple examiners.

Scientific Interpretation and Reporting of Results

The success of hair analyses to make a positive identification is limited in important ways. Most hair examiners would opine only that hairs exhibiting the same microscopic characteristics "could" have come from a

---

[80] Ibid., p. 179.

[81] Ibid., p. 180.

[82] M.M. Houck, R.E. Bisbing, T.G. Watkins, and R.P. Harman. 2004. Locard exchange: The science of forensic hair comparisons and the admissibility of hair comparison evidence: *Frye* and *Daubert* considered. *Modern Microscopy Journal* Available at www.modernmicroscopy.com/main.asp?article=36&searchkeys=Houck%2BBisbing.

[83] See www.collaborativetesting.com.

particular individual. Moreover, the "best" or most reliable characteristics will vary by case. For example, "color" may be a critical determinant in a case where it is artificial, because that introduces additional independent variables, such as the time since treatment and the actual hair color, while a natural hair might provide less information.

However, several members of the committee have experienced courtroom cases in which, despite the lack of a statistical foundation, microscopic hair examiners have made probabilistic claims based on their experience, as occurred in some DNA exoneration cases in which microscopic hair analysis evidence had been introduced during trial. Aitken and Robertson discuss some probabilistic concepts with respect to hair analysis.[84]

The availability of DNA analysis has lessened the reliance on hair examination. In a very high proportion of cases involving hair evidence, DNA can be extracted, even years after the crime has been committed. Although the DNA extraction may consist of only mitochondrial DNA (mtDNA), such analyses are likely to be much more specific than those conducted on the physical features of hair. For this reason, cases that might have relied heavily on hair examinations have been subjected more recently to additional analyses using DNA.[85] Because of the inherent limitations of hair comparisons and the availability of higher-quality and higher-accuracy analyses based on mtDNA, traditional hair examinations may be presented less often as evidence in the future, although microscopic comparison of physical features will continue to be useful for determining which hairs are sufficiently similar to merit comparisons with DNA analysis and for excluding suspects and assisting in criminal investigations.

Summary Assessment

No scientifically accepted statistics exist about the frequency with which particular characteristics of hair are distributed in the population. There appear to be no uniform standards on the number of features on which hairs must agree before an examiner may declare a "match." In one study of validity and accuracy of the technique, the authors required exact agreement on seven "major" characteristics and at least two agreements among six "secondary" characteristics.[86] The categorization of hair features depends heavily on examiner proficiency and practical experience.

An FBI study found that, of 80 hair comparisons that were "associ-

---

[84] C.G.G. Aitken and J.A. Robertson. 1986. A contribution to the discussion of probabilities and human hair comparisons. *Journal of Forensic Sciences* 32(3):684-689.

[85] M.M. Houck and B. Budowle. 2002. Correlation of microscopic and mitochondrial DNA hair comparisons. *Journal of Forensic Sciences* 47(5):964-967.

[86] R.A. Wickenheiser and D.G. Hepworth. 1990. Further evaluation of probabilities in human hair comparisons. *Journal of Forensic Sciences* 35(6):1323-1329.

ated" through microscopic examinations, 9 of them (12.5 percent) were found in fact to come from different sources when reexamined through mtDNA analysis.[87] This illustrates not only the imprecision of microscopic hair analyses, but also the problem with using imprecise reporting terminology such as "associated with," which is not clearly defined and which can be misunderstood to imply individualization.

In some recent cases, courts have explicitly stated that microscopic hair analysis is a technique generally accepted in the scientific community.[88] But courts also have recognized that testimony linking microscopic hair analysis with particular defendants is highly unreliable.[89] In cases where there seems to be a morphological match (based on microscopic examination), it must be confirmed using mtDNA analysis; microscopic studies alone are of limited probative value. The committee found no scientific support for the use of hair comparisons for individualization in the absence of nuclear DNA. Microscopy and mtDNA analysis can be used in tandem and may add to one another's value for classifying a common source, but no studies have been performed specifically to quantify the reliability of their joint use.

ANALYSIS OF FIBER EVIDENCE

Fibers associated with a crime—including synthetic fibers such as nylon, polyester and acrylic as well as botanical fibers such as ramie or jute, which are common in ropes or twines—can be examined microscopically in the same way as hairs, and with the same limitations. However, fibers also can be analyzed using the tools of analytical chemistry, which provide a more solid scientific footing than that underlying morphological examination. In some cases, clothing and carpets have been subjected to relatively distinctive environmental conditions (e.g., sunlight exposure or laundering agents) that impart characteristics that can distinguish particular items from others from the same manufacturing lot. Fiber examiners agree, however, that none of these characteristics is suitable for individualizing fibers (associating a fiber from a crime scene with one, and only one, source) and that fiber evidence can be used only to associate a given fiber with a class of fibers.[90]

---

[87] Houck and Budowle, op. cit.

[88] E.g., *State v. West*, 877 A.2d 787 (Conn. 2005); *Bookins v. State*, 922 A.2d 389 (Del. Supr, 2007).

[89] See P.C. Giannelli and E. West. 2001. Hair comparison evidence. *Criminal Law Bulletin* 37:514.

[90] See, e.g., R.R. Bresee. 1987. Evaluation of textile fiber evidence: A review. *Journal of Forensic Sciences* 32(2):510-521. See also SWGMAT. 1999. Introduction to forensic fiber examination. *Forensic Science Communications* 1(1). Available at www.fbi.gov/hq/lab/fsc/backissu/april1999/houcktoc.htm, which includes the following summarization in Section 5.4: "It can never be stated with certainty that a fiber originated from a particular textile because

Another type of fiber analysis consists of physically matching two remnants that appear to be torn from one another. By comparing the shapes of the mating edges, and aligning any patterns in the cloth, it can sometimes be possible to associate a fragment with the garment or other item from which it was torn. This is a form of pattern matching, analogous to the matching of shoe and tire prints, but it will not be discussed further here.

Sample Collection and Analysis

The collection of fibers and of a comparison group follows the same procedures as those for mounting hairs. If a macroscopic analysis (e.g., or color, texture, shape) suggests that the two samples appear to be the same, additional procedures such as the following are pursued:

1. Microscopy (reflected light)
2. Polarized light microscopy/fluorescence microscopy
3. Infrared microscopy (to determine man-made fiber composition, such as nylon, polyester)
4. Solubility in a medium
5. Melting point
6. Cross-sectional shape
7. Pyrolysis GC
8. Microspectrophotometry (MSP)
9. Raman spectroscopy

The last of these, Raman spectroscopy, often can provide additional information on polymer chain length (short, medium, long) and branching. Its use in forensic laboratories is rare, although research is under way to develop possible applications. A good overview of fiber evidence is provided by Grieve and Robertson.[91]

Summary Assessment

A group of experienced paint examiners, the Fiber Subgroup of the Scientific Working Group on Materials Analysis (SWGMAT), has produced guidelines,[92] but no set standards, for the number and quality of character-

---

other textiles are produced using the same fiber types and color. The inability to positively associate a fiber to a particular textile to the exclusion of all others, however, does not mean that a fiber association is without value."

[91] M. Grieve and J. Robertson. 1999. *Forensic Examination of Fibres*. London: Taylor and Francis Ltd.

[92] SWGMAT, op. cit. Available at www.fbi.gov/hq/lab/fsc/backissu/april1999/houcktoc.htm.

istics that must correspond in order to conclude that two fibers came from the same manufacturing batch. There have been no studies of fibers (e.g., the variability of their characteristics during and after manufacturing) on which to base such a threshold. Similarly, there have been no studies to inform judgments about whether environmentally related changes discerned in particular fibers are distinctive enough to reliably individualize their source, and there have been no studies that characterize either reliability or error rates in the procedures. Thus, a "match" means only that the fibers could have come from the same type of garment, carpet, or furniture; it can provide only class evidence.

Because the analysis of fibers is made largely through well-characterized methods of chemistry, it would be possible in principle to develop an understanding of the uncertainties associated with those analyses.[93] However, to date, that has not been done. Fiber analyses are reproducible across laboratories because there are standardized procedures for such analyses. Proficiency tests are routinely provided and taken annually, and the reports are available from Collaborative Testing Services.

QUESTIONED DOCUMENT EXAMINATION[94]

Questioned document examination involves the comparison and analysis of documents and printing and writing instruments in order to identify or eliminate persons as the source of the handwriting; to reveal alterations, additions, or deletions; or to identify or eliminate the source of typewriting or other impression marks. Questions about documents arise in business, finance, and civil and criminal trials, and in any matter affected by the integrity of written communications and records. Typical analyses include:

- determining whether the document is the output of mechanical or electronic imaging devices such as printers, copying machines, and facsimile equipment;
- identifying or eliminating particular human or machine sources of handwriting, printing, or typewriting;
- identifying or eliminating ink, paper, and writing instrument;
- establishing the source, history, sequence of preparation, alterations or additions to documents, and relationships of documents;

---

[93] Some relevant questions to be addressed are identified in Bresee, op. cit.

[94] This discussion is primarily based on *Standard Descriptions of Scope of Work Relating to Forensic Document Examiners (American Society for Testing and Materials [ASTM] Designation E 444-98)* (1998), *Standard Guide for Test Methods for Forensic Writing Ink Comparison (ASTM Designation E 1422-01)* (2001), *Standard Guide for Writing Ink Identification (ASTM Designation E 1789-04)* (2004), and *Standard Guide for Examination of Handwritten Items (ASTM Designation E 2290-03)* (2003).

- deciphering and restoring obscured, deleted, or damaged parts of documents;
- recognizing and preserving other physical evidence that may be present in documents; and
- determining the age of a document.

Questioned document examiners are also referred to as forensic document examiners or handwriting experts; questioned document examination includes the field of handwriting identification, while handwriting includes cursive or script style writing, printing by hand, signatures, numerals, or other written marks or signs. Forensic document examination does not involve a study of handwriting that purports to create a personality profile or otherwise analyze or judge the writer's personality or character.

Analyses

Equipment used in questioned document examination includes microscopes and other optical aids, photographic and other imaging devices, and a wide variety of imaging materials adaptable for use with numerous lighting methods, including those involving ultraviolet, visible, and infrared light, and other regions of the electromagnetic spectrum. Software tools recently have become available for the analysis of handwriting.[95] The analysis of papers and inks is similar to other forensic chemistry work. The principal procedures used for ink examination are nondestructive optical examinations and chemical examinations. Optical examinations include those that use visible and alternative light sources—for example, determining whether the class of ink is ballpoint pen; using ultraviolet examination to reveal indications that a document has been stained by chemicals; and employing reflected infrared to observe luminescence at different wavelengths. Chemical examination includes spot testing during which solvents are applied in small amounts to the ink line. For example, ballpoint inks, which are either oil based or glycol based, are highly soluble in pyridine. Inks formulated for fountain pens, porous point pens, and roller pens generally are water soluble in ethanol and water. Indelible markers are solvent based and generally would be soluble in pyridine.

Ink examination can have one of two objectives: class identification—for which the intention is to identify the ink formula or type based on a reference library of samples of inks—and comparison, for which the goal is to compare two ink samples to determine whether they are of common

[95] For an overview, see S.N. Srihari and G. Leedham. 2003. A survey of computer methods in forensic document examination. *Proceedings of the 11th International Graphonomics Society Conference*, pp. 278-281. Available at www.ntu.edu.sg/sce/labs/forse/PDF/docExam_7.pdf.

origin. Ink comparisons usually are performed to answer four basic categories of questions: (1) whether an ink is the same (in formula) as that on other parts of the same document or on other documents; (2) whether two writings with similar ink have a common origin (e.g., the same writing instrument or ink well); (3) whether the ink of entries over a period of time is consistent with varying ages or indicates preparation at one time; and (4) whether ink is as old as it purports to be.

Most problems with ink examinations arise from confounding factors that interact with the ink. These can be part of the writing process, such as blotting wet ink; variations in the papers; various forms of contamination on the document; or a combination of these factors. Most ink examinations must be performed on paper and without defacing the handwriting, and this creates a number of sampling and analytical challenges.

The examination of handwritten items typically involves the comparison of a questioned item submitted for examination along with a known item of established origin associated with the matter under investigation. Requirements for comparison are that the writing be of the same type (handwritten/cursive versus hand printed) and that it be comparable text (similar letter/word combinations). Special situations involving unnatural writing are forgery (an attempt to imitate/duplicate the writing of another person) and disguise (an attempt to avoid identification as the writer). The basis for comparison is that handwriting/handprinting/numerals can be examined to obtain writing characteristics (also referred to as features or attributes). The characteristics are further classified into class characteristics (the style that the writer was taught), individual characteristics (the writer's personal style), and gross/subtle characteristics.

Specific attributes used for comparison of handwriting are also referred to as discriminating elements, of which Huber and Headrick have identified 21.[96] Comparisons are based on the high likelihood that no two persons write the same way, while considering the fact that every person's writing has its own variabilities. Thus, an analysis of handwriting must compare interpersonal variability—some characterization of how handwriting features vary across a population of possible writers—with intrapersonal variability—how much an individual's handwriting can vary from sample to sample. Determining that two samples were written by the same person depends on showing that their degree of variability, by some measure, is more consistent with intrapersonal variability than with interpersonal variability. Some cases of forgery are characterized by signatures with too little variability, and are thus inconsistent with the fact that we all have intrapersonal variability in our writing.

---

[96] R.A. Huber and A. M. Headrick. 1999. *Handwriting Identification: Facts and Fundamentals.* Boca Raton, FL: CRC Press.

Scientific Interpretation and Reporting of Results

Terminology has been developed for expressing the subjective conclusions of handwriting comparison and identification, taking into account that there are an infinite number of gradations or opinions toward an identification or elimination. Several scales, such as a five-point scale and a nine-point scale, are used by questioned document examiners worldwide. The nine-point scale is as follows:

1. Identification (a definite conclusion that the questioned writing matches another sample)
2. Strong probability (evidence is persuasive, yet some critical quality is missing)
3. Probable (points strongly towards identification)
4. Indications [that the same person] did [create both samples] (there are a few significant features)
5. No conclusion (used when there are limiting factors such as disguise, or lack of comparable writing)
6. Indications [that the same person] did not [create both samples] (same weight as indications with a weak opinion)
7. Probably did not (evidence is quite strong)
8. Strong probably did not (virtual certainty)
9. Elimination (highest degree of confidence)[97]

Summary Assessment

The scientific basis for handwriting comparisons needs to be strengthened.[98] Recent studies have increased our understanding of the individuality and consistency of handwriting and computer studies[99] and suggest that

---

[97] *Standard Terminology for Expressing Conclusions of Forensic Document Examiners, ASTM Designation E 1658-04.*

[98] M. Kam, G. Fielding, and R. Conn. 1997. Writer identification by professional document examiners. *Journal of Forensic Sciences* 42(5):778-786, reports on proficiency tests given to more than 100 questioned document examiners and to a control group of individuals with similar educational backgrounds. Each subject made 144 pair-wise comparisons. Although the study showed that document examiners are much more accurate than lay people in determining whether or not two samples "match" (based on the "identification" and "strong probability" definitions of ASTM standard E1658), professionals nonetheless declared an erroneous match in 6.5 percent of the comparisons. A similar, more recent study, focusing on whether individual signatures were genuine, is reported in J. Sita, B. Found, and D. Rogers. 2002. Forensic handwriting examiners' expertise for signature comparison. *Journal of Forensic Sciences* 47:1117. That study found that professional handwriting examiners erred in 3.4 percent of their judgments.

[99] E.g., S.N. Sargur, S.-H. Cha, H. Arora, and S. Lee. 2002. Individuality of handwriting. *Journal of Forensic Sciences* 47(4):1-17.

there may be a scientific basis for handwriting comparison, at least in the absence of intentional obfuscation or forgery. Although there has been only limited research to quantify the reliability and replicability of the practices used by trained document examiners, the committee agrees that there may be some value in handwriting analysis.

Analysis of inks and paper, being based on well-understood chemistry, presumably rests on a firmer scientific foundation. However, the committee did not receive input on these fairly specialized methods and cannot offer a definitive view regarding the soundness of these methods or of their execution in practice.

ANALYSIS OF PAINT AND COATINGS EVIDENCE

Paint is a suspension of solid pigments in a polymeric binder that, after application by brushing, spraying, dipping, or other means, forms a protective and/or decorative coating. When two objects come in contact with one another and at least one of these objects is painted, a transfer of paint may occur. This transferred paint can be compared to the paint located near the point of damage to determine if the two samples have a common origin. Painted surfaces tend to be repainted over time, providing a characteristic history of layer sequence. Painted surfaces are encountered frequently at crime scenes in the form of vehicles, architectural structures, tools, bicycles, boats, and many other items. The results of the examinations often are valuable both during the investigation and as evidence if a trial results. Paint examinations by their nature can be useful in suggesting possible connections of evidence from the crime scene to its source and therefore are helpful in narrowing or excluding possible witnesses and suspects as well as in providing useful information for investigative leads.

Sample Data and Collection

There are many different types of paint and other coatings, including architectural, vehicular, and marine. Evidence collected from the crime scene may include painted surfaces such as automotive panels, tools, or victims' or suspects' clothing, or spray paint, smears, chips, or flakes. After documentation at the scene, the damaged painted surface is protected and preserved and then submitted to the laboratory. When it is not possible to bring the painted item or a portion of it to the laboratory, paint samples may be removed in such a way that the entire layer sequence is captured intact.

Analyses

The proper recognition and collection of paint evidence at the scene precedes the comparison of evidence occurring at the laboratory. The color, texture, type, layer sequence, and chemical composition of known and questioned paints are compared, and a conclusion is rendered. Additionally, in cases for which no suspect vehicle and questioned paint are available, it may be possible to provide at least an investigative lead based on the color and metallic/nonmetallic type of paint present. If appropriate, the Royal Canadian Mounted Police's PDQ (Paint Data Query) database may be searched, and vehicular information may be provided regarding the possible makes, models, and year range of vehicles that used the questioned paint system.

The examination and comparison of paint evidence requires microscopic and instrumental techniques and methods. The examination of questioned and known samples follows an analytical process that identifies and compares the class (or group) characteristics of the evidence.[100] Occasionally, identifying characteristics exist across edges that allow edge or piece fitting. These characteristics include irregular borders, brush stroke striations, polish mark striations, or surface abrasion markings. When paint fragments physically fit back to a sample from a known source, the fragments are identified as having come from that specific source. Only when physical fitting is possible can an individualized source determination be made

Examiners involved with the analysis of paint evidence in the laboratory typically possess an extensive scientific background, because many of the methods and analyses rely heavily on chemistry.[101] The suggested minimum education requirement is a bachelor's degree in a natural[102,103] or applied science,[104] with many candidates possessing a graduate degree. Coursework needs to include one year (or equivalent) of general chemistry with laboratory, organic chemistry with laboratory, analytical/instrumental analysis, and light microscopy to include basic polarized light microscopy—the latter obtained through structured coursework if it is not available at the graduate or undergraduate level.[105] On-the-job training continues in the laboratory, with its length depending on the examiner's experience. Before examiner trainees can work cases independently, they must observe and

[100] SWGMAT. 1999. Forensic paint analysis and comparison guidelines. *Forensic Science Communications* 1(2). Available at www.fbi.gov/hq/lab/fsc/backissu/july1999/painta.htm.

[101] SWGMAT. 2000. Trace evidence quality assurance guidelines. *Forensic Science Communications* 2(1). Available at www.fbi.gov/hq/lab/fsc/backissu/jan2000/swgmat.htm.

[102] G.S. Anderson (ed.). Canadian Society of Forensic Science. 2007. *CSFS Careers in Forensic Science*, p. 15. Available at www.csfs.ca/contentadmin/UserFiles/File/Booklet2007.pdf.

[103] SWGMAT 2000, op. cit.

[104] Ibid.

[105] Ibid.

work under the supervision of an experienced examiner. The completion of a laboratory's training program in paint analysis can range between 12 to 18 months.[106]

Scientific Interpretation and Reporting of Results

SWGMAT sets guidelines for this field, but it has not recommended report wording, and there are no set criteria for determining a conclusion, although a range of conclusions may be used to show the significance of the examination results. The strength of a conclusion depends on such variables as the number of layers present, the sample condition, and the type of paint (vehicular or structural). Terms such as "matched," "indistinguishable," "consistent," or "similar" are used along with the properties of the paints that were compared in stating the results of the comparison.

If there are no significant differences in the properties compared, the examiners may conclude that the paint or coating samples could have had a common origin. This does not mean they came from the same source to the exclusion of all others, but rather that they may have originated from the same source or from different sources that were painted or coated in the same manner. As the number of different layers associated increases (e.g., multiple different layers on a repainted surface), it may be concluded that it is unlikely that the questioned paint originated from any source other than that of the known paint.

SWGMAT has suggested forensic paint analysis and comparison guidelines[107,108] that discuss the examination procedure and instrumentation options, and ASTM has published the general guidelines.[109] However, neither includes report wording suggestions. Additional work should be done to provide standard language for reporting conclusions and sources of uncertainty. Such work has been completed by working groups for other forensic disciplines. Proficiency testing requirements are agreed upon by the predominant accrediting organization, the American Society of Crime Laboratory Directors-Laboratory Accreditation Board (ASCLD/LAB), which requires testing (internal or external) once per calendar year.

---

[106] Anderson, op. cit.; SWGMAT.

[107] SWGMAT. 1999. Forensic paint analysis and comparison guidelines. *Forensic Science Communications* 1(2). Available at www.fbi.gov/hq/lab/fsc/backissu/july1999/painta.htm.

[108] SWGMAT. 2002. Standard guide for using scanning electron microscopy/X-ray spectrometry in forensic paint examinations. *Forensic Science Communications* 4(4). Available at www.fbi.gov/hq/lab/fsc/backissu/oct2002/bottrell.htm.

[109] Ibid.

Summary Assessment

As is the case with fiber evidence, analysis of paints and coatings is based on a solid foundation of chemistry to enable class identification. Visual and microscopic examinations are typically the first step in a forensic examination of paints and coatings because of the ability to discriminate paints/coatings based on properties determined with these examinations. Several studies have been conducted that included hundreds of random automotive paint samples.[110] These studies have concluded that more than 97 percent of the samples could be differentiated based on microscopic examinations coupled with solubility and microchemical testing. Another study[111] determined that more than 99 percent of 2,000 architectural paint samples could be similarly differentiated. However, the community has not defined precise criteria for determining whether two samples come from a common source class.

ANALYSIS OF EXPLOSIVES EVIDENCE AND FIRE DEBRIS

Explosives evidence encompasses a wide range of materials from unburned, unconsumed powders, liquids, and slurries, to fragments of an explosive device, to objects in the immediate vicinity of an explosion thought to contain residue from the explosive. A typical analytical approach would be to identify the components and construction of an explosive device and conduct an analysis of any unconsumed explosives and residues. In addition to the analysis and identification of low and high explosives, chemical reaction bottle bombs are also analyzed. The scene of an explosion can require special investigative attention. What may appear to be a small piece of scrap metal could in fact be an important piece of the device that caused the explosion. The very nature of an explosion has a direct impact on the quality of evidence recovered. Pristine devices or device fragments, or appreciable amounts of unconsumed explosive material, should not be expected.

Analyses

Generally speaking, laboratories will not accept devices until they have been rendered safe. Examiners involved with the analysis of explosives evidence in the laboratory typically have an extensive scientific background, because the methods used entail a large amount of chemistry and instru-

[110] S.G. Ryland and R.J. Kopec. 1979. The evidential value of automobile paint chips. *Journal of Forensic Sciences* 24(1):140-147; J.A. Gothard. 1976. Evaluation of automobile paint flakes as evidence. *Journal of Forensic Sciences* 21(3):636-641.

[111] C.F. Tippet. 1968. The evidential value of the comparison of paint flakes from sources other than vehicles. *Journal of the Forensic Sciences Society* 8(2-3):61-65.

mentation. The Technical Working Group for Fire and Explosives (TWGFEX), a group of fire debris and explosives examiners, suggests that an explosives examiner be required to possess a bachelor's degree in a natural or applied science, with recommended coursework in chemistry and instrumental analysis.[112] The group also recommends that the examiner complete a training program that includes the analysis of low and high explosives, instruction in the use of instrumentation used in routine analyses, the construction of explosive devices, and participation in a postblast investigation course. Although there is no official certification program for explosives examiners, TWGFEX has devised a suggested training guide. The guide is divided into seven modules, each with a reading list, practical exercises, and methods of evaluation.[113] To ensure that examiners maintain a level of competency, proficiency testing (internal or external) is required by ASCLD/LAB once per calendar year.[114]

The ultimate goal of an explosives examination is the identification of the explosive material used, whether it is through the analysis of an intact material or of the residue left behind when the material explodes. Intact material lends itself to being more easily identified. The individual components of postblast residue may often be identified (e.g., potassium chloride and potassium sulfate). The training and experience of examiners allows them to deduce what types of explosive material were originally present from possible combinations of explosive materials.

Whether it is a low explosive or high explosive, the analysis of an intact explosive material follows a procedure that begins with a macroscopic and microscopic examination of the material, followed by a burn test, when appropriate. The results of the initial observations will dictate how the rest of the analysis will proceed. Typically it will involve the use of instrumentation that provides both elemental and structural information about the material, such as X-ray diffraction, scanning electron microscope-energy dispersive X-ray analysis, or infrared spectroscopy. TWGFEX has devised guidelines for the analysis of intact explosives that categorize the instruments that can be used based on the level of information they provide.[115] The information gathered, if sufficient, can be useful in identifying the material.

The analysis of postblast explosive residues begins much like the analy-

---

[112] TWGFEX Explosive Examiners Job Description. Undated. Available at http://ncfs.ucf.edu/twgfex/documents.html.

[113] TWGFEX Training Guide for Explosives Analysis Training. Undated. Available at http://ncfs.ucf.edu/twgfex/Documents.html.

[114] American Society of Crime Laboratory Directors International. 2006. *Supplemental Requirements for the Accreditation of Forensic Science Testing Laboratories*, p. 20. See www.ascld-lab.org/international/indexinternational.html.

[115] TWGFEX Recommended Guidelines for Forensic Identification of Intact Explosives. Undated. Available at http://ncfs.ucf.edu/twgfex/documents.html.

sis of intact explosives, with the macroscopic and microscopic analysis of the evidence submitted (whether it is an expended device, fragments of a device, or debris from near the site of the explosion). If no intact explosive material is found, a sequence of extracts may be used to capture any organic and/or inorganic residues present. These extracts are then analyzed employing the same instrumentation used for intact explosives. However, the results produced differ in their specificity, and it is here that the training and expertise of the examiner plays a large role. To interpret the results properly, the examiner must have knowledge of the composition of explosives and the reaction products that form when they explode. Interpretation can be further complicated by the presence of contaminants from, for example, the device or soil.[116]

Examination conclusions for postblast residues range from "the residue present was consistent with an explosive material" to "the residue is only indicative of an explosive" to "no explosive residues were present." TWGFEX recently has developed a set of guidelines for the analysis of postblast explosive residues,[117] but has yet to make any recommendations for report wording.

The examination of fire debris not associated with explosions often aims to determine whether an accelerant was used. To assess the effects of an accelerant, one might design an experiment, under a range of conditions (e.g., wind speed, temperature, presence/absence of other chemicals) with two groups: one in which materials are burned in the presence of an accelerant ("treatment") and one with no accelerant ("control"). The measured outcomes on the burned materials might be measures that characterize the damage patterns (e.g., depth of char, size of bubbles on surfaces). Differences in the ranges of these measurements from the materials in the two groups (treatment versus control) suggest a hypothesis about the effects of an accelerant. Following this exploration, one should design validation studies to confirm that these measures do indeed characterize the differences in materials treated or untreated with an accelerant.

Summary Assessment

The scientific foundations exist to support the analysis of explosions, because such analysis is based primarily on well-established chemistry. As part of the laboratory work, an analyst often will try to reconstruct the bomb, which introduces procedural complications, but not scientific ones.

---

116 C.R. Midkiff. 2002. Arson and explosive investigation. In: R. Saferstein (ed.). *Forensic Science Handbook*. Vol. 1, 2nd ed. Upper Saddle River, NJ: Prentice Hall.

117 TWGFEX Recommended Guidelines for Forensic Identification of Post-Blast Explosive Residues. 2007. Available at http://ncfs.ucf.edu/twgfex/action_items.html.

By contrast, much more research is needed on the natural variability of burn patterns and damage characteristics and how they are affected by the presence of various accelerants. Despite the paucity of research, some arson investigators continue to make determinations about whether or not a particular fire was set. However, according to testimony presented to the committee,[118] many of the rules of thumb that are typically assumed to indicate that an accelerant was used (e.g., "alligatoring" of wood, specific char patterns) have been shown not to be true.[119] Experiments should be designed to put arson investigations on a more solid scientific footing.

FORENSIC ODONTOLOGY

Forensic odontology, the application of the science of dentistry to the field of law, includes several distinct areas of focus: the identification of unknown remains, bite mark comparison, the interpretation of oral injury, and dental malpractice. Bite mark comparison is often used in criminal prosecutions and is the most controversial of the four areas just mentioned. Although the identification of human remains by their dental characteristics is well established in the forensic science disciplines, there is continuing dispute over the value and scientific validity of comparing and identifying bite marks.[120]

Many forensic odontologists providing criminal testimony concerning bite marks belong to the American Board of Forensic Odontology (ABFO), which was organized in 1976 and is recognized by the American Academy of Forensic Sciences as a forensic specialty. The ABFO offers board certification to its members.[121]

Sample Data and Collection

Bite marks are seen most often in cases of homicide, sexual assault, and child abuse. The ABFO has approved guidelines for the collection of evidence from bite mark victims and suspected biters.[122] The techniques for obtaining bite mark evidence from human skin—for example, various forms of photography, dental casts, clear overlays, computer enhancement, electron microscopy, and swabbing for serology or DNA—generally are

[118] J. Lentini. Scientific Fire Analysis, LLC. Presentation to the committee. April 23, 2007. Available at www7.nationalacademies.org/stl/April%20Forensic%20Lentini.pdf.

[119] NFPA 921 Guide for Explosion and Fire Investigations, 2008 Edition. Quincy, MA: National Fire Protection Association.

[120] E.g., J.A. Kieser. 2005. Weighing bitemark evidence: A postmodern perspective. *Journal of Forensic Science, Medicine, and Pathology* 1(2):75-80.

[121] American Board of Forensic Odontology at www.abfo.org.

[122] Ibid.

well established and relatively noncontroversial. Unfortunately, bite marks on the skin will change over time and can be distorted by the elasticity of the skin, the unevenness of the surface bite, and swelling and healing. These features may severely limit the validity of forensic odontology. Also, some practical difficulties, such as distortions in photographs and changes over time in the dentition of suspects, may limit the accuracy of the results.[123]

Analyses

The guidelines of the ABFO for the analysis of bite marks list a large number of methods for analysis, including transillumination of tissue, computer enhancement and/or digitalization of the bite mark or teeth, stereomicroscopy, scanning electron microscopy, video superimposition, and histology.[124] The guidelines, however, do not indicate the criteria necessary for using each method to determine whether the bite mark can be related to a person's dentition and with what degree of probability. There is no science on the reproducibility of the different methods of analysis that lead to conclusions about the probability of a match. This includes reproducibility between experts and with the same expert over time. Even when using the guidelines, different experts provide widely differing results and a high percentage of false positive matches of bite marks using controlled comparison studies.[125]

No thorough study has been conducted of large populations to establish the uniqueness of bite marks; theoretical studies promoting the uniqueness theory include more teeth than are seen in most bite marks submitted for comparison. There is no central repository of bite marks and patterns. Most comparisons are made between the bite mark and dental casts of an individual or individuals of interest. Rarely are comparisons made between the bite mark and a number of models from other individuals in addition to those of the individual in question. If a bite mark is compared to a dental cast using the guidelines of the ABFO, and the suspect providing the dental cast cannot be eliminated as a person who could have made the bite, there is no established science indicating what percentage of the population or subgroup of the population could also have produced the bite. This follows from the basic problems inherent in bite mark analysis and interpretation.

As with other "experience-based" forensic methods, forensic odontology suffers from the potential for large bias among bite mark experts in evaluating a specific bite mark in cases in which police agencies provide the suspects for comparison and a limited number of models from which

123 Rothwell, op. cit.
124 American Board of Forensic Odontology, op. cit.
125 Bowers, op. cit.

to choose from in comparing the evidence. Bite marks often are associated with highly sensationalized and prejudicial cases, and there can be a great deal of pressure on the examining expert to match a bite mark to a suspect. Blind comparisons and the use of a second expert are not widely used.

Scientific Interpretation and Reporting of Results

The ABFO has issued guidelines for reporting bite mark comparisons, including the use of terminology for conclusion levels, but there is no incentive or requirement that these guidelines be used in the criminal justice system. Testimony of experts generally is based on their experience and their particular method of analysis of the bite mark. Some convictions based mainly on testimony by experts indicating the identification of an individual based on a bite mark have been overturned as a result of the provision of compelling evidence to the contrary (usually DNA evidence).[126]

More research is needed to confirm the fundamental basis for the science of bite mark comparison. Although forensic odontologists understand the anatomy of teeth and the mechanics of biting and can retrieve sufficient information from bite marks on skin to assist in criminal investigations and provide testimony at criminal trials, the scientific basis is insufficient to conclude that bite mark comparisons can result in a conclusive match. In fact, one of the standards of the ABFO for bite mark terminology is that, "Terms assuring unconditional identification of a perpetrator, or without doubt, are not sanctioned as a final conclusion."[127]

Some of the basic problems inherent in bite mark analysis and interpretation are as follows:

(1) The uniqueness of the human dentition has not been scientifically established.[128]

(2) The ability of the dentition, if unique, to transfer a unique pattern to human skin and the ability of the skin to maintain that uniqueness has not been scientifically established.[129]
   i. The ability to analyze and interpret the scope or extent of distortion of bite mark patterns on human skin has not been demonstrated.
   ii. The effect of distortion on different comparison techniques is not fully understood and therefore has not been quantified.

[126] Bowers, op. cit.
[127] American Board of Forensic Odontology, op. cit.
[128] Senn, op. cit.
[129] Ibid.

(3) A standard for the type, quality, and number of individual characteristics required to indicate that a bite mark has reached a threshold of evidentiary value has not been established.

Summary Assessment

Despite the inherent weaknesses involved in bite mark comparison, it is reasonable to assume that the process can sometimes reliably exclude suspects. Although the methods of collection of bite mark evidence are relatively noncontroversial, there is considerable dispute about the value and reliability of the collected data for interpretation. Some of the key areas of dispute include the accuracy of human skin as a reliable registration material for bite marks, the uniqueness of human dentition, the techniques used for analysis, and the role of examiner bias.[130] The ABFO has developed guidelines for the analysis of bite marks in an effort to standardize analysis,[131] but there is still no general agreement among practicing forensic odontologists about national or international standards for comparison.

Although the majority of forensic odontologists are satisfied that bite marks can demonstrate sufficient detail for positive identification,[132] no scientific studies support this assessment, and no large population studies have been conducted. In numerous instances, experts diverge widely in their evaluations of the same bite mark evidence,[133] which has led to questioning of the value and scientific objectivity of such evidence.

Bite mark testimony has been criticized basically on the same grounds as testimony by questioned document examiners and microscopic hair examiners. The committee received no evidence of an existing scientific basis for identifying an individual to the exclusion of all others. That same finding was reported in a 2001 review, which "revealed a lack of valid evidence to support many of the assumptions made by forensic dentists during bite mark comparisons."[134] Some research is warranted in order to identify the circumstances within which the methods of forensic odontology can provide probative value.

---

[130] Ibid.

[131] American Board of Forensic Odontology, op. cit.

[132] I.A. Pretty. 2003. A Web-based survey of odontologists' opinions concerning bite mark analyses. *Journal of Forensic Sciences* 48(5):1-4.

[133] C.M. Bowers. 2006. Problem-based analysis of bite mark misidentifications: The role of DNA. *Forensic Science International* 159 Supplement 1:s104-s109.

[134] I.A. Pretty and D. Sweet. 2001. The scientific basis for human bitemark analyses—A critical review. *Science and Justice* 41(2):85-92. Quotation taken from the abstract.

BLOODSTAIN PATTERN ANALYSIS

Understanding how a particular bloodstain pattern occurred can be critical physical evidence, because it may help investigators understand the events of the crime. Bloodstain patterns occur in a multitude of crime types—homicide, sexual battery, burglary, hit-and-run accidents—and are commonly present. Bloodstain pattern analysis is employed in crime reconstruction or event reconstruction when a part of the crime scene requires interpretation of these patterns.

However, many sources of variability arise with the production of bloodstain patterns, and their interpretation is not nearly as straightforward as the process implies. Interpreting and integrating bloodstain patterns into a reconstruction requires, at a minimum:

- an appropriate scientific education;
- knowledge of the terminology employed (e.g., angle of impact, arterial spurting, back spatter, castoff pattern);
- an understanding of the limitations of the measurement tools used to make bloodstain pattern measurements (e.g., calculators, software, lasers, protractors);
- an understanding of applied mathematics and the use of significant figures;
- an understanding of the physics of fluid transfer;
- an understanding of pathology of wounds; and
- an understanding of the general patterns blood makes after leaving the human body.

Sample Data and Collection

Dried blood may be found at crime scenes, deposited either through pooling or via airborne transfer (spatter). The patterns left by blood can suggest the kind of injury that was sustained, the final movements of a victim, the angle of a shooting, and more. Bloodstains on artifacts such as clothing and weapons may be crucial to understanding how the blood was deposited, which can indicate the source of the blood. For example, a stain on a garment, such as a shirt, might indicate contact between the person who wore the shirt and a bloody object, while tiny droplets of blood might suggest proximity to a violent event, such as a beating.

Analyses

Bloodstain patterns found at scenes can be complex, because although overlapping patterns may appear simple, in many cases their interpretations are difficult or impossible. [135,136] Workshops teach the fundamentals of basic pattern formation and are not a substitute for experience and experimentation when applying knowledge to crime reconstruction.[137] Such workshops are more aptly applicable for the investigator who needs to recognize the importance of these patterns so that he or she may enlist the services of a qualified expert. These courses also are helpful for attorneys who encounter these patterns in the course of preparing a case or when preparing to present testimony in court.

Although there is a professional society of bloodstain pattern analysts, the two organizations that have or recommend qualifications are the IAI and the Scientific Working Group on Bloodstain Pattern Analysis (SWGSTAIN). SWGSTAIN's suggested requirements for practicing bloodstain pattern analysis are outwardly impressive, as are IAI's 240 hours of course instruction. But the IAI has no educational requirements for certification in bloodstain pattern analysis.[138] This emphasis on experience over scientific foundations seems misguided, given the importance of rigorous and objective hypothesis testing and the complex nature of fluid dynamics. In general, the opinions of bloodstain pattern analysts are more subjective than scientific. In addition, many bloodstain pattern analysis cases are prosecution driven or defense driven, with targeted requests that can lead to context bias.

Summary Assessment

Scientific studies support some aspects of bloodstain pattern analysis. One can tell, for example, if the blood spattered quickly or slowly, but some experts extrapolate far beyond what can be supported. Although the trajectories of bullets are linear, the damage that they cause in soft tissue and the complex patterns that fluids make when exiting wounds are highly variable. For such situations, many experiments must be conducted to determine what characteristics of a bloodstain pattern are caused by particular actions during a crime and to inform the interpretation of those causal links and

---

[135] H.L. MacDonell. 1997. Bloodstain Patterns. Corning, NY: Laboratory of Forensic Science; S. James. 1998. *Scientific and Legal Applications of Bloodstain Pattern Interpretation.* Boca Raton, FL: CRC Press; P. Pizzola, S. Roth, and P. DeForest. 1986. Blood drop dynamics–II. *Journal of Forensic Sciences* 31(1): 36-49.

[136] Ibid.; R.M. Gardner. 2004. *Practical Crime Scene Processing and Investigation.* Boca Raton, FL: CRC Press; H.C. Lee; T. Palmbach and M.T. Miller. 2005. *Henry Lee's Crime Scene Handbook.* Burlington, MA: Elsevier Academic Press, pp. 281-298.

[137] W.J. Chisum and B.E. Turvey. 2007. *Crime Reconstruction.* Burlington, MA: Elsevier Academic Press.

[138] See "Bloodstain Pattern Examiner Certification Requirements." Available at theiai.org/certifications/bloodstain/requirements.php.

their variabilities. For these same reasons, extra care must be given to the way in which the analyses are presented in court. The uncertainties associated with bloodstain pattern analysis are enormous.

AN EMERGING FORENSIC SCIENCE DISCIPLINE: DIGITAL AND MULTIMEDIA ANALYSIS

The analysis of digital evidence deals with gathering, processing, and interpreting digital evidence, such as electronic documents, lists of phone numbers and call logs, records of a device's location at a given time, e-mails, photographs, and more. In addition to traditional desktop and laptop computers, digital devices that store data of possible value in criminal investigations include cell phones, GPS devices, digital cameras, personal digital assistants (PDAs), large servers and storage devices (e.g., RAIDS and SANS), video game consoles (e.g., PlayStation and Xbox), and portable media players (e.g., iPods). The storage media associated with these devices currently fall into three broad categories. The first, magnetic memory, includes hard drives, floppy discs, and tapes. The second, optical memory, includes compact discs (CDs), and digital versatile discs (DVDs). The third, electrical storage, includes USB flash drives, some memory cards, and some microchips. These items are the most commonly encountered in criminal and counterintelligence matters, but laboratories have been asked to examine such items as scuba dive watches in death investigations and black boxes in aircraft mishaps.

The proliferation of computers and related devices over the past 30 years has led to significant changes in and the expansion of the types of criminal activities that generate digital evidence. Initially, computers were either the weapon or the object of the crime. In the early days, most computer crime involved manipulating computer programs of large businesses in order to steal money or other resources. As computers became more popular, they became storage containers for evidence. Drug dealers, book makers, and white collar criminals began to keep computerized spreadsheets detailing their transactions. Digital cameras and the Internet have made child pornography increasingly available, and computers act as a digital file cabinet to hold this contraband material. Finally, digital media have become witnesses to daily activities. Many individuals have two cell phones with text messaging and/or e-mail capability, several computers, a home alarm system, a GPS in the car, and more; even children often possess some subset of these items. Workplaces use magnetic card readers to permit access to buildings. Most communication involves some kind of computer, and by the end of each day, hundreds of megabytes of data may have been generated about where individuals have been, how fast they got there, to whom they spoke, and even what was said. Suicide notes are written on computers. Sexual predators stalk their victims online via e-mail, chat, and instant messaging. Even get-away cars are equipped with GPS devices. Finally, computer systems have become (with ever-increasing frequency) the victims of unauthorized control or intrusions. These intrusions often result in the manipulation of files and the exfiltration of sensitive information. In addition, computers in automobiles that track speed, breaking, and turning are valuable in accident reconstruction. As a result, almost every crime could have digital evidence associated with it.

Sample Data and Collection

The best practices for the collection of digital evidence most often call for the person at the scene to disconnect the power cord for the computer and related peripheral equipments (e.g., monitor, printer) and seize these items, as well as any loose storage media such as thumb drives and CDs. This method works well in most cases. However, some data (like recently typed passwords, malicious programs, and active communication programs) are volatile and are stored in the electronic chips of the system. In these circumstances, this information is lost when the device is turned off. In intrusion investigations or in cases in which encryption software is being used, this volatile information could be the key to a successful analysis and prosecution.[139]

Recognizing potential sources of digital evidence is also an ongoing challenge. Investigators are likely to seize a desktop computer but walk past a PlayStation. Thumb drives can be fashioned to look like a pocket knife, writing pen, or even a piece of sushi. Cell phones and wireless Internet capability present another challenge: If these devices are turned on while in law enforcement custody, they could be remotely accessed and altered by a suspect.

Analyses

The typical approach to examining a computer involves two main phases. The first is the imaging phase. During this process, the storage device (most often a hard drive) is fitted with an appliance that prevents any new information from being written. Then, all of the data are copied to a new blank hard drive. The copy is compared with the original, most often by using a mathematical algorithm called Message Digest–5, otherwise known as MD5 Hash. The MD5 Hash value gives a unique series of numbers and letters for every file. In the examination phase, this forensi-

[139] See W.G. Kruse and J.G. Heiser. 2001. *Computer Forensics: Incident Response Essentials*. Boston: Addison-Wesley.

cally sound copy is examined for saved computer files with probative value. These so-called logical files often are pictures, documents, spreadsheets, and e-mail files that have been saved by the user in various folders or directories. Logical files are patent evidence. Next, the forensic copy is examined for files that have previously been deleted. The computer files are sometimes called physical, because the data are physically present on the hard drive but they are not logically available to the computer operating system. Such files constitute latent evidence.

Finally, system files that are created and saved by the operating system are examined. These files are analogous to a surveillance tape that shows programs that were running on the computer and files that were changed. The goal of most of these examinations is to find files with probative information and to discover information about when and how these files came to be on the computer.[140]

Digital evidence has undergone a rapid maturation process. This discipline did not start in forensic laboratories. Instead, computers taken as evidence were studied by police officers and detectives who had some interest or expertise in computers. Over the past 10 years, this process has become more routine and subject to the rigors and expectations of other fields of forensic science. Three holdover challenges remain: (1) the digital evidence community does not have an agreed certification program or list of qualifications for digital forensic examiners; (2) some agencies still treat the examination of digital evidence as an investigative rather than a forensic activity; and (3) there is wide variability in and uncertainty about the education, experience, and training of those practicing this discipline.

A publication of the Department of Justice Computer Crime and Intellectual Property Section, *Searching and Seizing Computers and Obtaining Electronic Evidence in Criminal Investigations*,[141] describes the challenging legal issues surrounding the examination of digital evidence. For example, sometimes the courts have viewed computers as a piece of evidence that is sent to a laboratory for forensic examination, and as having no special legal constraints, while other times, the courts have viewed computers as a virtual room or filing cabinet.[142] For the latter cases, a warrant must be

---

[140] See E. Casey. 2004. *Digital Evidence and Computer Crime*. San Diego, CA: Academic Press; E. Casey. 2001. *Handbook of Computer Crime Investigation: Forensic Tools & Technology*. San Diego, CA: Academic Press; B. Carrier. 2005. *File System Forensic Analysis*. Boston: Addison-Wesley; S. Anson and S. Bunting. 2007. *Mastering Windows Network Forensics and Investigation*. Indianapolis: Sybex; and H. Carvey and D. Kleiman. 2007. *Windows Forensic Analysis*. Burlington: Syngress.

[141] Available at www.usdoj.gov/criminal/cybercrime/s&smanual2002.htm.

[142] See, e.g., G.R. McLain, Jr., 2007. *United States v. Hill*: A new rule, but no clarity for the rules governing computer searches and seizures. *George Mason Law Review* 14(4):1071-1104; D. Regensburger, B. Bytes, and B. Bonds. 2007. An exploration of the law concerning

obtained that specifies how the examination will be conducted and which files can be recovered before the electronic device can be examined.

Finally, the analysis of digital evidence differs from other forensic science disciplines because the examination generates not only a forensic report, but also brings to light documents, spreadsheets, and pictures that may have probative value. Different agencies have handled these generated files in different ways: Some treat them as exhibits, while others treat them as derivative evidence that requires a chain of custody and special protection.

A growing number of colleges and universities offer courses in computer security and computer forensics. Still, most law enforcement agencies are understaffed in trained computer security experts.

CONCLUSIONS

The term "forensic science" encompasses a broad range of disciplines, each with its own set of technologies and practices. Wide variability exists across forensic science disciplines with regard to techniques, methodologies, reliability, error rates, reporting, underlying research, general acceptability, and the educational background of its practitioners. Some of the forensic science disciplines are laboratory based (e.g., nuclear and mitochondrial DNA analysis, toxicology, and drug analysis); others are based on expert interpretation of observed patterns (e.g., fingerprints, writing samples, toolmarks, bite marks, and specimens such as fibers, hair, and fire debris). Some methods result in class evidence and some in the identification of a specific individual—with the associated uncertainties. The level of scientific development and evaluation varies substantially among the forensic science disciplines.

---

the search and seizure of computer files and an analysis of the Ninth Circuit's decision in *United States v. Comprehensive Drug Testing, Inc. Journal of Criminal Law and Criminology* 97(4)1151-1208.

6

Improving Methods, Practice, and Performance in Forensic Science

In a presentation to the committee, Jennifer Mnookin, of the University of California, Los Angeles School of Law, cautioned against yielding to two extremes in developing expectations for the forensic science disciplines. The first is the risk of letting the "perfect" be the enemy of the "good." That is, many forms of forensic investigation and analysis may work relatively well once appropriate tasks have been set for them. "The opposite danger is the risk of overconfidence about what we think we know—the risk of making unjustified inferences on the basis of limited information, or sometimes a resistance to gaining new information that would help us do it better."[1]

Nonetheless, a number of the forensic science disciplines, as they are currently practiced, do not contribute as much to criminal justice as they could. This chapter discusses the improvements that are needed and makes four major recommendations. It does not evaluate the quality of evidence collection and management—steps that provide the inputs to forensic methods—although, obviously, the quality of those steps is critical in maximizing the investigative and probative value of that evidence.

INDEPENDENCE OF FORENSIC SCIENCE LABORATORIES

The majority of forensic science laboratories are administered by law enforcement agencies, such as police departments, where the laboratory administrator reports to the head of the agency. This system leads to

[1] J. Mnookin, Professor of Law, University of California, Los Angeles Law School. Presentation to the committee. April 23, 2007.

significant concerns related to the independence of the laboratory and its budget. Ideally, public forensic science laboratories should be independent of or autonomous within law enforcement agencies. In these contexts, the director would have an equal voice with others in the justice system on matters involving the laboratory and other agencies. The laboratory also would be able to set its own priorities with respect to cases, expenditures, and other important issues. Cultural pressures caused by the different missions of scientific laboratories vis-à-vis law enforcement agencies would be largely resolved. Finally, the forensic science laboratories would be able to set their own budget priorities and not have to compete with the parent law enforcement agencies.

UNCERTAINTIES AND BIAS

Few forensic science methods have developed adequate measures of the accuracy of inferences made by forensic scientists. All results for every forensic science method should indicate the uncertainty in the measurements that are made, and studies must be conducted that enable the estimation of those values. For the identification sciences (e.g., friction ridge analysis, toolmark analysis, handwriting analysis), such studies would accumulate data about the intraindividual variability (e.g., how much one finger's impressions vary from impression to impression, or how much one toolmark or signature varies from instance to instance) and the interindividual variability (e.g., how much the impressions of many fingerprints vary across a population and in what ways). With that information, one could begin to attach confidence limits to individualization determinations and also begin to develop an understanding of how much similarity is needed in order to attain a given level of confidence that a match exists. Note that this necessary step would change the way the word "individualization" is commonly used. The concept of individualization is that an object found at a crime scene can be uniquely associated with one particular source. By acknowledging that there can be uncertainties in this process, the concept of "uniquely associated with" must be replaced with a probabilistic association, and other sources of the crime scene evidence cannot be completely discounted. The courts already have proven their ability to deal with some degree of uncertainty in individualizations, as demonstrated by the successful use of DNA analysis (with its small, but nonzero, error rate).

Finally, as discussed in Chapter 4, the accuracy of forensic methods resulting in classification or individualization conclusions needs to be evaluated in well-designed and rigorously conducted studies. The level of accuracy of an analysis is likely to be a key determinant of its ultimate probative value.

Some initial and striking research has uncovered the effects of some biases in forensic science procedures,[2] but much more must be done to understand the sources of bias and to develop countermeasures.[3] Some principles employed in other fields should be useful, although some (e.g., blinding) may not be feasible for some types of forensics work. The forensic science disciplines are just beginning to become aware of contextual bias and the dangers it poses. The traps created by such biases can be very subtle, and typically one is not aware that his or her judgment is being affected. An overview of the effect of bias in the forensic science disciplines can be found in Risinger et al., 2002.[4] Decisions regarding what analyses need to be performed and in what order also can be influenced by bias and ultimately have the potential to skew results.

Forensic scientists who sit administratively in law enforcement agencies or prosecutors' offices, or who are hired by those units, are subject to a general risk of bias. Bias also is introduced through decisions made about evidence collection, which controls who is listed as a suspect. Evidence collection and crime scene investigation can require scientific knowledge and judgment, and these functions are normally outside the control of forensic scientists.

REPORTING RESULTS

There is a critical need in most fields of forensic science to raise the standards for reporting and testifying about the results of investigations. For example, many terms are used by forensic examiners in reports and in court testimony to describe findings, conclusions, and the degrees of association between evidentiary material (e.g., hairs, fingerprints, fibers) and particular people or objects. Such terms include but are not limited to "match," "consistent with," "identical," "similar in all respects tested," and "cannot be excluded as the source of." The use of such terms can have a profound effect on how the trier of fact in a criminal or civil matter perceives and evaluates evidence. Yet the forensic science disciplines have not reached agreement or consensus on the precise meaning of any of these

---

[2] E.g., I.E. Dror and D. Charlton. 2006. Why experts make errors. *Journal of Forensic Identification* 56 (4):600-616; I.E. Dror, D. Charlton, and A Peron. 2006. Contextual information renders experts vulnerable to making erroneous identifications. *Forensic Science International* 156(1):74-78; D.E. Krane, S. Ford, J.R. Gilder, K. Inman, A. Jamieson, R. Koppl, I.L. Kornfield, D.M. Risinger, N. Rudin, M.S. Taylor, and W.C Thompson. 2008. Sequential unmasking: A means of minimizing observer effects in forensic DNA interpretation. *Journal of Forensic Sciences* 53(4):1006-1007; L.S. Miller. 1987. Procedural bias in forensic science examinations of human hairs. *Law and Human Behavior* 11(2):157-163.

[3] See the discussion of biases provided in Chapter 4.

[4] D.M. Risinger, M.J. Saks, W.C. Thompson, and R. Rosenthal. 2002. The *Daubert/Kumho* implications of observer effects in forensic science: Hidden problems of expectation and suggestion. *California Law Review* 90:1-56; Krane, et al., op. cit.

terms. Although some disciplines have developed vocabulary and scales to be used in reporting results, they have not become standard practice. This imprecision in vocabulary stems in part from the paucity of research in forensic science and the corresponding limitations in interpreting the results of forensic analyses. Publications such as Evett et al.,[5] Aitken and Taroni,[6] and Evett[7] provide the essential building blocks for the proper assessment and communication of forensic findings.

As a general matter, laboratory reports generated as the result of a scientific analysis should be complete and thorough. They should describe, at a minimum, methods and materials, procedures, results, and conclusions, and they should identify, as appropriate, the sources of uncertainty in the procedures and conclusions along with estimates of their scale (to indicate the level of confidence in the results). Although it is not appropriate and practicable to provide as much detail as might be expected in a research paper, sufficient content should be provided to allow the nonscientist reader to understand what has been done and permit informed, unbiased scrutiny of the conclusion.

Some forensic laboratory reports meet this standard of reporting, but most do not. Some reports contain only identifying and agency information, a brief description of the evidence being submitted, a brief description of the types of analysis requested, and a short statement of the results (e.g., "The green, brown plant material in item #1 was identified as marijuana"). The norm is to have no description of the methods or procedures used, and most reports do not discuss measurement uncertainties or confidence limits. Many disciplines outside the forensic science disciplines have standards, templates, and protocols for data reporting. Although some of the Scientific Working Groups have a scoring system for reporting findings, they are not uniformly or consistently used.

Forensic science reports, and any courtroom testimony stemming from them, must include clear characterizations of the limitations of the analyses, including associated probabilities where possible. Courtroom testimony should be given in lay terms so that all trial participants can understand how to weight and interpret the testimony. In order to enable this, research must be undertaken to evaluate the reliability of the steps of the various identification methods and the confidence intervals associated with the overall conclusions.

[5] I.W. Evett, G. Jackson, J.A. Lambert, and S. McCrossan. 2000. The impact of the principles of evidence interpretation on the structure and content of statements. *Science and Justice* 40(4):233-239.

[6] C.G.G. Aitken and F. Taroni. 2004. *Statistics and the Evaluation of Evidence for Forensic Scientists*. 2nd ed. V. Barnett, ed. Chichester, UK: John Wiley & Sons Ltd.

[7] I.W. Evett. 1990. The theory of interpreting scientific transfer evidence. *Forensic Science Progress* 4:141-179.

THE NEED FOR RESEARCH

Barry Fisher, Director of the Crime Laboratory of the Los Angeles County Sheriff's Department, has said, "We run the risk of our science being questioned in the courts because there is so little research."[8] In 2001 Giannelli wrote, "In many areas [of forensic science] little systematic research has been conducted to validate the field's basic premises and techniques, and often there is no justification why such research would not be feasible."[9] As Smith et al. note, the United States has a renowned higher education system, and many basic research discoveries relating to the forensic science disciplines have been made in academia.[10] However, the forensic science disciplines suffer from an inadequate research base: Few forensic scientists have the opportunity to conduct research, few academics are positioned to undertake such research, and, importantly, the funding for forensic research is insufficient. Others believe that the field suffers because the research initiatives being funded and pursued lack an overarching strategic plan.[11]

There are several explanations for the relative lack of funding for basic and applied research in the forensic science disciplines. First, forensic practice was started in, and has grown out of, the criminal justice and law enforcement systems. Many forensic science techniques were developed to aid in the investigatory phase of law enforcement and then were adapted to the role of aiding in prosecution by providing courtroom testimony. Thus, forensic practitioners who work in public crime laboratories often are seen as part of the prosecution team, not as part of the scientific enterprise. Second, some of the forensic science disciplines rely on an apprenticeship model for training, rather than on codifying their methods in a scientific framework. Third, federal agencies that fund scientific work, such as the National Science Foundation, the National Institutes of Health, and the Department of Defense, generally have not considered forensic science as part of the science base they need to support. It has been only in recent years that the National Institute of Justice has taken interest in funding forensic science research, but the majority of these funds have been awarded to reduce case backlogs, especially for cases that involve the analysis of DNA (see Chapter 2).

---

[8] K. Pyrek. 2007. *Forensic Science Under Siege: The Challenges of Forensic Laboratories and the Medico-Legal Investigation System.* Burlington, MA: Academic Press, p. 231.

[9] P.C. Giannelli. 2001. Scientific evidence in civil and criminal cases. *Arizona State Law Journal* 103:112.

[10] F.P. Smith, R.H. Liu, and C.A. Lindquist. 1988. Research experience and future criminalists. *Journal of Forensic Sciences* 33(4):1074-1080.

[11] IAI Positions and Recommendations to the NAS Committee to Review the Forensic Sciences. September 19, 2007. See presentation by K.F. Martin, IAI President, to the committee. December 6, 2007.

The forensic science disciplines need to develop rigorous protocols for performing subjective interpretations, and they must pursue equally rigorous research and evaluation programs. The development of such research programs can benefit significantly from work in other areas, notably from the large body of research that is available on the evaluation of observer performance in diagnostic medicine and from the findings of cognitive psychology on the potential for bias and error in human observers.

In evaluating the accuracy of a forensic analysis, it is crucial to clarify the type of question the analysis is called upon to address. Thus, although some techniques may be too imprecise to permit the accurate identification of a specific individual, they may still provide useful and accurate information about questions of classification. For example, microscopic hair analysis may provide reliable evidence on the subpopulation of the individual from which the specimen was derived, even if it cannot associate reliably the hair with a specific individual. However, the definition of the appropriate question is only a first step in evaluating the performance of a forensic technique. The research design should address the questions that arise in the specific context of forensics.

A complete research agenda should include studies to establish the strengths and limitations of each procedure, sources of bias and variation, quantification of uncertainties created by these sources, measures of performance, procedural steps in the process of analyzing the forensic evidence, and methods for continual monitoring and improving the steps in that process.

CONCLUSIONS AND RECOMMENDATIONS

Wide variability is found across forensic science disciplines not only with regard to techniques and methodologies (see Chapter 5), but also with regard to reliability, error rates, reporting, research foundations, general acceptability, and published material. Some of the disciplines are laboratory based (e.g., nuclear and mitochondrial DNA analysis, toxicology and drug analysis, and analyses of fibers and fire debris); others are based on expert interpretation of observed patterns (e.g., of fingerprints, writing samples, toolmarks, bite marks, and hairs). The briefings and materials that informed this report illustrate that the level of scientific development and evaluation varies substantially among the forensic science disciplines.

In most areas of forensic science, no well-defined system exists for determining error rates, and proficiency testing shows that some examiners perform poorly. In some disciplines, such as forensic odontology, the methods of evidence collection are relatively noncontroversial, but disputes arise over the value and reliability of the resulting interpretations.

In most forensic science disciplines, no studies have been conducted of large populations to establish the uniqueness of marks or features. Yet, despite the lack of a statistical foundation, examiners make probabilistic claims based on their experience. A statistical framework that allows quantification of these claims is greatly needed. These disciplines also critically need to standardize and clarify the terminology used in reporting and testifying about the results and in providing more information.

Little rigorous systematic research has been done to validate the basic premises and techniques in a number of forensic science disciplines. The committee sees no evident reason why conducting such research is not feasible; in fact, some researchers have proposed research agendas to strengthen the foundations of specific forensic disciplines.[12] Much more federal funding is needed to support research in forensic science and forensic pathology in universities and in private laboratories committed to such work. The forensic science and medical examiner communities (see Chapter 9) will be improved by opportunities to collaborate with the broader science and engineering communities. In particular, collaborative efforts are urgently needed to: (1) develop new technical methods or provide in-depth grounding for advances developed in forensic science; (2) provide an interface between the forensic science and medical examiner communities and basic sciences; and (3) create fertile grounds for discourse among the communities. The proposed National Institute of Forensic Science (NIFS) should recommend, implement, and guide strategies for supporting such initiatives.

Although a long-term research agenda will require a thorough assessment of each of the assumptions that underlie forensic science techniques, many concerns regarding the forensic science disciplines can be addressed immediately through studies in which forensic science practitioners are presented with a standardized set of realistic training materials that vary in complexity. Such studies will not explore the components of the decision process, but they will permit an assessment of the extent to which skilled forensic science practitioners will reach the same or similar conclusions when presented with the types of materials that lead to disagreements.

Recommendation 2:

> **The National Institute of Forensic Science (NIFS), after reviewing established standards such as ISO 17025, and in consultation with its advisory board, should establish standard terminology to be used in reporting on and testifying about the results of forensic science investigations. Similarly, it should establish model laboratory reports for different forensic science disciplines and specify**

[12] See, e.g., L. Haber and R.N. Haber. 2008. Scientific validation of fingerprint evidence under *Daubert*. *Law, Probability and Risk* 7(2):87-109.

the minimum information that should be included. As part of the accreditation and certification processes, laboratories and forensic scientists should be required to utilize model laboratory reports when summarizing the results of their analyses.

Recommendation 3:

Research is needed to address issues of accuracy, reliability, and validity in the forensic science disciplines. The National Institute of Forensic Science (NIFS) should competitively fund peer-reviewed research in the following areas:

(a) **Studies establishing the scientific bases demonstrating the validity of forensic methods.**
(b) **The development and establishment of quantifiable measures of the reliability and accuracy of forensic analyses. Studies of the reliability and accuracy of forensic techniques should reflect actual practice on realisticcase scenarios, averaged across a representative sample of forensic scientists and laboratories. Studies also should establish the limits of reliability and accuracy that analytic methods can be expected to achieve as the conditions of forensic evidence vary. The research by which measures of reliability and accuracy are determined should be peer reviewed and published in respected scientific journals.**
(c) **The development of quantifiable measures of uncertainty in the conclusions of forensic analyses.**
(d) **Automated techniques capable of enhancing forensic technologies.**

To answer questions regarding the reliability and accuracy of a forensic analysis, the research must distinguish between average performance (achieved across individual practitioners and laboratories) and individual performance (achieved by the specific practitioner and laboratory). Whether or not a forensic procedure is sufficient under the rules of evidence governing criminal and civil litigation raises difficult legal issues that are outside the realm of scientific inquiry.

Recommendation 4:

To improve the scientific bases of forensic science examinations and to maximize independence from or autonomy within the law enforcement community, Congress should authorize and appropri-

ate incentive funds to the National Institute of Forensic Science (NIFS) for allocation to state and local jurisdictions for the purpose of removing all public forensic laboratories and facilities from the administrative control of law enforcement agencies or prosecutors' offices.

Recommendation 5:

The National Institute of Forensic Science (NIFS) should encourage research programs on human observer bias and sources of human error in forensic examinations. Such programs might include studies to determine the effects of contextual bias in forensic practice (e.g., studies to determine whether and to what extent the results of forensic analyses are influenced by knowledge regarding the background of the suspect and the investigator's theory of the case). In addition, research on sources of human error should be closely linked with research conducted to quantify and characterize the amount of error. Based on the results of these studies, and in consultation with its advisory board, NIFS should develop standard operating procedures (that will lay the foundation for model protocols) to minimize, to the greatest extent reasonably possible, potential bias and sources of human error in forensic practice. These standard operating procedures should apply to all forensic analyses that may be used in litigation.

7

Strengthening Oversight of Forensic Science Practice

Several commentators appearing before the committee noted that nearly anyone with a garage and some capital theoretically could open a forensics laboratory and start offering services. Although this might be a bit hyperbolic, the fact is that there are no requirements, except in a few states (New York, Oklahoma, and Texas), for forensics laboratories to meet specific standards for quality assurance or for practitioners to be certified according to an agreed set of standards.[1] Well-publicized problems in large crime laboratories have uncovered systematic deficiencies in quality control. For example, in 2002, the Houston Police Department Crime Laboratory and Property Room came under scrutiny because of a range of quality concerns that created "profound doubts about the integrity of important aspects of the criminal justice system in Harris County."[2] Problems included poor documentation, serious analytical and interpretive errors, the absence of quality assurance programs, inadequately trained personnel, erroneous reporting, the use of inaccurate and misleading statistics, and even "drylabbing" (the falsification of scientific results).[3] In most cases, existing efforts

[1] See N.Y. Exec. § 995-b (McKinney 1996); (accreditation by Forensic Science Commission); Okla. Stat. Ann. tit. 74 § 150.37 (requiring accreditation by the American Society of Crime Laboratory Directors/Laboratory Accreditation Board or the American Board of Forensic Toxicology); Tex. Crim. Proc. Code art. 38.35 (accreditation by the Department of Public Safety).

[2] M.R. Bromwich. 2007. *Final Report of the Independent Investigator for the Houston Police Department Crime Laboratory and Property Room.* June 13. Available at www.hpdlabinvestigation.org, p. 1.

[3] Ibid.

to impose standards and best practices in forensic science practice rely on the voluntary participation of some members of the forensic science community working diligently to improve overall quality in the field.

Despite important movement in recent years toward developing and implementing quality control measures in the forensic science disciplines, a lack of uniform and mandatory quality assurance procedures, combined with some highly publicized problems involving large crime laboratories, has led to heightened attention to efforts to remedy uneven quality among laboratories through the imposition of standards and best practices. The American Bar Association has recommended that, "Crime laboratories and medical examiner officers should be accredited, examiners should be certified, and procedures should be standardized and published to ensure the validity, reliability, and timely analysis of forensic evidence."[4]

In *Daubert v. Merrell Dow Pharmaceuticals*,[5] the Supreme Court cited as a relevant factor in assessing expert testimony the "existence and maintenance of standards controlling the technique's operation." Standards and best practices create a professional environment that allows organizations and professions to create quality systems, policies, and procedures and maintain autonomy from vested interest groups. Standards ensure desirable characteristics of services and techniques such as quality, reliability, efficiency, and consistency among practitioners. Typically standards are enforced through systems of accreditation and certification, wherein independent examiners and auditors test and audit the performance, policies, and procedures of both laboratories and service providers. In addition, requirements for quality control can be imposed on entities receiving federal funds, and professional groups can develop codes of ethics and conduct to serve as measures against which performance can be assessed.

This chapter addresses some of the traditional approaches used by technical professions to enhance the quality of performance—accreditation, certification (including proficiency testing), and oversight—tied to federal funding. In each approach, standards are used to measure the quality of institutions or organizations, either in terms of their policies and procedures or in terms of the proficiency and skills of an individual practicing the discipline. However, as mentioned above, with the exception of three states mandating accreditation (New York, Oklahoma, and Texas), the accreditation of laboratories and certification of forensic examiners remains voluntary.

---

[4] American Bar Association. 2006. *Report of the ABA Criminal Justice Section's Ad Hoc Innocence Committee to Ensure the Integrity of the Criminal Process. Achieving Justice: Freeing the Innocent, Convicting the Guilty*. P.C. Giannelli and M. Raeder (eds.). Chicago: American Bar Association.

[5] 509 U.S. 579 (1993).

ACCREDITATION

Accreditation is just one aspect of an organization's quality assurance program, which also should include proficiency testing where relevant, continuing education, and other programs to help the organization provide better overall services. In the case of laboratories, accreditation does not mean that accredited laboratories do not make mistakes, nor does it mean that a laboratory utilizes best practices in every case, but rather, it means that the laboratory adheres to an established set of standards of quality and relies on acceptable practices within these requirements. An accredited laboratory has in place a management system that defines the various processes by which it operates on a daily basis, monitors that activity, and responds to deviations from the acceptable practices using a routine and thoughtful method. This cannot be a self-assessing program. Oversight must come from outside the participating laboratory to ensure that standards are not self-serving and superficial and to remove the option of taking shortcuts when other demands compete with quality assurance. In addition, accreditation serves as a mechanism to strengthen professional community ties, transmit best practices, and expose laboratory employees directly to the perspectives and expectations of other leaders in the profession.

An example of a strong accreditation system is that required through the Clinical Laboratory Improvement Amendments of 1988 (CLIA).[6] Through this legislation, the Centers for Medicare & Medicaid Services (CMS) regulates all clinical laboratory testing (except research) performed on humans in the United States. In total, CLIA covers approximately 189,000 laboratory entities (see Box 7-1).

Some key elements of CLIA and of other accreditation programs that might be incorporated into a mandatory accreditation system for forensic science include:

- a national organization that can mediate the accreditation process;
- an application process with criteria by which organizations are eligible to apply;
- a process of self-evaluation;
- an external evaluation process, including site visits by external evaluators;
- an appeals process;
- a repeat cycle of evaluation and external evaluation, and;
- a set of standards by which entities can be evaluated.[7]

---

[6] 42 U.S.C. § 263a.

[7] Institute of Medicine. 2001. *Preserving Public Trust: Accreditation and Human Research Participation Protection Programs.* Washington, DC: National Academy Press.

Box 7-1
Clinical Laboratory Improvement Amendments of 1988 (CLIA)

The objective of the CLIA program is to ensure quality laboratory testing. All clinical laboratories must be properly certified to receive Medicare or Medicaid payments. CLIA requires all entities that perform even one test using "materials derived from the human body for the purpose of providing information for the diagnosis, prevention or treatment of any disease or impairment of, or the assessment of the health of, human beings" to meet certain federal requirements. If an entity performs tests for these purposes, it is considered to be covered by CLIA and must register with the CLIA program.

CMS and CDC develop standards for laboratory certification (it is actually a certificate of accreditation). In addition, CDC conducts studies and convenes conferences to help determine when changes in regulatory requirements are needed. Oversight is conducted through onsite inspections of laboratories conducted every two years using federal surveyors or surveyors of deemed organizations or state-operated CLIA programs approved for this purpose. Oversight includes a comprehensive evaluation of the laboratory's operating environment and personnel, as well as its proficiency testing, quality control, and quality assurance procedures. The laboratory director plays a critical role in assuring the safe and appropriate use of laboratory tests—he or she must meet required qualifications and must ensure that the test methodologies selected are capable of providing the quality of results required for patient care. Laboratory directors are required to take specific actions to establish a comprehensive quality assurance program.

Six organizations are deemed to offer accreditation of laboratories for CLIA. An accreditation organization that applies or reapplies to CMS for deeming authority, or a state licensure program that applies or reapplies to CMS for exemption from CLIA program requirements of licensed or approved laboratories within the state, must provide extensive documentation of its process. This includes a detailed description of the inspection process, a description of the steps taken to monitor the correction of deficiencies, a description of the process for monitoring performance, procedures for responding to and for the investigation of complaints against its laboratories, and a list of all its current laboratories and the expiration dates of their certification.

CLIA also provides for sanctions that may be imposed on laboratories found to be out of compliance with one or more of the conditions of accreditation (e.g., unsuccessful participation in proficiency testing). These include suspension, limitation, or revocation of the certificate; civil suit to enjoin any laboratory activity that constitutes a significant hazard to the public health; and imprisonment or fine for any person convicted of the intentional violation of CLIA requirements. The regulations also require that the Department of Health and Human Services Secretary annually publish a list of all laboratories that have been sanctioned during the preceding year. Sanctions can be appealed.

SOURCE: www.cms.hhs.gov/clia/.

In addition, accrediting organizations typically offer education and training programs to help the participating entities comply with the standards. Accreditation cannot guarantee high quality—that is, it cannot guard against those who intentionally disobey or ignore requirements. However, over time it can reduce the likelihood that violations will occur, and reports of infractions should trigger increased scrutiny by an accrediting body. And, by requiring that education be a standard that must be met as a condition of accreditation, incremental change and quality improvement can be achieved individual by individual.

Development of Current Forensic Laboratory Accrediting Organizations

In the 1970s, FBI Director Clarence Kelley and FBI Laboratory Director Briggs White organized a group of crime laboratory directors that eventually became known as the American Society of Crime Laboratory Directors, or ASCLD. ASCLD's Committee on Laboratory Evaluation and Standards was focused on developing quality assurance standards, and in 1981 the ASCLD/Laboratory Accreditation Board (ASCLD/LAB) was formed. In 1988, it was officially incorporated as a not-for-profit organization.

In 1994, the passage of the DNA Identification Act established a DNA Advisory Board (DAB) to develop and enforce quality assurance standards for crime laboratories seeking access to the FBI's national database of DNA profiles (see below). The DAB recommended that crime laboratories seek accreditation as quickly as possible. According to the *Crime Lab Report*, "Because ASCLD/LAB policies and procedures would not allow accreditation to be awarded to a single work unit, laboratories that were not prepared to undergo a full ASCLD/LAB accreditation assessment seemed to have no other alternative but to forfeit access to the DNA database until they were ready for a full accreditation audit."[8]

In 1995, the private not-for-profit corporation National Forensic Science Technology Center (*NFSTC*) was formed by the ASCLD executive board for training, education, and support of accreditation.[9] *NFSTC* could support and assist crime laboratories preparing for a full *ASCLD/LAB accreditation as well as* audit and temporarily certify DNA units that complied with DNA-specific quality assurance standards.[10,11] NFSTC subsequently formed a new independent accreditation corporation, Forensic Quality Services (*FQS), with the idea that its program* would be based on

---

[8] *Crime Lab Report*. December 20, 2007. Available at www.crimelabreport.com/monthly_report/12-2007.htm.

[9] See http://nfstc.org/aboutus/history/history.htm.

[10] Ibid.

[11] DNA procedures are regulated under the DNA Identification Act of 1994. DNA Identification Act of 1994, 42 U.S.C. § 14132 (1994).

the new ISO/IEC 17025 international standard for testing and calibration laboratories.[12]

In 2003, the ASCLD/LAB Delegate Assembly approved the implementation of an ISO/IEC 17025 program, and ASCLD/LAB began offering these accreditations in April 2004. Accreditations for forensic science laboratories are now conducted using *General requirements for the competence of testing and calibration laboratories 17025 ISO/IEC* (2005),[13] the same requirements under which private and public laboratories are accredited. The international standards are developed through technical committees to deal with particular fields of technical activity. In order for sector specific requirements for forensic laboratories to be addressed, ISO allows for the amplification of requirements or supplemental requirements, such as *ASCLD/LAB-International Supplemental requirements for the accreditation of forensic science testing laboratories* (2006).

ASCLD/LAB's areas of focus are laboratory management and operations, personnel qualifications, and the physical plant. The following must be in place for accreditation:

- procedures to protect evidence from loss, cross-transfer, contamination, and/or deleterious change;
- validated and documented technical procedures;
- the use of appropriate controls and standards;
- calibration procedures;
- complete documentation of all evidence examination;
- documented training programs that include competency testing;
- technical review of a portion of each examiner's work product;
- testimony monitoring of all who testify; and
- a comprehensive proficiency testing program.[14]

The ASCLD/LAB accreditation cycle is five years, with annual reports required from each accredited laboratory that consist of any changes in management, staff, facilities, methodologies, proficiency testing, and testimony monitoring. All accredited laboratories must maintain written copies of appropriate technical procedures, including descriptions of sample preparation methods, controls, standards, and calibration procedures, as well as a discussion of precautions, sources of possible error, and literature references. In addition, ASCLD/LAB has a policy regarding the reporting of noncompliance with requirements, a portion of which is excerpted below:

---

[12] See www.forquality.org.

[13] See www.iso.org/iso/catalogue_detail?csnumber=39883.

[14] R. Stacey, President, ASCLD/LAB. Presentation to the committee. January 25, 2007.

> In keeping with the stated objective of 'identifying those laboratories which meet established standards,' the ASCLD/LAB Board has determined that, as an accrediting body, we must be timelier in reviewing instances of significant non-compliance. To further this objective, all accredited laboratories must disclose to ASCLD/LAB all substantive occurrences of non-compliance within 30 calendar days of determining that the non-compliance has occurred.[15]

In addition to this particular requirement, the ISO program has a requirement for an annual surveillance visit. During this site visit, any issues that may have come to the attention of ASCLD/LAB and/or requirements selected by ASCLD/LAB are reviewed. The accreditation programs are managed by a paid staff member working under the direction of a board of directors, which is elected by the Delegate Assembly. The Delegate Assembly is composed of the directors of all accredited laboratories and laboratory systems. Inspectors must complete a training program and must be employed in an accredited laboratory. At any time, if an issue is brought to the attention of ASCLD/LAB, the board of directors can, after determining that the claim is substantive, implement an interim inspection of that particular issue and the entire laboratory. The program also includes a system of sanctions and an appeal process.

Status of Accreditation

ASCLD/LAB's international program has accredited 60 laboratories as of April 2008, in addition to 337 laboratories accredited under the original Legacy program.[16] FQS-International (FQS-I) has accredited just over 50 laboratories in one or more disciplines; however, FQS-I allows forensic laboratories to customize their accreditation by phasing in one discipline at a time.[17] A survey of International Association for Identification (IAI) members, who tend to work in settings other than traditional crime laboratories, revealed that only 15 percent of respondents are accredited.[18]

Only a few jurisdictions require that their forensics laboratories be accredited. According to the 2005 census of 351 publicly funded crime laboratories, more than three-quarters of laboratories (78 percent) were

---

[15] 2008 version of the ASCLD/LAB Legacy Accreditation Manual.

[16] See www.ascld-lab.org/legacy/aslablegacylaboratories.html.

[17] See www.forquality.org/fqs_I_Labs.htm.

[18] T.S. Witt. Director, Bureau of Business and Economic Research, West Virginia University. Presentation to the committee. December 6, 2007.

accredited by ASCLD/ LAB.[19] Another 3 percent were accredited by some other professional organization, such as the ISO. State-operated laboratories (91 percent) were more likely to be accredited than laboratories serving county (67 percent) or municipal (62 percent) jurisdictions. Among the 230 laboratories providing accreditation information in both the 2002[20] and 2005 censuses, the accreditation rate increased during the three years from 75 to 87 percent.

However, identification units—that is, those forensic entities outside crime laboratories—do not participate in accreditation systems and are not required to do so. Given that some disciplines are practiced largely outside the laboratory environment (e.g., 66 percent of fingerprint analyses are not conducted in crime laboratories), there is a substantial gap in the number of programs participating in accreditation.[21,22]

As mentioned previously, DNA analysis is regulated under the DNA Identification Act of 1994, which created an advisory board on quality assurance, tasked with promulgating standards for proficiency testing of laboratories and analysts. The terms of the original advisory board expired, and now the FBI Quality Assurance Standards apply to DNA laboratories receiving federal funds. The standards require periodic (every other year) audits using the FBI Quality Assurance Standards to ensure compliance. The FBI guidelines require that two proficiency tests be completed annually by DNA examiners as well as by technical support personnel performing relevant analytical techniques. The tests must be administered by a source external to the laboratory. The FBI is responsible for developing and maintaining a DNA audit document for assessing compliance with DNA standards and also provides DNA auditor instruction to all ASCLD/LAB inspectors, in addition to the forensic DNA community, on how to interpret the DNA standards. The FBI also reviews audit findings and remedial action, if any. Once all standards are met, it notifies the laboratory of full compliance.

---

[19] M.R. Durose. 2008. *Census of Publicly Funded Forensic Crime Laboratories, 2005*. U.S. Department of Justice, Office of Justice Programs, Bureau of Justice Statistics. Available at www.ojp.usdoj.gov/bjs/pub/pdf/cpffcl05.pdf.

[20] J.L. Peterson and M. J. Hickman. 2005. *Census of Publicly Funded Forensic Crime Laboratories, 2002*. U.S. Department of Justice, Office of Justice Programs, Bureau of Justice Statistics. Available at www.ojp.usdoj.gov/bjs/pub/pdf/cpffcl02.pdf.

[21] Witt, op. cit.

[22] Accreditation is also available for other more specific forensic science disciplines. For example, the National Association of Medical Examiners (NAME) operates an accreditation program for coroners and medical examiners offices (see Chapter 9). The American Board of Forensic Toxicology accredits toxicology laboratories.

STANDARDS AND GUIDELINES FOR QUALITY CONTROL

Standards provide the foundation against which performance, reliability, and validity can be assessed. Adherence to standards reduces bias, improves consistency, and enhances the validity and reliability of results. Standards reduce variability resulting from the idiosyncratic tendencies of the individual examiner—for example, setting conditions under which one can declare a "match" in forensic identifications. They make it possible to replicate and empirically test procedures and help disentangle method errors from practitioner errors. Importantly, standards not only guide practice but also can serve as guideposts in accreditation and certification programs. Many forensic science disciplines have developed standards, but others have not, which contributes to questions about the validity of conclusions.

Several groups produce standards for use in the forensic science disciplines. For example, ASTM International (ASTM), originally known as the American Society for Testing and Materials, is an international standards organization that develops and publishes voluntary technical standards for a wide range of materials, products, systems, and services. In the area of forensic science it offers, for example:

- Standard Guide for Minimum Training Requirements for Forensic Document Examiners
- Standard Guide for Forensic Paint Analysis and Comparison
- Standard Guide for Nondestructive Examination of Paper
- Standard Guide for Forensic Analysis of Fibers by Infrared Spectroscopy
- Standard Terminology for Expressing Conclusions of Forensic Document Examiners

At the federal level, the National Institute of Standards and Technology (NIST) conducts research to establish standards in a limited number of forensic areas, for example, organic gunshot residue analysis, trace explosives detectors, and improvised explosive devices.[23] Its laboratories develop tests, test methods, produce reference data, conduct proof-of-concept implementations, and perform technical analyses. They also develop guides to help forensic organizations formulate appropriate policies and procedures, such as those concerning mobile phone forensic examinations. These guides are not all-inclusive and they do not prescribe how law enforcement and

[23] B. MacCrehan. National Institute of Standards and Technology. Analytical Chemistry Division. Presentation to the committee. September 21, 2007.

incident response communities should handle investigations. Instead, they provide principles for establishing policies and procedures.[24]

In accordance with ISO/IEC 17025, which states that all technical procedures used by a science laboratory should be fully validated before they are used in casework, the European Network of Forensic Science Institutes has developed a guidance document for its member laboratories to use in validating techniques employed in forensic casework.[25]

The FBI initiated the first Scientific Working Groups (SWGs) in the early 1990s to facilitate consensus around forensic science operations among federal, state, and local agencies.[26] Each SWG has a formal structure and functions in accordance with its bylaws. Membership is at the discretion of the chair of the working group. Most SWGs include members from both public and private organizations. Meetings held at least once a year allow SWG members to discuss issues of concern and reach consensus on documents drafted throughout the year. The SWGs create, prepare, and publish standards and guidelines for their constituents in the forensic science community. These documents provide crime laboratories a basis for operational requirements, although the committee found that some standards and guidelines lack the level of specificity needed to ensure consistency. However, enforcement of the guidelines is left to the appropriate governing agency and each group's internal policies. The SWGs generate voluntary guidelines and protocols, which carry no force of law. Nonetheless, the SWGs have been a source of improved standards for the forensic science disciplines and represent the results of a profession that is working to strengthen its professional services with only limited resources.

The FBI Laboratory currently sponsors the following groups:

- Scientific Working Group for Firearms and Toolmarks (SWGGUN)
- Scientific Working Group for Forensic Document Examination (SWGDOC)
- Scientific Working Group for Materials Analysis (SWGMAT)
- Scientific Working Group on Bloodstain Pattern Analysis (SWGSTAIN)
- Scientific Working Group on DNA Analysis Methods (SWGDAM)
- Scientific Working Group on Dog and Orthogonal Detector Guidelines (SWGDOG)
- Scientific Working Group on the Forensic Analysis of Chemical Terrorism (SWGFACT)

---

[24] B. Guttman. National Institute of Standards and Technology National Software Reference Library. Presentation to the committee. September 21, 2007.

[25] European Network of Forensic Science Institutes Standing Committee for Quality and Competence (QCC). 2006. *Validation and Implementation of (New) Methods.*

[26] Federal Bureau of Investigation. 2000. Scientific Working Groups. Available at www.fbi.gov/hq/lab/fsc/backissu/july2000/swgroups.htm.

- Scientific Working Group on the Forensic Analysis of Radiological Materials (SWGFARM)
- Scientific Working Group on Friction Ridge Analysis, Study and Technology (SWGFAST)
- Scientific Working Group on Microbial Genetics and Forensics (SWGMGF)
- Scientific Working Group on Shoeprint and Tire Tread Evidence (SWGTREAD)

Additional SWGs may be sponsored by other FBI divisions or other agencies. For example, the U.S. Drug Enforcement Administration supports the Scientific Working Group for the Analysis of Seized Drugs (SWGDRUG) (see Box 7-2).

Despite the proliferation of standards in many of the forensic science disciplines, their voluntary nature and inconsistent application make it difficult to assess their impact. Ideally, standards should be consistently applicable and measurable. In addition, mechanisms should be in place

Box 7-2
A Sampling of SWGs

SWGDRUG[a]

In 1997, the Drug Enforcement Agency and the Office of National Drug Control Policy created and sponsored a Technical Working Group for the Analysis of Seized Drugs (TWGDRUG), which was renamed a Scientific Working Group (SWGDRUG) in 1999. The stated objectives of SWGDRUG include the specification of requirements for forensic drug practitioners, the promotion of professional development, the exchange of information within the forensic science community, the promotion of ethical standards of practitioners, the provision of minimum standards for drug examinations and reporting, the establishment of quality assurance requirements, the consideration of relevant international standards, and the promotion of international acceptance of SWGDRUG recommendations. Individual subcommittees currently are devoted to evaluating analytical methods, setting standards for quality assurance, estimating uncertainty, formatting draft and final recommendations, and maintaining a glossary. The subcommittee develops recommendations, which the core committee votes to accept or reject. If accepted, draft documents are released for public comment for at least 60 days. Following public comment and possible revision, the core committee holds a final vote. Three-quarters of the core committee must be present, and two-thirds of those present must vote affirmatively in order to confer official status to a proposed recommendation.

Box 7-2 Continued

SWGDRUG has produced guidelines for quality assurance protocols, methods of analysis and identification of seized drugs, and education and training materials for forensic practitioners. Quality assurance guidelines emphasize the integrity and storage of evidence, the validation and documentation of procedures, and the verification of standards. Among SWGDRUG's recommendations for education is a requirement that entry level forensic drug analysts possess at least a bachelor's degree in a natural science, with coursework in general, organic, and analytical chemistry. Guidelines on methods and analyses categorize analytical techniques into three groups, according to discriminating ability: "A" techniques are deemed the most discriminating, and "C" techniques are considered the least discriminating. For the purposes of identifying substances, SWGDRUG recommends the use of at least one "A" technique and one other additional test for validation. When an "A" technique cannot be used, at least two uncorrelated "B" tests and one additional method are suggested. SWGDRUG also has released supplementary documents to assist in implementing these guidelines.

SWGGUN[b]

The FBI established SWGGUN in 1998 and has continued to fund the initiative in subsequent years. Subcommittees of a 20-member board draft guidelines in conjunction with external experts. Guidelines are posted on the SWGGUN Web site for public comment before the board finalizes the recommendations with an affirmative vote by two-thirds of the members present at a meeting.[c] Currently, SWGGUN offers guidelines on trigger pull analysis, education and experience requirements for firearm and toolmark examiners and trainees, laboratory training manuals, laboratory quality assurance programs, the range of possible conclusions when comparing toolmarks, projectile path reconstruction, and the examination of silencers. The SWGGUN website also offers an "admissibility resource kit," which offers arguments intended to satisfy the prongs of the *Daubert* standard.

SWGMAT[d]

Since 1996, SWGMAT has been issuing voluntary guidelines addressing trace evidence, including hair comparison. Quality assurance guidelines, published in 2000, advise that two examiners separately analyze samples and suggest minimum levels for training and qualifications for examiners and laboratories. Hair comparison guidelines, published in 2005, address techniques for collecting hair samples, examining and interpreting protocols for microscopic examination, and using DNA testing in hair analysis. Notably, the use of DNA testing of hair is advised only after an initial microscopic analysis is conducted. In contrast to the larger forensic science community's recent interest in blind testing and statistical verification, SWGMAT proposes the following approach: The examiner should consider what meaning can be attached to an exclusion or association based upon the known case circumstances. Probabilities and population statistics should not be used in the interpretation of microscopic hair comparisons. Databases, from which population statistics can be generated (as is done in DNA analysis), are not practical or realistic for hair analysis.

***SWGFAST*[e]**

In 1995, the FBI created a Technical Working Group on Friction Ridge Analysis, Study, and Technology (TWGFAST). The group was renamed as a Scientific Working Group (SWGFAST) in 1998 and has continued to provide guidelines on fingerprint evidence, with funding from the FBI. Additionally, a National Institute of Justice grant has supported the development of a forthcoming SWGFAST reference manual.

The SWGFAST bylaws allow for up to 40 members and require biannual meetings. Members have included agency employees from federal, state, local, and foreign bodies and from the academic and private sectors. Proposed guidelines are released to the community for comment after receiving an affirmative vote by two-thirds of the SWGFAST members present at a meeting. A draft document is adopted following community review and feedback, if two-thirds of the members present at a meeting again vote in favor of such action. Accepted guidelines are reconsidered five years after adoption. Existing SWGFAST guidelines address automation training, digital imaging, friction ridge analysis for latent print examination, latent print proficiency testing, professional conduct, minimum qualifications and competency for latent print trainees, quality assurance, interpretation and conclusions, and validation research.[f]

Like all other SWG documents, SWGFAST's guidelines have no inherent authority or force of law. However, in collaboration with academic institutions, law enforcement agencies, and industry, SWGFAST has participated in the development of a standard data format for the Interchange of Fingerprint, Facial, & Scar Mark and Tattoo Information, through the American National Standard for Information Systems-NIST (ANSI-NIST-ITL 1-2007). Additionally, crime laboratories have purportedly relied on SWGFAST guidelines in order to meet the ASCLD/LAB accreditation Standards.[g]

---

[a] N. Santos. 2007. "Drug Identification." Presentation to the committee. April 23, 2007.

[b] P. Striupaitis, Chair, IAI Firearm/Toolmark Committee, and member, SWGGUN. Presentation to the committee. April 23, 2007.

[c] Ibid.

[d] R.E. Bisbing, Executive Vice President, McCrone Associates, Inc., and member SWGMAT. Presentation to the committee. April 24, 2007.

[e] S. Meagher, Fingerprint Specialist, Federal Bureau of Investigation, and Vice-Chair SWGFAST. Presentation to the committee. April 24, 2007.

[f] See www.theiai.org/guidelines/swgfast/index.php.

[g] Meagher, op. cit.

for their enforcement, with sanctions imposed against those who fail to comply. As such, standards should be developed with a consideration of the relevant measures that will be used to provide a meaningful evaluation of an organization's or individual's level of compliance. Appropriate standards must be coupled with effective systems of accreditation and/or certification that include strong enforcement mechanisms and sanctions.

Individual laboratories undergoing accreditation develop their own laboratory protocols. Whether these protocols adhere to the SWG standards depends on the individual examiners in the discipline in the laboratory in question. Accrediting bodies require that the methods meet a level of acceptable practice. Currently, most of these practices are slight variations of the SWG guidelines, with adjustments to accommodate differences in equipment.

PROFICIENCY TESTING

Although many forensic science disciplines have engaged in proficiency testing for the past several decades, several courts have noted that proficiency testing in some disciplines is not sufficiently rigorous.[27] ASCLD/LAB's Web site states that "Proficiency testing is an integral part of an effective quality assurance program. It is one of many measures used by laboratories to monitor performance and to identify areas where improvement may be needed. A proficiency testing program is a reliable method of verifying that the laboratory's technical procedures are valid and that the quality of work is being maintained." [28] Similarly, ISO/IEC 17025 policies state:

> Proficiency testing is one of the important tools used by laboratories and Accreditation Bodies for monitoring test and calibration results and for verifying the effectiveness of the accreditation process. As such, it is an important element in establishing confidence in the competence of Signatories and their accredited laboratories covered by this Arrangement.[29]

---

[27] See *United States v. Crisp*, 324 F.3d 261, 274 (4th Cir. 2003); *United States v. Llera Plaza*, 188 F. Supp. 2d 549, 565, 558 (E.D. Pa. 2002); *United States v. Lewis*, 220 F. Supp. 2d 548, 554 (S.D. W.Va. 2002).

[28] See www.ascld-lab.org/legacy/pdf/aslabinternproficiencyreviewprogram.pdf. It is worth noting that several studies have assessed or published crime laboratory proficiency testing results, which generally reveal the need for improvement; J.L. Peterson, E.L. Fabricant, K.S. Field, and J.I. Thornton. 1978. *Crime Laboratory Proficiency Testing Research Program*. Washington, DC: U.S. Government Printing Office; J.L. Peterson and P. Markham. 1995. Crime laboratory proficiency testing results, 1978-1991, I: Identification and classification of physical evidence. *Journal of Forensic Sciences* 40(6):994-1008; J.L. Peterson and P. Markham, 1995. Crime laboratory proficiency testing results, 1978-1991, II: Resolving questions of common origin. *Journal of Forensic Sciences* 40(6):1009-1029.

[29] See www.iso.org/iso/catalogue_detail?csnumber=39883.

There are several types of proficiency tests, with the primary distinction among them being whether the examiner is aware that he or she is being tested (an open or declared test) or does not realize that the sample presented for analysis is a test sample and not a real case (a blind test). Tests can be generated externally, by another laboratory (sometimes called an interlaboratory test), or internally. Another type of testing involves random case reanalysis, in which an examiner's completed prior casework is randomly selected for reanalysis by a supervisor or another examiner.[30]

Interlaboratory testing can be conducted for a number of purposes:

(1) to determine the performance of individual laboratories for specific tests or measurements and to monitor laboratories' continuing performance;
(2) to identify problems in laboratories and initiate remedial actions, which may be related to, for example, individual staff performance or the calibration of instrumentation;
(3) to determine the performance characteristics of a method and to establish the effectiveness and comparability of new tests or measurement methods; or
(4) to assign values to reference materials and assess their suitability for use in specific tests or measurement procedures.[31]

Blind proficiency testing is recommended, but not required, by ASCLD/LAB—not as a way to determine error rates, but as a more precise test of a worker's accuracy. Initially, mandatory blind testing was proposed as part of the federal DNA Identification Act. A Department of Justice (DOJ) panel designed blind tests, evaluated them, and estimated it would cost $500,000 to $1 million annually for one test per laboratory.[32] In appropriate circumstances, proficiency testing should include blind testing.

ASCLD/LAB has a detailed proficiency testing program that requires all active examiners to take at least one proficiency test per year (two tests per year in DNA), that each discipline within the laboratory participate in an external proficiency test that is reviewed by a proficiency test review

[30] Refer to ISO/IEC Guide 43-1:1997(E) Section 4 for a list of proficiency testing schemes. Refer to ASTM E 1301 Section 6 for an overview of organization and design of proficiency tests. SWGs also provide guidelines for proficiency testing in the relevant discipline.

[31] European Network of Forensic Science Institutes. 2005. *Guidance on the Conduct of Proficiency Tests and Collaborative Exercises Within ENFSI*. Available at www.enfsi.eu/uploads/files/QCC-PT-001-003.pdf.

[32] J.L. Peterson, G. Lin, M. Ho, Y. Chen, and R.E. Gaensslen. 2003. The feasibility of external blind DNA proficiency testing. Available at www.astm.org/JOURNALS/FORENSIC/PAGES/4241.htm.

panel, and that any proficiency test that is not successfully completed be immediately reported to ASCLD/LAB along with a corrective action plan. To retain accredited status for a full five-year term, a laboratory must continue to meet the standards under which it was accredited. One of the means by which ASCLD/LAB monitors compliance is by reviewing proficiency testing reports submitted by approved test providers.

According to the 2002 BJS census,[33] 274 of the 351 publicly funded laboratories were engaged in proficiency testing. Proficiency testing was slightly less common among smaller laboratories and those serving municipal jurisdictions (8 laboratories did not engage in such testing, and 69 did not answer the survey question). Among the laboratories engaged in proficiency testing, almost all use declared tests. Slightly more than half engaged in proficiency testing use random case reanalysis. Twenty-six percent of the laboratories engaged in proficiency testing use blind tests. In addition, the BJS survey reported that almost all laboratories engaged in proficiency testing used tests that were generated externally (thus allowing comparative analysis). In addition to external tests, 74 percent of laboratories engaged in proficiency testing also used internally generated tests. Data on proficiency testing were not collected for the 2005 census.

CERTIFICATION

The certification of individuals complements the accreditation of laboratories for a total quality assurance program. In other realms of science and technology, professionals, including nurses, physicians, professional engineers, and some laboratorians, typically must be certified before they can practice.[34] The same should be true for forensic scientists who practice and testify. Although the accreditation process primarily addresses the management system, technical methods, and quality of the work of a laboratory (which includes the education and training of staff), certification is a process specifically designed to ensure the competency of the individual examiner.

The American Bar Association has recommended that certification standards be required of examiners, including "demanding written examinations, proficiency testing, continuing education, recertification procedures,

---

[33] Peterson and Hickman, op. cit.

[34] T. Ortelli. 2008. Characteristics of candidates who have taken the Certified Nurse Educator: CNE examination: A two-year review. *Nursing Education Perspectives* 29(2):120; P. Nowak. 2008. Get IT-certified: Having employees with the right certifications can help dealers and integrators qualify for business and gain access to IT networks. *Network Technology* 38(3):123; S. Space. 2007. Investigator certification. *Issues in Clinical Trials Management* 8(2):73.

an ethical code, and effective disciplinary procedures."[35] In addition to improving quality, certification programs can enhance the credibility of certificate holders. An excellent description of the certification process is contained in the following excerpt from the National Association of Medical Examiners (NAME) Web site:

> In general, certification boards consist of respected professionals in a particular area of professional practice who develop standards for education, training, and experience that are required before one can become 'certified' in a particular professional discipline. Successful completion of a written and/or practical examination is also usually required. In essence, 'certification' usually means that a particular individual has completed a defined course of education, training, and experience, and has passed an examination prepared by peers which demonstrates that the individual has obtained at least the minimum level of competence required to practice the specific discipline. A number of 'Certification Boards' exist for people in various scientific disciplines. . . .[36]

The professional forensic science community supports the concept of certification. ASCLD recommends that laboratory managers support peer certification programs that promote professionalism and provide objective standards. In 2002, the Technical Working Group on Forensic Science Education recommended certification of an individual's competency by an independent peer-based organization, if available, from a certifying body with appropriate credentials. In addition, IAI supports certification of forensic science practitioners.[37]

Some organizations, such as the American Board of Criminalists (ABC), offer examiner certification programs, but some certification organizations appear to lack stringent requirements.[38] In response, the American Academy of Forensic Sciences has formed a Forensic Specialties Accreditation Board to accredit certifying organizations. Organizations are invited to participate if they meet established requirements, such as periodic recertification, a sufficient knowledge base for certification, a process for providing credentials, and a code of ethics.[39] Currently accredited boards include:

- American Board of Criminalistics

---

[35] American Bar Association, op. cit., p. 7.

[36] See http://thename.org/index.php?option=com_content&task=view&id=80&Itemid=41.

[37] K.F. Martin, President, IAI. Presentation to the committee. September 19, 2007.

[38] See M. Hansen. 2000. Expertise to go. *ABA J.* 86:44-45; E. MacDonald. 1999. "The Making of an Expert Witness: It's in the Credentials." *Wall Street Journal.* February 8, p. B1.

[39] See FABS Standards for Accrediting Forensic Specialty Certification Boards at www.thefsab.org/standards_20070218.pdf.

- American Board of Forensic Document Examiners
- American Board of Forensic Toxicology
- American Board of Medicolegal Death Investigators
- Board of Forensic Document Examiners
- International Institute of Forensic Engineering Sciences

IAI also has established certification programs in:

- Bloodstain Pattern Analysis
- Crime Scene Investigation
- Footwear
- Forensic Art
- Forensic Photography/Imaging
- Latent Print
- Tenprint Fingerprint[40]

Other certification programs exist for (but are not limited to) the following forensic science disciplines:

- Document Examination (The American Board of Forensic Document Examiners [ABFDE])
- Drug Analysis, Fire Debris Analysis, Molecular Biology, Trace Analysis, and General Criminalistics (ABC)
- Firearms and ToolMark Identification (Association of Firearm and ToolMark Examiners [AFTE])
- Forensic Odontology (The American Board of Forensic Odontology [ABFO])
- Forensic Pathology (The American Board of Pathology [ABP])
- Toxicology (American Board or Forensic Toxicology [ABFT])

Each of these entities has specific educational, training, and experience requirements, including a series of competency tests—both written and practical—and participation in proficiency testing, and provide continuing education/active participation by means of publication, presentation, and membership in professional organizations.

OVERSIGHT AS A REQUIREMENT OF PAUL COVERDELL FORENSIC SCIENCE IMPROVEMENT GRANTS

One way of enforcing quality control is through the conditional funding of programs. The *Justice for All Act of 2004* (P.L. 108-405) that created

40 K.F. Martin, President, IAI. Presentation to the committee. September 19, 2007.

the Coverdell Forensic Science Improvement Grants required that grant recipients certify that they have a process in place for independent, external investigations if allegations arise of "serious negligence or misconduct substantially affecting the integrity of the forensic results."[41]

In December 2005, the Office of the Inspector General (OIG) of DOJ issued a report of an audit that found that the Office of Justice Programs (OJP), which administers the program, "had not enforced or exercised effective oversight over the external investigation requirement for the Fiscal Year (FY) 2005 Coverdell Program."[42] OJP did not require grant applicants to identify the government entities that they certified could perform independent external investigations:

> Our review found that NIJ did not enforce the Act's certification requirement. NIJ's FY 2005 Coverdell Grant Program Announcement did not give applicants necessary guidance on what constitutes an independent external investigation or how to make the required certification. In addition, the announcement did not provide examples of external investigation certifications and did not require an applicant to name the government entity responsible for conducting independent, external investigations. NIJ was aware of the shortcomings in the announcement because of questions it received from potential applicants and concerns expressed by the OIG, but failed to correct them.[43]

The OIG made three recommendations to improve the program announcement and application process (see Box 7-3).

A second audit of the program was released in January 2008.[44] Again, it reported that not all forensic laboratories that had received FY 2006 grant funds were covered by a government entity with the authority and capability to independently investigate allegations of serious negligence or misconduct. "Further, OJP's guidance does not require grantees and subgrantees (forensic laboratories) to refer allegations of serious negligence and misconduct to entities for investigation."[45] The OIG found that 78 of the 231 entities contacted did not meet the external investigation certification requirement. It also found that "OJP did not adequately review the information it did obtain to ascertain that the certifications submitted by

---

[41] 42 U.S.C. § 3797k(4).

[42] U.S. Department of Justice, Office of the Inspector General. 2005. *Review of the Office of Justice Programs' Forensic Science Improvement Grant Program,* Evaluation and Inspections Report I-2006-002. Available at www.usdoj.gov/oig/semiannual/0605/ojp.htm.

[43] Ibid.

[44] U.S. Department of Justice, Office of the Inspector General. 2008. *Review of the Office of Justice Programs' Forensic Science Improvement Grant Program,* Evaluation and Inspections Report I-2008-001.

[45] Ibid., p, ii.

the grantees were properly completed."[46] The OIG made three recommendations to OJP to correct its certification process (see Box 7-3).

CODES OF ETHICS

A code of ethics is another mechanism for encouraging the development and use of professional standards of conduct. However, there is disagreement about how effective such codes are in achieving that goal.[47] In 1991, Ladd argued that codes of ethics serve no good purpose and that reliance on such codes confuses ethics with law.[48] Some authors have noted that although practicing professionals rarely turn to their codes of ethics for guidance, the adoption of a code of ethics is critical to the professionalization of a group, because it indicates that the group recognizes an obligation to society that transcends its own self-interest.[49] However, codes of ethics can serve to provide rational bases for punishments, such as exiling violators from the community.

In the field of engineering, Davis asserts that codes of ethics should be understood as conventions among professionals:

> The code is to protect each professional from certain pressures (for example, the pressure to cut corners to save money) by making it reasonably likely . . . that most other members of the profession will not take advantage of her good conduct. A code protects members of a profession from certain consequences of competition. A code is a solution to a coordination problem.[50]

Also in the field of engineering, Harris et al. argue that codes can serve as a collective recognition by members of a profession of its responsibilities, creating an environment in which ethical behavior is the norm.[51] Moreover, a code of ethics can serve as an educational tool, providing a starting point for discussion in coursework and professional meetings.

---

[46] Ibid., p. iii.

[47] A series of articles published in the *Journal of Forensic Sciences* 34(3) (May 1989) addressed a range of ethical dilemmas facing individuals practicing science in the criminal justice system.

[48] J. Ladd. 1991. The quest for a code of professional ethics: An intellectual and moral confusion. In: D.G. Johnson (ed.). *Ethical Issues in Engineering*. Englewood Cliffs, NJ: Prentice-Hall, pp. 130-136.

[49] H.C. Luegenbiehl. 1983. Codes of ethics and the moral education of engineers. *Business and Professional Ethics Journal* 2:41-61; D.G. Johnson (ed.). 1991. *Ethical Issues in Engineering*. 1991. Englewood Cliffs, NJ: Prentice-Hall, pp. 137-154.

[50] M. Davis. 1991. Thinking like an engineer: The place of a code of ethics in the practice of a profession. *Philosophy and Public Affairs* 20(2):150-167, p. 154.

[51] C.E. Harris, M.S. Pritchard, and M.J. Rabins. 1995. *Engineering Ethics: Concepts and Cases*. Belmont, CA: Wadsworth Publishing.

Box 7-3
Recommendations from Two Reviews of the Coverdell Grant Program

2005 - We believe that Coverdell Grant Program Announcements must provide necessary guidance to applicants and request the information required for NIJ to evaluate the external investigation certifications and conduct effective oversight of the grants. To meet the requirements of the Justice for All Act of 2004, we recommend that OJP, as part of its oversight of NIJ:

1. Require that all Coverdell Grant Program Announcements contain guidance on what constitutes an independent external investigation and examples of government entities and processes that could satisfy the certification requirement.
2. Require that each Coverdell Grant applicant, prior to receiving funds, provide the name of the government entity with a process in place to conduct independent external investigations into allegations of serious negligence or misconduct.
3. Consider requiring each Coverdell Grant applicant, prior to receiving funds, to submit a letter from the government entity that will conduct independent external investigations acknowledging that the entity has the authority and process to investigate allegations of serious negligence or misconduct.

2006 - To improve OJP's administration of the Coverdell Program and better ensure that allegations of negligence or misconduct are subject to independent external investigation, the OIG recommends that OJP take the following actions:

1. Revise the certification template to require that applicants name the government entities and confirm that the government entities have:
   a. the authority,
   b. the independence,
   c. a process in place that excludes laboratory management, and
   d. the resources to conduct independent external investigations into allegations of serious negligence or misconduct by labs that will received Coverdell funds.
2. Provide applicants with guidance that allegations of serious negligence or misconduct substantially affecting the integrity of forensic results are to be referred to the certified government entities.
3. Revise and document the Coverdell Program application review process so that only applicants that submit complete external investigation certifications are awarded grants.

SOURCE: U.S.DOJ Office of the Inspector General. 2005. *Review of the Office of Justice Programs' Forensic Science Improvement Grant Program,* Evaluation and Inspections Report I-2006-002. Available at www.usdoj.gov/oig/semiannual/0605/ojp.htm; U.S. DOJ OFFICE of Inspector General. 2008. Review of the Office of Justice Programs' Forensic Science Improvement Grant Program, Evaluation and Inspections Report I-2008-001.

Many forensic science organizations—such as the American Academy of Forensic Sciences, the California Association of Criminalists, and ASCLD—have codes of ethics or codes of professional practice imploring members to act with honesty, integrity, and objectivity; to work within the bounds of their professional competence; to present testimony and reports in a clear and objective manner; and to avoid conflicts of interest and potential bias, among other things. The codes that do exist are generally comprehensive, but they vary in content. As a consequence, there is no single code of ethics to which all members of the forensic science profession subscribe. As the committee concluded its work, it learned of an effort by ASCLD/LAB to develop a uniform code of ethics.

CONCLUSIONS AND RECOMMENDATIONS

Although some areas of the forensic science disciplines have made notable efforts to achieve standardization and best practices, most disciplines still lack any consistent structure for the enforcement of "better practices," operating standards, and certification and accreditation programs. Accreditation is required in only three states—New York, Oklahoma, and Texas. In other states, accreditation is voluntary, as is individual certification. Certification, while broadly accepted by the forensic science community, is not uniformly offered or required.

Although many forensic science organizations have codes of ethics, these codes can be enforced to regulate only the practices of persons who belong to a given organization. A uniform code of ethics should be in place across all forensic organizations to which all forensic practitioners and laboratories should adhere.

Recommendation 6:

> **To facilitate the work of the National Institute of Forensic Science (NIFS), Congress should authorize and appropriate funds to NIFS to work with the National Institute of Standards and Technology (NIST), in conjunction with government laboratories, universities, and private laboratories, and in consultation with Scientific Working Groups, to develop tools for advancing measurement, validation, reliability, information sharing, and proficiency testing in forensic science and to establish protocols for forensic examinations, methods, and practices. Standards should reflect best practices and serve as accreditation tools for laboratories and as guides for the education, training, and certification of professionals. Upon completion of its work, NIST and its partners should report find-**

ings and recommendations to NIFS for further dissemination and implementation.

Recommendation 7:

Laboratory accreditation and individual certification of forensic science professionals should be mandatory, and all forensic science professionals should have access to a certification process. In determining appropriate standards for accreditation and certification, the National Institute of Forensic Science (NIFS) should take into account established and recognized international standards, such as those published by the International Organization for Standardization (ISO). No person (public or private) should be allowed to practice in a forensic science discipline or testify as a forensic science professional without certification. Certification requirements should include, at a minimum, written examinations, supervised practice, proficiency testing, continuing education, recertification procedures, adherence to a code of ethics, and effective disciplinary procedures. All laboratories and facilities (public or private) should be accredited, and all forensic science professionals should be certified, when eligible, within a time period established by NIFS.

Recommendation 8:

Forensic laboratories should establish routine quality assurance and quality control procedures to ensure the accuracy of forensic analyses and the work of forensic practitioners. Quality control procedures should be designed to identify mistakes, fraud, and bias; confirm the continued validity and reliability of standard operating procedures and protocols; ensure that best practices are being followed; and correct procedures and protocols that are found to need improvement.

Recommendation 9:

The National Institute of Forensic Science (NIFS), in consultation with its advisory board, should establish a national code of ethics for all forensic science disciplines and encourage individual societies to incorporate this national code as part of their professional code of ethics. Additionally, NIFS should explore mechanisms of enforcement for those forensic scientists who commit serious ethical violations. Such a code could be enforced through a certification process for forensic scientists.

8

Education and Training in Forensic Science

Forensic examiners must understand the principles, practices, and contexts of science, including the scientific method. Training should move away from reliance on the apprentice-like transmittal of practices to education at the college level and beyond that is based on scientifically valid principles, as discussed in Chapter 4. For example, in addition to learning a particular methodology through a lengthy apprenticeship or workshop during which a trainee discerns and learns to copy the skills of an experienced examiner, the junior person should learn what to measure, the associated population statistics (if appropriate), biases and errors to avoid, other threats to the validity of the evidence, how to calculate the probability that a conclusion is valid, and how to document and report the analysis. Among many skills, forensic science education and training must provide the tools needed to understand the probabilities and the limits of decisionmaking under conditions of uncertainty.

To correct some of the existing deficiencies, the starting place must be better undergraduate and graduate programs, as well as increased opportunities for continuing education. Legitimating practices in the forensic science disciplines must be based on established scientific knowledge, principles, and practices, which are best learned through formal education and training and the proper conduct of research.

Education and training in the forensic science disciplines serve at least three purposes. First, educational programs prepare the next generation of forensic practitioners. The number of secondary and postsecondary students interested in the forensic science disciplines has grown substantially in recent years. In response, colleges and universities have created new certificate and degree programs to prepare students for forensic science careers. There are several types of forensic practitioners, including criminalists (those who work in crime laboratories), who make up a large part of the forensic science workforce and who often enter the profession with a bachelor's degree, and other forensic science practitioners (e.g., pathologists, odontologists, entomologists, toxicologists, anthropologists), who typically have advanced degrees, often Ph.D.s, and who might work part time in forensic science activities. Another group of forensic examiners include crime scene investigators, who usually do not have advanced degrees; many do not have college degrees above the associate level.

Second, forensic science practitioners require continuing professional development and training. Scientific advances in forensic science techniques and research in the forensic science disciplines are of interest to practitioners who must be aware of these new developments. Forensic science practitioners also may need to complete additional training for certification purposes or may desire to learn new skills as part of their career development. Training refers to the "formal, structured process through which a forensic scientist reaches a level of scientific knowledge and expertise required to conduct specific forensic analyses."[1] Continuing professional development is the "mechanism through which a forensic scientist remains current or advances to a higher level of expertise, specialization, or responsibility."[2]

Third, there is a need to educate the users of forensic science analyses, especially those in the legal community. Judges, lawyers, and law students can benefit from a greater understanding of the scientific bases underlying the forensic science disciplines and how the underlying scientific validity of techniques affects the interpretation of findings. These three objectives are explored in more detail in this chapter.

STATUS OF FORENSIC SCIENCE EDUCATION

Demand for Forensic Science Practitioners

Demand for more and better-skilled forensic science practitioners is rising at both the macro and micro levels. At the macro level, the appropriate question to ask is, what is the need for forensic science expertise in the United States? At the micro level, the question to ask is, what are the needs of a crime laboratory in hiring new forensic science personnel?

---

[1] National Institute of Justice. 2004. *Education and Training in Forensic Science: A Guide for Forensic Science Laboratories, Educational Institutions, and Students*. Washington, DC: National Institute of Justice, p. 25.

[2] Ibid.

As the National Institute of Justice (NIJ) notes:

> In recent years, the demand for forensic scientists has increased for many reasons, including population demographics, increased awareness of forensic science by law enforcement, increased numbers of law enforcement officers, database automation in several categories of physical evidence, jury expectations, legal requirements, accreditation and certification requirements of laboratories and personnel, impending retirement of a large number of currently practicing forensic scientists, and increased public awareness of forensic science through the popular media.[3]

One manifestation of the need for more examiners is the backlog of requests for forensic services at crime laboratories. As noted in previous chapters of this report (based on the 2005 Census of Publicly Funded Forensic Crime Laboratories), many forensic laboratories experience large backlogs in requests for forensic services. To achieve a 30-day turnaround on all 2005 requests, the different forensic science disciplines would have needed varying increases in the number of full-time examiners performing that work—ranging from an estimated 73 percent increase in DNA examiners to an estimated 6 percent increase in examiners conducting toxicology analysis.[4]

The most recent *Occupational Outlook Handbook*, prepared by the Bureau of Labor Statistics at the U.S. Department of Labor, found that job growth for forensic science technicians will grow much faster than average, with 13,000 jobs available in 2006 and a projected 31 percent rise, or 17,000 jobs, projected by 2016.[5] Yet one analyst argued that "existing science programs overproduce graduates relative to the actual labor market" in criminalistics.[6] Having an accurate picture of demand—as well as the capacity of employers to absorb new forensic science professionals—is important for colleges and universities that are educating and training the future workforce. Additional information on such factors as retirement and attrition rates and on trends in funding for laboratory personnel could assist educational providers in obtaining a more accurate picture of future employment prospects for their students.

The micro level focuses on the skills that individuals need to gain

---

[3] Ibid., p. 3.

[4] M.R. Durose. 2008. *Census of Publicly Funded Forensic Crime Laboratories, 2005*. U.S. Department of Justice, Office of Justice Programs, Bureau of Justice Statistics. Available at www.ojp.usdoj.gov/bjs/pub/pdf/cpffcl05.pdf.

[5] Bureau of Labor Statistics, Department of Labor. "Science Technicians." In: *Occupational Outlook Handbook, 2008-09 edition*. Available at www.bls.gov/oco/ocos115.htm#projections_data.

[6] R.E. Gaensslen. 2003. How do I become a forensic scientist? Educational pathways to forensic science careers. *Analytical and Bioanalytical Chemistry* 376:1151-1155.

TABLE 8-1 Educational Pathways to Some Forensic Science Careers

Forensic Discipline	Educational Requirements
Crime scene investigation	Jobs are typically held by law enforcement personnel. Meet requirements for joining the law enforcement agency. For federal jobs, a college degree is required.
Computer crime investigation/forensic computer science	B.S. in computer science or computer engineering; M.S. may be common.
Criminalistics	B.S. in the physical sciences, with background in chemistry
Forensic engineering	B.S. in engineering; practitioners may also be licensed as professional engineers (PEs).
Forensic pathology	Appropriate college degree; M.D.; internship and pathology residency; and specialized training in forensic pathology; additionally requires state license and board certification.
Forensic odontology	Appropriate college degree; D.D.S. or D.D.M.; may include additional specialty training; additionally requires state license and board certification.
Forensic entomology	Ph.D. in entomology.
Forensic anthropology	M.S. or M.A. at minimum; many have Ph.D.s.
Forensic psychiatry	Similar to forensic pathology, with residency in psychiatry.
Forensic psychology	M.S.W. or Ph.D. in psychology; often must meet state requirements for clinical practice and may be certified.

SOURCE: Gaensslen, 2003.

entry into forensic science careers (see Table 8-1). As a starting point, one needs an appropriate degree. The required minimum degree for entry-level forensic science positions ranges from a bachelor's degree to a doctoral or medical degree.[7] Almirall and Furton[8] suggest that it is possible to begin a career as a crime scene investigator or in firearms, documents, or fingerprints with an associate degree.

It should be noted that the preferred degree is often higher than an

[7] Gaensslen, op. cit.

[8] R. Almirall and K.G. Furton. 2003. Trends in forensic science education: Expansion and increased accountability. *Analytical and Bioanalytical Chemistry* 376:1156-1159.

associate degree. Almirall and Furton posit that future trends favor a minimum of a graduate degree in almost all areas of forensic science.[9]

An issue that has received much attention is the degree requirements for positions in crime laboratories. A requirement for an entry-level position in most crime laboratories is at least a bachelor's degree in a natural science or forensic science, and many laboratories require a year or two of experience, with a master's degree. Over the years, most crime laboratory hires have been and continue to be graduates with degrees in chemistry or biology.

Several studies have focused on the needs of crime laboratories. In 1988 Siegel conducted a survey of undergraduate students at Michigan State University, forensic science practitioners employed by the Michigan State Police, and 240 members of the American Society of Crime Laboratory Directors (ASCLD).[10] Survey respondents expressed a strong preference for a master's degree in forensic science and a lack of preference for the B.S. in criminalistics/forensic science. One explanation noted by the respondents was "that too many programs passing themselves off as forensic science programs were actually little more than criminal justice programs with a forensic science internship and a smattering of 'hard' science."[11] Another finding was the importance of chemistry in the backgrounds of prospective forensic science examiners.

Also in 1988, Higgins and Selavka surveyed laboratory managers.[12] Similar to the findings of Seigel, "chemical knowledge was the most important ability they considered when evaluating potential employees. . . ."[13] In 1996, Furton et al. surveyed members of the ASCLD, primarily drug chemists and trace evidence analysts.[14] This survey found that "the majority of crime lab directors responding require applicants to have B.S. degrees with a preference for chemistry/biochemistry, followed by biology and forensic science with a requirement for a substantial number of chemistry and other natural science courses."[15]

---

[9] Ibid.

[10] J.A. Siegel. 1988. The appropriate educational background for entry level forensic scientists: A survey of practitioners. *Journal of Forensic Sciences* 33(4):1065-1068.

[11] Ibid., pp. 1067-1068.

[12] K.M. Higgins and C.M. Selavka. 1988. Do forensic science graduate programs fulfill the needs of the forensic science community? *Journal of Forensic Sciences* 33(4):1015-1021.

[13] Ibid., p. 1017.

[14] K.G. Furton, Y.L. Hsu, and M.D. Cole. 1999. What educational background is required by crime laboratory directors? *Journal of Forensic Sciences* 44:128-132.

[15] Ibid., p. 130.

Proliferation of Forensic Science Programs

In recent years, increasing attention has been paid to the forensic science disciplines by the media in the form of many new books, movies, high-profile court cases, and, especially, television shows such as *Crime Scene Investigation* (or CSI).[16] This media attention has resulted in explosive demand by college (as well as primary and secondary school) students for academic courses and degree programs that will prepare them for careers in forensic science that are like those portrayed in the media. Evidence of this is the dramatic rise in enrollments in forensic science courses on college campuses.[17]

One issue facing academic forensic science programs is combating Hollywood's version of the career of a forensic practitioner. "Students who enter forensic science programs often expect to work in conditions similar to the television crime shows they watch. Many find they are unprepared for the reality of a career in the field. 'A lot of new students come to our programs looking for an exciting career. Unfortunately, they come with unrealistic expectations,' says Charles Tindall, director of forensic science at the Metropolitan State College of Denver."[18]

Until recently, there were few academic programs in the forensic science disciplines. The earliest forensic science degree programs and the oldest continually functioning educational degree programs in forensic science in the United States were established at Michigan State University in 1946 and the University of California at Berkeley in 1950.[19] A survey conducted in the mid-1970s located 22 colleges and universities in the United States offering degrees (in one case a certificate) in criminalistics/forensic science, although some of these institutions offered multiple degrees.[20]

---

16 See, e.g., S. Smallwood. 2002. As seen on TV. *Chronicle of Higher Education* 48(45): A8-A10.

17 There have been similar increases in demand at the K-12 level. Forensic science has become a popular component of science teaching. An informal survey conducted in 2004 by the National Science Teachers Association found that, "Of the 450 middle and high school science educators who responded to an informal survey, 77 percent indicated that their school or school district is using forensic investigations to teach science. When asked if the popularity of forensic-based TV shows had ignited students' interest in science, the response was a resounding 'yes' (78 percent)." *NSTA Survey Reveals Forensic Science Is Hottest New Trend in Science Teaching*. Available at http://science.nsta.org/nstaexpress/nstaexpress_2004_10_25_forensic.htm.

18 National Institute of Justice. 2007. *Addressing Shortfalls in Forensic Science Education*. InShort, NCJ 216886. Washington, DC: U.S. Department of Justice, National Institute of Justice.

19 A. Vollmer, Chief of Police, Berkeley, California, established the School of Criminology at the University of California at Berkeley.

20 J.L. Peterson, D. Crim, and P.R. De Forest. 1977. The status of forensic science degree programs in the United States. *Journal of Forensic Sciences* 22(1):17-33.

In the 1980s, a contraction of programs occurred—particularly at the graduate level. Stoney argues that this was because of a lack of financial and administrative support.[21] Higgins and Selavka suggest that the end of funding provided by the Law Enforcement Assistance Administration in 1978 took important federal support away from many institutions.[22] Additionally, they suggest that the then-declining enrollment in graduate programs might have reflected the generally low-paying opportunities available to newly minted graduates.

In recent years, this trend has reversed itself. Many colleges and universities, seeing the potential revenue from increasing numbers of new students, have responded by creating all manner of new academic programs. The American Academy of Forensic Sciences (AAFS) now lists 138 undergraduate, 59 graduate, and 6 doctoral forensic science degree programs in the United States.[23] Not all are science based—many are criminal justice programs. The curricula of these degrees range from rigorous scientific coursework amounting to a degree in chemistry or biology with forensic science content, to little more than criminal justice degrees with an internship.

Doctoral Programs in Forensic Science

There is no doctoral program specifically in forensic science; the programs noted by AAFS offer Ph.D.s (mostly in chemistry) with a concentration in that area. Some scholars consider this to be a shortcoming in forensic science education. More than 20 years ago, Kobilinksy and Sheehan conducted a survey of crime laboratories throughout the United States and found that almost 73 percent of those responding believed there was a need for a Ph.D. program.[24] The advantages of a Ph.D. program lie in its positive effect on basic research in the field. Doctoral programs offer more research depth and capacity, have ties to other fields, have high expectations for quality, supply graduate student personnel to question and check past work and challenge conventional wisdom, and inspire more mentoring, which has two-way benefits.

---

[21] D.A. Stoney. 1988. A medical model for criminalistics education. *Journal of Forensic Sciences* 33(4):1086-1094.

[22] Higgins and Selavka, op. cit.

[23] See www.aafs.org.

[24] L. Kobilinksy and F.X. Sheehan. 1984. The desirability of a Ph.D. program in forensic science. *Journal of Forensic Sciences* 29(3):706-710.

CHALLENGES AND OPPORTUNITIES TO IMPROVE FORENSIC SCIENCE EDUCATION

The overarching challenges facing forensic science education, since its inception, have been inconsistent quality and insufficient funding. Commentators have noted repeatedly the deficiencies of forensic science education programs.[25] Because, until recently, no nationally recognized, mandated standards existed for forensic science degree programs at any level, consistent quality cannot be achieved. Peterson et al. note that while "the primary objective of all degree programs is similar, the capabilities of graduates from the respective institutions are not uniform. Laboratories are forced to evaluate each graduate student individually to determine his suitability for a given position."[26]

Unevenness in the quality of these programs has caused problems for students and future employers. The Council of Forensic Science Educators stated that, "Students completing these lesser programs expect to find employment in crime labs but are surprised to learn that lab management is not impressed by the curriculum."[27]

Additionally, the lack of applicants with a science or forensic background means that crime laboratories have to spend precious time and resources in the training of new scientists.[28] If forensic science education programs had sufficient rigor in science, law, and forensics, crime laboratories would have to spend less time and money for training,[29] thereby shortening as well the apprenticeship time needed. Forensic science methods should be taught in the framework of common scientific practice (see Chapters 4 through 6). Even if a student graduates with a science degree, he or she often lacks education in issues that are critical to the functioning of crime laboratories, including quality assurance and control, ethics, and expert testimony. Peterson et al. found that, "The faculty surveyed believes their students to be well prepared for entry into the field. This is not totally consistent with the feedback from some laboratories which have been less than satisfied with newly graduated recruits."[30] They continue to recommend that, "Measures should be taken to improve feedback from the laboratories to the schools to insure that the curriculum is not only comprehensive

[25] See, e.g., Peterson et al., op. cit; L.W. Bradford. 1980. Barriers to quality achievement in crime laboratory operations. *Journal of Forensic Sciences* 25(4):902-907; Stoney, op. cit.; NIJ, op. cit.

[26] Peterson et al., op. cit., p. 31.

[27] See www.criminology.fsu.edu/COFSE/default.htm.

[28] Stoney, op. cit.

[29] NIJ, 2007, op. cit.

[30] Peterson et al., op cit., p. 32.

from an academic standpoint but also meets the practical requirements of operating laboratories."[31]

Over the past few years, major strides have been taken in bringing a measure of standardization to forensic science education programs and boosting their quality. The NIJ report, *Forensic Science: Review of Status and Needs,* called in part for an accreditation system for such programs. Following this report, in 2001, NIJ established a Technical Working Group for Education and Training in Forensic Science (TWGED)—consisting of 47 experts, including educators, judges, attorneys, crime laboratory directors, and subject matter scientists—that developed recommended curricular guidelines for undergraduate and graduate forensic science programs. These were provided in a 2004 report.[32] In 2002, the American Academy of Forensic Sciences created an ad hoc committee, the Forensic Education Program Accreditation Committee, to look into issues regarding an accreditation system. The committee was made a standing committee in 2004, at which time the name was changed to the Forensic Science Education Program Accreditation Commission (FEPAC). FEPAC is made up of five forensic science educators, five crime laboratory directors, and one public member. FEPAC created a process for accrediting undergraduate and graduate forensic science programs using the TWGED standards.[33]

FEPAC standards are divided into three parts (see Table 8-2). There are general standards that all programs must meet and then additional standards for undergraduate and graduate programs.

An important note regarding the accreditation process is that the program must award at least a bachelor's degree in either forensic science or a natural science with a concentration in forensic science at both the bachelor's and master's levels. Programs that award certificates or associate degrees are ineligible for accreditation in this system. Additionally, at this time only U.S. programs are eligible for accreditation.

To summarize the general standards, such programs shall:

- have an explicit process for evaluating and monitoring its overall efforts to fulfill its mission, goals, and objectives; for assessing its effectiveness in serving its various constituencies; for modifying

[31] Programs accredited by FEPAC are required to complete periodic self-assessments, which include job placement statistics and employer satisfaction surveys.

[32] Technical Working Group for Education and Training in Forensic Science. 2004. *Education and Training in Forensic Science: A Guide for Forensic Science Laboratories, Educational Institutions and Students,* Special Report. Washington, DC: U.S. Department of Justice, National Institute of Justice. NCJ 203099.

[33] See FEPAC Accreditation Standards. Available at www.aafs.org/pdf/FEPAC%20 Accreditation%20Standards%20_082307_.pdf.

TABLE 8-2 Major Areas of FEPAC Standards

General Standards for All Programs
- Eligibility
- Planning and Evaluation
- Institutional Support
- Student Support Services
- Recruiting and Admissions Practices, Academic Calendars, Catalogs, Publications, Grading, and Advertising
- Record of Student Complaints
- Distance Learning and Other Alternative Delivery Mechanisms

Undergraduate Program Standards
- Mission, Goals, and Objectives
- Undergraduate Admissions Requirements
- Curriculum
- Program Director
- Faculty
- Success with Respect to Student Achievement
- Professional Involvement

Graduate Program Standards
- Mission, Goals, and Objectives
- Graduate Admissions Requirements
- Curriculum
- Program Director
- Faculty
- Success with Respect to Student Achievement
- Professional Involvement

SOURCE: www.aafs.org.

the curriculum as necessary, based on the results of its evaluation activities; and for planning to achieve its mission in the future;

- have adequate institutional support in the form of financial resources, facilities, instructional, and support services;
- provide adequate student support services, such as mentoring, advising, and career placement;
- have policies and procedures for student recruitment and admissions, with advisers to students regarding requirements for employment;
- have procedures for handling student complaints; and
- consider the use of distance learning as an instructional technique, demonstrating that all required laboratory experiences are hands-on for all students.

Concerning the undergraduate curriculum, it should, at a minimum, ensure that each student (1) obtain a thorough grounding in the natural sciences; (2) build upon this background by taking a series of more advanced science classes; and (3) develop an appreciation of issues specific to forensic science through course work and laboratory-based instruction.

Forensic science undergraduates in the chemistry track should take, at a minimum, chemistry courses required for chemistry majors—general chemistry, organic chemistry, physical chemistry, analytical chemistry, instrumental analysis, and biochemistry. Forensic science students in the biology track should take those chemistry courses required for biology majors and biology courses for biology majors, including general biology, biochemistry, instrumental analysis, genetics, molecular biology, and population genetics. All forensic science students should, at the earliest point possible, take a hands-on crime scene investigation course that teaches the principles of evidence, including its collection, preservation, and value. Additionally, the forensic science courses in drug analysis, criminalistics, and forensic biology (including DNA analysis) should be at the highest level. All forensic science majors should take a capstone course.

For graduate programs, the curriculum should, at a minimum, ensure that each student (1) understand essential issues in the forensic science disciplines, including the reduction of error rates; (2) develop an understanding of the areas of knowledge that are essential to forensic science; (3) acquire skills and experience in the application of basic forensic science concepts and of specialty knowledge to problem solving; (4) be oriented in professional values, concepts and ethics; and (5) demonstrate integration of knowledge and skills through a capstone experience, such as a formal, objective tool (e.g., the American Board of Criminalistics Forensic Science Aptitude Test) or another comprehensive examination or a thesis and/or research project.

Depending on the specialty track of interest, graduate students should take advanced courses in specialty areas of interest—drug analysis, toxicology, criminalistics, forensic biology, and forensic DNA analysis (including mtDNA sequencing, low copy number techniques, and SNPs). The criminalistics and forensic biology courses should be advanced beyond those seen at the undergraduate level. If the student has not had those lower-level courses, they should be taken first. Graduate students also should take a hands-on crime scene investigation class that covers investigation techniques and evidence association, including its examination, collection, and preservation. In addition, in-service work with a collaborating institution can provide significant practical training.

Finally, the standards lay out a suggested curriculum for forensic science education programs. At the undergraduate level, coursework includes several classes in the natural sciences (with a focus on chemistry); specialized science courses (e.g., microbiology, genetics, biochemistry); forensic science courses—which cover courtroom testimony; introduction to law; quality assurance; ethics; professional practice; evidence identification, collection and processing; a survey of the forensic science disciplines; and additional courses in the student's area of specialization. Laboratory work must be complemented with hands-on training that closely mimics the experiences of the crime laboratory. At the graduate level, students should take core forensic science topics, such as physical evidence concepts and ethics and professional responsibilities; courses in specialized areas; and a graduate seminar—all aimed at developing skills for conducting independent research.

FEPAC began a pilot accreditation program in the fall of 2003, accrediting five programs,[34] and the number of accredited programs has continued to grow (see Table 8-3). As of January 2008, 16 programs have met FEPAC's rigorous standards and accordingly have been accredited by FEPAC.

Accredited forensic science programs are listed on the AAFS Web site. Accreditation is seen as providing a "seal of quality to an institution;" helping faculty to improve their curricula; creating a standard for measuring the quality of forensic science programs; and benefiting laboratories by reducing the need for in-house training.[35] Accreditation should become the norm. The committee believes that, to encourage accreditation, a mechanism could be developed whereby only accredited programs would be eligible to receive certain federal grants and/or scholarships for its students. If the forensic science disciplines are to grow in stature and be recognized for their scientific rigor and high standards of quality, their research base must be broadened and strengthened. This will occur only if significant federal research funds are made available to universities by scientific granting agencies such as the National Institutes of Health and the National Science Foundation. Crime laboratories would be the beneficiaries of a wave of well-educated workers who would elevate the scientific standards of the field. The forensic science degree programs that are not sufficiently rigorous eventually would disappear, because their graduates would not be competitive in the employment arena. Consequently, employers would be more confident in the capabilities of graduates of forensic science programs and hence would be more inclined to hire them.

[34] Cedar Crest College (Allentown, Pennsylvania), Eastern Kentucky University (Richmond, Kentucky), Florida International University (Miami, Florida), Metropolitan State College of Denver (Denver, Colorado), and Michigan State University (East Lansing, Michigan).

[35] NIJ, 2000, op. cit.

TABLE 8-3 FEPAC Accredited Programs, 2008

Programs	Degree Program
Albany State University	Bachelor of Science Degree in Forensic Science
Arcadia University	Master of Science Degree Program in Forensic Science
Cedar Crest College	Bachelor of Science Degree Program in Chemistry, Biochemistry, Biology, and Genetic Engineering, with a concentration in Forensic Science
Eastern Kentucky University	Bachelor of Science Degree Program in Forensic Science
Florida International University	Certificate Programs in Conjunction with the Bachelor of Science in a Natural Science such as Chemistry or Biology
Florida International University	Master of Science Degree Program in Forensic Science
Marshall University	Master of Science Degree Program in Forensic Science
Metropolitan State College of Denver	Bachelor of Science Degree Program in Chemistry with a concentration in Criminalistics
Michigan State University	Master of Science Degree Program (biology and chemistry tracks)
University of Mississippi	Bachelor of Science Degree in Forensic Chemistry
Ohio University	Bachelor of Science Degree in Forensic Chemistry
SUNY at Albany	Master of Science Degree in Forensic Molecular Biology
Virginia Commonwealth University	Bachelor of Science Degree in Forensic Science
Virginia Commonwealth University	Master of Science Degree in Forensic Science
West Chester University	Bachelor of Science Degree Program In Forensic and Toxicological Chemistry
West Virginia University	Bachelor of Science Degree—Forensic and Investigative Science Program

SOURCE: www.aafs.org.

RESEARCH AS A COMPONENT OF FORENSIC SCIENCE EDUCATION PROGRAMS

Student research and exposure to research is a critical component of an appropriate forensic science education.[36] Research funding supports both faculty and graduate student research. Funding also supports the acquisition and maintenance of equipment and major research instrumentation and laboratory renovation.[37] As noted in Chapter 2, the level of funding for forensic science research programs is seen by many observers as inadequate. Fisher notes that "labs are looking for more forensic scientists at the master's and doctorate level. For universities to run graduate-level programs in the science, research dollars must be made available. However, the amounts of such R&D funds available to support forensic science at the National Institute of Justice are small and are all but non-existence [sic] from the National Science Foundation, and other funding sources."[38] Likewise, NIJ reported in 2004 that, "Currently, no sustainable source of State or Federal funding exists to support graduate education or research in forensic science. Nor should state and local governments fund research, as their funds have to support the service mission of the laboratories. The National Institute of Justice has traditionally provided virtually all federal research funding for forensic science, but additional funding from alternative sources is essential."[39]

Many forensic degree programs are found at small colleges or universities with few graduate programs in science and where research resources are limited. The lack of research funding has discouraged universities in the United States from developing research-based forensic degree programs, which leads to limited opportunities to attract graduate students into such programs. Only a few universities offer Ph.D.-level education and research opportunities in forensic science, and these are chemistry or biology programs with a forensic science focus. Most graduate programs in forensic science are master's programs, where financial support for graduate study is limited.

In addition, the lack of research funds means that universities are unlikely to develop research programs in forensic science. This lack of funding discourages top scientists from exploring the many scientific issues in the forensic science disciplines. This has become a vicious cycle during

---

36 To receive accreditation by FEPAC, a graduate program must include a component in which each student completes an independent research project leading to a thesis or written report, presented orally in a public forum for evaluation.

37 NIJ, 2004, op. cit., p. 23.

38 B.A.J. Fisher. 2003. Field needs adequate funding, national forensic science commission. *Forensic Focus*. See http://forensicfocusmag.com/articles/3b1persp1.html.

39 NIJ, 2004, op. cit., p. 22.

which the lack of funding keeps top scientists away and their unavailability discourages funding agencies from investing in forensic science research. Traditional funding agencies have never had a mission to support forensic science research.

STATUS OF TRAINING

Continuing education and in-service training in forensic science have been significant issues for many years. Funding programs initially were offered in the early 1970s through the Law Enforcement Assistance Administration. As forensic science grew, the needs for ongoing training and continuing education also grew. Several studies funded by NIJ have been undertaken since 1999—*Forensic Sciences: Review of Status and Needs* (1999); [40] *Education and Training in Forensic Science: A Guide for Forensic Science Laboratories, Educational Institutions, and Students* (2004),[41] developed by TWGED; and a report prepared by ASCLD for NIJ, published in May 2004, which has become known as the *180-day Study Report: Status and Needs of United States Crime Laboratories.*[42]

The issues addressed in all of these reports are the same ones confronting this committee today, namely the need for continuing education and the ongoing training of working examiners in the various disciplines:

> Prior to conducting analysis on evidence, forensic scientists require both basic scientific education and discipline-specific training. To be in compliance with widely-accepted accreditation standards, scientists in each of the disciplines must have, at a minimum, a baccalaureate degree in a natural science, forensic science, or a closely-related field. Each examiner must also have successfully completed a competency test (usually after a training period) prior to assuming independent casework.[43]

After the initial training period, continuing training is necessary to maintain and update knowledge and skills in new technology, equipment, and methods.

Accreditation and certification programs require some type of continuing education, and the various Scientific Working Groups (SWGs) recom-

---

[40] National Institute of Justice. 1999. *Forensic Sciences: Review of Status and Needs.* Washington, DC: National Institute of Justice.

[41] National Institute of Justice. 2004. *Education and Training in Forensic Science: A Guide for Forensic Science Laboratories, Educational Institutions, and Students.* Washington, DC: National Institute of Justice.

[42] American Society of Crime Laboratory Directors. 2004. *180-day Study Report: Status and Needs of United States Crime Laboratories.* Largo, FL: ASCLD.

[43] Ibid., p. 12.

mend such programs (see Chapter 7). Continuing professional development also is a means of expanding expertise and career advancement.

Training Needs

As described by ASCLD:

> When a new analyst or examiner is hired, usually a recent university graduate, that individual requires initial training to build competency. The length of the initial training provided to an analyst depends upon the laboratory specialty area the trainee will enter.
>
> For example, controlled substance analysts may require only six to twelve months of training. Those training in experience-based disciplines such as latent prints examinations, firearms and toolmarks analyses, and questioned documents examinations may require up to three years of training before being permitted to perform independent casework. During their training period, individuals in experience-based disciplines serve much like an apprentice to a senior examiner.[44]

NIJ describes a variety of training needs for forensic scientists in crime laboratories by position.[45] For operational scientists, training is needed to stay up to date in theoretical and practical issues (such as applying methods and performing analyses). Everyone in a laboratory needs orientation in such topics as the criminal justice system, the legal system, ethics, professional organizations, the basic philosophy of forensic science, overview of disciplines of forensic science, quality control (e.g., good laboratory practice), effective expert testimony, and safety. First-line supervisors need training in quality assurance, case file review, and basic supervision skills; and managers need training in fiscal management, quality systems management, leadership, project management, human resource management, and customer service. Training can be done in-service or through short courses. The 1999 NIJ report identifies a number of examples of such courses.

On-the-job training involves specific challenges; it is labor intensive and can be expensive.[46] The costs of training include the salary of the trainee as well as the opportunity cost of the lost productivity of the trainer. Moreover, there are no uniform recommendations on the content of training in the forensic science disciplines. ASCLD has suggested some examples of efforts to make training more efficient, including conducting some training in conjunction with universities (essentially conducting training while forensic

---

[44] ASCLD, op. cit., p. 15.

[45] NIJ, 1999, op. cit.

[46] Ibid.

scientists are students and before they are full-time employees), and some laboratories have tried collaborating to train employees.

Continuing Education

Continuing education is critical for all personnel working in crime laboratories as well as for those in other forensic science disciplines, such as forensic pathologists or anthropologists. Some commonly used approaches to continuing education are instructor led, professional conferences/seminars, distributed learning, apprenticeship, residency, internship, teaching and presentations by trainee/employee, and independent learning.[47]

The greatest issue for continuing education is quality. TWGED has provided guidelines for training courses. First, there should be specific eligibility requirements. Specified minimum and experiential requirements should be consistent with recognized, peer-defined standards (e.g., SWGs, ASCLD/Laboratory Accreditation Board). Factors such as drug use, credit and criminal history, and personal references may affect career opportunities. Second, the structure of the training programs should include: learning objectives; instructor qualifications; student requirements; a detailed syllabus; performance goals; periodic assessments; and competency testing. Third, program content can include a mix of discipline-specific and core elements. Core elements are essential topics that lay the foundation for entry into professional practice, regardless of the specialty area. They include the following:

- Standards of conduct—includes professional ethics training.
- Safety—includes biological, chemical, and physical hazards.
- Policy—includes such administrative and laboratory policies as standard operating procedures, quality assurance, accreditation, and security.
- Legal—includes expert testimony, depositions, rules of evidence, criminal and civil law and procedures, and evidence authentication.
- Evidence handling—includes interdisciplinary issues; recognition, collection, and preservation of evidence; and chain of custody.
- Communication—includes written, verbal, and nonverbal communication skills; report writing; exhibit and pretrial preparation; and trial presentation.

Discipline-specific elements include such topics as the history of the discipline, relevant literature, methodologies and validation studies, instru-

---

[47] NIJ, 2004, op. cit.

mentation, statistics, knowledge of related fields, and testimony. Finally, individuals should be assessed through mechanisms such as oral examinations, written examinations, laboratory practicals and laboratory exercises, mock trials, and the assessment of technical performance by appropriate senior staff.

EDUCATION IN THE LEGAL SYSTEM

The forensic science community needs to educate those who use their services and therefore needs to understand the services and their terminology. Users of forensic science analyses include law enforcement officers, forensic pathologists, the bar, the judiciary, the general public, and policymakers. This section focuses on education for the legal community of judges, lawyers, and juries.

In recent years, some judges have struggled to understand increasingly complex scientific evidence. Sophisticated epidemiology and toxicology studies often are introduced in mass tort litigation. Complex econometric models are common in antitrust cases. Disputes over sophisticated engineering principles often are at the core of patent litigation. Failure to consider such evidence in a thoughtful and thorough manner threatens the integrity and independence of the judiciary. Following the *Daubert* decision, the Federal Judicial Center published the *Reference Manual on Scientific Evidence*, and a second edition was issued in 2000 to "facilitate the process of identifying and narrowing issues concerning scientific evidence by outlining for judges the pivotal issues in the areas of science that are often subject to dispute."[48] In addition, the courts have responded to the growing complexity of evidence by developing science-based judicial education programs that explain scientific issues as they may arise in the context of litigation. However, these courses are not mandatory, there is no fixed routine of continuing education in legal practice with regard to science, and there are no good ways to measure the proficiency of judges who attend these programs.

Pfefferli suggests that it is important to tailor education programs to the needs of judges:

> Forensic educational programs directed towards proficiency in evidence matter must meet the needs of judicial magistrates, which goes beyond a better understanding of the scientific principles and technical methods applied to criminal investigations to demonstrate the existence of a crime. These programs have to look at a variety of different kinds of forensic evidence and their interacting processes, giving special attention to individualization/identification process; evidential value and evaluation of

[48] Federal Judicial Center. 2000. *Reference Manual on Scientific Evidence*. 2nd ed., p. vi.

evidence; critical issues and quality assurance, and deterministic versus probabilistic opinions of experts."[49]

Pfefferli further notes that different members of the judicial community should benefit from customized training. For example, prosecutors and defense attorneys might benefit from a focus on the interpretation of and requirements for evidence; and judges may benefit from information on evaluating the scientific rigor of expert testimony and the reliability of forensic evidence.

At the end of the 1990s, NIJ noted that training for the judiciary was sporadic at the federal, state, and local levels and rare in general.[50] Virginia is one state that provides annual seminars for the judiciary, and ASCLD formerly provided training to judges.

Reliance on DNA technology for identification purposes in forensic science spurred the development of judicial education programs. As part of the President's DNA Initiative, the Department of Justice developed a series of publications and online training programs designed for officers of the courts, including judges. The course, "Principles of Forensic DNA for Officers of the Court," released in 2006, is designed "to educate criminal justice professionals and other practitioners about the science of DNA analysis and the legal issues regarding the use of DNA in the courtroom."[51] The 15 training modules in the course include:

- information on the biology of DNA;
- the history of forensic DNA analysis;
- how to understand a forensic DNA laboratory report;
- factors in postconviction DNA testing requests;
- information about forensic DNA databases;
- issues involved in presenting DNA evidence in the courtroom;
- information on the admissibility issues regarding the use of DNA evidence; and
- an extensive glossary with basic definitions relating to forensic DNA analysis.

But other than this initiative, judicial education programs have not focused on the forensic science disciplines.

---

[49] P.W. Pfefferli. 2003. *Forensic Education & Training of Judges and Law Enforcement Magistrates*. Presentation at the International Society for the Reform of Criminal Law, 17th International Conference, The Hague. Available at www.isrcl.org/Papers/Pfefferli.pdf, p. 2.

[50] NIJ, 1999, op. cit.

[51] Office of Justice Programs, U.S. Department of Justice. 2006. *Department of Justice Releases Interactive Training Tool on Principles of Forensic DNA*. Available at www.ojp.usdoj.gov/newsroom/pressreleases/2006/NIJ06036.htm.

Another avenue for education would be courses taught by forensic science education programs, but geared to continuing education participants rather than full-time students. The University of Florida, for example, offers a distance learning, continuing education course for Florida lawyers that is certified by the Florida Bar Association and that covers a variety of forensic science topics. Professional organizations also have offered courses. For example, the National District Attorneys Association founded the American Prosecutors Research Institute (APRI) as a nonprofit research, technical assistance, and program development resource for prosecutors at all levels of government. In the past, APRI has offered training opportunities in forensic science, although its programs have decreased in recent years. The National College of District Attorneys and the National Association of Criminal Defense Attorneys also periodically offer courses in forensic science. A third option is for law schools to offer more courses in the forensic disciplines, statistics, or basic science methodology, or to provide credit for students wishing to take courses in those fields.

Unfortunately, it might be too late to effectively train most lawyers and judges once they enter their professional fields. Training programs are beneficial in the short term, because they offer responsible jurists a way to learn what they need to know. For the long term, however, the best way to get lawyers and judges up to speed is for law schools to offer better courses in forensic science in their curricula.

Juries and Scientific Evidence

Despite common stereotypes about jury incompetence and runaway juries, research has demonstrated a consistency between jury and bench trial verdicts, regardless of the level of scientific complexity involved.[52] Even in cases in which jurors express incomplete and flawed understandings of scientific and technical evidence, researchers have described jury results as generally justified.[53] Moreover, it has been suggested that jurors' errors in interpreting evidentiary information are often traceable in part to misleading presentations and instructions by attorneys and judges.[54]

However, juries have been described as least comfortable and compe-

[52] V.P. Hans, D.H. Kaye, M.B. Dann, E.J. Farley, and S. Albertson. 2007. *Science in the Jury Box: Jurors' Views and Understanding of Mitochondrial DNA Evidence.* Cornell Law School Legal Studies Research Paper No. 07-02. Available at http://ssrn.com/abstract=1025582; T. Eisenberg, P.L. Hannaford-Agor, V.P. Hans, N.L. Mott, G.T. Munsterman, S.J. Schwab, and M.T. Wells. 2005. Judge-jury agreement in criminal cases: A partial replication of Kalven & Zeisel's *The American Jury*. *Journal of Empirical Legal Studies* 2:171-206.

[53] Hans, op. cit.

[54] Ibid.

tent with regard to statistical evidence.[55] Interestingly, juries are often hesitant to give as much credence as experts suggest to the statistics associated with DNA evidence.[56] Juries frequently raise concerns about laboratory error and sample contamination, even when opposing counsel does not introduce such issues.[57]

Jurors' use and comprehension of forensic evidence is not well studied. Better understanding is needed in this area, and recommendations are needed for programs or methods that will better prepare juries in appropriate, unbiased ways for trials in which scientific evidence is expected to play a large or pivotal role. However, several studies indicate that trial judges agree with jury verdicts in an overwhelming proportion of criminal cases.[58]

CONCLUSIONS AND RECOMMENDATION

Despite major strides made in recent years in bringing a measure of standardization to forensic science education programs and boosting their quality, more information is required on the number of programs that are available and the depth and breadth of the course offerings. It appears that there are no formal and systematically applied standards or standardization requirements for forensic science education programs, making the quality and relevance of existing programs uncertain. Moreover, there are no requirements or incentives in place to ensure that forensic science education programs must be accredited in order to receive federal funds.

Current funding is insufficient for developing graduate training programs that cut across organizational, programmatic, and disciplinary boundaries and that can attract students in the life and physical sciences to pursue graduate studies in multidisciplinary fields critical to forensic science. Similarly, too few funding sources exist for research conducted in association with forensic science graduate programs.

In addition, forensic researchers, legal scholars, and forensic practitioners and members of the bench and bar do not have sufficient opportuni-

---

[55] Ibid. See also W.C. Thompson and E.L. Schumann. 1987. Interpretation of statistical evidence in criminal trials: The prosecutor's fallacy and the defense attorney's fallacy. *Law and Human Behavior* 11:167-187; W.C. Thompson. 1989. Are juries competent to evaluate statistical evidence? *Law and Contemporary Problems* 52:9-41.

[56] J.J. Koehler. 2001. When are people persuaded by DNA match statistics? *Law and Human Behavior* 25:493-513; D.A. Nance and S.B. Morris. 2002. An empirical assessment of presentation formats for trace evidence with a relatively large and quantifiable random match probability. *Jurimetrics Journal* 42:403-448; J. Schklar and S.S. Diamond. 1999. Juror Understanding of DNA evidence: An empirical assessment of presentation formats for trace evidence with a relatively small random-match probability. *Journal of Legal Studies* 34:395-444.

[57] Schklar and Diamond, op. cit.

[58] Hannaford-Agor, Hans, and Munsterman, op. cit.

ties and venues for interaction and sharing information. This impedes the translation of advances in forensic science to legal scholars and litigators (including civil litigators, prosecutors, and criminal defense counsel), federal, state, and local legislators, members of the judiciary, and law enforcement officials. The result is needless delay in improvements in criminal and civil laws and procedures, law enforcement practices, litigation strategies, and judicial decisionmaking.

Lawyers and judges often have insufficient training and background in scientific methods, and they often fail to fully comprehend the approaches employed by different forensic science disciplines and the strengths and vulnerabilities of forensic science evidence offered during trials.

Forensic science examiners need additional training in the principles, practices, and contexts of scientific methodology, as well as in the distinctive features of their specialty. Training should move well beyond intern-like transmittal of practices to teaching that is based on scientifically valid principles. In addition to the practical experience and learning acquired during an internship, a trainee should acquire rigorous interdisciplinary education and training in the scientific areas that constitute the basis for the particular forensic discipline and should also receive instruction on how to document and report the analysis. A trainee in addition should have working knowledge of basic probability and statistics as they relate to the tasks he or she may need to address in the applicable discipline.

To correct some of the existing deficiencies, it is crucially important to improve undergraduate and graduate forensic science programs. The legitimization of practices in the forensic science disciplines must be based on established scientific knowledge, principles, and practices, which are best learned through formal education. Apprenticeship has a secondary role; under no circumstances can it supplant the need for the scientific basis of education and of the practice of forensic science. In addition, lawyers and judges often have insufficient training and background in scientific methodology, and they often fail to fully comprehend the approaches employed by different forensic science disciplines and the degree of reliability of forensic science evidence that is offered in trial. Such training is essential, because any checklist for the admissibility of scientific or technical testimony (such as the *Daubert* standards) is imperfect. Conformance with items on a checklist can suggest that testimony is reliable, but it does not guarantee it. Better connections must be established and promoted among experts in forensic science and legal scholars and practitioners. The fruits of any advances in the forensic science disciplines should be transferred directly to legal scholars and practitioners (including civil litigators, prosecutors, and criminal defense counsel), federal, state, and local legislators, members of the judiciary, and law enforcement officials, so that appropriate adjustments can be made in criminal and civil laws and procedures, model jury instructions, law enforcement practices, litigation strategies, and judicial decisionmaking. Law schools should enhance this connection by offering courses in forensic science, by offering credit for forensic science courses students take in other colleges, and by developing joint degree programs.

Recommendation 10:

> **To attract students in the physical and life sciences to pursue graduate studies in multidisciplinary fields critical to forensic science practice, Congress should authorize and appropriate funds to the National Institute of Forensic Science (NIFS) to work with appropriate organizations and educational institutions to improve and develop graduate education programs designed to cut across organizational, programmatic, and disciplinary boundaries. To make these programs appealing to potential students, they must include attractive scholarship and fellowship offerings. Emphasis should be placed on developing and improving research methods and methodologies applicable to forensic science practice and on funding research programs to attract research universities and students in fields relevant to forensic science. NIFS should also support law school administrators and judicial education organizations in establishing continuing legal education programs for law students, practitioners, and judges.**

9

Medical Examiner and Coroner Systems: Current and Future Needs

The role of coroner emerged in England in the ninth or tenth century. In the twelfth century, under King Richard I, the role of coroner was formalized in the Articles of Eyre.[1] Coroners or "crowners" were "guardians of the crown's pleas." The office originally was created to provide a local official whose primary duty was to protect the financial interest of the crown in criminal proceedings. On behalf of the crown, the crowner was responsible for inquests to confirm the identity of the deceased, determine the cause and manner of death, confiscate property, collect death duties, and investigate treasure troves. Through the implementation of British Common Law, settlers in North America brought coroner laws to the early colonies.[2] Moreover, early state constitutions explicitly mentioned the position of coroner, often without defining the role.[3] Georgia's state constitution was the first. Article XL stated that, "[i]n the absence of the chief justice, the senior justice on the bench shall act as chief justice with the clerk of the county, attorney for the State, sheriff, coroner, constable, and the jurors."[4]

The first formal acknowledgment of the need for medical training for coroners occurred in 1860, when Maryland passed legislation allowing coroners to require that a physician be present at an inquest. In 1877, Massachusetts became the first state to replace its coroners with medical

[1] Institute of Medicine (IOM). 2003. *Medicolegal Death Investigation System: Workshop Summary*. Washington, DC: The National Academies Press, p. 8.

[2] Ibid.

[3] Ibid.

[4] GA. CONST. of 1777, art. XL.

examiners, who were required to be physicians. Physician medical examiners began performing autopsies for coroners in Baltimore in 1890. In 1918, New York City instituted a medical examiner system.[5]

The National Academy of Sciences first addressed the state of death investigation in 1928. The National Research Council's (NRC's) Committee on Medical Legal Problems, whose members included Roscoe Pound, Dean of Harvard Law School, and John Henry Wigmore, Dean of Northwestern Law School, released a harshly critical report entitled *The Coroner and the Medical Examiner*.[6] In its first four recommendations, the 1928 committee suggested the following: (1) that the office of coroner be abolished. It is an anachronistic institution which has conclusively demonstrated its incapacity to perform the functions customarily required of it; (2) that the medical duties of the coroner's office be vested in the office of medical examiner; (3) that the office of medical examiner be headed by a scientifically trained and competent pathologist, selected and retained under civil service, and compensated by a salary which will attract men of genuine scientific training and ability; and (4) that the office of medical examiner be provided with the services of a staff competent in toxicology, bacteriology and other sciences necessary in the scientific investigation of causes of death, and with adequate scientific equipment. . . .[7]

Additionally, the 1928 committee recommended the development of medicolegal institutes, which would affiliate medical examiners with hospitals and universities.[8] In 1932, another NRC committee produced a review of existing medicolegal collaborations, which were mostly located in Europe.[9] This committee again advised a larger role for medical doctors within forensic science and criminal proceedings.[10]

In 1954, the National Conference of Commissioners on Uniform State Laws issued the Model Post-Mortem Examinations Act (the Model Act).[11] In its prefatory note, the Model Act stated the following:

> The purpose of the Post-Mortem Examinations Act is to provide a means whereby greater competence can be assured in determining causes of death where criminal liability may be involved. Experience has shown that many

---

[5] IOM, 2003, op. cit.

[6] Bulletin of the National Research Council, No. 64. 1928. *The Coroner and the Medical Examiner.* Washington, DC: National Research Council.

[7] Ibid., p. 89.

[8] Ibid., p. 90.

[9] Bulletin of the National Research Council, No. 87. 1932. *Possibilities and Need for Development of Legal Medicine in the United States*. Washington, DC: National Research Council.

[10] Ibid., pp. 111-112.

[11] The model act has been posted by the National Association of Medical Examiners (NAME) at http://thename.org/index.php?option=com_content&task=view&id=97&Itemid=41.

> elected coroners are not well trained in the field of pathology, and the Act should set up in each state an Office headed by a trained pathologist, this Office to have jurisdiction over post-mortem examinations for criminal purposes. The Office would supersede the authority of Coroner's Offices in this field.[12]

Following the release of the Model Act, a number of states implemented the proposed guidelines. Between 1960 and 1979, 12 states converted from coroners to medical examiners.[13] However, in the subsequent decades, updates to death investigation organizations slowed considerably. Between 1980 and 1999, only three states converted from coroner to medical examiner systems.[14] Since then, 11 states with coroners have remained unchanged, and only a handful of individual counties have independently implemented recommendations from the Model Act.[15] Several of the remaining coroner states have provisions in their state constitutions requiring that coroners be elected.[16] Although these provisions may be amended or removed, to do so will require political momentum. However, these provisions do not prohibit the addition of appointed medical examiners. For example, Kentucky has maintained county coroners, as dictated by its constitution, while also implementing medical examiners to serve at the state and district levels.[17]

MEDICAL EXAMINERS AND CORONERS (ME/C)

About 2,342 medical examiner and coroner offices provided death investigation services across the United States in 2004.[18] Individual state statutes determine whether a medical examiner or coroner delivers death investigation services, which include death scene investigations, medical investigations, reviews of medical records, medicolegal autopsies, determination of the cause and manner of death, and completion of the certificate of death.

---

[12] Ibid.

[13] Hanzlick, 2003, op. cit.

[14] Ibid.

[15] Ibid.

[16] ARK. CONST. art. VII, § 46; COLO. CONST. art. XIV, § 8; IDAHO CONST. art. XVIII, § 6; IND. CONST. art. VI, § 2; MISS. CONST. ANN. art. V, § 135.

[17] KY. CONST. § 99; KY. REV. STAT. ANN § 72.210 (2007).

[18] Hanzlick, 2007, op. cit. The Bureau of Justice Statistics omits Louisiana and classifies Texas as a medical examiner state, and accordingly reports the total as 1,998. According to Hanzlick, many of Texas's 254 counties maintain justice of the peace/coroner's offices.

ME/C JURISDICTION

ME/C jurisdiction is determined by each state code and generally extends to deaths that are sudden and unexpected, deaths that have no attending physician, and all suspicious and violent deaths. The actual classes of death over which the ME/C assumes jurisdiction vary from state to state. Classes may include deaths resulting from injury, such as by violence or poisoning; by circumstance, such as related to fire or under anesthesia; by decedent status, such as prisoners or mental health patients; or by timeframe, such as deaths that occur within 24 hours of admission to a hospital. About 1 percent of the U.S. population (about 2.6 million people) dies each year. In 2004, ME/C offices received nearly 1 million reports of deaths, constituting between 30 to 40 percent of all U.S. deaths, and accepted about one half of those (500,000, or 1 in 6 deaths) for further investigation and certification.[19] Depending on the jurisdiction, about 40 to 50 percent of deaths referred to the ME/C will, after investigation and examination, be attributed to natural causes, 27 to 40 percent to accident, 12 to 15 percent to suicide, 7 to 10 percent to homicide, and 1 percent as undetermined.[20]

ME/C MISSIONS

ME/Cs serve dual purposes. First, they serve the criminal justice system as medical detectives by identifying and documenting pathologic findings in suspicious or violent deaths and testifying in courts as expert medical witnesses. Second, as public health officers, they surveil for index cases of infection or toxicity that may herald biological or chemical terrorism, identify diseases with epidemic potential, and document injury trends.

Additional ME/C responsibilities include the response to and investigation of all deaths resulting from all hazards, including terrorism and mass fatality events, and the identification of the unidentified dead. In addition, some 13,000 unidentified individuals are currently entered into databases for the unidentified dead, and many thousands more are entered as missing persons, as thousands of families search for them. Accessing these databases and matching them to the many thousands of individuals entered as missing persons is a major challenge for all organizations. Eighty percent of surveyed ME/C systems "rarely or never" utilize the National Crime Information Center Unidentified and Missing Persons (NCIC UP/MP) files to match their dead bodies to those reported as missing by law enforcement

---

[19] J.M. Hickman, K.A. Hughes, K.J. Strom, and J.D. Ropero-Miller. 2004. *Medical Examiners and Coroners' Offices, 2004*. U.S. Department of Justice, Bureau of Justice Statistics Special Report NCJ216756.

[20] *Office of the Chief Medical Examiner's Annual Report: 2006*. Available at www.vdh.state.va.us/medExam/Reports.htm.

agencies, even though NCIC recently granted access to the files by ME/Cs. Access, however, is not uniform, and the information that may be available could be limited.[21]

The newly established National Institute of Justice (NIJ) Office of Justice Programs, National Missing and Unidentified Persons System, NamUs, remains underutilized. Identification efforts for either of the national government databases require multiple investigative as well as data entry skills, and they are labor intensive. ME/Cs need a functional death investigation system; staff to develop identification features; and the necessary education, training, and equipment to utilize the multiple databases that are necessary to identify the unidentified dead and to meet the increasing societal expectations that ME/C systems should be able to identify the unidentified.[22] Critically needed is a federal requirement that ME/C systems enter information on the unidentified into federal databases. A later section in this report discusses the medical examiner/coroner role in homeland security.

VARIATIONS IN ME/C SYSTEMS

As of 2004, administratively, 16 states had a centralized statewide medical examiner system, 14 had a county coroner system, 7 had a county medical examiner system, and 13 had a mixed county ME/C system.[23] Eight states had hybrid arrangements, with coroners and a state medical examiner office that performed medicolegal duties. The District of Columbia relies on a medical examiner system (see Figure 9-1). In large cities and counties, forensic pathologists serve both as medical examiners and pathologists. A few large systems, such as those of Los Angeles, California, and Cuyahoga County, Ohio, bear the historical name of a coroner system, but function essentially under a medical examiner structure. Eighty percent of ME/C offices are run by county coroners.

In total, there are approximately 2,342 separate death investigation jurisdictions.[24] Of 1,590 coroner offices in the United States, 82 serve jurisdictions with more than 250,000 people; 660 medium-sized offices serve between 25,000 and 249,999 people; and 848 offices serve small jurisdictions

---

[21] J.C.U. Downs, Board Member and Chair, Governmental Affairs Committee, National Association of Medical Examiners; Vice Chair, Consortium of Forensic Science Organizations; Coastal Regional Medical Examiner, Georgia Bureau of Investigation. Presentation to the committee. June 5, 2007.

[22] National Missing and Unidentified Persons System, NamUS. See www.namus.gov.

[23] Downs, op. cit.

[24] R. Hanzlick. "An Overview of Medical Examiner/Coroner Systems in the United States–Development, Current Status, Issues, and Needs." Presentation to the committee. June 5, 2007.

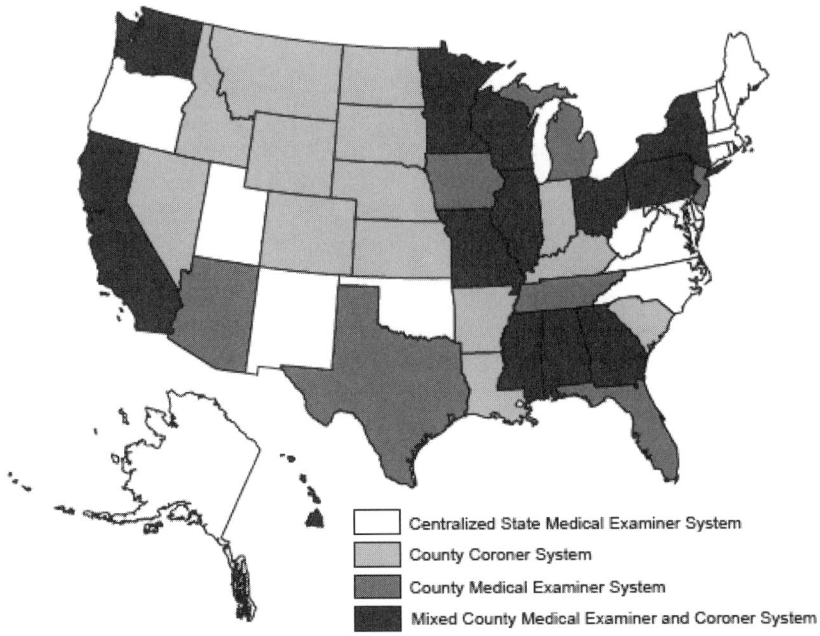

FIGURE 9-1 Death investigation systems in the United States, 2004.

SOURCE: J.M. Hickman, K.A. Hughes, K.J. Strom, and J.D. Ropero-Miller. 2004. Medical Examiners and Coroners' Offices, 2004. U.S. Department of Justice, Bureau of Justice Statistics Special Report NCJ216756. (In 2007, Kentucky became legally a mixed county ME/C system.[a])

[a] Constitution of the State of Kentucky, § 99.

of fewer than 25,000 people.[25] The hodgepodge and multiplicity of systems and controlling statutes makes standardization of performance difficult, if not impossible. Some observers believe that a revisiting of the model code is required, as has been proposed by numerous study groups over the years, in order to work toward the development of a modern model code for death investigation systems that utilizes new and available technologies that are responsive to the needs of the citizens.[26]

[25] Ibid.
[26] Ibid.

QUALIFICATIONS OF CORONERS AND MEDICAL EXAMINERS

Jurisdictions vary in terms of the required qualifications, skills, and activities for death investigators. Coroners are constitutional officers, with 82 percent being elected and 18 percent appointed.[27] Coroners as elected officials fulfill requirements for residency, minimum age, and any other qualifications required by statute. They may or may not be physicians, may or may not have medical training, and may or may not perform autopsies (see Box 9-1). Some serve as administrators of death investigation systems, while others are responsible solely for decisions regarding the cause and manner of death. Typical qualifications for election as a coroner include being a registered voter, attaining a minimum age requirement ranging from 18 to 25 years, being free of felony convictions, and completing a training program, which can be of varying length. The selection pool is local and small (because work is inconvenient and pay is relatively low), and medical training is not always a requirement. Coroners are independent of law enforcement and other agencies, but as elected officials they must be responsive to the public, and this may lead to difficulty in making unpopular determinations of the cause and manner of death.

Recently a 17-year-old high school senior successfully completed the coroner's examination and was appointed a deputy coroner in an Indiana jurisdiction.[28] In one state, justices of the peace are charged with determining cause and manner of death, but they are not medical death investigators. Whether coroners refer cases to pathologists for autopsy is largely budget driven (an autopsy costs about $2,000), although access to pathologists may be an issue if regional interjurisdictional arrangements do not exist. Even so, 84 percent of coroner offices see a need for professional standards,[29] and they identify resources for infrastructure, staff, and training as continuing needs.

Options for improving death investigation by coroners include (1) replacing coroner systems with medical examiner systems; (2) increasing the statutory requirements for performance of coroners; or (3) infusing funding to improve the capabilities of coroners.[30]

Some coroners have suggested establishing a "Coroner College."[31] Coroners want grants for equipment, accreditation incentives, and access to forensic laboratories, NCIC, and automated fingerprint identification

---

[27] P.M. Murphy, Coroner, Clark County Coroner's Office, Las Vegas, Nevada. "The Coroner System." Presentation to the committee. June 5, 2007.

[28] "Teen Becomes Indiana's Youngest Coroner." See http://happynews.com/news/5122007/teen-becomes-indiana-youngest-coroner.htm.

[29] Murphy, op. cit.

[30] Ibid.

[31] Ibid.

Box 9-1
What Is an Autopsy?

An autopsy is the systematic external and internal examination of a body to establish the presence or absence of disease by gross and microscopic examination of body tissues. The pathologist makes a surgical incision from shoulder to shoulder and from the midpoint of the shoulder to shoulder incision to the pubic bone. The skin is reflected, and each organ in the chest, including the neck structures, abdomen, and pelvis is removed and carefully examined. An incision is also made from the mastoid bone on the right to the mastoid bone on the left, and the scalp is pulled forward and the bony cap removed to reveal the brain. The brain is removed and examined. The pathologist takes a small sample or biopsy of all tissues and archives them in formalin to maintain them for future reference. In medicolegal autopsies, all tissues other than the biopsies are replaced in the body, except for perhaps the brain or heart, which may be retained and examined by consultants for diagnoses causing or contributing to death. For hospital autopsies, depending on the list of permissions given by the person qualified to give permission, tissues and organs may be retained for study, research, or other investigations. The pathologist submits small 2 × 2 cm sections of tissue to the histology laboratory, where thin slices a few microns thick are subjected to chemical treatment to preserve them. The tissue blocks are shaved, so that a thin layer can be mounted on a glass slide and stained with dyes to differentiate cells. The pathologist can recognize diseases in the stained tissue. Medicolegal autopsies are conducted to determine the cause of death; assist with the determination of the manner of death as natural, suicide, homicide, or accident; collect medical evidence that may be useful for public health or the courts; and develop information that may be useful for reconstructing how the person received a fatal injury.

systems.[32] Lack of direct access to laboratories and insufficient funding for testing impair the expertise of coroners. Some coroners are amenable to protocols that would ensure the use of forensic pathologists for autopsy. However, even with these improvements, the assessment of the dead for disease, injury, medical history, and laboratory studies is a medical decision, as opposed to a decision that would be made by a lay person with investigative and some medical training. The disconnect between the determination a medical professional may make regarding the cause and manner of death and what the coroner may independently decide and certify as the cause and manner of death remains the weakest link in the process.

In contrast, medical examiners are almost always physicians, are appointed, and are often pathologists or forensic pathologists. They bring

[32] Murphy, op. cit.

the body of knowledge of medicine to bear when assessing the history and physical findings and when deciding on the appropriate laboratory studies needed to determine the cause and manner of death. In statewide systems, cities and counties have local medical examiners that are physicians trained to receive the reports of death, decide jurisdiction, examine the body, and make a determination of the cause and manner of death. They certify locally many obvious natural and accidental deaths. In statewide and regionalized statewide systems, local medical examiners do not need to be forensic pathologists and do not perform autopsies, but they do refer, according to protocols, deaths from violence—particularly suicides, homicides, and deaths occurring under suspicious circumstances—to a central or regional autopsy facility for autopsy and further follow-up by a forensic pathologist. In hybrid or mixed state systems, coroners may refer cases for autopsy to forensic pathologists, but there is no supervision or quality assurance to ensure that the coroner's certification of the cause of death and manner of death is concordant with the pathologist's conclusions.

ME/C ADMINISTRATION AND OVERSIGHT

ME/Cs have varying forms of organizational oversight. Forty-three percent of the U.S. population is served by systems that are independent, 33 percent by offices residing administratively in public safety or law enforcement organizations, 14 percent by offices in health departments, and 10 percent by offices within a forensic laboratory. Government reports over the years have recommended that a medical examiner system should be an independent agency or should report to a commission so that it avoids any conflicts of interest and so that it reports directly to the jurisdictional governing body. When this is not possible, incorporation into a health department, instead of into law enforcement agencies, seems to provide the next most compatible location.[33]

ME/C STAFFING AND FUNDING

ME/C offices serving populations of less than 25,000 people employ 1 to 2 full-time equivalent (FTE) staff members, while offices serving populations of 1 million or more employ an average of 50 FTEs.[34] Competent death investigations require that trained medical death investigators attend scenes; medically credentialed persons perform external physical examinations; and forensic pathologists perform medicolegal autopsies, employ and

[33] V. Weedn. "Legal Impediment to Adequate Medicolegal Death Investigation." Presentation to the committee. June 5, 2007.

[34] Downs, op. cit.

interpret radiographs, prepare records, maintain databases, and provide competent and credible testimony in courts. Staff requires training and expensive equipment to utilize and integrate new technologies. Efforts are restricted by budgets, and budgets vary widely, ranging from $18,000 to $2.5 million annually for county systems, depending on the size of the population. A 2007 survey conducted for the National Association of Medical Examiners (NAME) by Hanzlick revealed that county systems' per capita cost ranged from $1.31 to $9.19, with a mean of $2.89. State systems benefit from economies of scale and function more economically at $.64 to $2.81, with a mean of $1.76. [35] The large variation in qualifications, staffing, budgets, and the multiple skills required for competent death investigations, especially in small jurisdictions, has resulted in marked variation in the quantity and quality of death investigations in the United States.

Physical facilities also vary in adequacy. Only one-third of offices have in-house facilities to perform the histology needed to make microscopic diagnoses on tissues sampled at autopsy. Only one-third have in-house toxicology capabilities to identify drugs present in the deceased that either contributed to or were the primary cause of death. One-third do not have radiology services in-house that would allow the identification of missiles, disease, bony injury or identification features in decedents.[36] Some coroner systems do not have any physical facility at all.

It is clear that death investigations in the United States rely on a patchwork of coroners and medical examiners and that these vary greatly in the budgets, staff, equipment, and training available to them, and in the quality of services they provide. No matter what the level of quality of other forensic science disciplines that are supported by a particular jurisdiction may be, if the death investigation does not include competent death investigation and forensic pathology services, both civil and criminal cases may be compromised.

All ME/Cs share the following deficiencies to some degree:

- imperfect legal structure/code controlling death investigations;
- inadequate expertise to investigate and medically assess decedents;
- inadequate resources to perform competent death investigations;
- inadequate facilities and equipment for carrying out body views and conducting autopsies;
- inadequate technical infrastructure (laboratory support);
- inadequate training of personnel in the forensic science disciplines;

---

[35] R. Hanzlick. "An Overview of Medical Examiner/Coroner Systems in the United States—Development, Current Status, Issues, and Needs." Presentation to the committee. June 5, 2007.

[36] Murphy, op. cit.

- lack of best practices and information standards;
- lack of quality measures and controls;
- lack of information systems; and
- lack of translational research and associations with university research.[37]

THE MOVEMENT TO CONVERT CORONER SYSTEMS TO MEDICAL EXAMINER SYSTEMS

As mentioned above, the movement to improve death investigations by bringing in medical expertise in the form of medical examiner systems is not new. Early NRC reports were followed in 2003 by an Institute of Medicine Workshop on the Medicolegal Death Investigation System, which also concluded that the medical examiner system is the best organizational structure for utilizing medical expertise to assess the presence or absence of disease and injury and for correlating the medical findings and investigative information to arrive at a determination of cause of death and manner of death. Progress has been very slow.

Additional impediments to progress include the need for some states to change state constitutions or codes, the political constituent base underpinning local coroners, insufficient population and budget to support a competent independent system in small localities, an unwillingness to develop cooperative regionalization for provision of autopsy services, the shortage of physicians—especially pathologists and forensic pathologists—and lack of interest, advocacy, or the perception of need.[38] To implement such conversions, the United States will require a national vision, a model code, increased numbers of forensic pathologists, and funding for infrastructure, staff, education, training, and equipment.

One possible model for providing incentives for these conversions could be an initiative similar to the Law Enforcement Assistance Administration (LEAA). LEAA was a federal agency operating from 1968 to 1982 with the purpose of funneling federal funding to state and local law enforcement agencies. The agency created state planning agencies and funded educational programs, research, and matching grants for physical plants and a variety of local crime control initiatives. For example, an $8 million grant to Virginia established the Virginia Department of Forensic Science, a premier state forensic laboratory that provides forensic science services to all state agencies and the Medical Examiner System in Virginia. [39] If

[37] Downs, op. cit.

[38] Downs, op. cit; Weedn, op. cit., Hanzlick, op. cit.

[39] Law Enforcement Assistance Administration at www.archives.gov/research/guide-fed-records/groups/423.html.

the capitalization of a medical examiner system is the major impediment to progress, an LEAA model can remove that barrier. However, a Medical Examiner Assistance Administration, or MEAA, would need to be structured so that the medical examiner would not be considered a servant of law enforcement and thus would not be placed in a position in which there is even an appearance of conflict of interest. Sensitive cases, such as police shootings and police-encounter deaths, jail and prison deaths, deaths in public institutions, and others, require an unbiased death investigation that is clearly independent of law enforcement. All previous studies have recommended that the medical examiner be independent of other agencies, or if they are to be under the umbrella of a central agency that the reporting chain should be through a health department. The medical examiner is first and foremost a physician, whose education, training, and experience is in the application of the body of medicine to situations that have a legal dimension that must be answered by a practitioner of medicine.

UTILIZATION OF BEST PRACTICES

The tremendous variation in death investigation systems also impedes interagency and interjurisdictional communication and the development of standardized best practices both in death investigation and in the performance of medicolegal autopsies.

NIJ and NAME have attempted to provide guidance for best practices. The NIJ document *Death Investigation: A Guide for the Scene Investigator; Medicolegal Death Investigator: A Systematic Training Program for the Professional Death Investigator*; the NAME Autopsy Standards and Inspection Checklist; and NAME's Forensic Pathology Autopsy Standards are available, but there is no incentive for death investigation systems to adopt them for use.[40]

Compliance is further limited because of heavy case loads, deficiencies in trained staff, absence of equipment, nonavailability of required day-to-day and consultative services, and the presence of contradictory policies and practices.

[40] U.S. Department of Justice, Office of Justice Programs, National Institute of Justice. *Death Investigation: A Guide for the Scene Investigator*. Available at www.ojp.usdoj.gov; S.C. Clark, M.F. Ernst, W.D. Haglund, and J.M. Jentzen. 1996. Medicolegal Death Investigator: A Systematic Training Program for the Professional Death Investigator. Occupational Research and Assessment. Grand Rapids; NAME Autopsy Standards and Inspection Checklist at www.thename.org; and G. Peterson and S. Clark. 2006. Forensic Autopsy Performance Standards at www.thename.org.

POTENTIAL SCIENTIFIC ADVANCES THAT MAY ASSIST ME/CS

In addition to current technologies, which are often unavailable and underutilized, new technologies are on the horizon to assist death investigators, medical examiners, and forensic pathologists.

Computerization of case records and the development of case information databases should be standard in any death investigation office, so that death data may be tracked for trends, response to public health and public safety interventions can be streamlined and accelerated, and continuing quality assurance measures can be implemented. There is no standard method of sample and data collection for ME/C systems. Multiple systems are commercially available that can be structured to meet the particular needs of any death investigation system. The initial cost of such systems is significant, and they require continuing maintenance, which rules out their utilization by small and/or underfunded offices. Even if such computer systems were present in each office, there is no standardization that would allow them to talk to one another, a necessity in a multijurisdictional event such as the Hurricane Katrina disaster, for which databases across states were critical to the identification of the dead and the tracking of survivors.

Laboratory information systems are available for the management of medical evidence, laboratory specimens, laboratory data, forensic samples, and personal effects. Effective database management allows information to be gathered and utilized by staff and analyzed for trends and quality issues. Effective databases are essential for managing any multiple fatality event. Rapid electronic transmission of reports is feasible if encryption software is available. At this time, ME/C information systems are less interoperable than current Automated Fingerprint Identification Systems (see Chapter 10). Although the standard autopsy report generally covers the internal examination by organ systems, reporting formats are not standardized among jurisdictions. And, although the NAME Forensic Autopsy Performance Standards provide a model for reporting autopsy findings,[41] it is not widely used.

Imaging equipment is critical to documenting findings sufficient for courts, for review by outside experts, and for reevaluation as medical knowledge advances. Fluoroscopy is helpful for locating missiles. Computed tomography scanning and nuclear magnetic resonance imaging may often present a better visual picture of some injuries and would likely reduce the number of autopsies carried out to rule out occult injury and to document in greater detail the extent of injury in accidents. The "Virtual

[41] G. Peterson and S. Clark. 2006. Forensic Autopsy Performance Standards. Available at www.thename.org.

Autopsy," or "virtopsy," utilizes multislice computed tomography and magnetic resonance imaging combined with 3-D imaging technology to create vivid images of the interior of the human body.[42]

The advantages of the virtopsy are that it is not invasive or destructive of tissue and can provide dramatic pictures of skeletal and soft tissue injury. It also provides some information when there is a religious objection to autopsy. Virtopsy has the potential to detect internal bleeding, missile paths, bone and missile fragmentation, fracture patterns, brain contusion, and gas embolism, in addition to occult fractures that are technically difficult to demonstrate during the traditional autopsy. Although a standard forensic autopsy is needed to recover evidence such as bullets or bomb fragments within the body and to collect specimens for testing, virtopsy offers a valuable tool for examination when dissection of the body is not feasible, when evidence is hard to visualize, or when a more complete assessment of injury is desired in noncriminal cases. For example, instead of a simple external examination for an obviously lethal injury in a vehicular violence death, virtopsy would permit more extensive cataloging of the injury to help automotive engineers design safer vehicles. The same technology can enhance bite mark impressions and some patterned injuries. Only a few ME/Cs have access to virtopsy at this time, and very few have the budget to purchase the expensive equipment or to build a suitable facility and staff and maintain it.

Scanning electron microscopy is not new but few ME/Cs have access to it to assist in identifying the metal conductor(s) in electrocution injuries, gunpowder residues in gunshot injuries, and other trace metals on skin or in tissues.

The anthrax bioterrorism attack that occurred in Connecticut, Maryland, New York, Virginia, and Washington, DC, highlighted the need to have biosafety capability for autopsy facilities. Currently, most autopsy facilities are 20 years old, on average, and are outdated in physical plant, technology, and biosafety capability. One-third of them lack design/airflow control of pathogens, and most function at biosafety level 2 rather than level 3.[43] Upgrading facilities to handle the potential biohazards associated with bioterrorism will require a massive infusion of funds that localities currently are unable or unwilling to provide. Laboratory safety in an era in which bioterrorism is a real threat remains an ongoing issue.

In-house toxicology services utilizing state-of-the-art equipment are essential for identifying drugs, intoxicants, and poisons and for detecting unsuspected homicides, suicides, and child and elder abuse. Yet only 37

---

[42] See www.nlm.nih.gov/visibleproofs/galleries/technologies/virtopsy.html.

[43] Downs, op. cit.

percent of systems have in-house toxicology capabilities.[44] The cost for complete toxicology utilizing private sector laboratories for cases is high, resulting in insufficient toxicology screening and minimal testing on cases even when they are clearly indicated.

Molecular diagnosis conducted on blood and tissue samples is routine in hospital laboratories to diagnose disease. Investigations of unexplained sudden deaths, especially in young people and infants, would benefit from greater access to molecular diagnostics. Molecular diagnostic procedures are available, but most ME/C offices cannot afford to conduct these procedures and do not have the medical expertise to request them or the skills to interpret them. For example, testing for inborn errors of metabolism should be a part of any examination of the unexpected death of an infant or toddler, and testing for long QT syndrome is important in determining the cause of cardiac death in young people or in those whose family pedigree discloses other sudden unexpected deaths. Molecular testing is available for the etiology of multiple causes of sudden cardiac death, including abnormalities in ion channels in cell membranes or channelopathies, hypertrophic cardiomyopathy, long QT syndrome, Marfan syndrome, right ventricular cardiomyopathy, dilated cardiomyopathy, and Ehlers-Danlos syndrome.[45]

Some testing can be carried out on a dried blood sample long after death has occurred.[46] Some molecular diseases are heritable, and it could be argued that the ME/C has a duty to identify these diseases and alert families about their presence. Many medical examiner offices archive a card with a dried blood sample on decedents, primarily to document personal identification, should the need arise, but also for future study. In the future, kin may request the archived blood cards, as the molecular diagnosis of disease improves and families seek to identify their risk. Thus, ME/Cs need education and training in and access to the specialized laboratory testing available to establish the molecular basis of disease and of sudden unexpected natural death.

---

[44] Ibid.

[45] S.E. Lehnart, M.J. Ackerman, D.W. Benson, R. Brugada, C.E. Clancy, J.K. Donahue, A.L. George, A.O. Grant, S.C. Groft, C.T. January, D.A. Lathrop, W.J. Lederer, J.C. Makielski, P.J. Mohler, A. Moss, J.M. Nerbonne, Y.M. Olson, D.A. Przywara, J.A. Towbin, L.H. Wang, A.R. Marks. Inherited arrhythmias: a National Heart, Lung, and Blood Institute and Office of Rare Diseases workshop consensus report about the diagnosis, phenotyping, molecular mechanisms, and therapeutic approaches for primary cardiomyopathies of gene mutations affecting ion channel function. *Circulation* 13;116(20):2325-2345.

[46] Personal communication between M.J. Ackerman and Marcella Fierro. June 16, 2008.

THE SHORTAGE OF MEDICAL EXAMINERS AND FORENSIC PATHOLOGISTS

Medical examiners are physicians who are appointed and charged with determining the cause and manner of death. In some states, medical examiners are forensic pathologists, while in other statewide systems, local, city, and county medical examiners are physicians but do not need to be forensic pathologists. They receive death investigation training and are responsible for examining bodies that do not require medicolegal autopsy and, according to system guidelines, for referring cases that need autopsy to regional offices where forensic pathologists perform the examinations and initiate further investigation as needed. Well-trained local medical examiners keep costs in line by reducing transportation costs to regional or central offices and are more accessible than pathologists in distant offices. Changes in the delivery of health care, increased patient caseloads, the inconvenience of attending scenes, the need for before and after hours examination of decedents, and the level of remuneration have made it difficult for statewide systems to recruit busy physicians to serve as community or local medical examiners. If this trend continues, systems will rely more heavily on lay medical death investigators and will need to develop training programs that assure competency.

Forensic pathology is the subspecialty of medicine devoted to the investigation and physical examination of persons who die a sudden, unexpected, suspicious, or violent death. Forensic pathology derives its name from "forensis" (public), or pertaining to the forum, and "pathos" (suffering), referring to pathos or suffering. The term ultimately evolved to encompass the study of deaths due to injury and disease and of deaths that are of interest to the legal "forum." Forensic pathologists are physicians who have completed, at a minimum, four years of medical school and three to four years of medical specialty training in anatomical pathology or anatomical and clinical pathology, followed by an accredited fellowship year in forensic pathology. They are certified by examination and assessment of their credentials by the American Board of Pathology in, at a minimum, anatomical pathology, and by subspecialty examination, as having special competence in forensic pathology.

As of 2008, approximately 38 forensic pathology residency programs accredited by the Accreditation Council for Graduate Medical Education sponsored approximately 70 training fellowships. Some positions are unfunded, and others did not find suitable candidates. Forty-two candidates were certified in forensic pathology by the American Board of Pathology in January 2008. Pathologists must recertify by examination every 10 years to maintain their certifications, in addition to maintaining a professional license in the state in which they are practicing, by submitting a description of practice for pathologists that do not practice as hospital staff and by earning continuing medical education credits.[47]

Forensic pathologists examine the dead to identify specific classes of injury, collect medical evidence, determine the presence or absence of natural disease, and determine the physiological cause of death. They document their findings in reports for the civil and criminal courts and provide information to family members and others who have a legitimate need to know. They may sign the death certificate describing the manner or circumstances under which death occurred (natural, accident, suicide, homicide, or undetermined). The examinations forensic pathologists carry out may be inspections or "views" of the external surfaces of a body or a medicolegal autopsy, which comprises an external and internal examination of the head, thorax, abdomen, and any other body region pertinent to the case. The nature of the death and its circumstances dictate which type of examination the forensic pathologist performs on an individual case. Pathologists who are not certified in forensic pathology perform many of the medicolegal autopsies in the United States.

Forensic pathologists practice in multiple settings. Most operate within death investigation systems and are appointed as civil servants and serve as medical examiner forensic pathologists. Some function as private practitioners, while others serve as consultants. They may operate under a fee-for-service agreement or be under contract to a city or county jurisdiction to provide medical examiner services. Others may serve as coroner's pathologists, and perform autopsies and prepare reports for coroners, who by statute assign the cause and manner of death and sign the death certificate.

An estimated 1,300 pathologists have been certified in forensic pathology since the American Board of Pathology first offered the certification in 1959 (about 5,000 medical residents enter internal medicine programs each year). Currently, approximately 400 to 500 physicians practice forensic pathology full time. Although there are only about 70 positions available each year, recent data indicate that only 70 percent of the slots are filled. NAME recommends an autopsy caseload of no more than 250 cases per year. The estimated need is for about 1,000 forensic pathologists; about 10 percent of available positions are vacant because of manpower shortages and/or insufficient funding of pathologist positions.[48] Although many forensic pathologists earn between $150,000 and $180,000 annually, this range is much lower than the average income of most hospital-based pathologists starting at the entry level.

An Association of American Medical Colleges (AAMC) survey indi-

---

[47] American Board of Pathology at www.abpath.org/200801newsltr.htm; *ABP Examiner* 39. January 1, 2008 at www.abpath.org/200802newsltr.htm.

[48] Hanzlick, 2007, op. cit.

cates that the average medical school graduate in 2006 finished with debt in excess of $130,571 (including premedical school borrowing), with 72 percent having a debt of at least $100,000.[49] Interested pathology residents are less likely to elect to practice forensic pathology as a career if they are already burdened by debt load, and a program of loan forgiveness for years of service in a medical examiner system would be a major enticement to students who are considering a career in pathology. The shortage of qualified forensic pathologists required to staff aspiring medical examiner systems constitutes a major challenge not only for offices that are currently seeking staff, but for the future as well.

STANDARDS AND ACCREDITATION FOR DEATH INVESTIGATION SYSTEMS

Currently, the standard for quality in death investigation for medical examiner offices is accreditation by NAME. Accreditation attests that an office has a functional governing code, adequate staff, equipment, training, and a suitable physical facility and produces a forensically documented accurate, credible death investigation product. Of all ME/C systems nationally, only 54 are accredited by NAME. The NAME accreditation checklist is available online and describes the requirements for accreditation.[50] Accreditation is for a period of five years. NAME also offers an individualized assessment program to enable jurisdictions to identify what they need to meet accreditation standards. Impediments to developing systems that meet accreditation requirements include the following:

- Most coroner systems cannot qualify for accreditation because of problems related to size, insufficient staff and equipment, and insufficiently trained personnel, which inhibit their ability to perform a competent physical examination, make and/or exclude medical diagnoses on dead bodies, and make determinations of the cause and manner of death. The historic role of the coroner is insufficient to accurately perform the medicolegal and public health functions related to sudden, unexpected, or violent death.
- Many medical examiner systems are constrained by budget, lack of staff, lack of equipment, and insufficient facilities and cannot meet NAME standards.
- The accreditation process requires considerable staff work, including written policies and procedures.

[49] Association of American Medical Colleges at www.ama-assn.org/ama/pub/category/5349.html.

[50] NAME Autopsy Standards and Inspection Checklist at www.thename.org.

- The process requires renewal.
- There is administrative cost of the process.
- Many offices do not see any benefit to accreditation.

Federal incentives are lacking for states to perform an assessment of death investigation systems to determine status and needs, using as a benchmark and goal compliance with NAME current professional standards, guidelines, and accreditation requirements.

QUALITY CONTROL AND QUALITY ASSURANCE

Quality control and quality assurance begin with the implementation of standardized policies and procedures by qualified staff. For lay medical investigators, registration and certification by the American Board of Medicolegal Death Investigators requires standard performance procedures as outlined in the NIJ document *Death Investigation: A Guide for the Scene Investigator* and other published education and training documents.[51] For forensic pathologists, basic competence is initially documented by examination and certification and subsequently by recertification by the American Board of Pathology. Written office and morgue policies and procedures with scheduled reviews and updates help ensure consistent performance over time. Professional performance parameters, such as the NIJ investigation guidelines for investigators and the NAME forensic autopsy standards, are offered as national documents that all systems should be able to follow. Professional continuing education must be available and supported, and it should be mandatory.

CONTINUING MEDICAL EDUCATION

For pathologists to maintain professional standing they must earn Continuing Medical Education (CME) credits in accordance with the number required by their state medical licensing board. Attendance at forensic educational meetings, such as the annual meetings of NAME and the American Academy of Forensic Sciences (AAFS), help keep medical staff current. Other opportunities that offer valuable CME credits are meetings that focus on pediatric forensic issues and general pathology updates. AAFS meetings are multidisciplinary and afford an opportunity for updating in forensic anthropology, forensic odontology, and other forensic disciplines. The American Society of Clinical Pathologists offers CheckSample exercises and

---

[51] U.S. Department of Justice, Office of Justice Programs, National Institute of Justice. *Death Investigation: A Guide for the Scene Investigator*. Available at www.ojp.usdoj.gov.

quizzes on forensic subjects prepared by experts.[52] Regular in-house training on emerging technologies in pathology and forensic science, and journal clubs covering a broad spectrum of journals, can help educate and reeducate forensic pathologists and investigators. Medical death investigators may attend the same meetings. The College of American Pathologists offers self-assessment programs in anatomical and forensic pathology, as well as a continuing education program of forensic pathology case challenges.[53]

HOMELAND SECURITY

As part of homeland security, the National Response Plan (National Response Framework as of March 2008) identifies ME/Cs under Emergency Support Function 8 as responsible for management of the dead resulting from any hazardous event.[54] All deaths resulting from any form of terrorism are under the jurisdiction of the ME/C. MED-X, the bioterrorism surveillance program provided by the Centers for Disease Control and Prevention (CDC) for ME/Cs, utilizes syndromic surveillance of primarily out-of-hospital deaths (deaths occurring before the opportunity occurs for hospitalization and medical assessment and testing) to quickly identify deaths resulting from bioterrorism.[55]

With the exception of some large city, county, and state systems, the level of preparedness of ME/C jurisdictions is generally very low. Larger medical examiner systems may be able to manage events causing several hundred simultaneous single-site recoverable bodies with minimal outside assistance. Any event with thousands of fatalities would require federal assistance. Some statewide systems have developed consortia with neighboring states to supplement staff and equipment, but smaller cities and counties will need to rely entirely on federal assets such as Disaster Mortuary Operational Response Teams and the DOD Joint Task Force Civil Support.[56] Homeland security and disaster response would be well served by universal improvement in ME/C offices to manage mass fatality events such as the multistate Hurricane Katrina tragedy and the World Trade Center attacks, while also surveilling for the links between bioterrorism

---

[52] American Society of Clinical Pathologists CheckSample. Available at www.ascp.org/Education/selfStudyPublications/checkSample/default.aspx.

[53] See http://cap.org/apps/cap.portal.

[54] Homeland Security National Response Plan (known as the National Response Framework after March 2008) at www.dhs.gov.

[55] Ibid; K.B. Nolte, S.L. Lathrop, M.B. Nashelsky, J.S. Nine, M.M. Gallaher, E.T. Umland, J.L. McLemore, R.R. Reichard, R.A. Irvine, P.J. McFeeley, R.E. Zumwalt. 2007. "Med-X": A medical examiner surveillance model for bioterrorism and infectious disease mortality. *Human Pathology* 38:718-725.

[56] Disaster Mortuary Operational Response Team at www.dmort.org; Joint Task Force Civil Support at http://jtfcs.northcom.mil.

deaths. Multiple fatality management across jurisdictional lines, such as was needed in response to Hurricane Katrina, is nearly impossible under current conditions, given the absence of medical expertise in some systems, the absence of standards of performance, and the noninteroperability of systems and procedures. The recent infusion of funds to the states through the Department of Health and Human Services (DHHS) and the Department of Homeland Security (DHS) is of little assistance when there are no competent systems able or willing to employ those funds. Uniform statewide and interstate standards of operation, consolidation of small systems, regionalization of services, and standardization of staff training are needed to assist in the management of interstate and cross-jurisdictional events. A software program is needed that is universally usable and available, and its use should be promulgated by ME/C systems for multiple fatality management. (See also Chapter 11.)

FORENSIC PATHOLOGY RESEARCH

Currently, little research is being conducted in the areas of death investigation and forensic pathology in the United States. Individual ME/C offices mainly utilize their databases for epidemiological retrospective reviews. Individual forensic pathologists operating in any system carry heavy caseloads and often have no dedicated time, expertise, facilities, or funding for research. Research is further limited because many offices operate training programs independent of university medical schools. Occasionally, a specific case may inspire "litigation research" directed to the elucidation of a specific problem related to a case that is being litigated actively, but this does not replace broad and systematic research of a forensic issue. Few university pathology departments promote basic pathology research in forensic problems such as time of death, injury response and timing, or tissue response to poisoning. In general, research interest often is inspired by a national goal that is funded through grants. A review of the forensic literature for basic research in forensic pathology reveals that efforts are originating largely from Europe, Scandinavia, and Japan. In other countries, universities house a department of legal medicine and/or departments of forensic medicine and pathology where forensic pathologists have the time, expertise, and funding needed to perform basic forensic research.

The Accreditation Council for Graduate Medical Education (ACGME) requires forensic pathology training programs to provide fellows an opportunity for scholarly research or other scholarly activities.[57] These research projects are usually small and limited in scope because of the constraints of a one-year fellowship, legislation that does not permit most basic research

[57] Accreditation Council for Graduate Medical Education. Available at www.acgme.org/acWebsite/downloads/RRC_progReq/310forensicpath07012004.pdf.

on tissues that are available upon autopsy without the permission of next of kin, lack of funding, and lack of space. Historically, the consent issue derives from the fact that forensic autopsies are carried out for medicolegal purposes and thus do not require permission from the next of kin. But without this permission, research that utilizes tissue from medical examiner offices does not take place. The time constraints for the performance of medicolegal autopsies make finding families and obtaining consent difficult. Many projects consist of epidemiological reviews that while of interest are not basic science.

Some U.S. universities may administer some forensic pathology fellowship programs, while others may include forensic pathologists within their departments of pathology. In these instances, the forensic pathologist usually supervises a departmental autopsy service that performs hospital and forensic autopsies. A university connection usually provides the university with the opportunity to rotate pathology residents and medical students through an ME/C office for a brief period, usually several months, and provides exposure to forensic pathology as part of an overall education program for medical students or as required by ACGME for training residents in general pathology. Even in universities that have a department of forensic science, research is limited to the forensic science disciplines, and little or no research is devoted to forensic pathology or forensic medicine. In some cases, there may be collaborative, ongoing epidemiological activities, such as when forensic pathologists work with members of departments of trauma surgery to develop statistical studies or when a forensic pathologist presents data at surgical or pediatric death review conferences. Of the many impediments to academic research in forensic pathology in the United States, the most significant are the lack of understanding of forensic research challenges, the lack of a perceived need and national goals, the lack of grant funding of any kind to support research, the lack of forensic pathology researchers, and the lack of recognition for efforts directed to forensic pathology research within the university community. Grant funding drives research, but virtually no funding is available to encourage departments of pathology to make forensic pathology research a focus, and there is little tradition of collaboration between academic and forensic pathologists.

Translational research bridges the gap between basic science discoveries and their practical applications. In the case of forensic pathology/medicine, this means taking basic science research knowledge to the autopsy table.[58] Given the large numbers of autopsies performed in the

[58]NIH Roadmap for Medical Research: Re-engineering the Clinical Research Enterprise–Translational Research. Available at http://nihroadmap.nih.gov/clinicalresearch/overview-translational.asp.

United States in medical examiner offices, there is a great need for new knowledge that will filter down to the autopsy pathologist and for opportunities for practicing forensic pathologists to identify problems that need basic research.

COMMON METHODS OF SAMPLE AND DATA COLLECTION

State statute determines the sample or collection of cases that ME/Cs investigate and examine. The minimal data collected on each case is demographic and is entered on the certificate of death by the state division of vital records and death statistics, which also maintains the data. The data are reported nationally each year to the National Center for Health Statistics. ME/C offices with databases may keep records pertaining to their particular jurisdiction and collect additional data on specific diagnoses, or classes, of death. They collect useful death data through child fatality review teams, adult fatality review teams, surveillance programs for family and intimate partner violence, and the National Violent Death Review System.[59] None of these data collection projects is federally mandated, and for small systems there is no perceived benefit. ME/C reports are available to next of kin and others as provided by statute. ME/C investigations recognize product and equipment failures leading to death and report them to appropriate agencies. Before 2005, when funding was withdrawn, CDC maintained the Medical Examiner and Coroner Information Sharing Program (MECISP) to receive reports of product-associated deaths, which allowed early recognition of problem products.[60] Originally, MECISP was established to obtain data from all deaths investigated by ME/Cs and to share such information with relevant agencies. The major goals of MECISP were to improve medicolegal death investigation and to facilitate the sharing of death investigation information.[61] Many agencies depend on ME/C investigations and autopsies to complete their work, such as the Occupational Health and

---

[59]National Violent Death Reporting System. Available at www.cdc.gov/ncipc/profiles/nvdrs/default.htm.

[60] Centers for Disease Control and Injury Prevention Medical Examiner Coroner Information Sharing Project. Available at www.cdc.gov/ncphi/disse/nndss/contact.htm#mecisp.

[61] MECISP was established in 1986 by CDC with goals that included improving the quality of death investigation in the United States mainly by achieving uniformity and improving the quality of information obtained during the investigation of deaths by ME/Cs. The program was active and productive and very well received by medical examiners. It constituted the major interface between the public health and the ME/C systems. Approximately 10 years ago, CDC went through a period of internal reorganization and administratively began decreasing the budget for MECISP. MECISP was moved from the CDC National Center for Environmental Health to the CDC Epidemiology Program Office. The budget was eliminated in 2004, despite the efforts of NAME. R. Hanzlick. 2006. Medical examiners, coroners, and public health. *Archives of Pathology and Laboratory Medicine* 130:1247-1282.

Safety Administration, social services agencies, victim witness compensation programs, and workers compensation agencies.

Systems with in-house forensic pathologists may collect autopsy data, but often the data are collected in a format that is different from the one used for the underlying (proximate) cause of death data as listed on death certificates. The reporter may use a pathology classification system such as SNOMED (Systematized Nomenclature of Medicine) or an individually devised system that tracks diseases or injuries of personal or system-specific interest.[62] There is no universally accepted or required system for collection or maintenance of autopsy data by medical examiners and coroners. Analysis of data may be local or regional, and it may be conducted by review teams or by national organizations or agencies with interests in specific classes of data.

Scientific interpretation and summaries of the results are included in the reports generated by each ME/C office. Reports by medical death investigators that describe the circumstances of death are descriptive and vary in quality depending on the standards of the office. Pathologists produce the autopsy reports and may or may not provide an interpretive summary of findings. Reports vary from the academic pathology report that lists each organ system and any deviations from normal to the problem-oriented autopsy report that prioritizes diagnoses from the most important leading to death followed by any contributory and then noncontributory pathology of interest. Not all pathologists follow the NAME autopsy standards. The general expectation, at least for the legal forum, is that each autopsy will have documented the findings in sufficient detail through narrative and photographs and that review by another pathologist will confirm the adequacy of the examination.

Requiring the adoption of standards for death investigations and autopsies as well as accreditation of all ME/C offices would benefit all parties, including the recipients of ME/C services. Because the credibility of unaccredited offices is rarely challenged, implementing and enforcing standards will require major incentives as well as negative consequences for nonadherence.

CONCLUSIONS AND RECOMMENDATION

ME/C systems function at varying levels of expertise, often with deficiencies in facilities, equipment, staff, education, and training. And, unfortunately, most systems are under budgeted and understaffed. As with other forensic science fields, there are no mandated national qualifications or certifications required for death investigators. Nor is medical expertise

[62] SNOMED. Available at www.snomed.org.

always required. In addition, there is no one recognized set of performance standards or best practices for ME/C systems nor are there incentives to implement one recognized set. Also lacking are universally accepted or promulgated methods of quality control or quality assurance. It is clear that the conversion of coroner systems to medical examiner systems as recommended by many studies has essentially halted and requires federal incentives to move forward.

The Model Post-Mortem Examination Act of 1954 needs to be revisited and updated to include the elements of a progressive and responsive death investigation law. The revised code should include standards for administration, staffing, and training. Any changes to the system will require federal incentives to implement the changes in each state.

The shortage of forensic pathologists speaks to the need to provide incentives for young physicians to train in forensic pathology. Systems with authorized positions cannot fill them, because of this shortage and budget deficits. The National Forensic Sciences Improvement Act (NFSIA) must be fully funded to support the core needs of ME/C grantees for equipment and facilities, training and education, and infrastructure.

Many ME/C systems do not utilize up-do-date technologies that would help in making accurate medical diagnoses. Moreover, many are unable to make use of advances in forensic technology because of staff educational deficiencies, untrained staff, and budget stringencies. Basic and translational forensic pathology research are nearly nonexistent.

Homeland security is compromised because operating units related to forensic pathology are not standardized, and the multiplicity of systems precludes meaningful communication among units. Surveillance for bioterrorism and chemical terrorism is not universal, and database systems cannot operate across jurisdictional lines to share data or manage multiple fatality incidents.

Although steps have been taken to transform the medicolegal death investigation system, the shortage of resources and the lack of consistent educational and training requirements prevent investigators from taking full advantage of tools, such as CT scans and digital X-rays, that the health care system and other scientific disciplines offer. In addition, more rigorous efforts are needed in the areas of accreditation and adherence to standards. Currently, requirements for practitioners vary from an age and residency requirement to certification by the American Board of Pathology in forensic pathology.

Funds are needed to assess and modernize the medicolegal death investigation system, using as a benchmark the current requirements of NAME related to professional credentials, standards, and accreditation. As it now stands, ME/Cs are essentially ineligible for direct federal funding and cannot receive grants from DHHS (including the National Institutes of Health [NIH]) and the Department of Justice or DHS. The Paul Coverdell NFSIA is the only federal grant program that names ME/Cs as eligible for grants. However, ME/Cs must compete with public safety agencies for Coverdell grants; as a result, the funds available to ME/Cs have been significantly reduced. NFSIA is not funded sufficiently to provide significant improvements in ME/C systems. In addition to more direct funding, other initiatives could be pursued to improve medicolegal death investigation practices.

AAMC and other appropriate professional organizations might organize collaborative activities in education, training, and research to strengthen the relationship between the medical examiner community and its counterparts in the larger academic medical community. Medical examiner offices with training programs affiliated with medical schools should be encouraged to compete for funds. Funding should be available to support pathologists who are seeking forensic fellowships. In addition, forensic pathology fellows could apply for medical school loan forgiveness if they stay full time at a medical examiner's office for a reasonable period of time.

Additionally, the proposed National Institute of Forensic Science (NIFS) should seek funding from Congress to allow it, CDC, and DHS, jointly, to design programs of interest to medical examiners and medical examiner offices in national disaster planning, preparedness, and consequence management. Uniform statewide and interstate standards of operation would be needed to assist in the management of cross-jurisdictional and interstate events. NIFS also might consider whether to support a federal program underwriting the development of software for use by ME/C systems for the management of multisite, multistate, or multiple fatality events.

NIFS also could work with groups such as the National Conference of Commissioners on Uniform State Laws, the American Law Institute, and NAME, in collaboration with other appropriate professional groups, to update the 1954 Model Post-Mortem Examinations Act and draft legislation for a modern model death investigation code. An improved code might, for example, include the elements of a competent medical death investigation system and clarify the jurisdiction of the medical examiner with respect to organ donation. Although these ideas must be developed in greater detail before any concrete plans can be pursued, the committee makes a number of specific recommendations, which, if adopted, will help to modernize and improve the medicolegal death investigation system. These recommendations deserve the immediate attention of NIFS and Congress.

Recommendation 11:

To improve medicolegal death investigation:

(a) Congress should authorize and appropriate incentive funds to the National Institute of Forensic Science (NIFS) for allocation to states and jurisdictions to establish medical examiner systems, with the goal of replacing and eventually eliminating existing coroner systems. Funds are needed to build regional medical examiner offices, secure necessary equipment, improve administration, and ensure the education, training, and staffing of medical examiner offices. Funding could also be used to help current medical examiner systems modernize their facilities to meet current Centers for Disease Control and Prevention-recommended autopsy safety requirements.

(b) Congress should appropriate resources to the National Institutes of Health (NIH) and NIFS, jointly, to support research, education, and training in forensic pathology. NIH, with NIFS participation, or NIFS in collaboration with content experts, should establish a study section to establish goals, to review and evaluate proposals in these areas, and to allocate funding for collaborative research to be conducted by medical examiner offices and medical universities. In addition, funding, in the form of medical student loan forgiveness and/or fellowship support, should be made available to pathology residents who choose forensic pathology as their specialty.

(c) NIFS, in collaboration with NIH, the National Association of Medical Examiners, the American Board of Medicolegal Death Investigators, and other appropriate professional organizations, should establish a Scientific Working Group (SWG) for forensic pathology and medicolegal death investigation. The SWG should develop and promote standards for best practices, administration, staffing, education, training, and continuing education for competent death scene investigation and postmortem examinations. Best practices should include the utilization of new technologies such as laboratory testing for the molecular basis of diseases and the implementation of specialized imaging techniques.

(d) All medical examiner offices should be accredited pursuant to NIFS-endorsed standards within a timeframe to be established by NIFS.
(e) All federal funding should be restricted to accredited offices that meet NIFS-endorsed standards or that demonstrate significant and measurable progress in achieving accreditation within prescribed deadlines.
(f) All medicolegal autopsies should be performed or supervised by a board certified forensic pathologist. This requirement should take effect within a timeframe to be established by NIFS, following consultation with governing state institutions.

10

Automated Fingerprint Identification Systems

In the late 1970s and early 1980s law enforcement agencies across the Nation began adopting Automated Fingerprint Identification Systems (AFIS) to improve their efficiency and reduce the amount of time it took to identify (or not exclude) a given individual from a fingerprint or to conduct a background investigation. AFIS introduced an enormous improvement in the way local, state, and federal law enforcement agencies managed fingerprints and identified people. Before the use of AFIS, the fingerprint identification process involved numerous clerks and fingerprint examiners sifting through thousands of tediously classified and cataloged paper fingerprint cards, while dealing with delays and challenges caused by the realities of exchanging information with other agencies by mail, fax, or other means. With AFIS, fingerprint examiners use computer workstations to mark the features of a scanned fingerprint image (e.g., ridge endings, bifurcations), encode the resulting data in a machine-readable format, and then search for similar fingerprints in an associated database of known fingerprints and records. AFIS searches are fast, and they often allow examiners to search across a larger pool of candidates. Although challenging cases can be time consuming, depending on the size of the database being searched and the system's workload, AFIS often can return results to the examiner within minutes.

AFIS searches today fall into two distinct categories:

10-print searches, which typically involve comparing relatively high-quality, professionally obtained fingerprint images—for example, prints taken during an arrest or booking or as part of a background check—

with fingerprint records in an agency database, such as the FBI's Integrated Automated Fingerprint Identification System (IAFIS) or a state's criminal fingerprint database; and

Latent print searches, which are considerably more complicated than 10-print searches. In a latent print search, a fingerprint examiner attempts to identify an individual by comparing a full or partial latent fingerprint from a crime scene with the records contained in an AFIS database. Latent prints are regularly of poor quality and may be only a partial print, and often fingerprint examiners may not even know from which finger a given latent print came.

A third category (albeit one that includes elements of both categories listed above) might also be called "unidentified burned, decomposed, or fragmented prints," which may be either a complete 10-print card to be compared with known prints on file to confirm identity or partial prints recovered from the skin or dermis of damaged fingers of an unknown decedent to determine identity. This third category can include prints from single individuals recovered from a small single event or victims of a mass casualty event resulting from naturally occurring catastrophes or terrorism. In either case, AFIS systems have reduced the time required to accomplish many identifications from weeks to hours.

Today, the process of populating AFIS systems with records is managed primarily by uploading 10-print records from police bookings and background checks. Because images from these sources are generally of good quality (indeed, poor-quality 10-print records are normally redone at the time they are taken), an automated algorithm is adequate for extracting the features used to index an image for retrieval. Computer algorithms work well for performing comparisons of 10-print records (e.g., to see if the prints taken when one applies for a security clearance match the prints taken during a previous background check). However, submitting a latent print for comparison is a more customized process, requiring fingerprint examiners to mark or adjust the features manually to retrieve stored prints with the same features in analogous places. Because latent print images normally are not as clear or as complete as images from a 10-print card, the image processing algorithms used for 10-prints are not as good as the human eye in spotting features in poor images.

AFIS has been a significant improvement for the law enforcement community over the past decades, but AFIS deployments today are still far from optimal. Many law enforcement AFIS implementations are stand-alone systems or are part of relatively limited regional networks with shared databases or information-sharing agreements—the Western Identification

Box 10-1
The Western Identification Network

WIN was formed in May 1988 to facilitate the creation of a multistate AFIS implementation. A year later, the state legislatures of Alaska, California, Idaho, Oregon, Nevada, Utah, Washington, and Wyoming appropriated the necessary funding to begin work on the system.

The initial WIN AFIS was installed in Sacramento, California, with remote subsystems in Cheyenne, Wyoming; Salt Lake City, Utah; Boise, Idaho; Carson City, Nevada; and Salem and Portland, Oregon. Booking terminals also were installed in numerous locations throughout these states, and existing similar stand-alone systems in Alaska, California, and Washington were connected to WIN in 1990 to complete the initial network. At first, WIN's centralized automated database included 900,000 fingerprint records, but after connecting to Alaska, California, and Washington, the number of searchable fingerprint records increased to more than 14 million. Today, WIN members have access to more than 22 million fingerprint records from the western United States.

NOTE: For information about WIN, see www.winid.org/winid/who/documents/WINService StrategyJanuary2008.pdf.

Network (WIN) is one example of such a regional network (for more information on WIN, see Box 10-1).

Today, AFIS systems from different vendors most often cannot interoperate with one another. Indeed, different versions of similar systems from the same vendor sometimes cannot share fingerprint data with one another. In addition, many law enforcement agencies also access the FBI's IAFIS database[1] through an entirely separate stand-alone system—a fact that often forces fingerprint examiners into entering fingerprint data for one search multiple times (at least once for each system being searched).

There is no doubt that much good work has been done in recent years aimed at improving the interoperability of AFIS implementations and databases (see Box 10-2), but the committee believes that, given the potential benefits of more interoperable systems, the pace of these efforts to date has been too slow, and greater progress needs to be made toward achieving meaningful, nationwide AFIS interoperability.

---

[1] See www.fbi.gov/hq/cjisd/iafis.htm.

Box 10-2
Working Toward AFIS Interoperability

As early as 1986, the American National Standards Institute (ANSI) and the National Bureau of Standards (now known as the National Institute of Standards and Technology, or NIST) were working on ways to facilitate the exchange of fingerprint data. Their collaboration produced a standard defining minutiae data and both low- and high-resolution fingerprint images. The standard was not successful, however, because of conflicts with proprietary systems.

In 1993, ANSI and NIST teamed up again to create another fingerprint data standard, a standard later updated in 1997. It defined standards for minutiae data and low- and high-resolution fingerprint images in both binary and grayscale format, as well as methods for compressing and decompressing image data.

In the late 1990s, the International Association for Identification's AFIS Committee successfully demonstrated a method of conducting remote fingerprint searches across jurisdictions and across equipment from different vendors.[a]

In 2003, the ANSI/NIST standard was updated again. It grew to include 16 record types in total, with the addition of standards for such things as palm print data and latent print data.[b] The standard was recently updated once more and has subsequently been approved by ANSI's Board of Standards Review as an ANSI standard.[c]

The NIST-sponsored Minutiae Interoperability Exchange Test (MINEX) program is an ongoing series of coordinated development efforts aimed at improving the performance and interoperability of fingerprint minutiae standards. In 2004, the original project undertook to determine the feasibility of using minutiae data (rather than image data) as the interchange medium for fingerprint information between different fingerprint matching systems.[d]

---

[a] The committee's final report is available at www.onin.com/iaiafis/IAI_AFIS_071998_Report.pdf.

[b] For more information on the ANSI/NIST standards, see P. Komarinski. 2005. *Automated Fingerprint Identification Systems*. Boston: Elsevier Academic Press, pp. 162-166.

[c] This approved revision of the ANSI/NIST-ITL 1-2000 standard is now available as NIST Special Publication 500-271: *Data Format for the Interchange of Fingerprint, Facial, & Other Biometric Information-Part 1* (ANSI/NIST-ITL 1-2007) at http://fingerprint.nist.gov/standard/Approved-Std-20070427.pdf.

[d] More information about the work of the MINEX series is available at http://fingerprint.nist.gov/minexII/.

INTEROPERABILITY CHALLENGES

Despite the work done to date to achieve broader AFIS interoperability and its potential benefits (i.e., more crimes solved, quicker and more efficient searches, and better use of limited law enforcement resources), several persistent challenges to reaching this goal remain.

Technical Challenges

The technical challenges to AFIS interoperability involve both those that are encountered and addressed by the information technology community in other disciplines (such as data sharing and algorithmic performance) and those that are specific to AFIS and the sharing of fingerprint information (e.g., feature identification, reliability of latent print comparisons). In addition, systems will need to be designed with the flexibility to handle other kinds of biometric data in the future (e.g., iris and palm scans and possibly genomic data). As these latter challenges are addressed, retrieval algorithms within proprietary AFIS systems also may tend to converge, which could simplify the broader interoperability challenges.

Creating useful technical standards is never a simple undertaking, especially given a diverse array of stakeholders, proprietary systems, and ever-advancing technological capabilities (e.g., improved pattern recognition, better hardware, increased data compression). However, the successful interoperability of other distributed information networks—such as modern banking systems (e.g., ATM machines[2]), information sharing networks in the real estate world,[3] the Centers for Disease Control and Prevention's Public Health Information Network,[4] and even the Internet itself, each of which functions only by reliance on a number of finely crafted and agreed standards and protocols—is proof that efforts to develop and implement standards pay off in the end by allowing greater collaboration and sharing of information.

One other major area of technical challenge to achieving AFIS interoperability involves the algorithms that systems use to identify features in fingerprint images (e.g., how a system determines that a given pattern of pixels corresponds to a true ridge ending or bifurcation and how it infers what type of feature those pixels actually represent). To date, these algorithms

[2] Indeed, financial card transactions are facilitated by their own ISO standard (ISO 8583-1:2003). For more information, see www.iso.org/iso/iso_catalogue/catalogue_tc/catalogue_detail.htm?csnumber=31628.

[3] See, e.g., the Metropolitan Regional Information System (MRIS) at www.mris.com/about/WhoWeAre.cfm.

[4] CDC's Public Health Information Network is a national initiative to improve the capacity of the public health community to use and exchange information electronically by promoting the use of standards and defining functional and technical requirements. The network employs a messaging system (PHINMS) to rapidly and securely share sensitive health information among CDC and other local, state, and federal organizations over the Internet—information such as HIV records, pandemic information, and information on bioterrorism. Complete information about PHIN and PHINMS is available at www.cdc.gov/phin/.

have been largely proprietary and vendor specific (i.e., different for each type of system). In fact, experienced latent print examiners have found that different systems will retrieve different stored prints in response to a given input map of features, and they have learned system-specific ways of annotating features on a latent print in order to maximize the success of each system's (inferred) search algorithms. However, achieving broad-based AFIS interoperability will require baseline standards for these algorithms, so that fingerprint examiners can be assured of consistent feature mapping across systems. As mentioned previously, fingerprint examiners have learned by experience to provide different inputs to different vendors' systems, often purposely leaving out information—knowing that the added input will degrade the search quality:

> The examiner does not necessarily encode every point he can find in the latent print. LPU [latent print unit] examiners have learned through experience with the IAFIS program which types of points are most likely to yield a correct match. LPU Unit Chief Meagher told the OIG [Office of Inspector General] that examiners are taught to avoid encoding points in areas of high curvature ridge flow, such as the extreme core of a print. Unit Chief Wieners and Supervisor Green told the OIG that IAFIS does not do well when asked to search prints in which points have been encoded in two or more clusters separated by a gap. One reason is that IAFIS gives significant weight to the ridge count between points. If the ridge count between two clusters of points in a latent is unclear, IAFIS may fail to retrieve the true source of the print. Thus, an examiner will not necessarily encode every point that can be seen in a latent fingerprint, but rather may limit his encoding to points in a defined area in which the ridge count between points is clear.[5]

The fact that today's systems often do not effectively utilize most of the available feature information and require substantial input from fingerprint examiners suggests that there is significant room for improvement. An ideal, comprehensive AFIS, for example, would be capable of automated:

- reading of latent prints;
- encoding of most features of usable quality, including those features identified as Level 1 (fingerprint classes such as whorl, arch), Level 2 (minutiae), Level 3 (pores, cuts), and ridge paths, together with a provision for including other features that could be defined by the vendor/user;

[5] Office of the Inspector General, Oversight and Review Division, U.S. Department of Justice. 2006. *A Review of the FBI's Handling of the Brandon Mayfield Case*, p. 119.

- recognizing absent, blurred, double/multioverlap, poor-quality sections of an observed print and encoding the system to downweight, or omit entirely, during the search process;
- recognizing any orientation information;
- conducting database searches;
- providing "best matches"; and
- collecting statistical data based on the quality of the print and numbers/types of features.

Other technical challenges might include the development and use of a secure Web interface (or an analogous system) that would permit authorized latent print examiners in any jurisdiction to submit queries to IAFIS and other federated AFIS databases, as well as the development of standard procedures for maintaining AFIS databases securely, removing redundancies, ensuring that fingerprint data are entered properly, and conducting quality control and validation of searches (i.e., ensuring that queries are actually searching an entire database). Although some of the capabilities mentioned here are present in today's commercially available systems, significant improvement still can be realized.

Support from Policymakers

Given the complexity of the AFIS interoperability challenge and the large number of players whose contributions and cooperation will be necessary to meet that challenge, it is clear that no effort aimed at nationwide interoperability will succeed without strong, high-level support from policymakers in federal and state government. Resources available to law enforcement agencies for the deployment, use, and maintenance of AFIS systems vary greatly from jurisdiction to jurisdiction, and the considerable expenses associated with purchasing, maintaining, training for, operating, and upgrading an AFIS implementation—which can easily cost millions of dollars[6]—must be well thought out and weighed against other competing costs and interests facing law enforcement.

The committee hopes that this report will help convince policymakers of the benefits to nationwide interoperability and move them to provide much-needed support to law enforcement agencies, vendors, and researchers to help them achieve this goal. Indeed, the committee believes that true AFIS interoperability can be achieved in a timely manner only if policymakers provide a strong, clear mandate and additional funding from federal and state governments—both to support the research and development

---

[6] See P. Komarinski. 2005. *Automated Fingerprint Identification Systems*. Boston: Elsevier Academic Press, p. 145.

work necessary to achieve truly interoperable systems and to assist law enforcement agencies in purchasing, implementing, and managing systems and training personnel.

Vendors

As suggested above, AFIS equipment and service vendors must cooperate to ensure nationwide AFIS interoperability. However, to date—and as one could reasonably expect in a technology sector in which product differentiation and the maintenance of competitive advantages are prime concerns—vendors have had little incentive to design their systems to enable them to share information with competitors' systems. The committee believes that increased cooperation among AFIS vendors is a key to achieving meaningful interoperability. For example, one can imagine how it might prove useful if AFIS vendors could collaborate (perhaps through work facilitated by the proposed National Institute of Forensic Science [NIFS]) on developing standard (or baseline) retrieval algorithms. Such a step conceivably could make it less time consuming for fingerprint examiners to run searches on many different systems because they would not have to manually *tune* their searches to work on the systems of different vendors.

Administrative, Legal, and Policy Issues

As noted earlier, most AFIS implementations are either stand-alone systems or are part of relatively limited regional databases. To achieve truly interoperable systems, jurisdictions must work more closely together to craft acceptable agreements and policies to govern the routine sharing of fingerprint information. NIFS can facilitate the development of standard agreements along these lines, which could include issues such as the extent of system access to other jurisdictions, the management of search priorities, and the recovery of costs associated with processing the requests from outside agencies. In addition, many jurisdictions also might want assurances that they will not be held responsible for any possible misuse of fingerprint information that is provided to other law enforcement agencies.

CONCLUSIONS AND RECOMMENDATION

Great improvement is possible with respect to AFIS interoperability. Many crimes no doubt go unsolved today simply because investigating agencies cannot search across all the individual databases that might hold a suspect's fingerprints or contain a match for an unidentified latent print from a crime scene. It is possible that some perpetrators have gone free because of the limitations on fingerprint searches.

The committee believes that, in addition to the technical challenges noted above, a number of other critical obstacles to achieving nationwide AFIS interoperability exist involving issues of practical implementation. These include (1) convincing federal and state policymakers to mandate nationwide AFIS interoperability; (2) persuading AFIS equipment vendors to cooperate and collaborate with the law enforcement community and researchers to create and use baseline standards for sharing fingerprint image and minutiae data and interfaces that support all searches; (3) providing law enforcement agencies with the resources necessary to develop interoperable AFIS implementations; and (4) coordinating jurisdictional agreements and public policies that would allow law enforcement agencies to share fingerprint data more broadly.

Given the disparity in resources and information technology expertise available to local, state, and federal law enforcement agencies, the relatively slow pace of interoperability efforts to date, and the potential gains that would accrue from increased AFIS interoperability, the committee believes that a new emphasis on achieving nationwide fingerprint data interoperability is needed.

Recommendation 12:

Congress should authorize and appropriate funds for the National Institute of Forensic Science (NIFS) to launch a new broad-based effort to achieve nationwide fingerprint data interoperability. To that end, NIFS should convene a task force comprising relevant experts from the National Institute of Standards and Technology and the major law enforcement agencies (including representatives from the local, state, federal, and, perhaps, international levels) and industry, as appropriate, to develop:

(a) standards for representing and communicating image and minutiae data among Automated Fingerprint Identification Systems. Common data standards would facilitate the sharing of fingerprint data among law enforcement agencies at the local, state, federal, and even international levels, which could result in more solved crimes, fewer wrongful identifications, and greater efficiency with respect to fingerprint searches; and

(b) baseline standards—to be used with computer algorithms—to map, record, and recognize features in fingerprint images, and a research agenda for the continued improvement, refinement, and characterization of the accuracy of these algorithms (including quantification of error rates).

These steps toward AFIS interoperability must be accompanied by the provision of federal, state, and local funds to support jurisdictions in upgrading, operating, and ensuring the integrity and security of their systems; the retraining of current staff; and the training of new fingerprint examiners to gain the desired benefits of true interoperability. Additionally, greater scientific benefits can be realized through the availability of fingerprint data or databases for research purposes (using, of course, all the modern security and privacy protections available to scientists when working with such data). Once created, NIFS might also be tasked with the maintenance and periodic review of the new standards and procedures.

11

Homeland Security and the Forensic Science Disciplines

In its charge to the committee, Congress raised the question of the role of forensic science in homeland security. The committee recognized that, to address this issue thoroughly, it would need additional expertise and more time to fully undertake an analysis of the role that forensic science currently plays and could possibly play in the future. Such an analysis would require serious study of the current configuration of the Department of Homeland Security (DHS) and its relationships with the forensic science community, law enforcement, and national security. Indeed, as the committee began to explore this issue it became clear that the question of the role of forensic science in homeland security is a study unto itself. Not wanting to ignore this issue, the committee limited its analysis to the presentations made to the committee and the expertise of its membership. Consequently, this chapter should be viewed as a first step in addressing the role of forensic science in homeland security.

The development and application of the forensic science disciplines to support intelligence, investigations, and operations aimed at the prevention, interdiction, disruption, attribution, and prosecution of terrorism has been an important component of what is now termed "homeland security" for at least two decades. Major terrorist bombings in the United States and abroad in the 1980s and 1990s influenced the U.S. government to enhance federal investigative and forensic science entities to be able to respond more effectively. For example, forensic science played an important role in investigating the bombing of Pan Am Flight 103 (1988), the first bombing of the World Trade Center in New York City (1993), the Oklahoma City bombing (1995), the suspected attack or sabotage of Trans World Airline

Flight 800 (1996), the bombing of the USS Cole (2000), and the bombings of the U.S. Embassies in Kenya and Tanzania (1998). And even though the identification of the Unabomber (1996) occurred as a result of the cooperation of his brother with the authorities, the forensic evidence against Theodore Kaczynski was substantial and crucial to the case.

The nature of homeland security requires the integration of forensic science into the investigative process much earlier than is the case for criminal justice. That is, for homeland security, forensic science plays not only its traditional role of inferring what happened at a crime scene and who was involved, but also contributes more intensively to generating investigative leads and testing, directing, or redirecting lines of investigation. In this role, forensic science contributes to the gathering of effective and timely intelligence and investigative information on terrorists and terrorist groups. This requires both traditional forensic science tools and enhanced and specialized forensic analysis and information sharing—new tools that are being developed primarily by the intelligence and defense communities in the United States, with each community tailoring the new tools to its specialized needs and missions.

The intelligence and investigative capabilities thus build on a foundation of traditional forensic science expertise that exists in the military and the FBI. The Department of Defense (DOD), for example, includes the U.S. Army Criminal Investigation Laboratory, which, with its 137-member staff, carries out criminal investigations. It also conducts research activities to develop specialized techniques needed by the military. Some of the nontraditional forensic science capabilities available within that laboratory include methods suited to intelligence gathering and counter-intelligence and the ability to make inferences about foreign language documents. Plans for the future include developing capabilities such as increased integration of biometrics (used for security) and forensic science and improved accident investigation and reconstruction.[1]

Other DOD forensic science capabilities are found in the Armed Forces Institute of Pathology (with a staff of 25), the Cyber Crime Center (with a staff of approximately 190), the Joint POW/MIA Accounting Command Central Identification Laboratory (more than 46 staff members), and the Armed Forces DNA Identification Laboratory (with staff of approximately 138).[2] The Joint POW/MIA Accounting Command Central Identification Laboratory bills itself as the largest forensic anthropology laboratory in the world.[3] Also contributing to DOD's forensic science capabilities is its

[1] L.C. Chelko, Director, U.S. Army Criminal Investigation Laboratory. "Department of Defense Forensic Capabilities." Presentation to the committee. September 21, 2007.

[2] Ibid.

[3] Ibid.

Biometrics Task Force, which leads in the development and implementation of biometric technologies for combatant commands, military services, and other DOD agencies.[4] The DOD forensic science capabilities are not centrally managed.[5]

DOD has a particular interest in DNA identification, both of its own people and of enemies. The department has a repository of five million DNA samples, primarily from military service members, intended mostly for casualty identification. DOD also pools data with intelligence and law enforcement programs to build and maintain the Joint Federal Agencies Intelligence DNA Database, a searchable database of DNA profiles from detainees and known or suspected terrorists.[6]

The DOD forensic science laboratories are relatively well resourced, according to the Director of the U.S. Army Criminal Investigation Laboratory, and DOD personnel are active in professional forensic science organizations, national certification/accreditation bodies, and national scientific working groups. Of particular note is that all of DOD's institutional laboratories are nationally accredited,[7] unlike many civilian law enforcement laboratories.

An example of federal efforts to develop forensic science methods of importance to homeland security is the relatively new National Biodefense Forensic Analysis Center, established by DHS in 2004. The center's mission is to provide a national capability to conduct and coordinate forensic analyses of evidence from biocrime and bioterror investigations. It is supported by DHS research to fill short- and long-term capabilities gaps, but the center itself is devoted to actual casework. Before its establishment, the Nation had no dedicated biocontainment laboratories, staff, or equipment to conduct bioforensic analysis. It had no methods to enable the handling of biothreat agent powders, no methods to support traditional forensic analyses of evidence contaminated with a biothreat agent, and no place in which to receive large quantities or large pieces of evidence contaminated with a biothreat agent. There were no established methods for handling evidence and conducting analysis, no quality guidelines or peer review of methodologies, and no central coordination for bioforensic analyses. These gaps became very apparent during the Nation's response to the anthrax attacks of 2001.[8]

[4] T. Cantwell, Senior Forensic Analyst, Biometric Task Force and Leader, Forensic Integrated Product Team, Department of Defense, "Latent Print Analysis." Presentation to the committee. December 6, 2007.

[5] Chelko, op. cit.

[6] Ibid.

[7] Ibid.

[8] J. Burans, Director, National Bioforensics Analysis Center. "The National Biodefense Analysis and Countermeasures Center." Presentation to the Committee. September 21, 2007.

Bioforensics, which is sometimes referred to as microbial forensics, or as forensic microbiology, is a developing interdisciplinary field of microbiology devoted to the development, assessment, and validation of methods for fully characterizing microbial samples for the ultimate purpose of high-confidence comparative analyses. It supports attribution investigations involving pathogens or toxins of biological origin used in a biological attack. The bioforensics toolkit includes diagnostic assay systems that can identify infectious agents rapidly, as well as organic and inorganic analytical chemistry, electron microscopy, and genetic engineering. Much of the work must be conducted according to stringent safety and containment protocols, and dedicated laboratories are now under construction. The center's capabilities enable the identification and/or characterization of biological threats, physical and chemical analyses, and the generation of data that can help in investigations and ultimate attribution. In addition to conducting casework, the center aims to develop and evaluate assays for high-consequence biological agents that threaten humans, animals, and plants, achieve accreditation for bioforensic casework and then continue to expand the scope of accreditation for newly established capabilities, and establish and maintain reference collections of biological agents for comparative forensic identifications.[9]

Another component of forensic science for homeland security is found in the Office of the Director of National Intelligence, which coordinates the various elements of the intelligence community. Within that office is a National Counterproliferation Center that also carries out work in bioforensics.[10] The considerable threat of the acquisition, development, and use of weapons of mass destruction (WMD; chemical, biological, radiological, and nuclear weapons) has led U.S. government agencies to develop new forensic science capabilities. In 1996, this development was begun with the establishment of a specialized forensic hazardous materials unit in the FBI Laboratory, which came at a time of greater awareness of and concern over WMD in the hands of terrorists and in preparing for the 1996 Olympic Games in Atlanta. Interest and investment in this type of capability has diversified and expanded since that time in the FBI as well as in DOD, the Department of Energy, the Intelligence Community, and DHS. The programs described above are visible evidence of the government's commitment to forensic science and infrastructure as integral components of homeland security. At the time of this writing, the importance of forensic science and its potential for improving the attribution of WMD are also active topics in discussions internationally.

---

[9] Ibid.

[10] C.L. Cooke Jr., Office of the Deputy Director for Strategy & Evaluation, National Counterproliferation Center. "Microbial Forensics: Gaps, Opportunities and Issues." Presentation to the committee. September 21, 2007.

The traditional U.S. forensic science community generally has not been included directly in planning, preparedness, resourcing, response, training, and the exercising of large-scale or specialized forensic science capabilities for terrorism and homeland security, although the FBI Laboratory provides a link between homeland security applications of forensic science and traditional uses in criminal justice. One reason for this segmentation is that the traditional community has heavy commitments to day-to-day law enforcement requirements, timelines, and backlogs. Also, many of the homeland security applications of forensic science require specialized expertise and infrastructure that are not widespread, and they might require access to information that is protected by security classification. Although major metropolitan law enforcement agencies and forensic laboratories, such as those in New York City and Los Angeles, have developed some specialized tactical capacities of these types, most of the U.S. forensic science enterprise does not and will not legitimately invest in such capacities and will rely instead on agencies such as the FBI and those who are part of the FBI-led Joint Terrorism Task Forces[11] in some 100 U.S. cities.

For the most part, the specialized capacities and capabilities needed for homeland security are not warranted for most civilian forensic science laboratories and medical examiner offices, although there are exceptions, and some of the skills embodied in these new forensic efforts may have direct applicability to traditional forensic science disciplines. However, the skills embodied within the traditional forensic science and medical examiners communities are potentially an important asset for assisting in homeland security. The geographic dispersion of those communities is an additional asset, because a security event or natural disaster can occur anywhere, beyond the quick reach of specialized federal capabilities. In addition, to the extent that members of the forensic science and medical examiners communities might respond to WMD attacks before specialized experts can, it is important to train those local responders sufficiently so that they can properly preserve critical evidence while protecting themselves from harmful exposure. More generally, there would be value in strengthening the links between civil forensic scientists and those affiliated with DOD and DHS, so that all sectors can pool their knowledge.

The medical examiner community, in particular, could be viewed as a geographically distributed and rapidly deployable "corps" that can augment federal experts in efforts to monitor emerging public health threats or respond to catastrophes. When a catastrophic event takes place, whether it is the result of nature or terrorism, a large contingent of medical examin-

---

[11] *Protecting America Against Terrorist Attack: A Closer Look at the FBI's Joint Terrorism Task Forces*. Federal Bureau of Investigation. December 2004. Available at www.fbi.gov/page2/dec04/jttf120114.htm.

ers is sometimes needed on short notice. Yet medical examiners have not been appropriately funded or trained in the management of mass fatality incidents. (See Chapter 9 for a more complete discussion of the medical examiner's role in homeland security.) Plans and policies must be developed that enable this contingent use of medical examiners.

In written input to the committee, Barry A.J. Fisher, Director of the Scientific Services Bureau of the Los Angeles County Sheriff's Department, stated the needs and opportunities as follows:

> . . . [C]onsider a situation where there are multiple events in the US and aboard occurring simultaneously. Resources could be stretched to the breaking point, not to mention the concept of *surge capacity*. There is not an unlimited supply of forensic scientists available to the FBI. But there are probably 5,000+ public forensic scientists at State and local crime labs who could be enlisted to help. Some jurisdictions have plans in place to use local talent. Others do not. It varies from region to region.
>
> Forensic scientists are often called to crime scenes to assist in the collection of evidence. Yet few would recognize that they were looking at a potential improvised explosive lab. There is little training available at the national level. Much of the information is classified. State and local forensic scientists have no need for security clearances but often go through law enforcement background checks. This creates a classic 'Catch 22' situation. State and local forensic personnel can't be given classified information to recognize terrorist devices which they might be able to disable before they and others are injured.
>
> The identification of victims in mass casualties is another area where State and local forensic labs could play a part. (They could, for example, provide fingerprint identification services.) While few labs have the capacity to mount a major DNA testing effort, personnel are knowledgeable in evidence collection and can assist in such efforts. Again there are no consistent plans for using local or regional resources.
>
> Medical examiners and coroners use a system of volunteers called D-MORT (Disaster Mortuary Operational Response Team) to assist in mass casualty events whether natural or caused by terrorist incidents. A similar program could be considered to enlist State and local forensic scientist to assist in major incident situations. [12]

This chapter illustrates the overlap between the capabilities of forensic science and the needs of homeland security, but ideally, the forensic science community and homeland security communities should be more integrated with better communication. However, the committee limited its recom-

---

[12] B.A.J. Fisher. June 12, 2007. "Contemporary Issues in Forensic Science," unpublished paper submitted to the committee.

mendations on this matter because it recognized two critical factors: (1) the forensic science system is in need of a major overhaul (see Chapters 2 through 8), and until these issues are addressed it makes little sense to expand the efforts of state and local forensic scientists into homeland security operations and (2) many issues that would arise from such integration (e.g., federal jurisdiction, national security issues, restrictions on sharing of information) go beyond the charge and principal focus of the committee.[13]

CONCLUSIONS AND RECOMMENDATION

Good forensic science and medical examiner practices are of clear value from a homeland security perspective because of their roles in bringing criminals to justice and in dealing with the effects of natural and human-made mass disasters. Forensic science techniques (e.g., the evaluation of DNA fragments) enable the thorough investigations of crime scenes. Routine and trustworthy collection of digital evidence, and improved techniques and timeliness for its analysis, can be of great potential value in identifying terrorist activity. Therefore, a strong and reliable forensic science community is needed to maintain homeland security. However, to capitalize on this potential, the forensic science and medical examiner communities must be well interfaced with homeland security efforts, so that they can contribute when needed. To be successful, this interface will require: (1) the establishment of good working relationships among federal, state, and local jurisdictions; (2) the creation of strong security programs to protect data transmittals across jurisdictions; (3) the development of additional training for forensic scientists and crime scene investigators; and (4) the promulgation of contingency plans that will promote efficient team efforts on demand. Although policy issues relating to the enforcement of homeland security are beyond the scope of this report, it is clear that improvements in the forensic science community and the medical examiner system could greatly enhance the capabilities of homeland security.

Recommendation 13:

> **Congress should provide funding to the National Institute of Forensic Science (NIFS) to prepare, in conjunction with the Centers for Disease Control and Prevention and the Federal Bureau of Investigation, forensic scientists and crime scene investigators for their potential roles in managing and analyzing evidence from**

---

[13] See Institute of Medicine. 2008. *Research Priorities in Emergency Preparedness and Response for Public Health Systems* and workshop summaries of the Disasters Roundtable, dels.nas.edu/dr/

events that affect homeland security, so that maximum evidentiary value is preserved from these unusual circumstances and the safety of these personnel is guarded. This preparation also should include planning and preparedness (to include exercises) for the interoperability of local forensic personnel with federal counterterrorism organizations.

Appendix A

Biographical Information of Committee and Staff

Harry T. Edwards (Co-chair) was appointed to the United States Court of Appeals for the District of Columbia Circuit by President Carter in 1980. He served as Chief Judge from September 15, 1994, until July 16, 2001. Judge Edwards graduated from Cornell University, B.S., 1962, and the University of Michigan Law School, J.D., 1965, with distinction and honors. He was a member of the Michigan Law Review and was elected to the Order of the Coif. Before joining the bench, Judge Edwards practiced law in Chicago from 1965 to 1970. Between 1970 and 1980, he was a tenured Professor of Law at the University of Michigan and at Harvard Law School. He also served as Visiting Professor at the University of Brussels and as a member of the faculty at the Institute for Educational Management at Harvard University. Since joining the bench, he has taught at numerous law schools, including Duke, Georgetown, Harvard, Pennsylvania, Michigan, and New York University, where he has been a member of the faculty since 1990. Judge Edwards is currently a Visiting Professor of Law at the New York University School of Law. During his years as Chief Judge of the D.C. Circuit, Judge Edwards directed numerous automation initiatives at the Court of Appeals; oversaw a complete reorganization of the Clerk's Office; implemented case management programs that helped to cut the court's case backlog and reduce case disposition times; successfully pursued congressional support for the construction of the William B. Bryant Annex to the E. Barrett Prettyman U.S. Courthouse; presided over the court's hearings in *United States v. Microsoft*; established programs to enhance communications with the lawyers who practice before the court; and received high praise from members of the bench, bar, and press for fostering collegial relations among the members of the court. Judge Edwards' many positions have included Chairman of the Board of Directors of AMTRAK; member of the Board of Directors of the National Institute for Dispute Resolution; member of the Executive Committee of the Order of the Coif; member of the Executive Committee of the Association of American Law Schools, and Chairman of the Minority Groups Section; Vice President of the National Academy of Arbitrators; and member of the President's National Commission on International Women's Year. He also has received many awards for outstanding service to the legal profession and numerous Honorary Doctor of Laws degrees. Judge Edwards is a member of the American Law Institute; the American Academy of Arts and Sciences; the American Judicature Society; the American Bar Foundation; the American Bar Association; and the Supreme Court Historical Society. He is director/mentor at the Unique Learning Center in Washington, D.C., a volunteer program to assist disadvantaged inner city youth. Judge Edwards is the coauthor of five books. His most recent book, coauthored by Linda A. Elliot, *Federal Courts—Standards of Review: Appellate Court Review of District Court Decisions and Agency Actions*, was published in 2007. He has also published scores of law review articles dealing with labor law, equal employment opportunity, labor arbitration, higher education law, alternative dispute resolution, federalism, judicial process, comparative law, legal ethics, judicial administration, legal education, and professionalism. One of his most significant publications, "The Growing Disjunction Between Legal Education and the Legal Profession," published in the *Michigan Law Review* in 1992, has been the source of extensive comment, discussion, and debate among legal scholars and practitioners in the United States and abroad.

Constantine Gatsonis (Co-chair) is Professor of Biostatistics at Brown University and the founding Director of the Center for Statistical Sciences. He is a leading authority on statistical methods for the evaluation of diagnostic tests and biomarkers and has extensive involvement in research in Bayesian biostatistics, meta-analysis, and statistical methods for health services and outcome research. He is Network Statistician of the American College of Radiology Imaging Network, a National Cancer Institute-funded national collaborative group conducting multicenter studies of imaging in cancer diagnosis and therapy. Dr. Gatsonis has served on numerous review and advisory panels, including the Immunization Safety Review Committee of IOM, the Committee on Applied and Theoretical Statistics of NAS, panels of the Center for Devices and Radiological Health of U.S. Food and Drug Administration, the HSDG Study Section of the Agency for Health Care Policy Research, the Commission of Technology Assessment of the American College of Radiology, the Data Safety and Monitoring Boards for the National Institute of Neurological Disorders and Stroke and the

U.S. Department of Veterans Affairs, and several National Institutes of Health grant review panels. He is co-convener of the Screening and Diagnostic Tests Methods Working Group of the Cochrane Collaboration and a member of the steering group of the Cochrane Diagnostic Reviews initiative to develop systematic reviews of diagnostic accuracy for the Cochrane Library. Dr. Gatsonis is the founding editor-in-chief of *Health Services and Outcomes Research Methodology* and serves as Associate Editor of the *Annals of Applied Statistics, Clinical Trials and Bayesian Analysis.* Previous editorial positions include membership of the editorial board of *Statistics in Medicine*, *Medical Decision Making*, and *Academic Radiology*. He was elected fellow of the American Statistical Association and the Association for Health Services Research.

Margaret A. Berger received her A.B. from Radcliffe College and her J.D. from Columbia University School of Law. She is widely recognized as one of the nation's leading authorities on scientific evidentiary issues and is a frequent lecturer across the country on these topics. Professor Berger is the recipient of the Francis Rawle Award for outstanding contribution to the field of postadmission legal education by the American Law Institute/American Bar Association for her role in developing new approaches to judicial treatment of scientific evidence and in educating legal and science communities about ways in which to implement these approaches. Professor Berger served as the Reporter for the Working Group on Post-Conviction Issues for the National Commission on the Future of DNA Evidence. She has been called on as a consultant to the Carnegie Commission on Science, Technology, and Government and has served as the Reporter to the Advisory Committee on the Federal Rules of Evidence. She is the author of numerous amicus briefs, including the brief for the Carnegie Commission on the admissibility of scientific evidence in the landmark case of *Daubert v. Merrell Pharmaceutical, Inc.* She also has contributed chapters to both editions of the Federal Judicial Center's Reference Manual on Scientific Evidence (1994, 2000). Professor Berger has been a member of the Brooklyn Law School faculty since 1973. She has served on the following National Academies committees: the Committee on Tagging Smokeless and Black Powder; the Committee on DNA Technology in Forensic Science: An Update; and the IOM Committee on Evaluation of the Presumptive Disability Decision-Making Process for Veterans. She currently serves as a member of the National Academies Committee on Science, Technology, and Law, on the Committee on Science, Engineering, and Public Policy, and on the Committee on Ensuring the Utility and the Integrity of Research Data.

Joe S. Cecil is a Senior Research Associate and Project Director in the Division of Research at the Federal Judicial Center. Currently, he is directing the center's Program on Scientific and Technical Evidence. As part of this program, he serves as principal editor of the Center's *Reference Manual on Scientific Evidence*. He has published several articles on the use of court-appointed experts and is currently examining changes in summary judgment practice in federal district courts over the past 30 years. Dr. Cecil received his J.D. and a Ph.D. in psychology from Northwestern University. He serves on the editorial boards of social science and legal journals. He has served as a member of several panels of NAS, and currently is serving as a member of the National Academies Committee on Science, Technology, and Law. Other areas of research interest include federal civil and appellate procedure, jury competence in complex civil litigation, claim construction in patent litigation, and judicial governance.

M. Bonner Denton is a Professor of Chemistry and a Professor of Geosciences at the University of Arizona. He received his B.S. and B.A. in 1967 from Lamar State College of Technology. In 1972, he received his Ph.D. from the University of Illinois. He is the recipient of the American Chemical Society Division of Analytical Chemistry Award in Spectrochemical Analysis, 2001; the Pittsburgh Spectroscopy Award, 1998; the University of Arizona Excellence in Teaching Award, 1993; and the SAS Lester Strock Award, 1991. Dr. Denton has served as the editor of four texts on scientific optical imaging and has authored more than 190 peer-reviewed manuscripts. He has served as President of the Society of Applied Spectroscopy; Chair of the Analytical Division of the American Chemical Society; a Galileo Fellow, College of Science, University of Arizona, 2004; Fellow, Royal Society of Chemistry, 2004; Fellow, Society for Applied Spectroscopy, 2006; and Fellow, National Association of the Advancement of Science, 2006. His research interests include analytical instrumentation and spectroscopy and mass spectrometry.

Marcella F. Fierro served as Chief Medical Examiner for the Commonwealth of Virginia, and Professor of Pathology and Professor and Chair of the Department of Legal Medicine at Virginia Commonwealth University from 1994 to 2008. Dr. Fierro oversaw the medical examiner investigations of all violent, suspicious, and unnatural deaths in Virginia. She teaches forensic pathology to medical schools, law students, law enforcement agencies, the Commonwealth's attorneys, and other interested groups. She received a B.A. in biology cum laude from D'Youville College, Buffalo, New York, and earned her M.D. from the State University of New York at Buffalo School of Medicine. She completed residency training in pathology at the Cleveland Clinic and the Medical College of Virginia, Virginia Commonwealth University. She was a fellow in forensic pathology and legal medicine at Virginia Commonwealth University and the Office of the

Chief Medical Examiner in Richmond, Virginia. Dr. Fierro is certified by the American Board of Pathology in anatomical, clinical, and forensic pathology. After serving as Deputy Chief Medical Examiner for Central Virginia for 17 years, Dr. Fierro accepted a position as Professor of Pathology at East Carolina University School of Medicine, where she served as a Professor of Pathology in the division of forensic pathology and taught general and forensic pathology until she returned to Virginia in 1994 as Chief. Dr. Fierro has been active in professional organizations as a member of the Forensic Pathology Council of the American Society of Clinical Pathologists and Chair of the Forensic Pathology Committee of the College of American Pathologists. She is past president of the National Association of Medical Examiners and served on the board of directors and the executive committee of that organization and currently serves on several committees. Dr. Fierro is a Fellow of the American Academy of Forensic Sciences, was a member of the Forensic Science Board for the Commonwealth, and has served as a consultant to the Federal Bureau of Investigation for the National Crime Information Center Unidentified and Missing Persons Files and on federal panels and committees that are developing best practices in mass fatality management. Dr. Fierro has been active in the legislative process, serving as a resource and advocate in Virginia for matters related to forensic and medical examiner issues. Recent activities include establishing child and maternal mortality review teams and the National Violent Death Reporting System and Family and Interpersonal Violence surveillance programs for Virginia. Dr. Fierro has published in professional journals, edited a textbook, contributed chapters to several books, and presented at international meetings. Dr. Fierro served as a reviewer for the American Journal of Forensic Medicine and Pathology. She received Virginia's Public Health Hero Award and the National Association of Medical Examiners Service award, and she was elected to Alpha Omega Alpha as a distinguished alumna of the School of Medicine, State University of New York at Buffalo.

Karen Kafadar is Rudy Professor of Statistics and Physics at Indiana University. She received her B.S. and M.S. degrees from Stanford and her Ph.D. in statistics from Princeton under John Tukey. Her research focuses on exploratory data analysis, robust methods, characterization of uncertainty in quantitative studies, and analysis of experimental data in the physical, chemical, biological, and engineering sciences. Previously, she was Professor and Chancellor's Scholar in the Departments of Mathematical Sciences and Preventive Medicine & Biometrics at the University of Colorado-Denver; Fellow at the National Cancer Institute (Cancer Screening section); and Mathematical Statistician at Hewlett Packard Company (R&D laboratory for RF/Microwave test equipment) and at the National Institute of Standards and Technology (where she continues as Guest Faculty Visitor on problems of measurement accuracy, experimental design, and data analysis). Previous engagements include consultancies in industry and government, as well as visiting appointments at the University of Bath, Virginia Tech, and Iowa State University. She has served on previous NRC committees and also on the editorial review boards for several professional journals as editor or associate editor and on the governing boards for the American Statistical Association, the Institute of Mathematical Statistics, and the International Statistical Institute. She is an Elected Fellow of the American Statistical Association and the International Statistical Institute, and she has authored more than 80 journal articles and book chapters and has advised numerous M.S. and Ph.D. students.

Peter M. Marone is the Executive Director of the Virginia Department of Forensic Sciences. He joined the department in 1978 and served as Central Laboratory Director from 1998 until 2005, when he was named Director of Technical Services. Mr. Marone began his forensic career at the Allegheny County Crime Laboratory in 1971 and remained in Pittsburgh until 1978. Mr. Marone is a member of the American Society of Crime Laboratory Directors (ASCLD), the American Academy of Forensic Sciences, the Mid-Atlantic Association of Forensic Scientists, and the International Association for Chemical Testing and the Forensic Science Society. He has served on the ASCLD's DNA Credential Review Committee (for DNA) and was Co-chair of the Undergraduate Curriculum Committee of the Technical Working Group for Forensic Science Training and Education. He is a past chair of the American Society of Crime Laboratory Directors Laboratory Accreditation Board, a member of the Forensic Education Program Accreditation Commission for the American Academy of Forensic Sciences, and the chair of the Board of Directors of the Consortium of Forensic Science Organizations. Mr. Marone received his B.S. and M.S. in chemistry from the University of Pittsburgh.

Geoffrey S. Mearns is the Dean of the Cleveland-Marshall College of Law at Cleveland State University. Before his appointment in July 2005, Dean Mearns was a practicing lawyer. His practice focused on federal criminal investigations and prosecutions and complex commercial litigation. While in private practice, he was also actively involved in pro bono work. Before commencing private practice in 1998, Dean Mearns had a distinguished nine-year career as a prosecutor with the U.S. Department of Justice. During his tenure with the Justice Department, he was an Assistant United States Attorney for the Eastern District of New York, where he was Chief of the Organized Crime and Racketeering Section. In that position, he was responsible for investigating, prosecuting, and supervising cases against members and associates of organized crime families charged with racketeering, murder, extortion, bribery, and obstruction of justice. Dean Mearns also was the First Assistant United States Attorney for the Eastern District of North Carolina. From 1997 to 1998, as Special Assistant to the United States Attorney General, he participated in the prosecution of Terry Nichols, one of two men convicted for bombing the Oklahoma City Federal Building. Dean Mearns received his undergraduate degree from Yale University in 1981, and he received his law degree from the University of Virginia in 1987. After graduating from law school, he clerked for the Honorable Boyce F. Martin, Jr., of the United States Court of Appeals for the Sixth Circuit. Dean Mearns has been active in professional and community service. Among other activities, he was twice Chair of the Merit Selection Committee on Bankruptcy Judgeships for the Northern District of Ohio; he was Chair of the Merit Selection Committee on United States Magistrate Judgeship for the Northern District of Ohio; and he was Chair of the Board of Trustees of Applewood Centers, Inc. He is a trustee of Wingspan Care Group, Inc., of the Cleveland Metropolitan Bar Association, and of the Sisters of Charity Foundation of Cleveland. Dean Mearns has been an adjunct professor at Case Western Reserve University School of Law and New York Law School. He has published articles on criminal litigation, and he is a frequent speaker and commentator on various criminal law issues, including counterterrorism.

Randall S. Murch is the Associate Director, Research Program Development, Research Division, National Capital Region, Virginia Tech. He holds Adjunct Professorships in the School of Public and International Affairs, College of Architecture and Urban Studies, and the Department of Plant Pathology, College of Agriculture and Life Sciences. He is also a Visiting Professor, Department of War Studies, King's College London, United Kingdom. Dr. Murch received his B.S. in biology from the University of Puget Sound, Tacoma, Washington, his M.S. in botanical sciences from the University of Hawaii in 1976, and his Ph.D. in plant pathology from the University of Illinois, Urbana-Champaign in 1979. He has extensive strategy, analysis, and leadership experience in the design, development, and implementation of advanced forensic capabilities for intelligence, counterterrorism. and other national security applications and purposes. Following brief service in the U.S. Army Reserve, Dr. Murch's first career was with the Federal Bureau of Investigation (FBI), where he was a Special Agent. He was assigned to the Indianapolis and Los Angeles Field Offices, where he performed counterterrorism, counterintelligence, and other investigations. During his career, Dr. Murch was assigned to the FBI Laboratory as a forensic biologist, research scientist, department head, and deputy director, at various times. Interdispersed with his Laboratory assignments were four assignments in the bureau's technical investigative program: as a program manager for complex operations planning, Intelligence Division; unit chief for a technology development and deployment group, Technical Services Division; squad supervisor, New York Field Office; and Deputy Director, Investigative Technology Division (formally Technical Services Division). Between his last Laboratory assignment and his last technical investigative program assignment, he was detailed to the Defense Threat Reduction Agency, Department of Defense, where he was the director of the Advanced Systems and Concepts Office and led advanced studies on complex current and future challenges dealing with weapons of mass destruction. He created the FBI's WMD forensic investigative program, served as the Bureau's science advisor to the 1996 Olympic Games, led forensic investigative aspects of a number of major terrorism cases, and initiated a number of new programs for both the FBI Laboratory and technical investigative program. In 1996, Dr. Murch created the FBI's Hazardous Materials Response Unit, the Nation's focal point for the forensic investigation of WMD threats, events and hoaxes. Throughout his FBI career, he also was involved with extensive liaison at the national and international levels in furthering science and technology for law enforcement, counterterrorism, and national security purposes. Dr. Murch retired from the FBI in November 2002, after nearly 23 years of service. From December 2002 through December 2004, Dr. Murch was employed as a Research Staff Member, Institute for Defense Analyses, a leading Federally Funded Research and Development Center, where he led and participated in studies for the defense, intelligence, and homeland security communities. He is still an adjunct staff member at the institute. He joined Virginia Tech in December 2004, where he now works in the areas of life science research program development, systems biology, microbial systems biology, microbial forensics, and biosecurity and university strategic planning. He has served or still serves on several advisory boards, including the Board of Life Sciences, NRC; the Defense Threat Reduction Agency's Threat Reduction Advisory Committee; the Defense Intelligence Agency's BioChem 2020; the FBI's Scientific Working Group on Microbial Genomics and Forensics, and a new standing committee of NAS for the Department of Homeland Security's National Biodefence Analysis and Countermeasures Center. He has also been a member of or advised study committees of NRC, NAS, IOM, the Defense Science Board, and the Threat Reduction Advisory Committee. Dr. Murch has been a member of the American Academy of Forensic Sciences and the American Society of Crime Laboratory Directors; has served on the Board of Directors, American Society of Crime Laboratory Directors; and has been a member of the National Institute of Justice DNA Proficiency Testing Panel. He also served as the Designated Federal Employee on the DNA Advisory Board.

Channing Robertson received his in B.S. in chemical engineering from the University of California, Berkeley; his M.S. in chemical engineering from Stanford University; and his Ph.D. in chemical engineering, with an emphasis on fluid mechanics and transport phenomena, from Stanford University. Professor Robertson began his career at the Denver Research Center of the Marathon Oil Company and worked in the areas of enhanced oil recovery, geophysical chemistry, and polyurethane chemistry. Since 1970, he has been on the faculty of Stanford's Department of Chemical Engineering and has educated and trained more 40 doctoral students, holds 7 patents, and has published more than 140 articles. He is Director of the Stanford-National Institutes of Health Graduate Training Program in Biotechnology. He was Co-director of the Stanford initiative in biotechnology known as BioX, which in part includes the Clark Center for Biomedical Engineering and Sciences. He directed the summer Stanford Engineering Executive Program. Dr. Robertson received the 1991 Stanford Associates Award for service to the university, the 1991 Richard W. Lyman Award, and the Society of Women Engineers Award for Teacher of the Year 2000 at Stanford. He is a Founding Fellow of the American Institute of Medical and Biological Engineering. Dr. Robertson serves on the Scientific Advisory Committee on Tobacco Product Regulation of the World Health Organization and on the Panel on Court-Appointed Scientific Experts of the American Association for the Advancement of Science. Because of his interests in biotechnology, he has consulted widely in the design of biomedical diagnostic devices. Dr. Robertson has also served as an expert witness in several trials, including the Copper-7 intrauterine contraceptive cases (United States and Australia), the Stringfellow Superfund case, and, most recently, the Minnesota tobacco trial.

Marvin E. Schechter has been a solo practitioner, specializing in criminal defense matters before state, federal, and appeals courts, since 1994. Mr. Schechter has held several positions with the Legal Aid Society of New York, including Deputy Attorney-in-Charge, Criminal Defense Division, Kings County. He is currently a member of the Board of Directors of the National Association of Criminal Defense Attorneys, a member of the Executive Committee of the Criminal Justice Section of the New York State Bar Association, and a past president of the New York State Association of Criminal Defense Attorneys. Mr. Schechter co-founded Getting Out/Staying Out, a program that provides 18- to 22-year-old Rikers Island Correctional Facility inmates with the opportunity to earn a GED and receive job counseling, employment, and housing. He has taught at the National Institute for Trial Advocacy programs at Hofstra University and Cardoza Law School and has been an adjunct professor for trial advocacy at Fordham University Law School. He received his J.D. from Brooklyn Law School.

Robert Shaler received his Ph.D. from Pennsylvania State University in 1968 and has had academic appointments at the University of Pittsburgh School of Medicine, the University of Pittsburgh School of Pharmacy, the City University of New York, New York University School of Medicine, and, most recently, at Pennsylvania State University. He joined the scientific staff of the Pittsburgh and Allegheny County Crime Laboratory in 1970, where, as a criminalist, he practiced forensic science, testified in court, and investigated crime scenes. He joined the Aerospace Corporation staff in 1977 and managed four Law Enforcement Assistance Administration contracts, one of which resulted in setting the bloodstain analysis standard for the Nation's crime laboratories until the mid 1980s. In 1978, he joined the staff of the New York City Medical Examiner's Office as the head of its serology laboratory, a position he held until 1987, when he moved to the Lifecodes Corporation, the Nation's first forensic DNA typing laboratory. As the Director of Forensic Science and Business Development, he introduced "DNA Fingerprinting" to the Nation's legal and law enforcement communities, through a series of nationwide, informational lectures. Dr. Shaler returned to the Medical Examiner's Office in 1990, where he created a modern Department of Forensic Biology, designed its current 300,000 square foot modern building, and established the city's first crime reconstruction team, which still operates from within the Medical Examiner's Office. In the wake of the 9/11 attacks on the World Trade Center, he assumed responsibility for the DNA identification effort, designing the testing strategy and coordinating the work of six different laboratories. In 2005, he published a book, *Who They Were—Inside the World Trade Center DNA Story: The Unprecedented Effort to Identify the Missing,* that told the story of the people working behind the scenes of the DNA work done at the Medical Examiner's Office in New York City. In July 2005, he retired from the Medical Examiner's Office and accepted a professorship at Pennsylvania State University, where he is the director of the university's forensic science program. His crime scene investigation course has attracted national attention, and his research interests are broad, focusing on applying science and technology to crime scene investigation and quantifying the biological response to trauma and stress. He has taught several workshops to working law enforcement professionals in crime scene investigation, crime reconstruction, and bloodstain pattern analysis.

Jay A. Siegel is Professor and Director of the Forensic and Investigative Sciences Program at Indiana University Purdue University, Indianapolis. He was Director of the Forensic Science Program at Michigan State University. He was Professor of Chemistry at Metropolitan State College in Denver, Colorado, and he spent three years as a forensic chemist with the Virginia Bureau of Forensic Sciences, where he analyzed illicit drugs and trace evidence. Dr. Siegel has testified as an expert witness more than 200 times in 7 states, as well as in federal and military courts. Dr. Siegel is a Fellow with the American Academy of Forensic Sciences, where he was awarded the Paul Kirk Award for outstanding service to the Criminalistics section in 2005. He is also a member of the American Chemical Society, the Midwest Association of Forensic Scientists, and the Forensic Science Society (United Kingdom). He is a member of the International Association for Identification and an Academic Affiliate member of the American Society of Crime Lab Directors. Dr. Siegel is an active researcher in forensic science, with many scientific publications. He currently serves as the principal investigator on a research grant from the National Institute of Justice on ink analysis, his second grant for this work. He also is the author of two textbooks in forensic science and is the editor in chief of the *Encyclopedia of Forensic Sciences*.

Sargur Srihari received a B.Sc. in physics and mathematics from the Bangalore University in 1967, a B.E. in electrical communication engineering from the Indian Institute of Science, Bangalore, in 1970, and a Ph.D. in computer and information science from the Ohio State University, Columbus, in 1976. Dr. Srihari is a State University of New York Distinguished Professor at the University of Buffalo in the Department of Computer Science and Engineering. He is the founding director of the Center of Excellence for Document Analysis and Recognition. He has supervised 30 completed doctoral dissertations. Dr. Srihari is a member of the Board of Scientific Counselors of the National Library of Medicine. He is chairman of CedarTech, a corporation for university technology transfer. Dr. Srihari has been general chairman of several international conferences and workshops: the Third International Workshop on Handwriting Recognition held in Buffalo, New York, in 1993, the Second International Conference on Document Analysis and Recognition, in Montreal, Canada, 1995, the Fifth International Conference on Document Analysis and Recognition, 1999, held in Bangalore, India, and the Eighth International Workshop on Handwriting Recognition, 2002, held in Niagara-on-the-Lake, Ontario, Canada. Dr. Srihari has served as chairman of TC-11 (technical committee on Text Processing) of the International Association for Pattern Recognition. He is currently Chair of the International Association for Pattern Recognition's Publicity and Publications Committee. Dr. Srihari received a New York State/United University Professions Excellence Award for 1991. He became a Fellow of the Institute of Electronics and Telecommunications Engineers (India) in 1992, a Fellow of the Institute of Electrical and Electronics Engineers in 1995, and a Fellow of the International Association for Pattern Recognition in 1996. He was named a distinguished alumnus of the Ohio State University College of Engineering in 1999.

Sheldon M. Wiederhorn (NAE) received his B.S. in chemical engineering from Columbia University in 1956 and his M.S. and Ph.D. from the University of Illinois, also in chemical engineering, with a minor in solid state physics. His Ph.D. topic was high pressure physics, with an emphasis on phase transformations in alkali halides. After finishing graduate school, he worked at DuPont at the Research Station in Wilmington, Delaware, during which time his research and scientific interests gradually changed toward materials science with a specialization in the mechanical behavior of ceramic materials. After three years, he began work at the National Bureau of Standards, where he carried out an independent research program on the mechanical behavior of glasses and ceramic materials. At the National Bureau of Standards, now the National Institute of Standards and Technology, Dr. Wiederhorn carried out a program on the mechanical reliability of brittle materials. He was one of the first to apply fracture mechanics techniques to study the fracture of ceramic materials. A result of his research was the development of techniques to assure the structural reliability of brittle ceramic materials. Techniques pioneered by Dr. Wiederhorn are now used to assure the reliability of glass windows in airplanes and in space vehicles. Dr. Wiederhorn is best known for the experiments he developed to study and to characterize subcritical crack growth in glasses. The results of these studies illustrated the complexity of subcritical crack growth, and a natural conclusion of his study was that the failure of glass was caused by the slow growth of cracks to a critical size, which determined the time-to-failure. In addition to his work on the fracture of glass, Dr. Wiederhorn directed a program to measure the deformation of structural ceramics at very high temperatures. The objective of this work was to develop ceramic materials that could be used as turbine blades in power turbines used for more efficient production of electricity. The program has resulted in the development of new measurement techniques for characterizing creep at elevated temperatures. A new mechanism of creep has also been discovered by Dr. Wiederhorn and his group, and ways have been suggested to improve the creep behavior of nonoxide materials at high temperatures. Dr. Wiederhorn has received many awards for his research and leadership at the National Institute of Standards and Technology. These include both a Silver and Gold Medal awarded by the Department of Commerce and the Samuel Wesley Stratton Award by the National Bureau of Standards. He is also a Fellow of the American Ceramic Society and has received a number of important awards for his research from this society, including the Jeppson Award for outstanding research on ceramic materials. He is now a Distinguished Lifetime Member of the American Ceramic Society. In 1991, Dr. Wiederhorn was elected a member of the National Academy of Engineering. At the National Institute of Standards and Technology, Dr. Wiederhorn is now a Senior Fellow and continues to carry out a research program on the mechanical properties of ceramic materials. His current interests are to use the Atomic Force Microscope to investigate the atomistics of crack growth in glasses and ceramic materials, with the hope of learning more about the crack growth process and the relation between crack growth and the microstructure of glass.

Ross E. Zumwalt is Chief Medical Investigator of the State of New Mexico. He received his undergraduate education from Wabash College in Crawfordsville, Indiana. Dr. Zumwalt graduated from the University of Illinois College of Medicine. He completed a rotating internship and one year of pathology residency at the Mary Imogene Bassett Hospital in Cooperstown, New York. Dr. Zumwalt then completed his pathology residency at the Southwestern Medical School and Parkland Hospital in Dallas. He received his forensic fellowship training at the Dallas County Medical Examiner's Office. Dr. Zumwalt served in the United States Navy as director of laboratories at the Navy Regional Medical Center in Camp Lejeune, North Carolina. He spent two years as deputy coroner in Cleveland, Ohio, and six years as deputy coroner in Cincinnati, Ohio, before coming to the Office of the Medical Investigator in 1987. Dr. Zumwalt is certified in anatomic and forensic pathology by the American Board of Pathology. He was a trustee of the American Board of Pathology from 1993 to 2004. He is currently a member of the Residency Review Committee for Pathology. Dr. Zumwalt has served as president of the National Association of Medical Examiners and is a member of the following professional organizations: The National Association of Medical Examiners; the American Academy of Forensic Sciences; the College of American Pathologists; the American Society of Clinical Pathologists; the United States and Canadian Academy of Pathology; the American Medical Association; and the American Association for the Advancement of Science.

Staff

Anne-Marie Mazza is Director of the Committee on Science, Technology and Law. She joined the National Academies in 1995. She has served as Senior Program Officer with both the Committee on Science, Engineering, and Public Policy and the Government-University-Industry Research Roundtable. In 1999 she was named the first director of the Committee on Science, Technology, and Law, a newly created program designed to foster communication and analysis among scientists, engineers, and members of the legal community. In 2007, she became the director of the Christine Mirzayan Science and Technology Graduate Policy Fellowship Program. Dr. Mazza has been the study director on numerous Academy reports, including *Science and Security in a Post 9-11 World, 2007; Reaping the Benefits* *of Genomic and Proteomic Research, 2005*; *Intentional Human Dosing Studies for EPA Regulatory Purposes: Scientific and Ethical Issues, 2004; The Age of Expert Testimony: Science in the Courtroom, 2002; Issues for Science and Engineering Researchers in the Digital Age, 2001;* and *Observations on the President's Fiscal Year 2000 Federal Science and Technology Budget, 1999.* Between October 1999 and October 2000, she divided her time between the Committee on Science, Technology, and Law and the White House Office of Science and Technology Policy, where she served as a Senior Policy Analyst responsible for issues associated with the government-university research partnership. Before joining the Academy, Dr. Mazza was a Senior Consultant with Resource Planning Corporation. She received a B.A., M.A., and Ph.D. from The George Washington University.

Scott T. Weidman is the Director of NRC's Board on Mathematical Sciences and Their Applications. He joined NRC in 1989 with the Board on Mathematical Sciences and moved to the Board on Chemical Sciences and Technology in 1992. In 1996, he established a new board to conduct annual peer reviews of the Army Research Laboratory, which conducts a broad array of science, engineering, and human factors research and analysis, and he later directed a similar board that reviews the work of the National Institute of Standards and Technology. He has worked full time with the Board on Mathematical Sciences and Their Applications since June 2004. During his NRC career, he has staffed studies on a wide variety of topics related to mathematical, chemical, and materials sciences; laboratory assessment; and science and technology policy. His current focus is on building NRC's capabilities and portfolio related to all areas of analysis and computational science. He holds bachelor degrees in mathematics and materials science from Northwestern University and an M.S. and Ph.D. in applied mathematics at the University of Virginia. Before joining NRC, he held positions with General Electric, General Accident Insurance Company, Exxon Research and Engineering, and MRJ, Inc.

David Padgham is Policy Director at the High Performance Computing Initiative Council on Competitiveness. Before joining the council, he was an associate program officer at the Computer Science and Telecommunications Board of NRC. His work there comprised a robust mix of writing, research, and project management, and he was involved in the production of numerous reports, including, most recently, *Software for Dependable Systems: Sufficient Evidence?*; *Engaging Privacy and Information Technology in a Digital Age*; and *Renewing U.S. Telecommunications Research*. Before joining the Computer Science and Telecommunications Board in 2006, Mr. Padgham was a policy analyst for the Association for Computing Machinery, where he worked closely with its public policy committee, USACM, to support the organization's policy principles and promote its policy interests. Mr. Padgham holds a master's degree in library and information science, from the Catholic University of America in Washington, D.C., and a B.A. in English, from Warren Wilson College in Asheville, North Carolina.

John Sislin is a Program Officer with the Board on Higher Education and Workforce. His work focuses on topics in international affairs, higher education, globalization, and the impact of science and technology on society and security. His work on international affairs includes developing a system to monitor compliance with international labor standards for the U.S. Department of Labor and development of a biographical database on world leaders with foreign education or employment experience sponsored by the MacArthur Foundation. Dr. Sislin's work in higher education has focused on gender (three projects on recruiting, retaining, and advancing women in science and engineering in higher education and academic careers) and the role of community colleges in educating future engineers. He has worked on program evaluations for the NIST, the United States Institute of Peace, and NSF. Other projects include a survey of life scientists' attitudes toward personal responsibility regarding dual-use research and biosecurity and a study of priorities in civil aeronautics research sponsored by NASA. Before coming to the Academies, Dr. Sislin's previous research focused on international and civil conflict, human rights, international security, and U.S. foreign policy. Dr. Sislin received a B.A. from the University of Michigan in Russian and East European Studies and a Ph.D. in Political Science from Indiana University.

Steven Kendall is Senior Program Associate for the Committee on Science, Technology, and Law. He is a Ph.D. candidate in the Department of the History of Art and Architecture at the University of California, Santa Barbara, where he is completing a dissertation on nineteenth-century British painting. Mr. Kendall received his M.A. in Victorian art and architecture at the University of London. Before joining The National Academies in 2007, he worked at the Smithsonian American Art Museum and The Huntington in San Marino, California.

Kathi E. Hanna is a science and health policy consultant, writer, and editor specializing in biomedical research policy and bioethics. She served as Research Director and Senior Consultant to President Clinton's National Bioethics Advisory Commission and as Senior Advisor to President Clinton's Advisory Committee on Gulf War Veterans Illnesses. More recently, she served as the lead author and editor of President Bush's Task Force to Improve Health Care Delivery for Our Nation's Veterans. In the 1980s and 1990s, Dr. Hanna was a Senior Analyst at the congressional Office of Technology Assessment, contributing to numerous science policy studies requested by congressional committees on science education, research funding, biotechnology, women's health, human genetics, bioethics, and reproductive technologies. In the past decade, she has served as an analyst and editorial consultant to the Howard Hughes Medical Institute, the National Institutes of Health, IOM, NAS, and several charitable foundations, voluntary health organizations, and biotechnology companies. Before coming to Washington, D.C., she was the Genetics Coordinator at Children's Memorial Hospital in Chicago, where she directed clinical counseling and coordinated an international research program in prenatal diagnosis. Dr. Hanna received an A.B. in biology from Lafayette College, an M.S. in human genetics from Sarah Lawrence College, and a Ph.D. from the School of Business and Public Management, The George Washington University.

Sara D. Maddox is a science and health policy editor who served as senior editor for reports to the President of the National Bioethics Advisory Commission, including *Ethical Issues in Human Stem Cell Research* and *Research Involving Human Biological Materials: Ethical Issues and Policy Guidance*. Earlier in her career she was a writer and editor at the Howard Hughes Medical Institute, and she has served as a science editor and writer for reports of the Secretary's Advisory Committee on Genetics, Health, and Society. Ms. Maddox participated in editing *Firepower in the Lab: Automation in the Fight Against Infectious Diseases and Bioterrorism*, a publication based on a colloquium on bioterrorism and laboratory-based data held at NAS. She has edited reports of the National Resource Council, including *Intentional Human Dosing Studies for EPA Regulatory Purposes: Scientific and Ethical Issues* and *Participants* and *Science and Security in a Post 9/11 World*. She also was editor for IOM's *Genes, Behavior, and the Social Environment: Moving Beyond the Nature/Nurture Debate*.

Appendix B

Committee Meeting Agendas

MEETING 1
WASHINGTON, D.C.
JANUARY 25, 2007

8:30 Welcome and Introductions

Committee Co-chairs
Harry T. Edwards, Judge, U.S. Court of Appeals for the District of Columbia Circuit
Constantine Gatsonis, Director, Center for Statistical Studies, Brown University

8:45 Charge to Committee

David W. Hagy, Deputy Assistant Attorney General for Policy Coordination, Office of Justice Programs, U.S. Department of Justice and Principal Deputy Director, National Institute of Justice, U.S. Department of Justice

9:10 Discussion

9:30 Importance of Study to the Forensics Community

Joe Polski, Chair, Consortium of Forensic Science Organizations

9:45 Discussion

10:15 Current State of Forensics: Census of Publicly Funded Forensic Crime Labs
Joseph L. Peterson, Director and Professor, School of Criminal Justice and Criminalistics, California State University, Los Angeles

Matthew J. Hickman, U.S. Department of Justice, Bureau of Justice Statistics

10:45 Discussion

11:15 Overview of Forensics Training and Education

Max M. Houck, Director, Forensic Science Initiative and Director, Forensic Business Development, College of Business and Economics, West Virginia University

Larry Quarino, Assistant Professor, Cedar Crest College

12:00 Discussion

12:15 Lunch

1:00 Daily Operations of Forensic Labs

Joseph A. DiZinno, Assistant Director, Laboratory Division, Federal Bureau of Investigation

Jan L. Johnson, Laboratory Director, Forensic Science Center at Chicago, Illinois State Police

Irma Rios, Assistant Director, City of Houston Crime Lab

2:15 Discussion

3:00 National Institute of Justice Research Program and Budget—Future Needs and Priorities

John Morgan, Deputy Director for Science and Technology, National Institute of Justice, DOJ

3:20 Discussion

3:45 Views from the Major Forensic Science Organizations: Issues and Challenges

Bruce A. Goldberger, President-Elect, American Academy of Forensic Sciences

Bill Marbaker, President, American Society of Crime Laboratory Directors

Robert Stacey, President, American Society of Crime Laboratory Directors, Laboratory Accreditation Board

Arthur Eisenberg, Board Member, Forensic Quality Services

Joe Polski, Chief Operations Officer, International Association for Identification

James Downs, Board Member and Chair, Government Affairs Committee, National Association of Medical Examiners

5:00 Discussion

5:30 Adjourn

JANUARY 26, 2007

8:30 Opportunities for Improvement: Critical Areas

Michael Risinger, Professor of Law, Seton Hall Law School

Peter Neufeld, Co-founder and Co-director, The Innocence Project

David Stoney, Chief Scientist, Stoney Forensic, Inc.

9:30 Discussion

10:00 Adjourn

MEETING 2
WASHINGTON, D.C.
APRIL 23, 2007

8:00 Welcome and Introductions

Harry T. Edwards and Constantine Gatsonis
Committee Co-chairs

8:10 Essential Elements of Science: Hypotheses, Falsifiability, Replication, Peer Review

Alan I. Leshner, Chief Executive Officer, American Association for the Advancement of Science

The Science of Statistics: Error Testing, Probabilities, Observer Bias

Jay Kadane, Senior Statistician, Department of Statistics, Carnegie Mellon University

9:00 Discussion

9:20 Forensic DNA

Science

Robin Cotton, Director, Biomedical Forensic Sciences Program, Boston University School of Medicine

Policy and Politics

Chris Asplen, Vice President, Gordon Thomas Honeywell Government Affairs and former Executive Director, U.S. Attorney General's National Commission on the Future of DNA Evidence

10:10 Discussion

10:45 The Science of Forensic Disciplines

What is the state of the art? Where is research conducted? Where is it published? What is the scientific basis that informs the interpretation of the evidence? Where are new developments coming from? What are the major problems in the scientific foundation or methods and in the practice? What research questions would you like to have answered?

Moderator: Constantine Gatsonis, Committee Co-Chair

10:50 Drug Identification

Joseph P. Bono, Laboratory Director, Forensic Services Division, U.S. Secret Service

11:15 Discussion

11:45 Lunch

12:30 Pattern Evidence with Fingerprints and Toolmarks as Illustrations

Fingerprints

Ed German, Latent Print Examiner, U.S. Army, Retired

Toolmarks

Peter Striupaitis, Chair, International Association for Identification, Firearm/Toolmark Committee and Member, Scientific Working Group for Firearms and Toolmarks (SWGGUN)

1:30 Discussion

2:00 Trace Evidence with Arson and Hair as Illustrations

Arson

John Lentini, Scientific Fire Analysis, LLC

Hair

Max M. Houck, Director, Forensic Science Initiative and Director, Forensic Business Development, College of Business and Economics, West Virginia University

3:00 Discussion

3:45 Forensic Odontology: Bite Marks
David R. Senn, Director, Center for Education and Research in Forensics and Clinical Assistant Professor, Department of Dental Diagnostic Science, The University of Texas Health Science Center at San Antonio

4:10 Discussion

4:30 Commentators

Robert E. Gaensslen, Head of Program in Forensic Science, College of Pharmacy, University of Illinois at Chicago

Jennifer Mnookin, Professor of Law, University of California, Los Angeles Law School

David Kaye, Regents' Professor of Law and Professor of Life Sciences, Arizona State University

5:15 Comments from the Floor

5:45 Adjourn

APRIL 24, 2007

8:00 Welcome and Introductions

Harry T. Edwards and Constantine Gatsonis
Committee Co-chairs

8:10 From Crime Scene to Courtroom: The Collection and Flow of Evidence

Barry A. J. Fisher, Director, Scientific Services Bureau, Los Angeles County Sheriff's Department and former President, American Academy of Forensic Sciences

8:45 Discussion

9:15 Practice and Standards: Scientific Working Groups

What is the process for establishing the guidelines and standards? What are the guidelines/standards for each of these disciplines? How is quality control/quality assurance monitored and enforced? What recommendations have these organizations made and have they been implemented? What is needed?

Moderator: Harry T. Edwards, Committee Co-chair

9:20 Drug Identification

Nelson A. Santos, Drug Enforcement Administration and Chair, Scientific Working Group for the Analysis of Seized Drugs (SWGDRUG)

9:40 Discussion

10:00 Pattern Evidence: Latent Prints

Stephen B. Meagher, Fingerprint Specialist, Federal Bureau of Investigation and Vice-Chair, Scientific Working Group on Friction Ridge Analysis, Study and Technology (SWGFAST)

10:30 Discussion

11:00 Trace Evidence: Hair Analysis

Richard E. Bisbing, Executive Vice President, McCrone Associates, Inc. and member, Scientific Working Group on Materials Analysis (SWGMAT)

11:20 Discussion

11:45 Commentators

Paul C. Giannelli, Weatherhead Professor, Case Western Reserve University School of Law

Carol Henderson, Director, National Clearinghouse for Science, Technology and the Law and Professor of Law, Stetson University

Michael J. Saks, Professor of Law & Psychology and Faculty Fellow, Center for the Study of Law, Science, & Technology, Sandra Day O'Connor College of Law, Arizona State University

12:30 Comments from the Floor

1:00 Adjourn

MEETING 3
WASHINGTON, D.C.
JUNE 5, 2007

8:15 Welcome and Introductions

Harry T. Edwards and Constantine Gatsonis
Committee Co-chairs

8:30 Forensic Sciences: Issues and Direction

Bruce Budowle, Senior Scientist, Laboratory Division, Federal Bureau of Investigation

9:30 Challenges for Crime Laboratories: City, County, and Private

Peter Pizzola, Director, New York Police Department Crime Laboratory

John Collins, Director, DuPage County Sheriff's Office Crime Laboratory

John E. Moalli, Group Vice President and Principal Engineer, Exponent

11:00 Emerging Issues: Cybercrime, fMRI (functional Magnetic Resonance Imaging) and Lie Detection, and Photographic Comparison Analysis

Eric Friedberg, Co-president, Stroz Friedberg, LLC

Hank Greely, Deane F. and Kate Edelman Johnson Professor of Law, Stanford University

Richard W. Vorder Bruegge, Supervisory Photographic Technologist-Examiner of Questioned Photographic Evidence, Federal Bureau of Investigation

12:30 Working Lunch: Continuation of Morning Session

1:15 Automated Fingerprint Identification Systems (AFIS) Interoperability

John Onstwedder III, Statewide AFIS Coordinator for the Forensic Sciences Command, Forensic Science Center at Chicago, Illinois State Police

Peter T. Higgins, Principal Consultant, The Higgins-Hermansen Group
Peter D. Komarinski, Komarinski & Associates, LLC

2:15 Medical Examiner System

Randy Hanzlick, Chief Medical Examiner, Fulton County Medical Examiner's Center, Fulton County, Georgia and Professor of Forensic Pathology, Emory University School of Medicine

James Downs, Board Member and Chair, Governmental Affairs Committee, National Association of Medical Examiners; Vice Chair, Consortium of Forensic Science Organizations; Coastal Regional Medical Examiner, Georgia Bureau of Investigation

Garry F. Peterson, Chief Medical Examiner Emeritus, Hennepin County Medical Examiner's Office, Minnesota; Chair, Standards, Inspection and Accreditation Committee and Standards Subcommittee and Past President, National Association of Medical Examiners

Victor W. Weedn, Medical Examiner

4:15 Comments from the Floor

5:00 Adjourn

MEETING 4
WOODS HOLE, MASSACHUSETTS
SEPTEMBER 20, 2007

1:30 Welcome

Harry T. Edwards and Constantine Gatsonis
Committee Co-chairs

1:35 Lessons Learned From the Houston Police Department Investigation

Michael R. Bromwich, Independent Investigator, Fried, Frank, Harris, Shriver & Jacobson LLP

2:45 200 Exonerations: A Look at the Cases Involving Faulty Forensic Evidence

Brandon L. Garrett, Associate Professor of Law, University of Virginia

Peter Neufeld, Co-Founder and Co-Director, The Innocence Project

4:15 Ethics in Forensic Science

Peter D. Barnett, Partner, Forensic Science Associates

5:00 Reducing Error Rates: A New Institutional Arrangement for Forensic Science

Roger G. Koppl, Director, Institute for Forensic Science Administration, Fairleigh Dickinson University

6:00 Adjourn

SEPTEMBER 21, 2007

8:15 Welcome

Harry T. Edwards and Constantine Gatsonis
Committee Co-chairs

8:20 The U.K. Forensics System

Carole McCartney, Centre for Criminal Justice Studies, School of Law, University of Leeds

9:20 The Role of Forensics in Homeland Security

Charles Cooke, Bio-Specialist, Office of the Deputy Director for Strategy and Evaluation, National Counterproliferation Center, Office of the Director of National Intelligence

James Burans, Bioforensics Program Manager, National Bioforensics Analysis Center, U.S. Department of Homeland Security

Larry Chelko, Director, U.S. Army Criminal Investigation Laboratory

Rick Tontarski, Chief, Forensic Analysis Division, U.S. Army Criminal Investigation Laboratory

11:00 Forensics at the National Institute of Standards and Technology

Michael D. Garris, Image Group Manager, National Institute of Standards and Technology

Barbara Guttman, Line Manager, National Software Reference Library, National Institute of Standards and Technology

William MacCrehan, Research Chemist, Analytical Chemistry Division, National Institute of Standards and Technology

12:20 Adjourn

MEETING 5
WASHINGTON, D.C.
DECEMBER 6, 2007

8:15 Welcome and Introductions

Harry T. Edwards and Constantine Gatsonis
Committee Co-chairs

8:30 Scientific Working Group on Friction Ridge Analysis, Study and Technology (SWGFAST)

Glenn Langenburg, Minnesota Bureau of Criminal Apprehension

9:15 Fingerprint Source Book

John Morgan, Deputy Director for Science and Technology, National Institute of Justice, U.S. Department of Justice

9:45 International Association of Identification: Key Issues

Kenneth F. Martin, Crime Scene Services, Massachusetts State Police

10:30 Forensic Science Issues at the U.S. Secret Service

Vici Inlow, Forensic Services Division, U.S. Secret Service

Deborah Leben, Forensic Services Division, U.S. Secret Service

11:10 Contextual Bias

Itiel Dror, School of Psychology, University of Southampton

12:00 Lunch

1:00 The Coroner System

Michael Murphy, Las Vegas Office of the Coroner

1:50 Survey of Non-Traditional Forensic Service Providers

Tom Witt, Bureau of Business and Economic Research, College of Business and Economics, West Virginia University

2:30 Department of Defense Latent Print Analysis

Thomas Cantwell, Senior Forensic Analyst, Biometric Task Force and Leader, Forensic Integrated Product Team, U.S. Department of Defense

3:15 Comments from the Floor

3:45 Adjourn

Index

B

D

E

G

H

I

J

L

M

N

O

P

Q

T

U

V

W